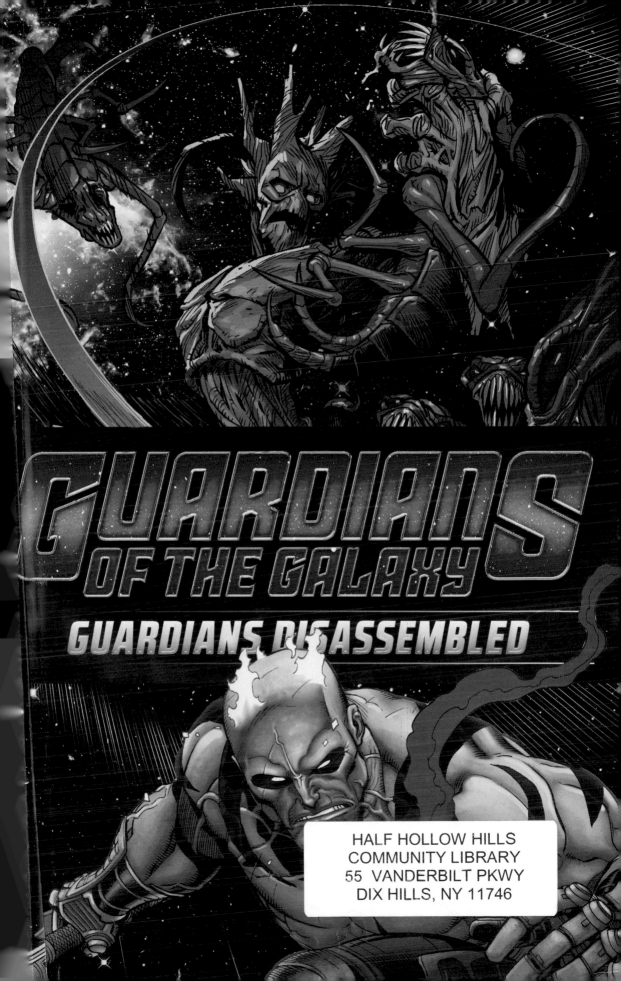

GUARDIANS
OF THE GALAXY

GUARDIANS DISASSEMBLED

GUARDIANS OF THE GALAXY

GUARDIANS DISASSEMBLED

PREVIOUSLY...

PETER QUILL'S ESTRANGED FATHER, THE KING OF SPARTAX, ALONG WITH THE LEADERS OF THE OTHER GALACTIC EMPIRES DECREED THAT NO ALIEN HAND MAY TOUCH THE PLANET EARTH. WHICH THE GUARDIANS PROMPTLY DISOBEYED. THEY HAVE BEEN FUGITIVES EVER SINCE. TO MAKE MATTERS WORSE, A BOUNTY HUNTER, UNDER CONTRACT FROM AN UNKNOWN SOURCE, HAS BEEN HUNTING GAMORA.

THE GUARDIANS RECENTLY MADE ENEMIES OF THE SHI'AR IMPERIAL GUARD AS WELL, WHILE HELPING THE TIME-DISPLACED ORIGINAL X-MEN RESCUE THE YOUNG JEAN GREY FROM THEIR CLUTCHES.

MEANWHILE, THE WARRIOR ANGELA HAS FOUND HERSELF TRANSPLANTED FROM HER OWN UNIVERSE THROUGH SOME ERROR IN THE SPACE-TIME CONTINUUM. UNIDENTIFIABLE AS ANY KNOWN SPECIES, SHE MUST NOW DETERMINE HER PLACE AND PURPOSE IN THE GALAXY.

GUARDIANS OF THE GALAXY VOL. 3: GUARDIANS DISASSEMBLED. Contains material originally published in magazine form as FREE COMIC BOOK DAY 2014 (GUARDIANS OF THE GALAXY) #1, GUARDIANS OF THE GALAXY #14-17, CAPTAIN MARVEL #1 and AMAZING SPIDER-MAN #654. First printing 2014. ISBN# 978-0-7851-5479-2. Published by MARVEL WORLDWIDE, INC., a subsidiary of MARVEL ENTERTAINMENT, LLC. OFFICE OF PUBLICATION: 135 West 50th Street, New York, NY 10020. Copyright © 2011, 2012 and 2014 Marvel Characters, Inc. All rights reserved. All characters featured in this issue and the distinctive names and likenesses thereof, and all related indicia are trademarks of Marvel Characters, Inc. No similarity between any of the names, characters, persons, and/or institutions in this magazine with those of any living or dead person or institution is intended, and any such similarity which may exist is purely coincidental. Printed in the U.S.A. ALAN FINE, EVP - Office of the President, Marvel Worldwide, Inc. and EVP & CMO Marvel Characters B.V.; DAN BUCKLEY, Publisher & President - Print, Animation & Digital Divisions; JOE QUESADA, Chief Creative Officer; TOM BREVOORT, SVP of Publishing; DAVID BOGART, SVP of Operations & Procurement, Publishing; C.B. CEBULSKI, SVP of Creator & Content Development; DAVID GABRIEL, SVP Print, Sales & Marketing; JIM O'KEEFE, VP of Operations & Logistics; DAN CARR, Executive Director of Publishing Technology; SUSAN CRESPI, Editorial Operations Manager; ALEX MORALES, Publishing Operations Manager; STAN LEE, Chairman Emeritus. For information regarding advertising in Marvel Comics or on Marvel.com, please contact Niza Disla, Director of Marvel Partnerships, at ndisla@marvel.com. For Marvel subscription inquiries, please call 800-217-9158. Manufactured between 9/12/2014 and 10/27/2014 by R.R. DONNELLEY, INC., SALEM, VA, USA.

10 9 8 7 6 5 4 3 2 1

STAR-LORD  GAMORA  ROCKET RACCOON  GROOT  DRAX  ANGELA

WRITER: **BRIAN MICHAEL BENDIS**

**FREE COMIC BOOK DAY 2014
(GUARDIANS OF THE GALAXY) #1**
PENCILER: NICK BRADSHAW
INKER: SCOTT HANNA
COLORIST: MORRY HOLLOWELL
LETTERER: VC'S CORY PETIT
COVER ART: SARA PICHELLI & JUSTIN PONSOR
LETTERER: VC'S CORY PETIT
EDITORS: STEPHEN WACKER & ELLIE PYLE

ISSUE #14
ARTISTS: NICK BRADSHAW WITH JASON MASTERS
& TODD NAUCK
INKERS: NICK BRADSHAW, WALDEN WONG,
JASON MASTERS & TODD NAUCK
COLORISTS: JUSTIN PONSOR WITH JASON KEITH
COVER ART: NICK BRADSHAW & JUSTIN PONSOR

"GROOT'S TALE"
WRITER: ANDY LANNING
PENCILER: PHIL JIMENEZ
INKER: LIVESAY
COLORIST: ANTONIO FABELA

"FIGHT FOR THE FUTURE"
WRITER: DAN ABNETT
ARTIST: GERARDO SANDOVAL
COLORIST: RACHELLE ROSENBERG

ISSUE #15
PENCILERS: NICK BRADSHAW & CAMERON STEWART
INKERS: NICK BRADSHAW, CAMERON STEWART
& WALDEN WONG
COLORIST: JUSTIN PONSOR
COVER ART: NICK BRADSHAW & JUSTIN PONSOR

ISSUE #16
ARTISTS: NICK BRADSHAW, DAVID MARQUEZ
& JASON MASTERS
COLORISTS: JUSTIN PONSOR, EDGAR DELGADO
& JOSE VILLARRUBIA
COVER ART: NICK BRADSHAW & JUSTIN PONSOR

ISSUE #17
ARTISTS: NICK BRADSHAW & MICHAEL OEMING
INKERS: NICK BRADSHAW, MICHAEL OEMING
& WALDEN WONG
COLORISTS: JUSTIN PONSOR
COVER ART: ED MCGUINNESS, MARK FARMER
& JUSTIN PONSOR
LETTERER: VC'S CORY PETIT
ASSISTANT EDITOR: XANDER JAROWEY
EDITOR: MIKE MARTS

CAPTAIN MARVEL #1 (2012)
WRITER: KELLY SUE DECONNICK
ARTIST: DEXTER SOY
LETTERER: VC'S JOE CARAMAGNA
COVER ARTISTS: ED MCGUINNESS, DEXTER VINES
& JAVIER RODRIGUEZ
ASSISTANT EDITOR: ELLIE PYLE
EDITOR: SANA AMANAT
SENIOR EDITOR: STEPHEN WACKER

**"REBIRTH"
FROM AMAZING SPIDER-MAN #654 (2011)**
WRITER: DAN SLOTT
PENCILERS: PAULO SIQUEIRA
& RONAN CLIQUET DE OLIVEIRA
INKERS: PAULO SIQUEIRA, ROLAND PARIS
& GREG ADAMS
COLORIST: FABIO D'AURIA
LETTERER: VC'S JOE CARAMAGNA
ASSISTANT EDITOR: ELLIE PYLE
SENIOR EDITOR: STEPHEN WACKER

COLLECTION EDITOR: **JENNIFER GRÜNWALD**
ASSISTANT EDITOR: **SARAH BRUNSTAD**
ASSOCIATE MANAGING EDITOR: **ALEX STARBUCK**
EDITOR, SPECIAL PROJECTS: **MARK D. BEAZLEY**
SENIOR EDITOR, SPECIAL PROJECTS: **JEFF YOUNGQUIST**
SVP PRINT, SALES & MARKETING: **DAVID GABRIEL**

EDITOR IN CHIEF: **AXEL ALONSO**
CHIEF CREATIVE OFFICER: **JOE QUESADA**
PUBLISHER: **DAN BUCKLEY**
EXECUTIVE PRODUCER: **ALAN FINE**

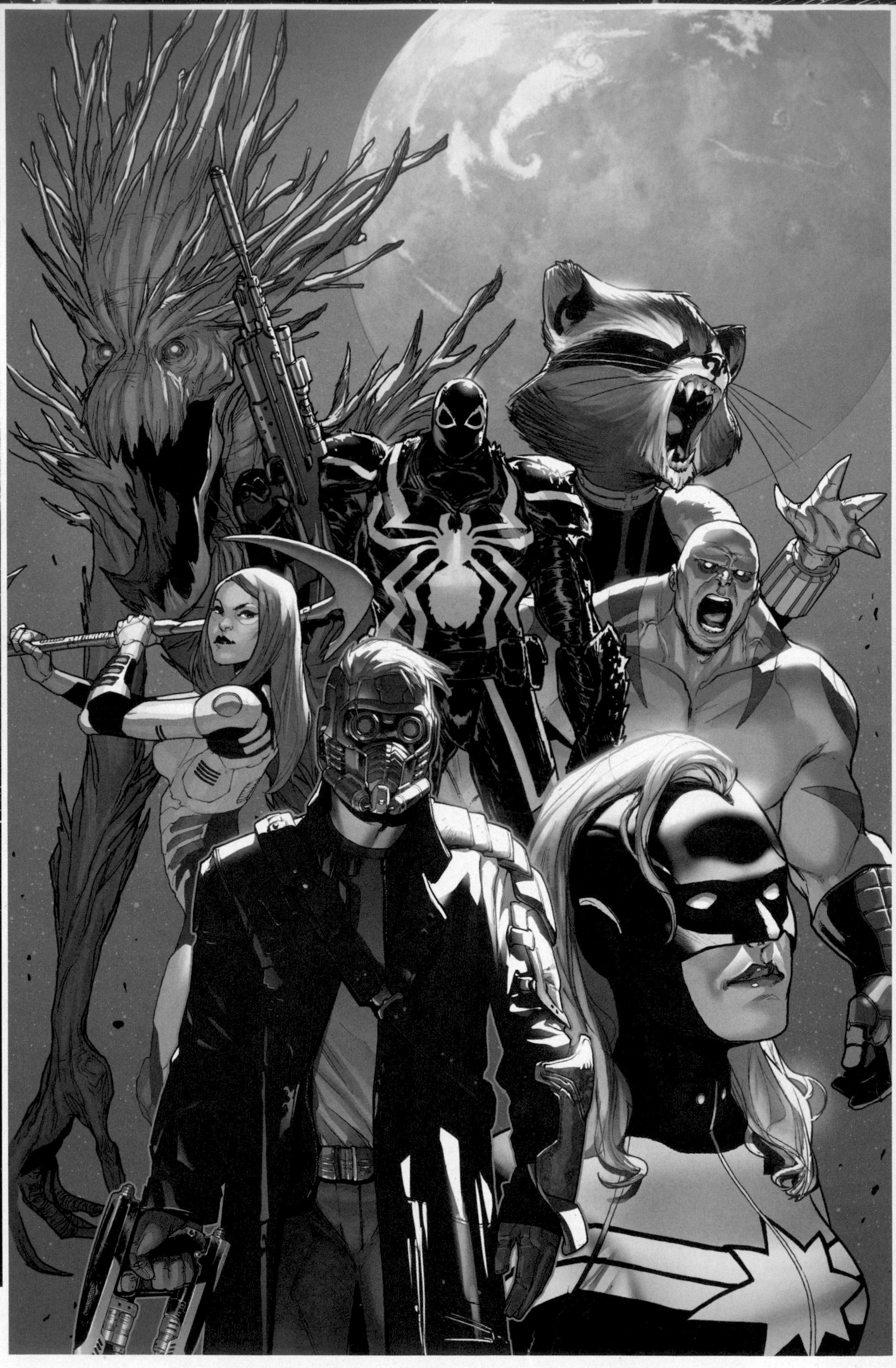

FREE COMIC BOOK DAY 2014 (GUARDIANS OF THE GALAXY) #1

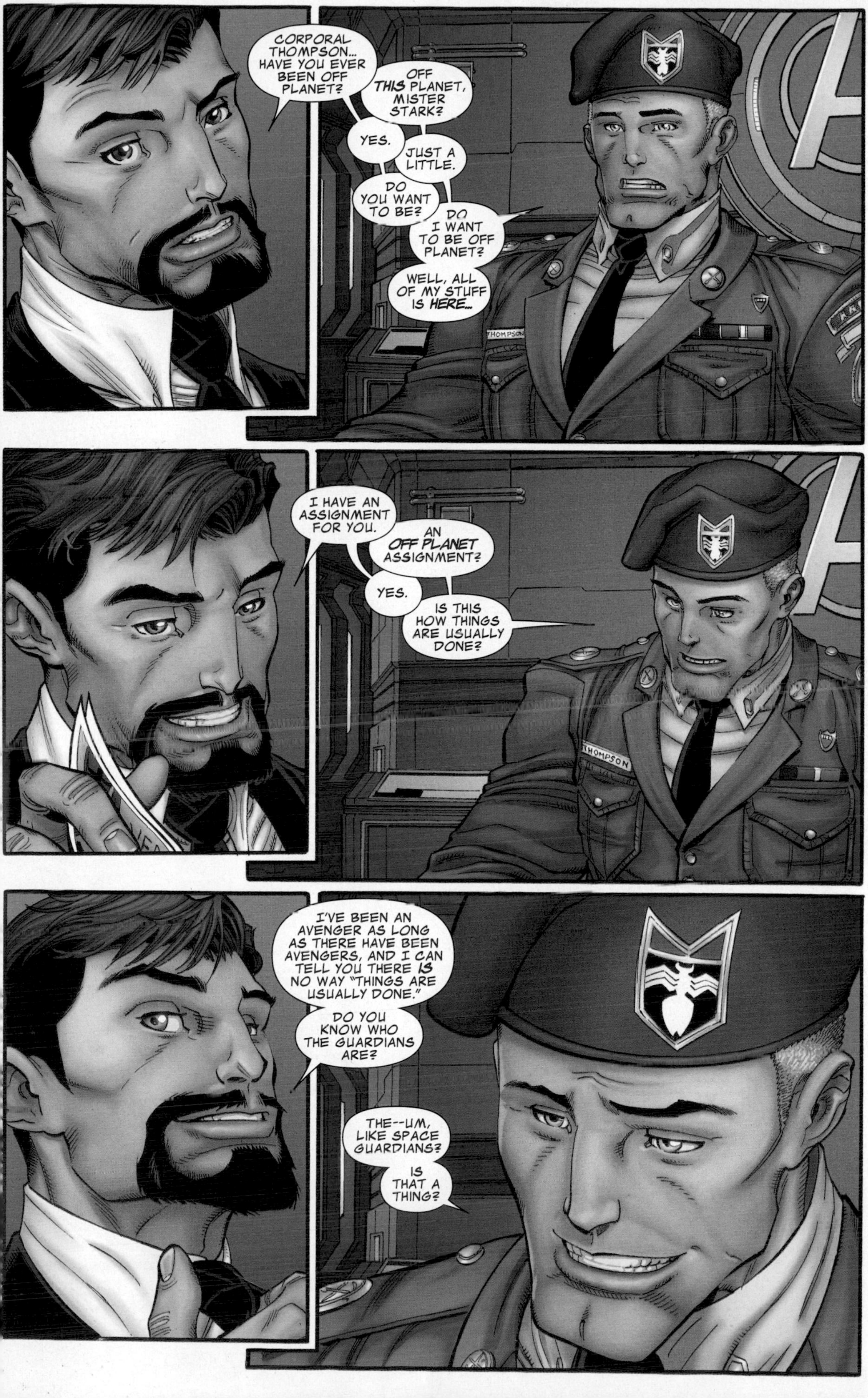
CORPORAL THOMPSON... HAVE YOU EVER BEEN OFF PLANET?
OFF THIS PLANET, MISTER STARK?
YES.
JUST A LITTLE.
DO YOU WANT TO BE?
DO I WANT TO BE OFF PLANET?
WELL, ALL OF MY STUFF IS HERE...
THOMPSON
I HAVE AN ASSIGNMENT FOR YOU.
AN OFF PLANET ASSIGNMENT?
YES.
IS THIS HOW THINGS ARE USUALLY DONE?
THOMPSON
I'VE BEEN AN AVENGER AS LONG AS THERE HAVE BEEN AVENGERS, AND I CAN TELL YOU THERE IS NO WAY "THINGS ARE USUALLY DONE."
DO YOU KNOW WHO THE GUARDIANS ARE?
THE--UM, LIKE SPACE GUARDIANS?
IS THAT A THING?

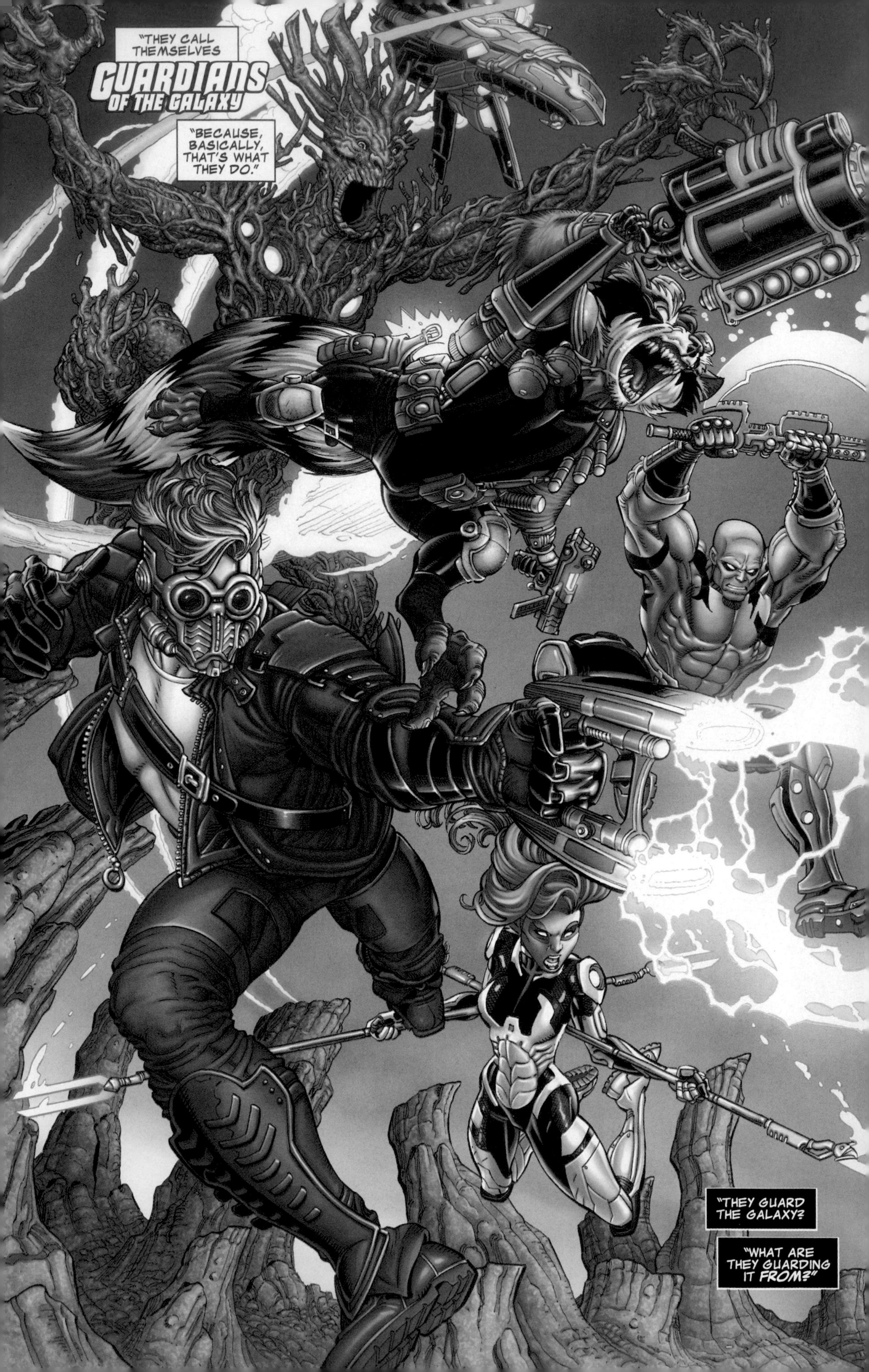
"THEY CALL THEMSELVES
GUARDIANS OF THE GALAXY
"BECAUSE, BASICALLY, THAT'S WHAT THEY DO."
"THEY GUARD THE GALAXY?
"WHAT ARE THEY GUARDING IT FROM?"

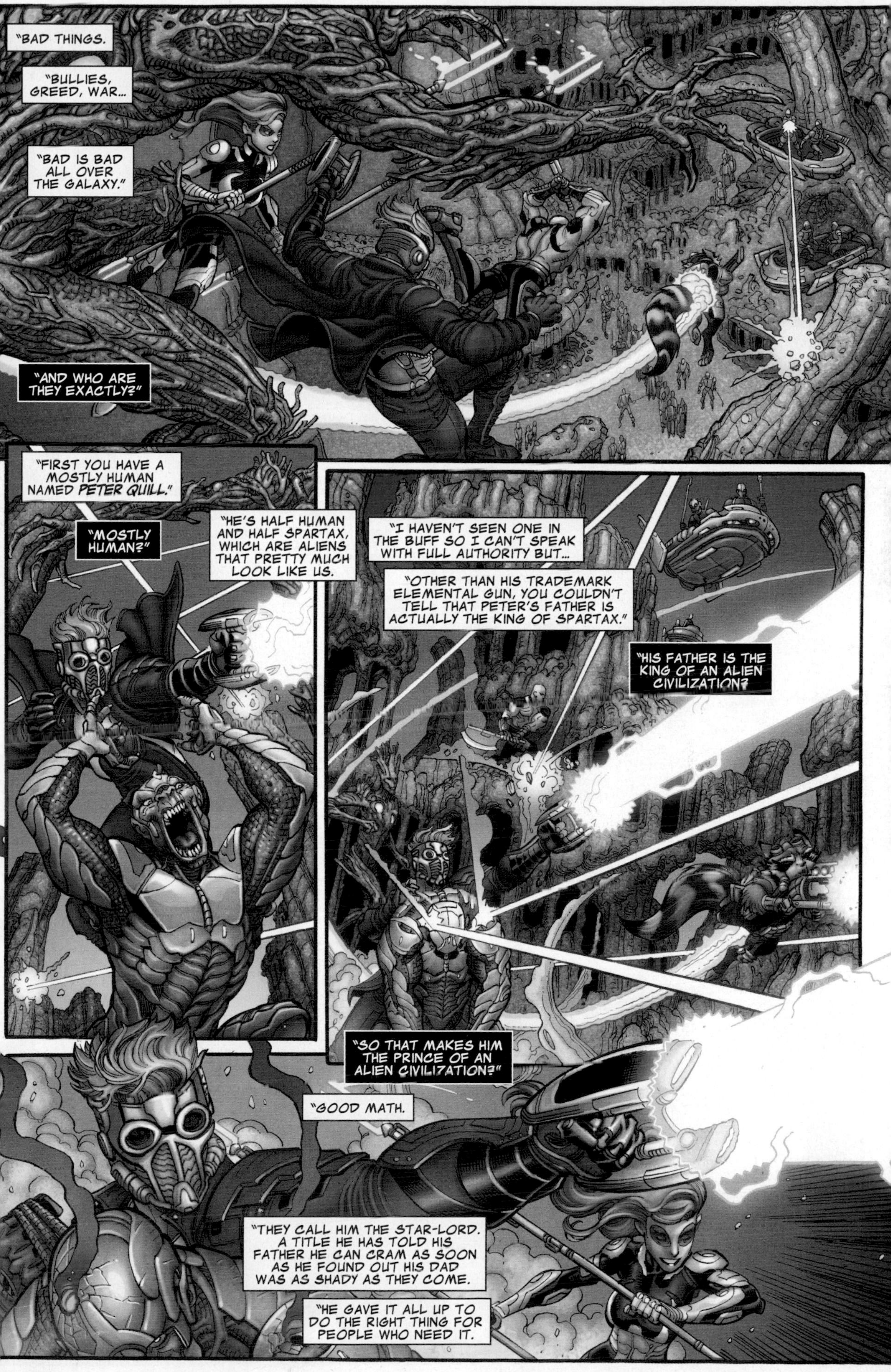
"BAD THINGS.
"BULLIES, GREED, WAR...
"BAD IS BAD ALL OVER THE GALAXY."
"AND WHO ARE THEY EXACTLY?"
"FIRST YOU HAVE A MOSTLY HUMAN NAMED PETER QUILL."
"MOSTLY HUMAN?"
"HE'S HALF HUMAN AND HALF SPARTAX, WHICH ARE ALIENS THAT PRETTY MUCH LOOK LIKE US.
"I HAVEN'T SEEN ONE IN THE BUFF SO I CAN'T SPEAK WITH FULL AUTHORITY BUT...
"OTHER THAN HIS TRADEMARK ELEMENTAL GUN, YOU COULDN'T TELL THAT PETER'S FATHER IS ACTUALLY THE KING OF SPARTAX."
"HIS FATHER IS THE KING OF AN ALIEN CIVILIZATION?
"SO THAT MAKES HIM THE PRINCE OF AN ALIEN CIVILIZATION?"
"GOOD MATH.
"THEY CALL HIM THE STAR-LORD. A TITLE HE HAS TOLD HIS FATHER HE CAN CRAM AS SOON AS HE FOUND OUT HIS DAD WAS AS SHADY AS THEY COME.
"HE GAVE IT ALL UP TO DO THE RIGHT THING FOR PEOPLE WHO NEED IT.

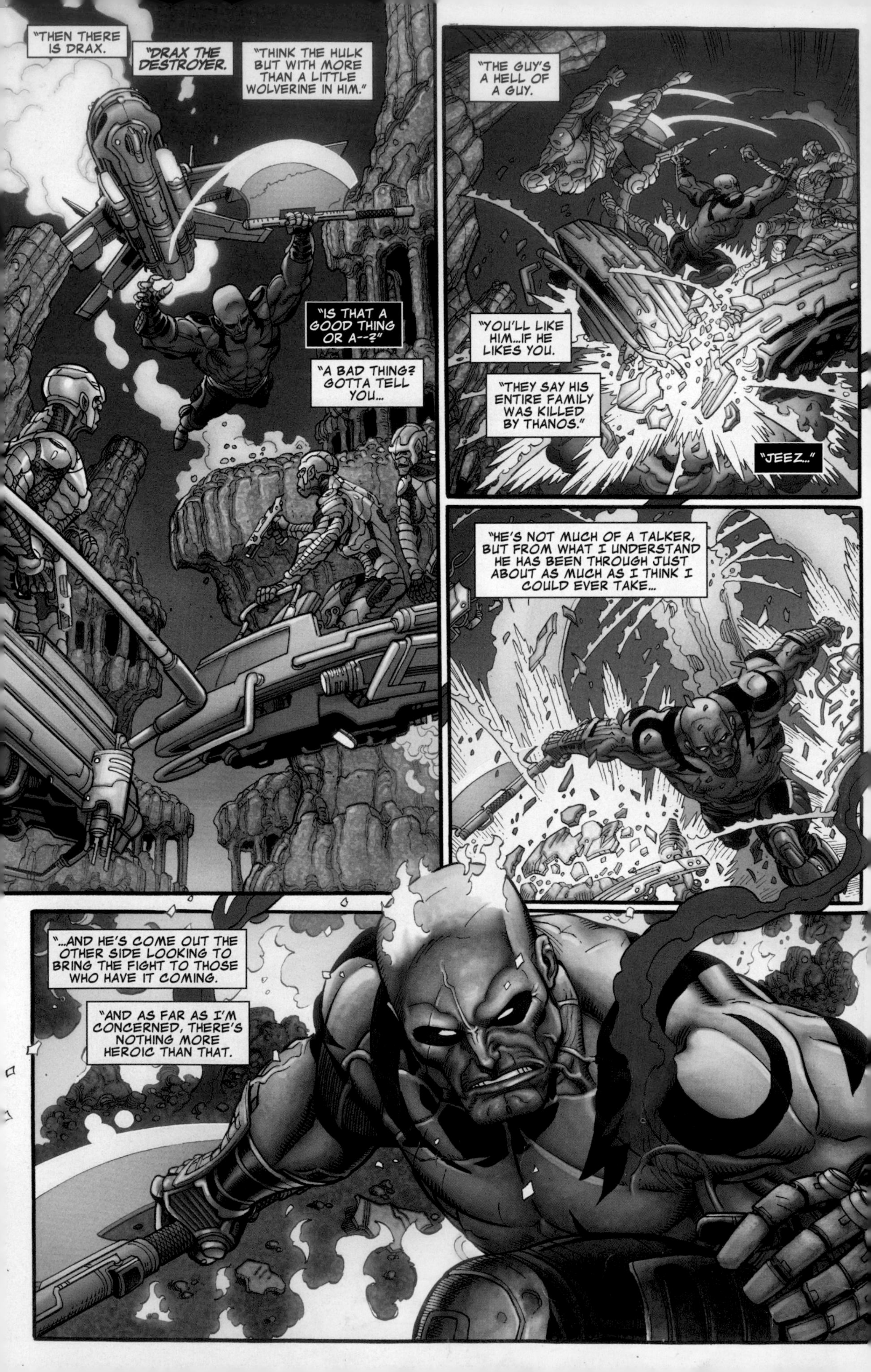
"THEN THERE IS DRAX.
"DRAX THE DESTROYER.
"THINK THE HULK BUT WITH MORE THAN A LITTLE WOLVERINE IN HIM."
"IS THAT A GOOD THING OR A--?"
"A BAD THING? GOTTA TELL YOU...
"THE GUY'S A HELL OF A GUY.
"YOU'LL LIKE HIM...IF HE LIKES YOU.
"THEY SAY HIS ENTIRE FAMILY WAS KILLED BY THANOS."
"JEEZ..."
"HE'S NOT MUCH OF A TALKER, BUT FROM WHAT I UNDERSTAND HE HAS BEEN THROUGH JUST ABOUT AS MUCH AS I THINK I COULD EVER TAKE...
"...AND HE'S COME OUT THE OTHER SIDE LOOKING TO BRING THE FIGHT TO THOSE WHO HAVE IT COMING.
"AND AS FAR AS I'M CONCERNED, THERE'S NOTHING MORE HEROIC THAN THAT.

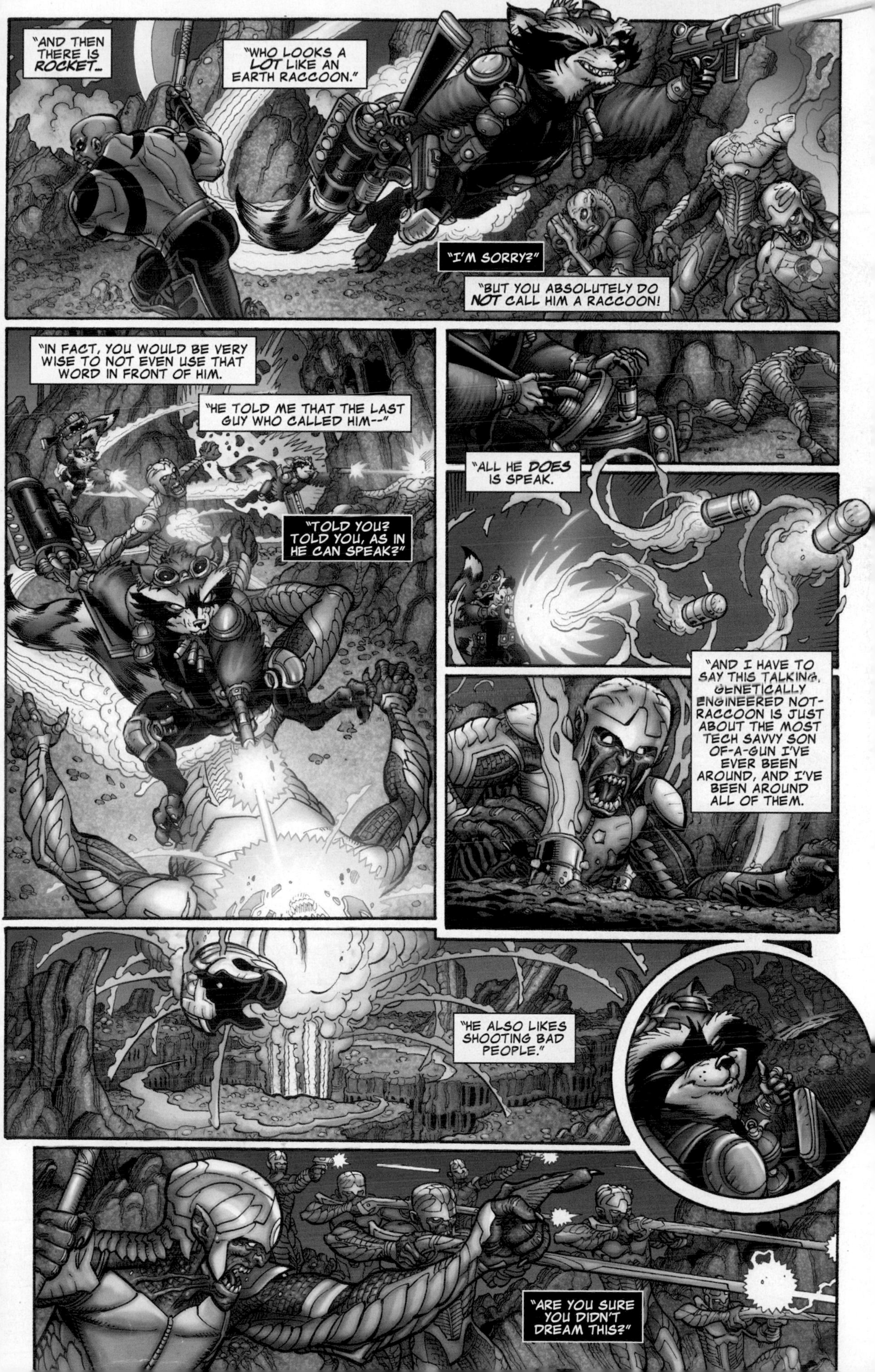

"AND THEN THERE IS ROCKET...
"WHO LOOKS A LOT LIKE AN EARTH RACCOON."
"I'M SORRY?"
"BUT YOU ABSOLUTELY DO NOT CALL HIM A RACCOON!
"IN FACT, YOU WOULD BE VERY WISE TO NOT EVEN USE THAT WORD IN FRONT OF HIM.
"HE TOLD ME THAT THE LAST GUY WHO CALLED HIM--"
"TOLD YOU? TOLD YOU, AS IN HE CAN SPEAK?"
"ALL HE DOES IS SPEAK.
"AND I HAVE TO SAY THIS TALKING, GENETICALLY ENGINEERED NOT-RACCOON IS JUST ABOUT THE MOST TECH SAVVY SON OF-A-GUN I'VE EVER BEEN AROUND, AND I'VE BEEN AROUND ALL OF THEM.
"HE ALSO LIKES SHOOTING BAD PEOPLE."
"ARE YOU SURE YOU DIDN'T DREAM THIS?"

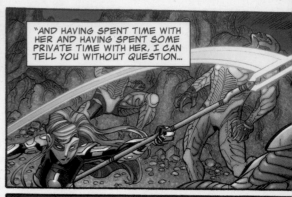

"AND HAVING SPENT TIME WITH HER AND HAVING SPENT SOME PRIVATE TIME WITH HER, I CAN TELL YOU WITHOUT QUESTION..."

"AND THEN THERE IS GAMORA.

"SHE IS KNOWN FAR AND WIDE AS THE MOST DANGEROUS WOMAN IN THE GALAXY.

"...THAT SHE IS THE MOST DANGEROUS WOMAN IN THE GALAXY.

"SHE WAS TRAINED FOR THIS SINCE BIRTH.

"SHE IS THANOS' DAUGHTER.

"YEAH, IMAGINE THAT.

"BUT THE GOOD NEWS IS SHE HATES HIM MORE THAN ALL OF US PUT TOGETHER."

"THANOS' DAUGHTER. CAN SHE BE TRUSTED?"

"WITH EVERYTHING YOU HAVE.

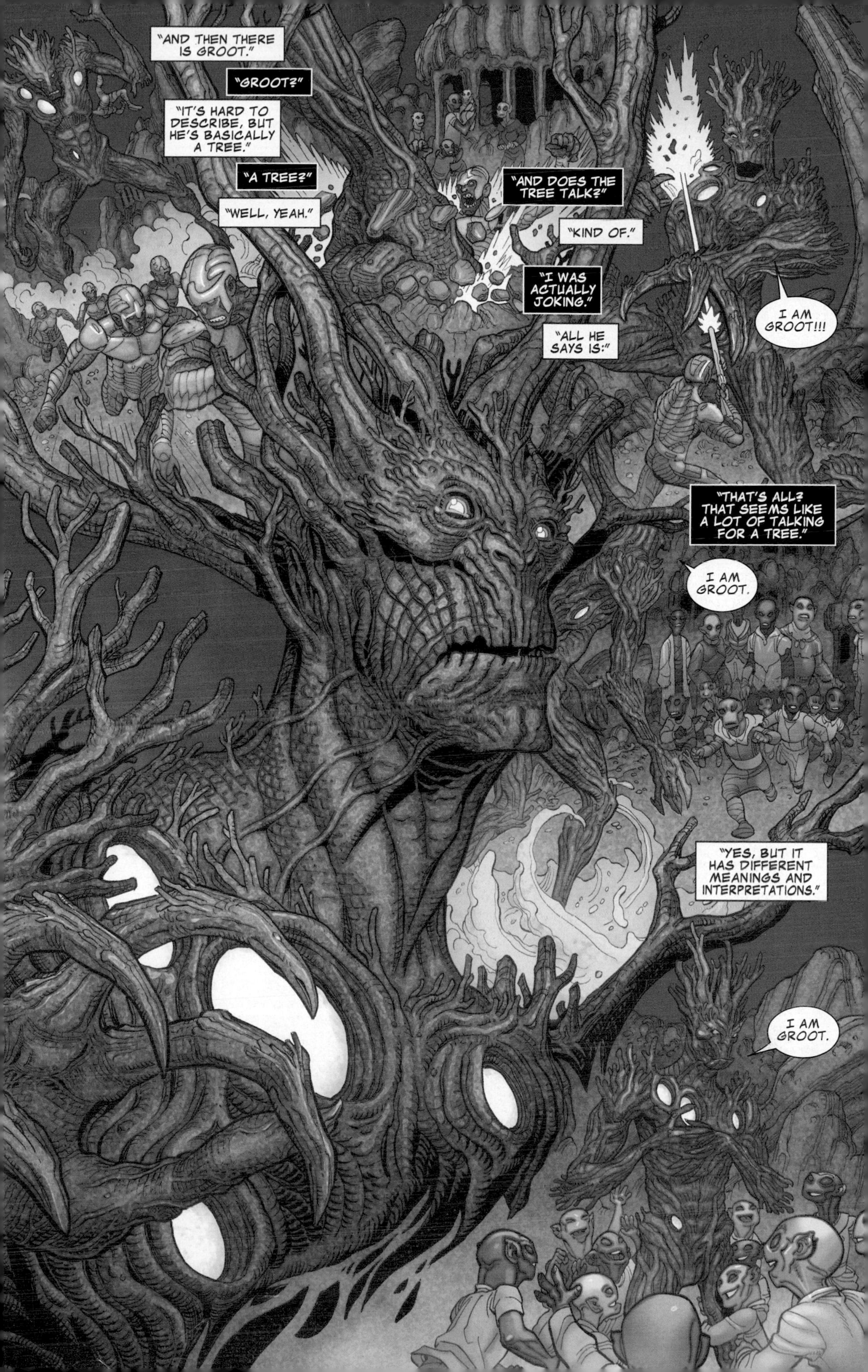
"AND THEN THERE IS GROOT."
"GROOT?"
"IT'S HARD TO DESCRIBE, BUT HE'S BASICALLY A TREE."
"A TREE?"
"WELL, YEAH."
"AND DOES THE TREE TALK?"
"KIND OF."
"I WAS ACTUALLY JOKING."
"ALL HE SAYS IS:"
I AM GROOT!!!
"THAT'S ALL? THAT SEEMS LIKE A LOT OF TALKING FOR A TREE."
I AM GROOT.
"YES, BUT IT HAS DIFFERENT MEANINGS AND INTERPRETATIONS."
I AM GROOT.

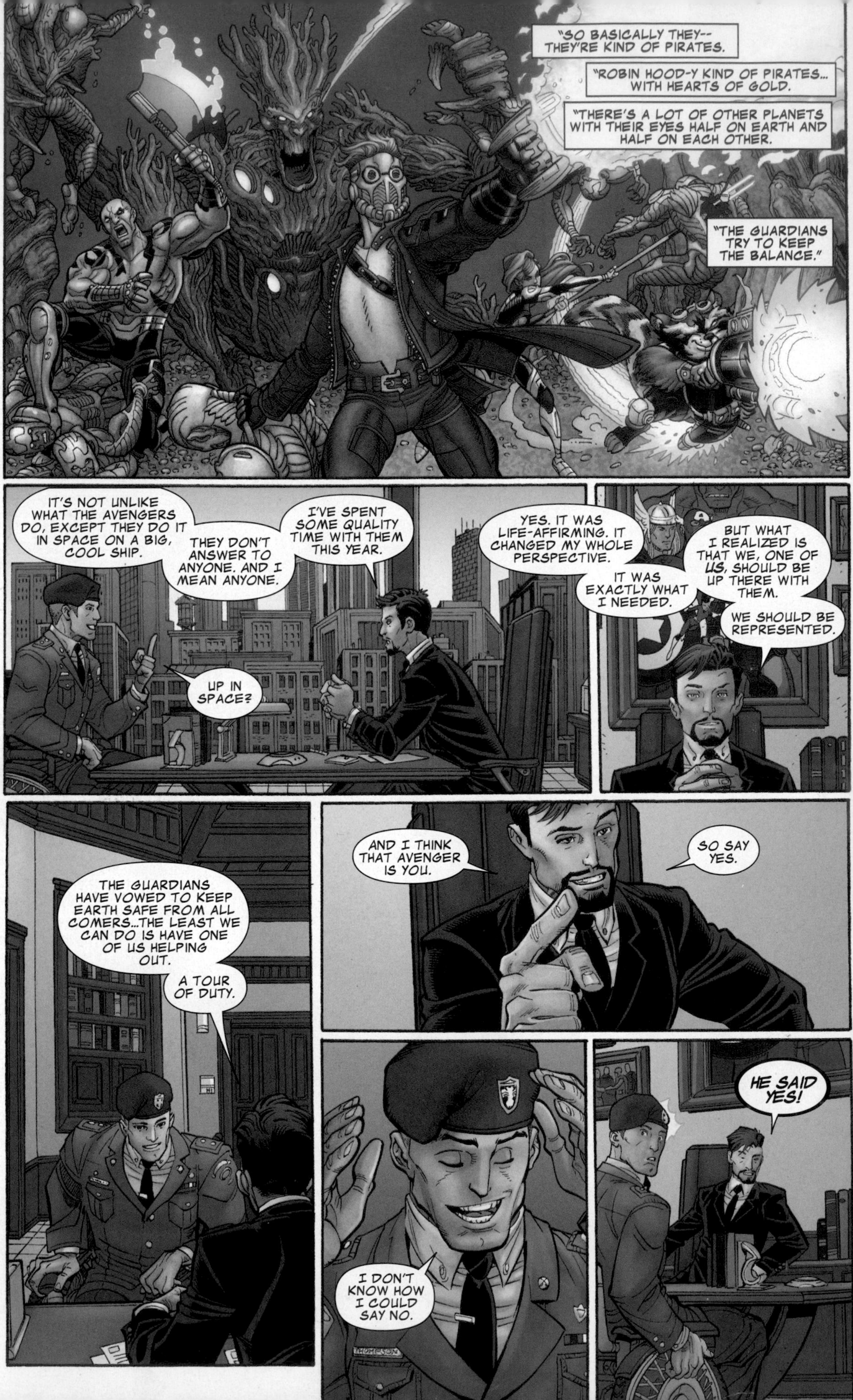

"SO BASICALLY THEY-- THEY'RE KIND OF PIRATES.
"ROBIN HOOD-Y KIND OF PIRATES... WITH HEARTS OF GOLD.
"THERE'S A LOT OF OTHER PLANETS WITH THEIR EYES HALF ON EARTH AND HALF ON EACH OTHER.
"THE GUARDIANS TRY TO KEEP THE BALANCE."
IT'S NOT UNLIKE WHAT THE AVENGERS DO, EXCEPT THEY DO IT IN SPACE ON A BIG, COOL SHIP.
THEY DON'T ANSWER TO ANYONE. AND I MEAN ANYONE.
I'VE SPENT SOME QUALITY TIME WITH THEM THIS YEAR.
UP IN SPACE?
YES. IT WAS LIFE-AFFIRMING. IT CHANGED MY WHOLE PERSPECTIVE.
IT WAS EXACTLY WHAT I NEEDED.
BUT WHAT I REALIZED IS THAT WE, ONE OF US, SHOULD BE UP THERE WITH THEM.
WE SHOULD BE REPRESENTED.
THE GUARDIANS HAVE VOWED TO KEEP EARTH SAFE FROM ALL COMERS...THE LEAST WE CAN DO IS HAVE ONE OF US HELPING OUT.
A TOUR OF DUTY.
AND I THINK THAT AVENGER IS YOU.
SO SAY YES.
I DON'T KNOW HOW I COULD SAY NO.
HE SAID YES!

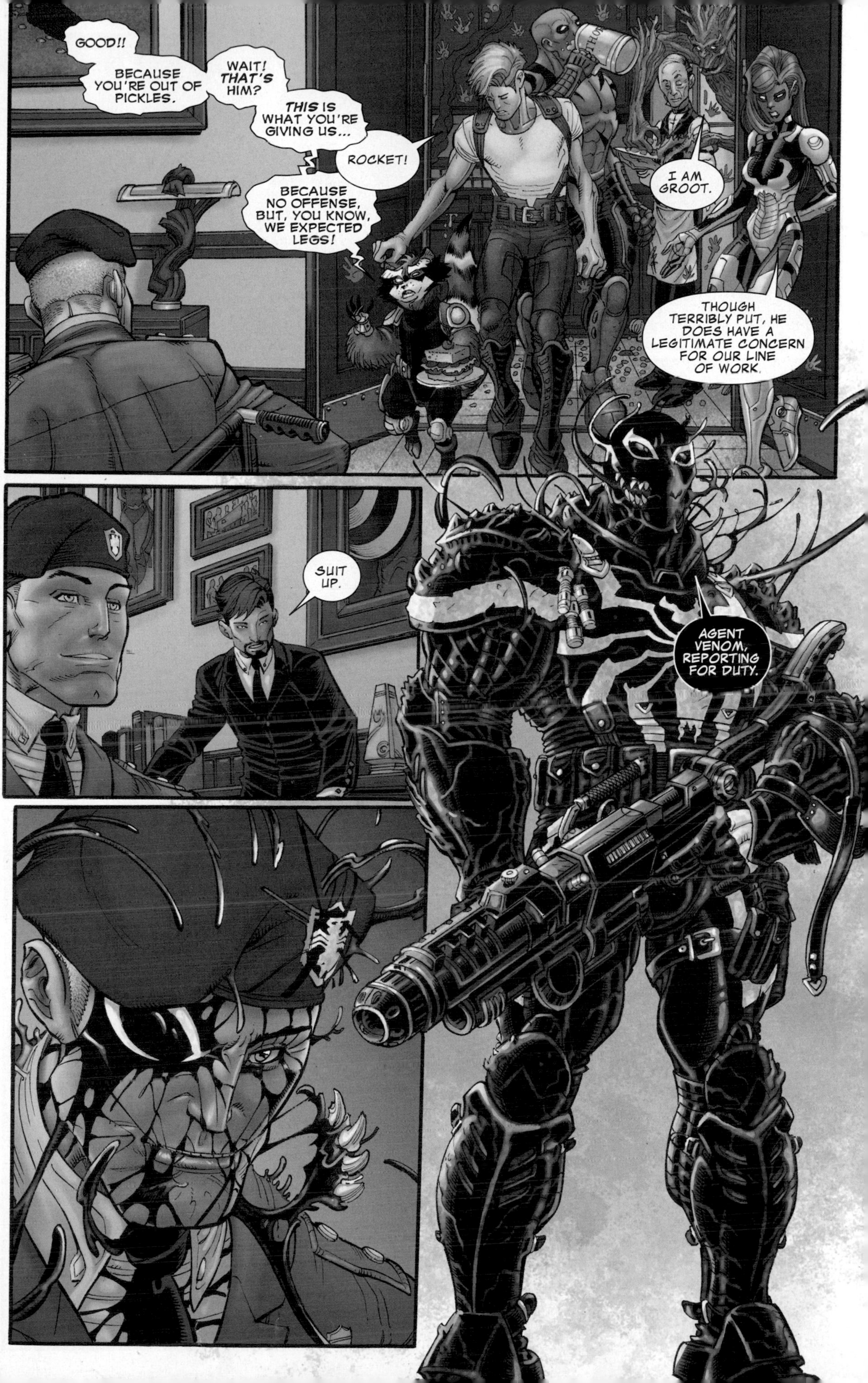
GOOD!!
BECAUSE YOU'RE OUT OF PICKLES.
WAIT! THAT'S HIM?
THIS IS WHAT YOU'RE GIVING US...
ROCKET!
BECAUSE NO OFFENSE, BUT, YOU KNOW, WE EXPECTED LEGS!
I AM GROOT.
THOUGH TERRIBLY PUT, HE DOES HAVE A LEGITIMATE CONCERN FOR OUR LINE OF WORK.
SUIT UP.
AGENT VENOM, REPORTING FOR DUTY.

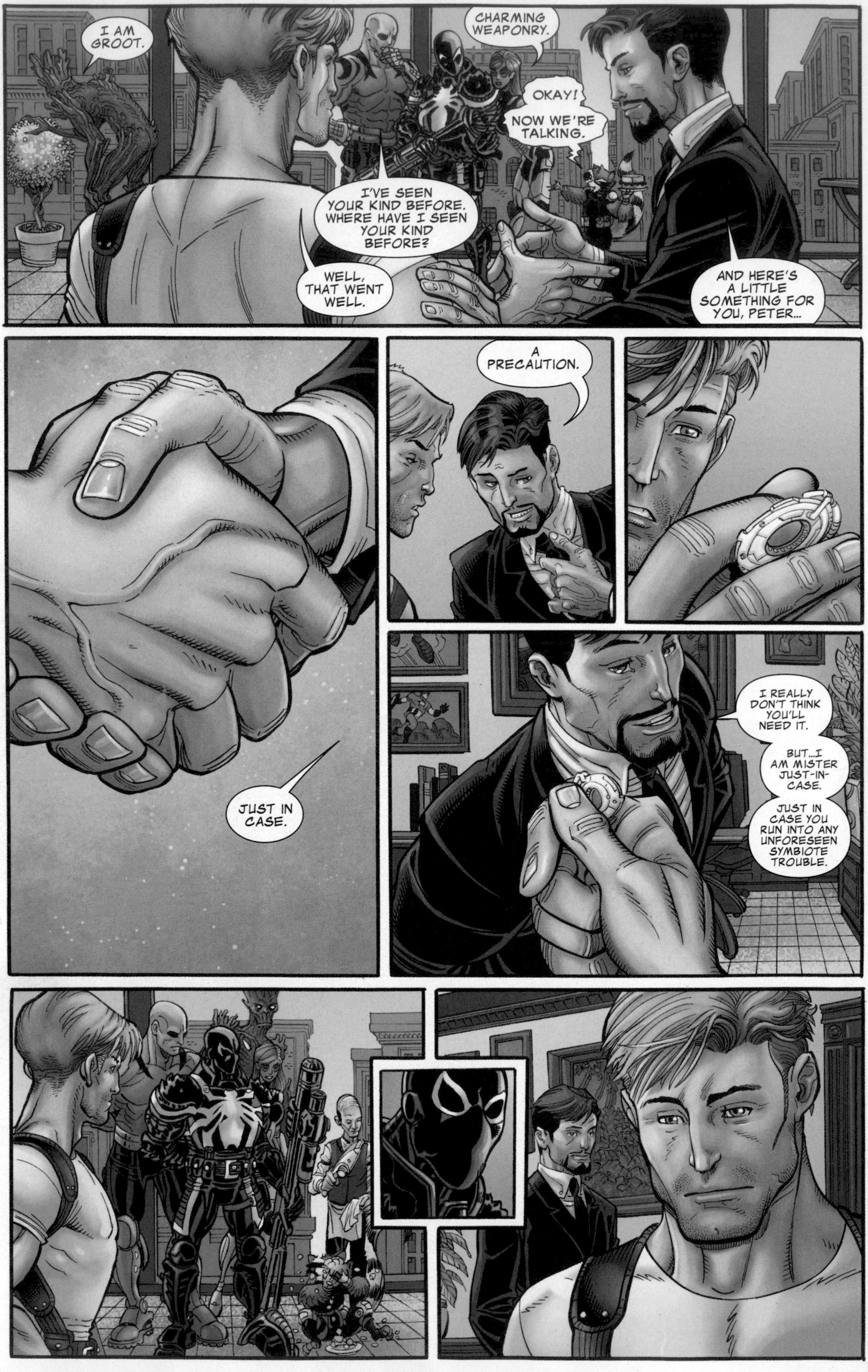
I AM GROOT.
CHARMING WEAPONRY.
OKAY!
NOW WE'RE TALKING.
I'VE SEEN YOUR KIND BEFORE. WHERE HAVE I SEEN YOUR KIND BEFORE?
WELL, THAT WENT WELL.
AND HERE'S A LITTLE SOMETHING FOR YOU, PETER...
JUST IN CASE.
A PRECAUTION.
I REALLY DON'T THINK YOU'LL NEED IT.
BUT...I AM MISTER JUST-IN-CASE.
JUST IN CASE YOU RUN INTO ANY UNFORESEEN SYMBIOTE TROUBLE.

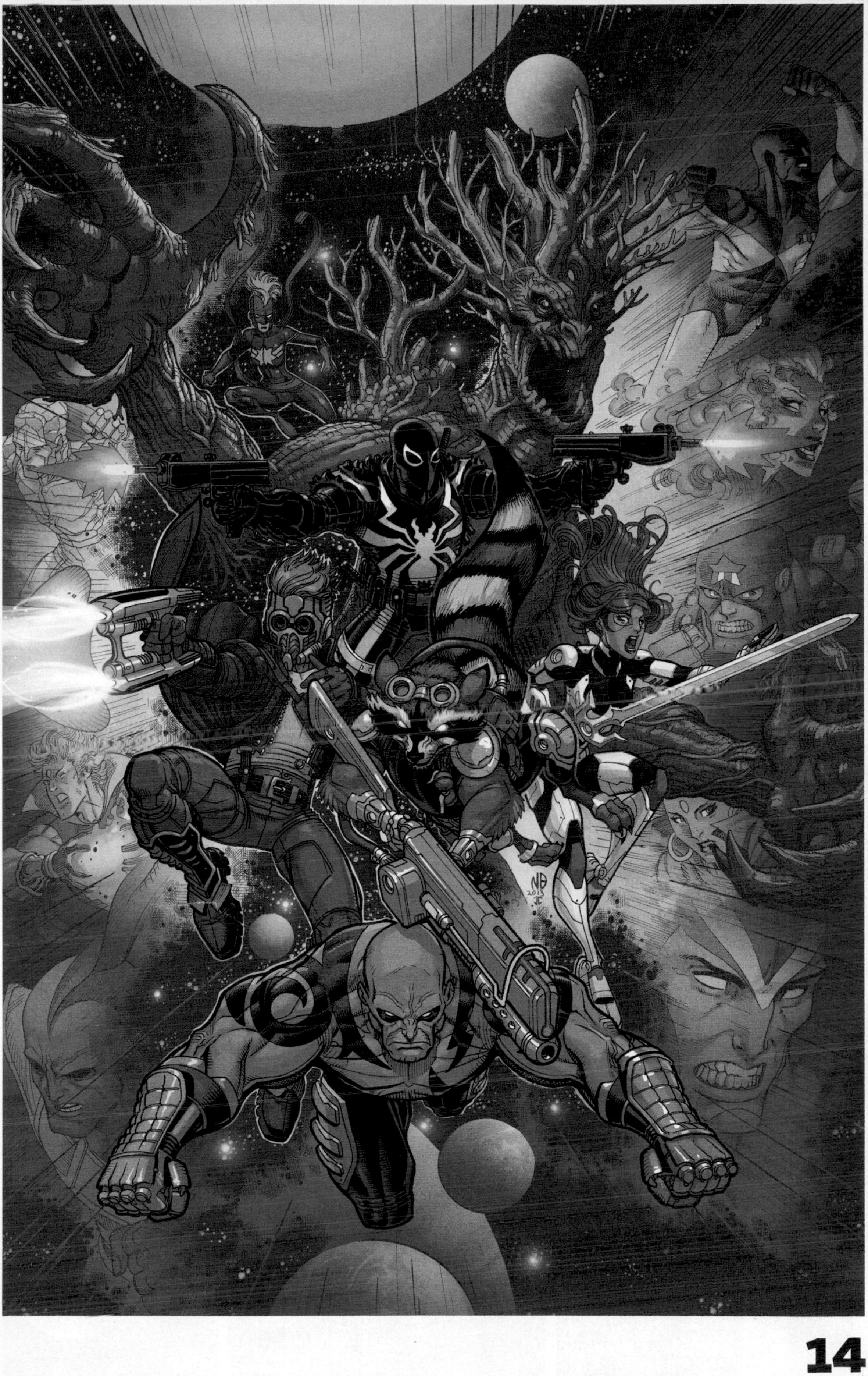

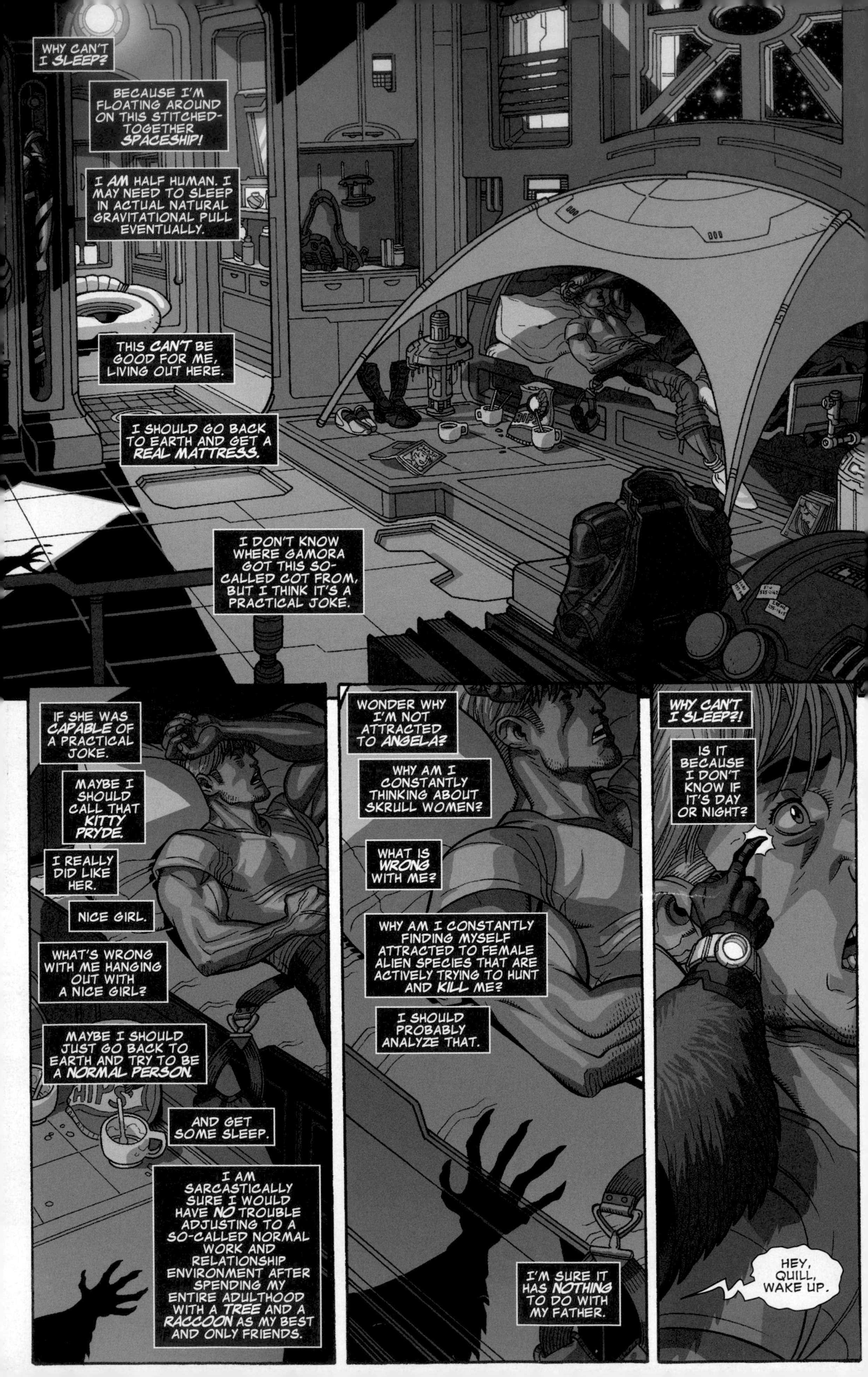

WHY CAN'T I SLEEP?
BECAUSE I'M FLOATING AROUND ON THIS STITCHED-TOGETHER SPACESHIP!
I AM HALF HUMAN. I MAY NEED TO SLEEP IN ACTUAL NATURAL GRAVITATIONAL PULL EVENTUALLY.
THIS CAN'T BE GOOD FOR ME, LIVING OUT HERE.
I SHOULD GO BACK TO EARTH AND GET A REAL MATTRESS.
I DON'T KNOW WHERE GAMORA GOT THIS SO-CALLED COT FROM, BUT I THINK IT'S A PRACTICAL JOKE.
IF SHE WAS CAPABLE OF A PRACTICAL JOKE.
MAYBE I SHOULD CALL THAT KITTY PRYDE.
I REALLY DID LIKE HER.
NICE GIRL.
WHAT'S WRONG WITH ME HANGING OUT WITH A NICE GIRL?
MAYBE I SHOULD JUST GO BACK TO EARTH AND TRY TO BE A NORMAL PERSON.
AND GET SOME SLEEP.
I AM SARCASTICALLY SURE I WOULD HAVE NO TROUBLE ADJUSTING TO A SO-CALLED NORMAL WORK AND RELATIONSHIP ENVIRONMENT AFTER SPENDING MY ENTIRE ADULTHOOD WITH A TREE AND A RACCOON AS MY BEST AND ONLY FRIENDS.
WONDER WHY I'M NOT ATTRACTED TO ANGELA?
WHY AM I CONSTANTLY THINKING ABOUT SKRULL WOMEN?
WHAT IS WRONG WITH ME?
WHY AM I CONSTANTLY FINDING MYSELF ATTRACTED TO FEMALE ALIEN SPECIES THAT ARE ACTIVELY TRYING TO HUNT AND KILL ME?
I SHOULD PROBABLY ANALYZE THAT.
I'M SURE IT HAS NOTHING TO DO WITH MY FATHER.
WHY CAN'T I SLEEP?!
IS IT BECAUSE I DON'T KNOW IF IT'S DAY OR NIGHT?
HEY, QUILL, WAKE UP.

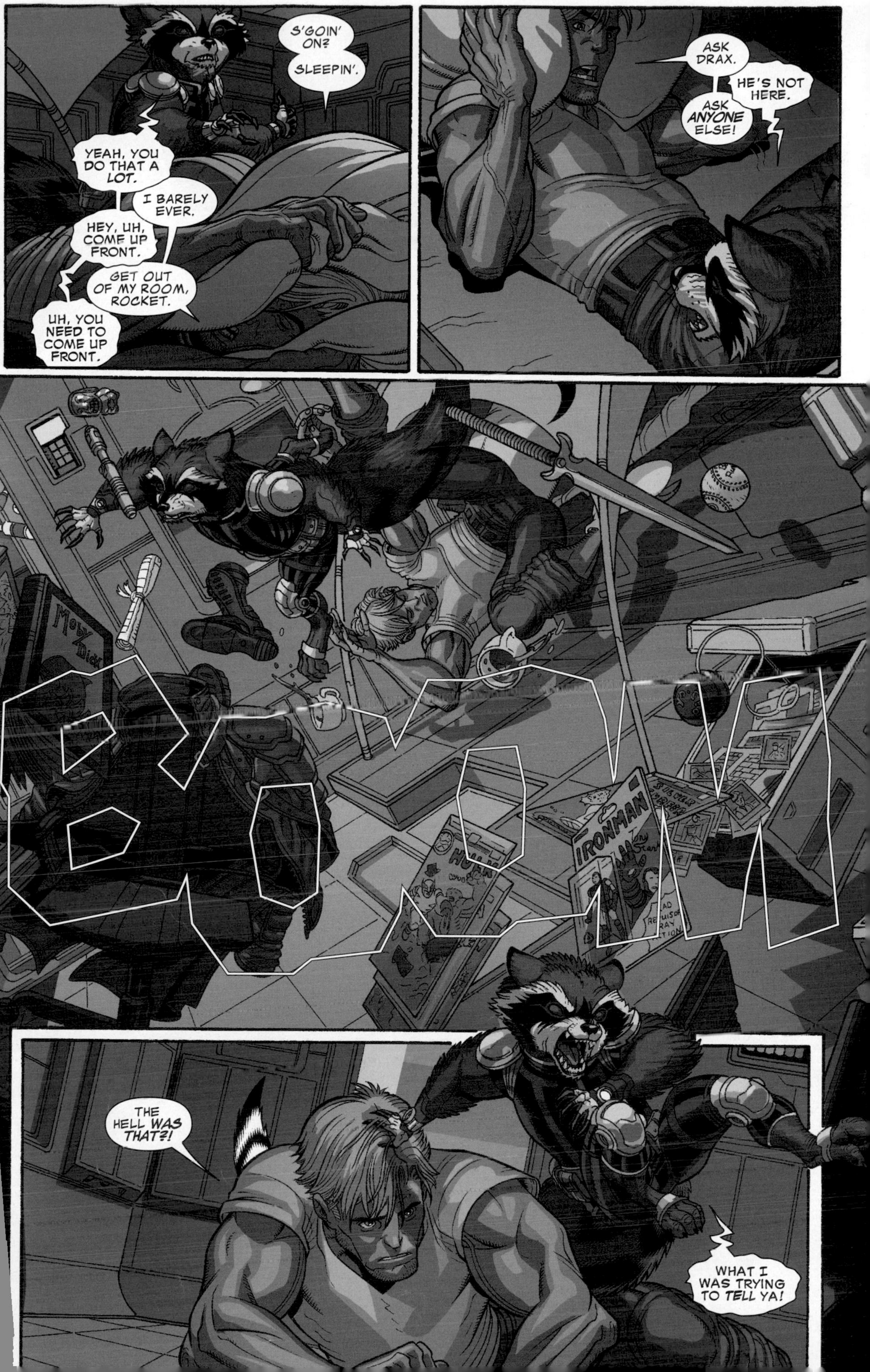
S'GOIN' ON?
SLEEPIN'.
YEAH, YOU DO THAT A LOT.
I BARELY EVER.
HEY, UH, COME UP FRONT.
GET OUT OF MY ROOM, ROCKET.
UH, YOU NEED TO COME UP FRONT.
ASK DRAX.
HE'S NOT HERE.
ASK ANYONE ELSE!
MOBY DICK
BOOM
HULK
IRONMAN
THE HELL WAS THAT?!
WHAT I WAS TRYING TO TELL YA!

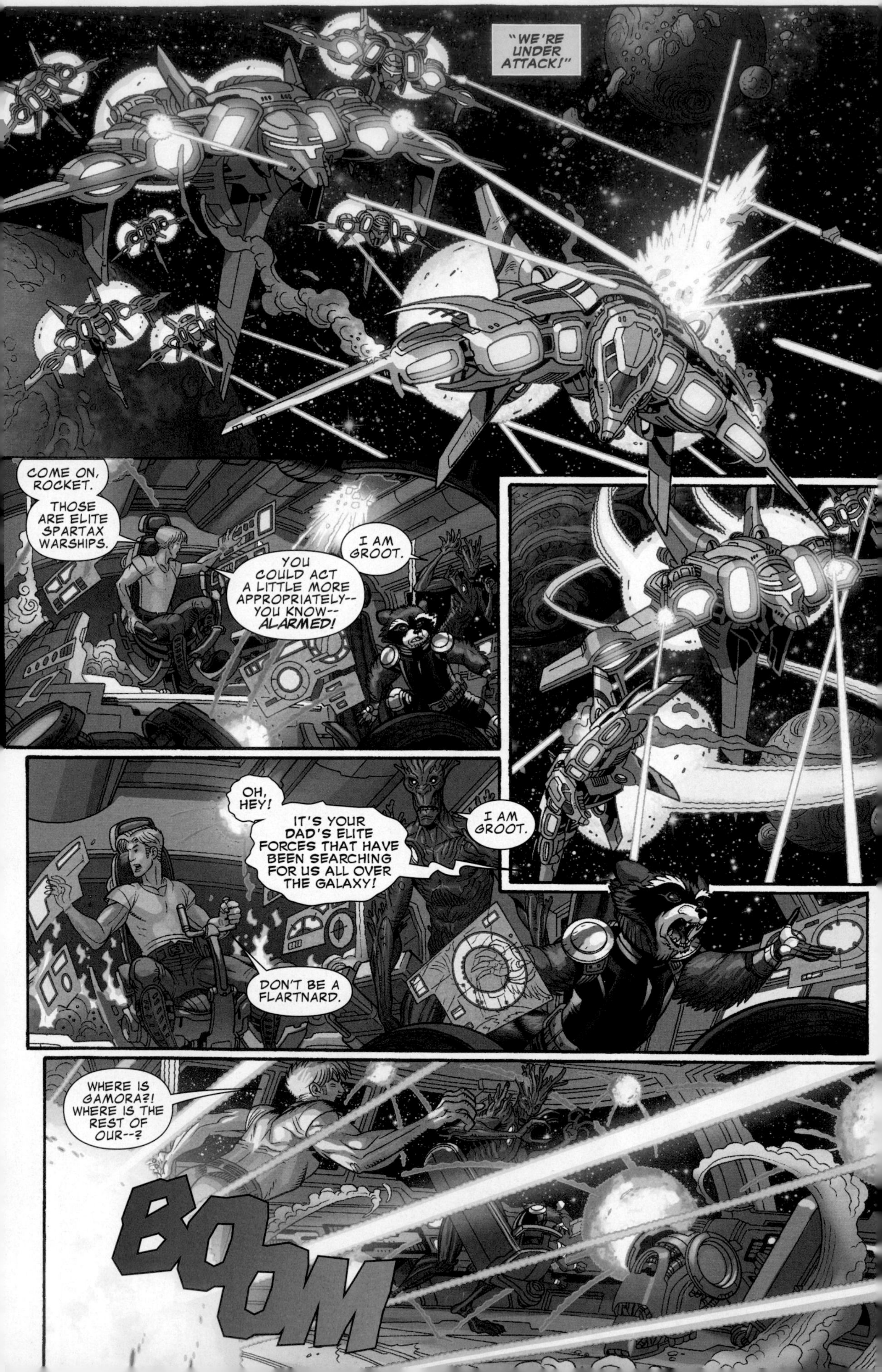
"WE'RE UNDER ATTACK!"
COME ON, ROCKET.
THOSE ARE ELITE SPARTAX WARSHIPS.
YOU COULD ACT A LITTLE MORE APPROPRIATELY-- YOU KNOW-- ALARMED!
I AM GROOT.
OH, HEY!
IT'S YOUR DAD'S ELITE FORCES THAT HAVE BEEN SEARCHING FOR US ALL OVER THE GALAXY!
I AM GROOT.
DON'T BE A FLARTNARD.
WHERE IS GAMORA?! WHERE IS THE REST OF OUR--?
BOOM

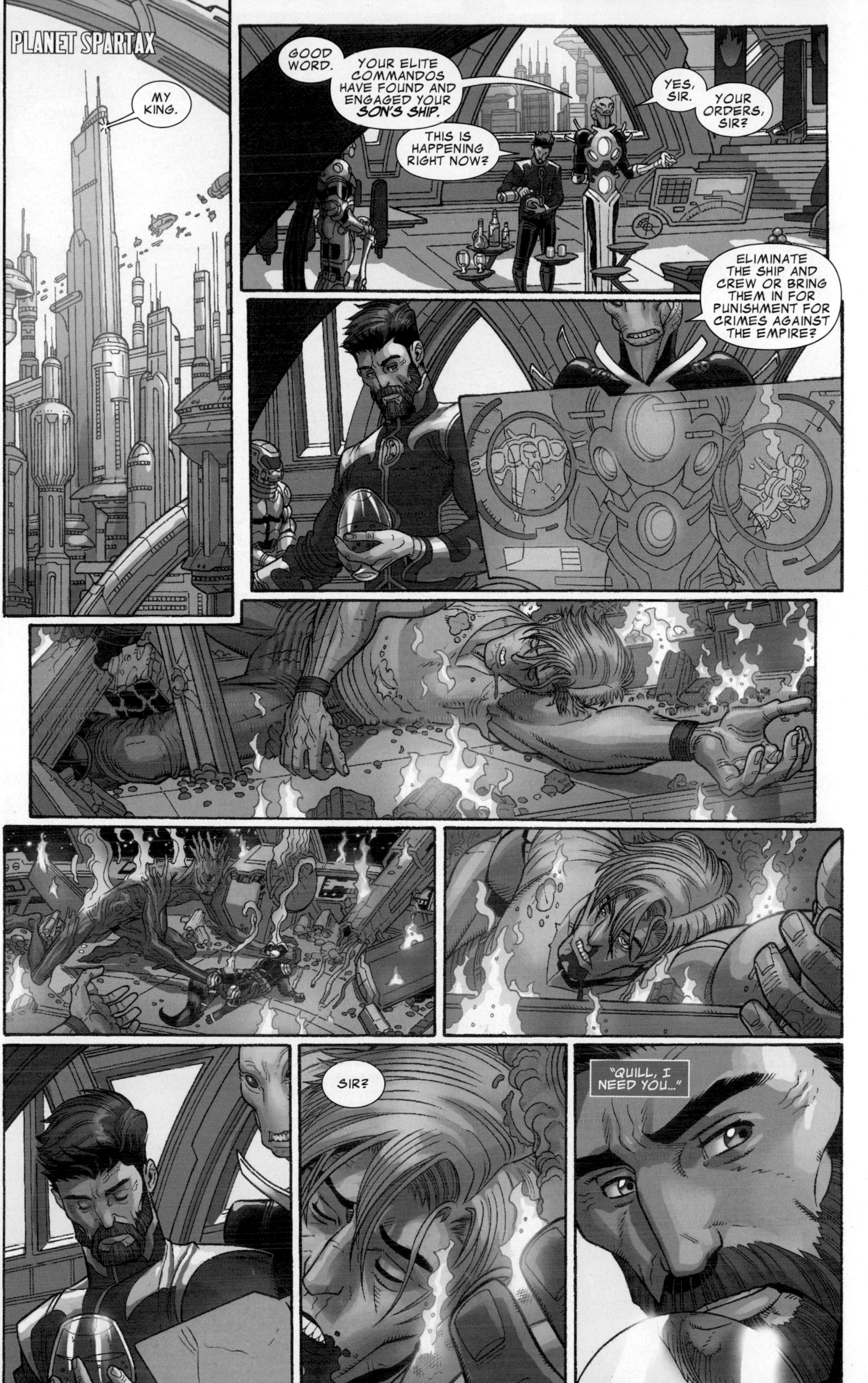
PLANET SPARTAX
MY KING.
GOOD WORD.
YOUR ELITE COMMANDOS HAVE FOUND AND ENGAGED YOUR SON'S SHIP.
THIS IS HAPPENING RIGHT NOW?
YES, SIR.
YOUR ORDERS, SIR?
ELIMINATE THE SHIP AND CREW OR BRING THEM IN FOR PUNISHMENT FOR CRIMES AGAINST THE EMPIRE?
SIR?
"QUILL, I NEED YOU..."

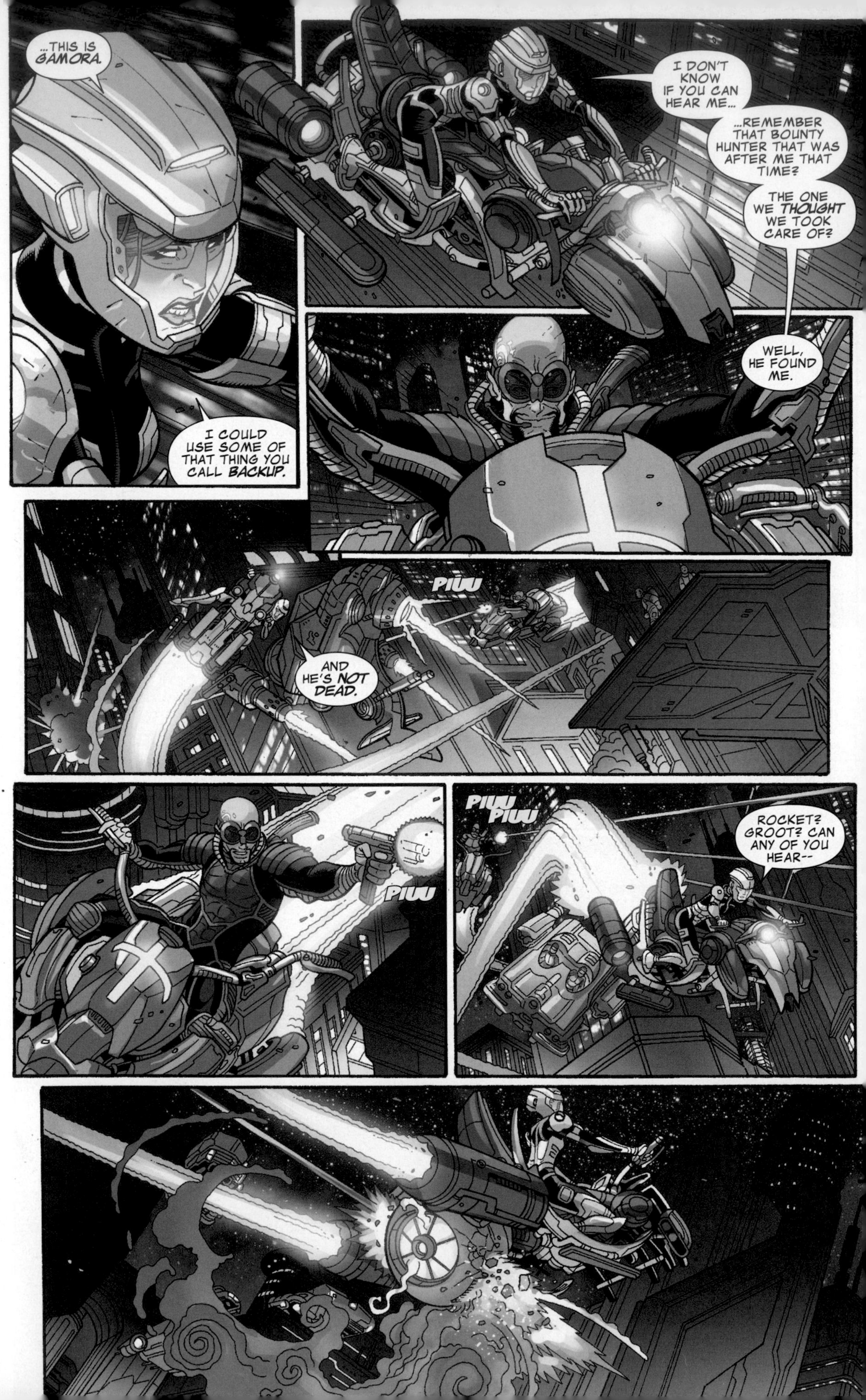
...THIS IS GAMORA.
I DON'T KNOW IF YOU CAN HEAR ME...
...REMEMBER THAT BOUNTY HUNTER THAT WAS AFTER ME THAT TIME?
THE ONE WE THOUGHT WE TOOK CARE OF?
I COULD USE SOME OF THAT THING YOU CALL BACKUP.
WELL, HE FOUND ME.
PIUU
AND HE'S NOT DEAD.
PIUU
PIUU PIUU
ROCKET? GROOT? CAN ANY OF YOU HEAR--

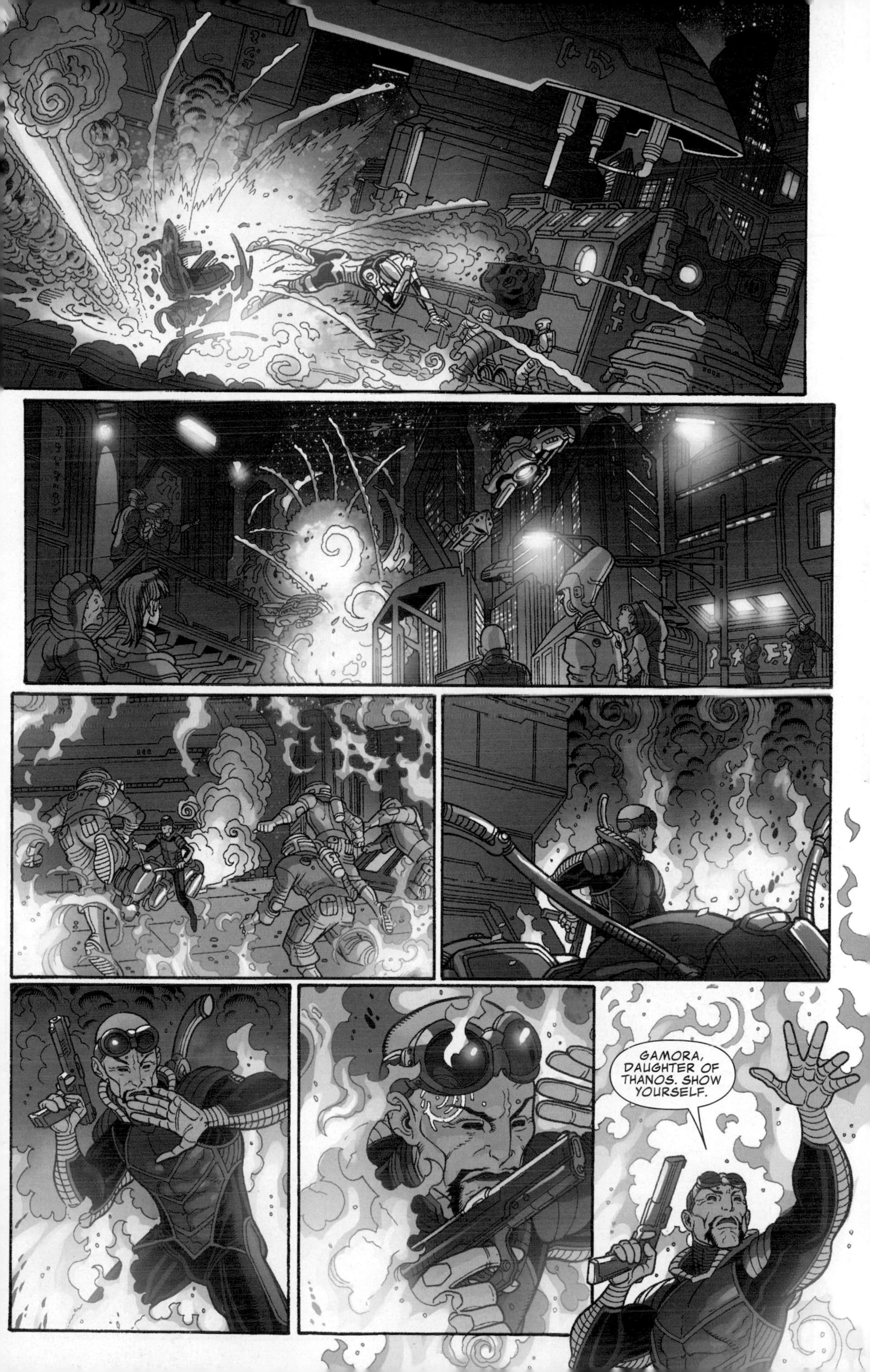
GAMORA, DAUGHTER OF THANOS. SHOW YOURSELF.

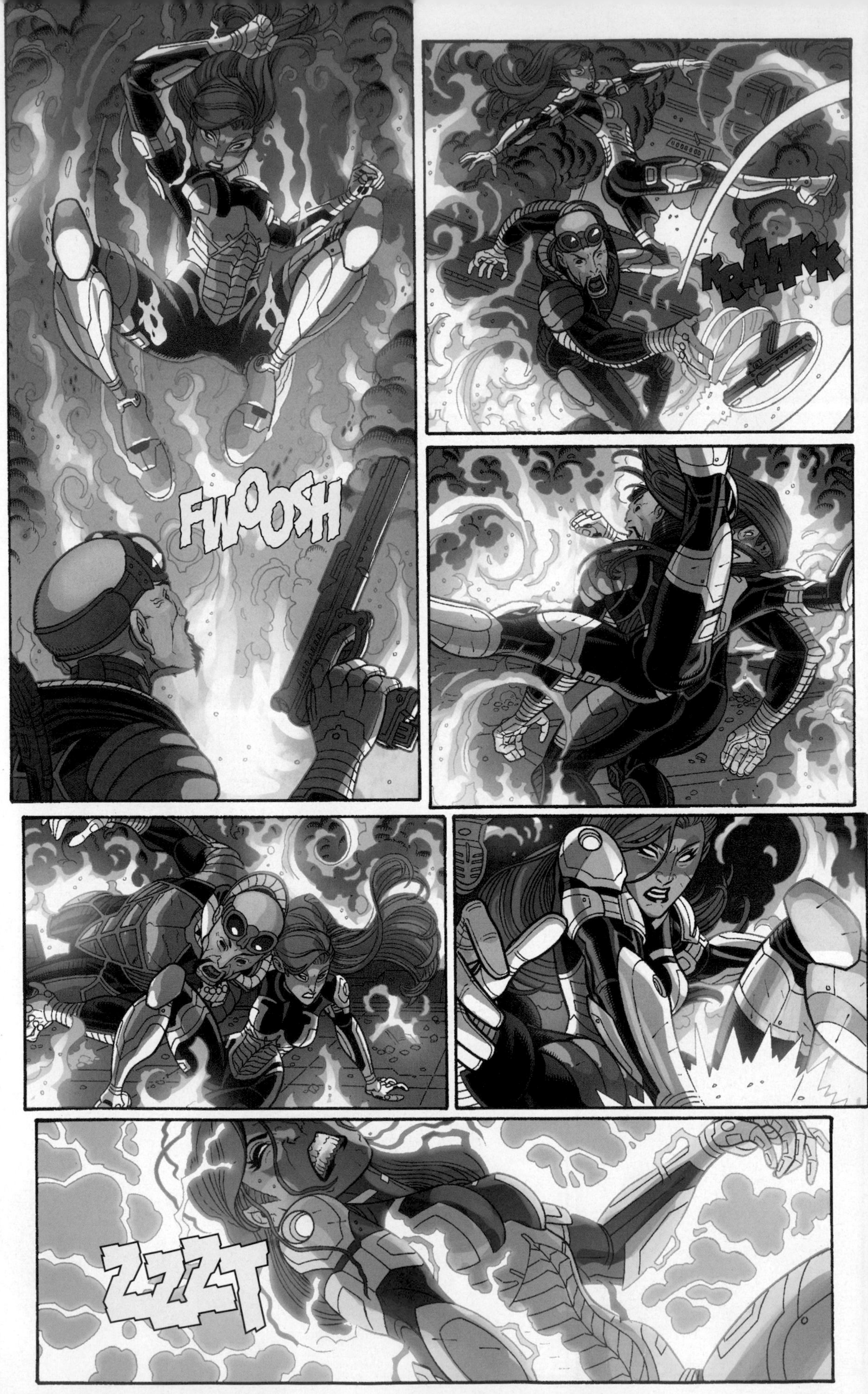
FWOOSH
KRAAKK
ZZZT

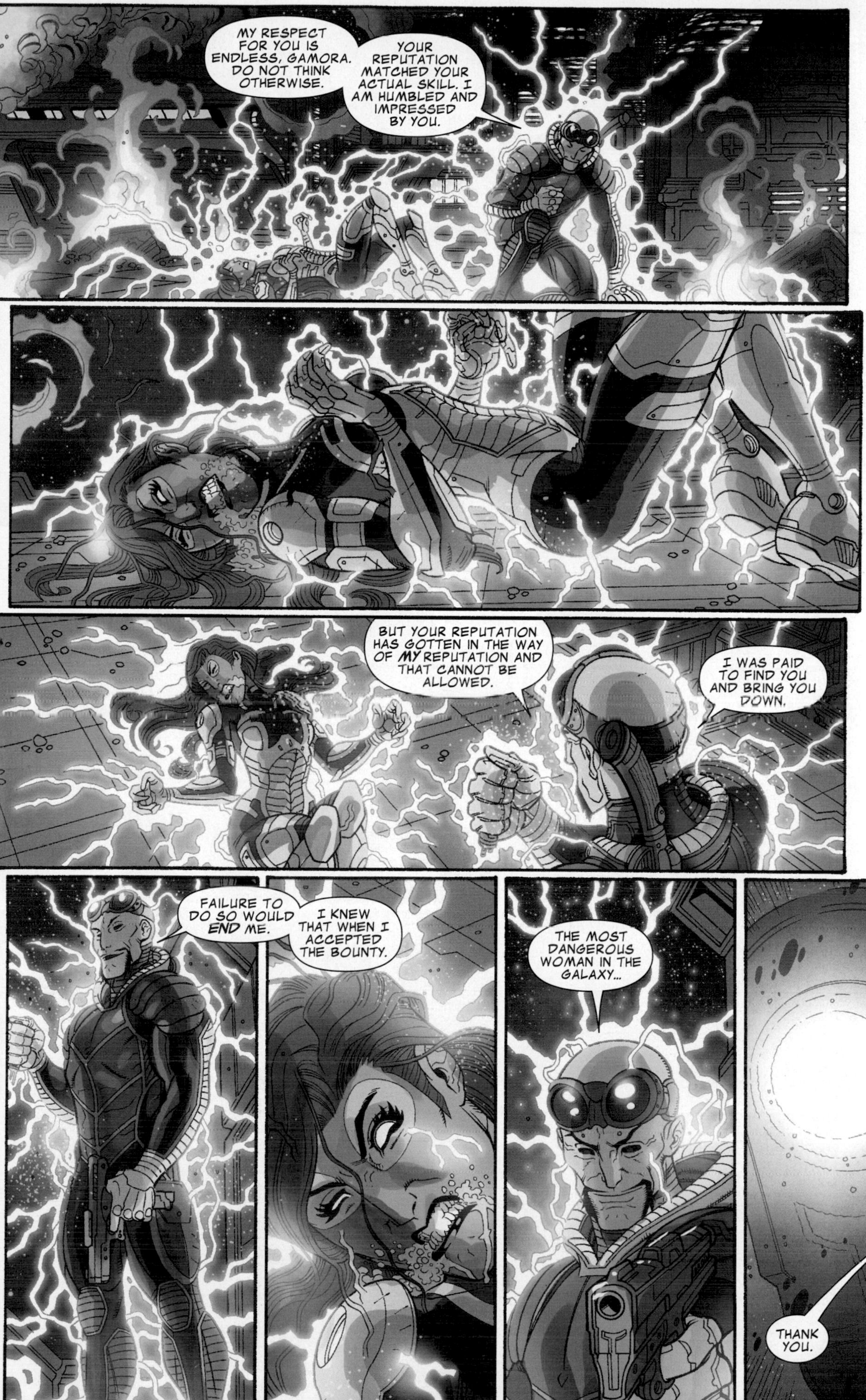
MY RESPECT FOR YOU IS ENDLESS, GAMORA. DO NOT THINK OTHERWISE.
YOUR REPUTATION MATCHED YOUR ACTUAL SKILL. I AM HUMBLED AND IMPRESSED BY YOU.
BUT YOUR REPUTATION HAS GOTTEN IN THE WAY OF MY REPUTATION AND THAT CANNOT BE ALLOWED.
I WAS PAID TO FIND YOU AND BRING YOU DOWN.
FAILURE TO DO SO WOULD END ME.
I KNEW THAT WHEN I ACCEPTED THE BOUNTY.
THE MOST DANGEROUS WOMAN IN THE GALAXY...
THANK YOU.

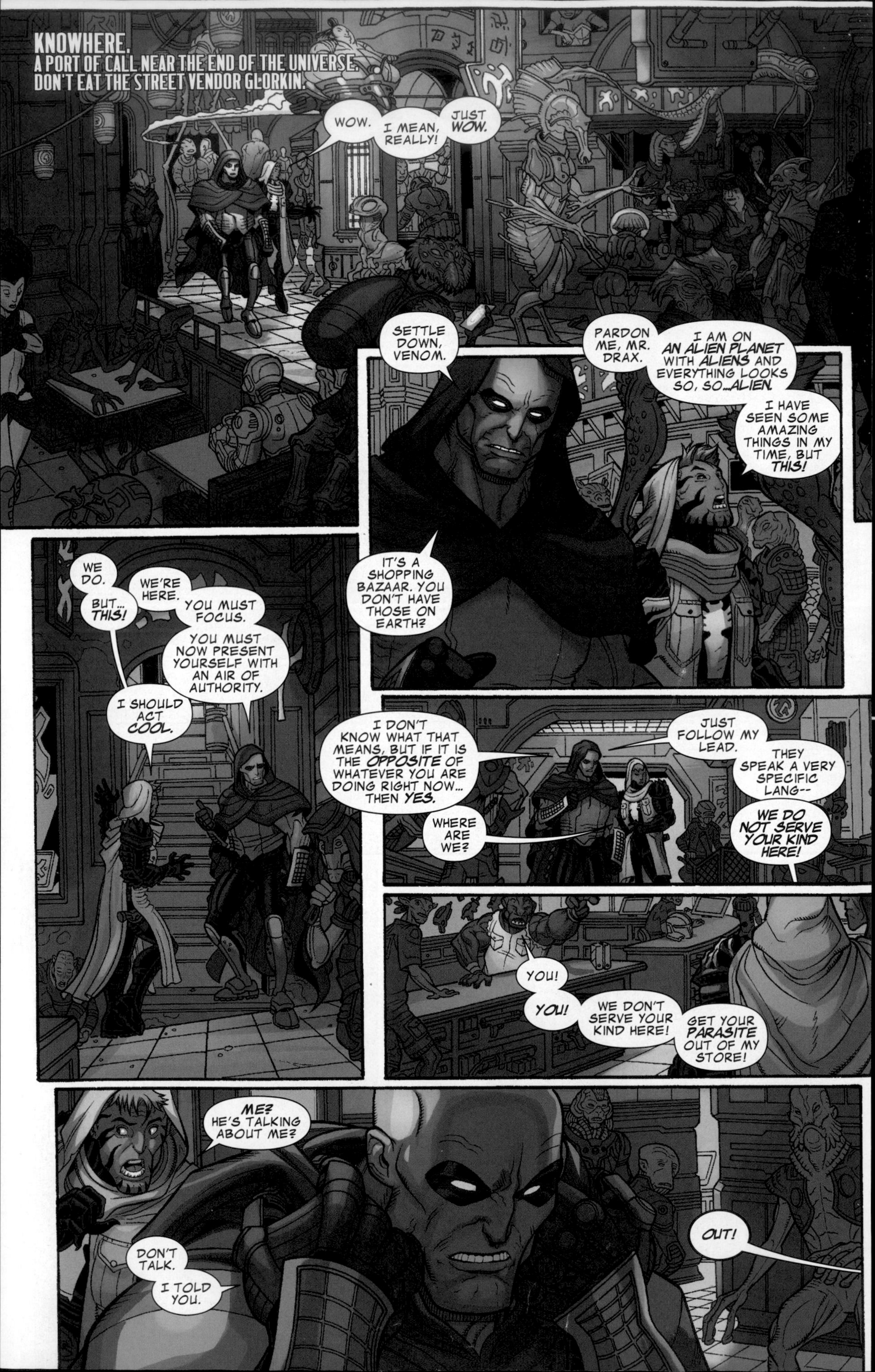
KNOWHERE.
A PORT OF CALL NEAR THE END OF THE UNIVERSE.
DON'T EAT THE STREET VENDOR GLORKIN.
WOW.
I MEAN, REALLY!
JUST WOW.
SETTLE DOWN, VENOM.
PARDON ME, MR. DRAX.
I AM ON AN ALIEN PLANET WITH ALIENS AND EVERYTHING LOOKS SO, SO...ALIEN.
I HAVE SEEN SOME AMAZING THINGS IN MY TIME, BUT THIS!
IT'S A SHOPPING BAZAAR. YOU DON'T HAVE THOSE ON EARTH?
WE DO.
BUT... THIS!
WE'RE HERE.
YOU MUST FOCUS.
YOU MUST NOW PRESENT YOURSELF WITH AN AIR OF AUTHORITY.
I SHOULD ACT COOL.
I DON'T KNOW WHAT THAT MEANS, BUT IF IT IS THE OPPOSITE OF WHATEVER YOU ARE DOING RIGHT NOW... THEN YES.
WHERE ARE WE?
JUST FOLLOW MY LEAD.
THEY SPEAK A VERY SPECIFIC LANG--
WE DO NOT SERVE YOUR KIND HERE!
YOU!
YOU!
WE DON'T SERVE YOUR KIND HERE!
GET YOUR PARASITE OUT OF MY STORE!
ME? HE'S TALKING ABOUT ME?
DON'T TALK.
I TOLD YOU.
OUT!

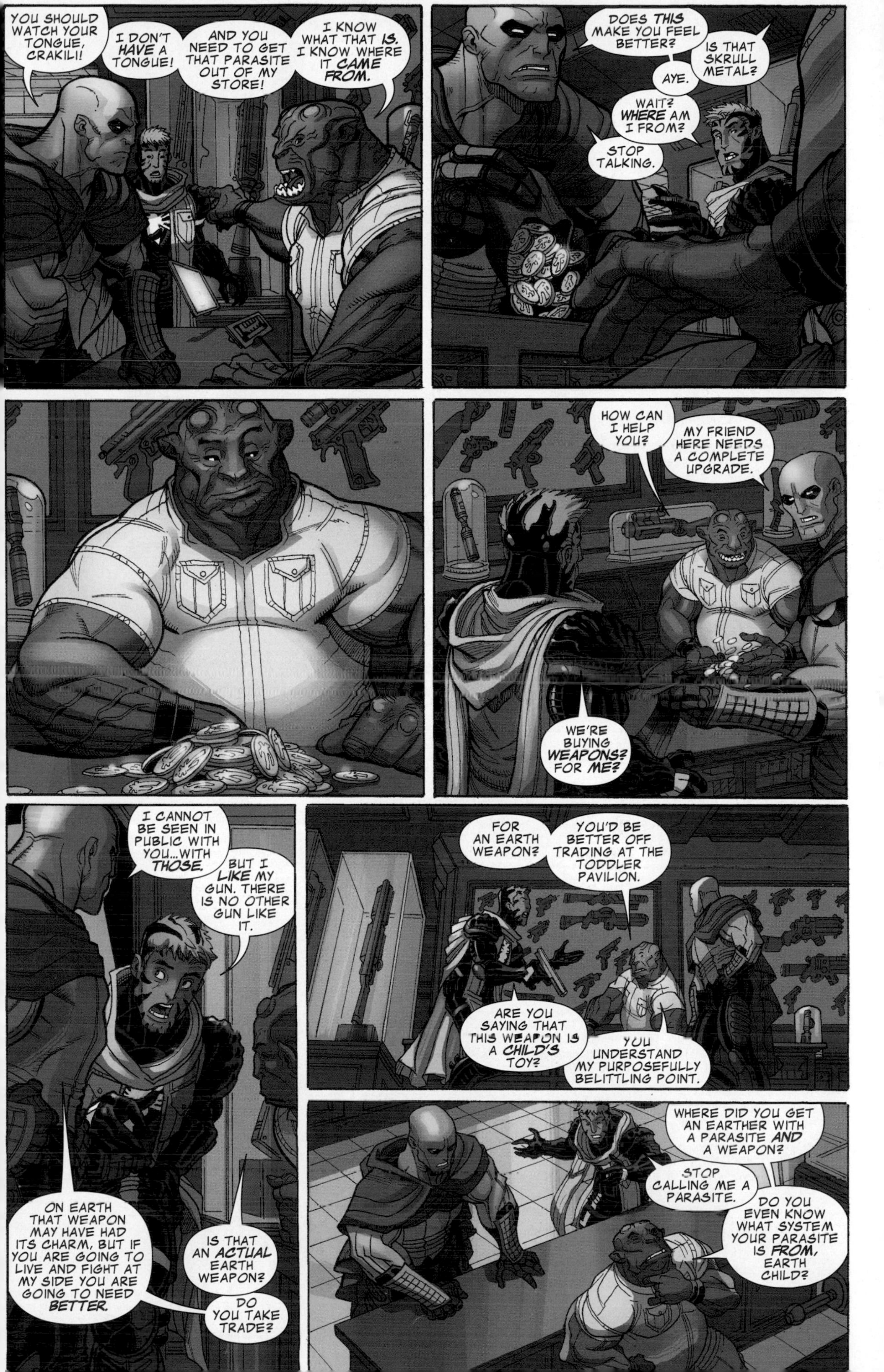
YOU SHOULD WATCH YOUR TONGUE, CRAKILI!
I DON'T HAVE A TONGUE!
AND YOU NEED TO GET THAT PARASITE OUT OF MY STORE!
I KNOW WHAT THAT IS. I KNOW WHERE IT CAME FROM.
DOES THIS MAKE YOU FEEL BETTER?
IS THAT SKRULL METAL?
AYE.
WAIT? WHERE AM I FROM?
STOP TALKING.
HOW CAN I HELP YOU?
MY FRIEND HERE NEEDS A COMPLETE UPGRADE.
WE'RE BUYING WEAPONS? FOR ME?
I CANNOT BE SEEN IN PUBLIC WITH YOU...WITH THOSE.
BUT I LIKE MY GUN. THERE IS NO OTHER GUN LIKE IT.
ON EARTH THAT WEAPON MAY HAVE HAD ITS CHARM, BUT IF YOU ARE GOING TO LIVE AND FIGHT AT MY SIDE YOU ARE GOING TO NEED BETTER.
IS THAT AN ACTUAL EARTH WEAPON?
DO YOU TAKE TRADE?
FOR AN EARTH WEAPON?
YOU'D BE BETTER OFF TRADING AT THE TODDLER PAVILION.
ARE YOU SAYING THAT THIS WEAPON IS A CHILD'S TOY?
YOU UNDERSTAND MY PURPOSEFULLY BELITTLING POINT.
WHERE DID YOU GET AN EARTHER WITH A PARASITE AND A WEAPON?
STOP CALLING ME A PARASITE.
DO YOU EVEN KNOW WHAT SYSTEM YOUR PARASITE IS FROM, EARTH CHILD?

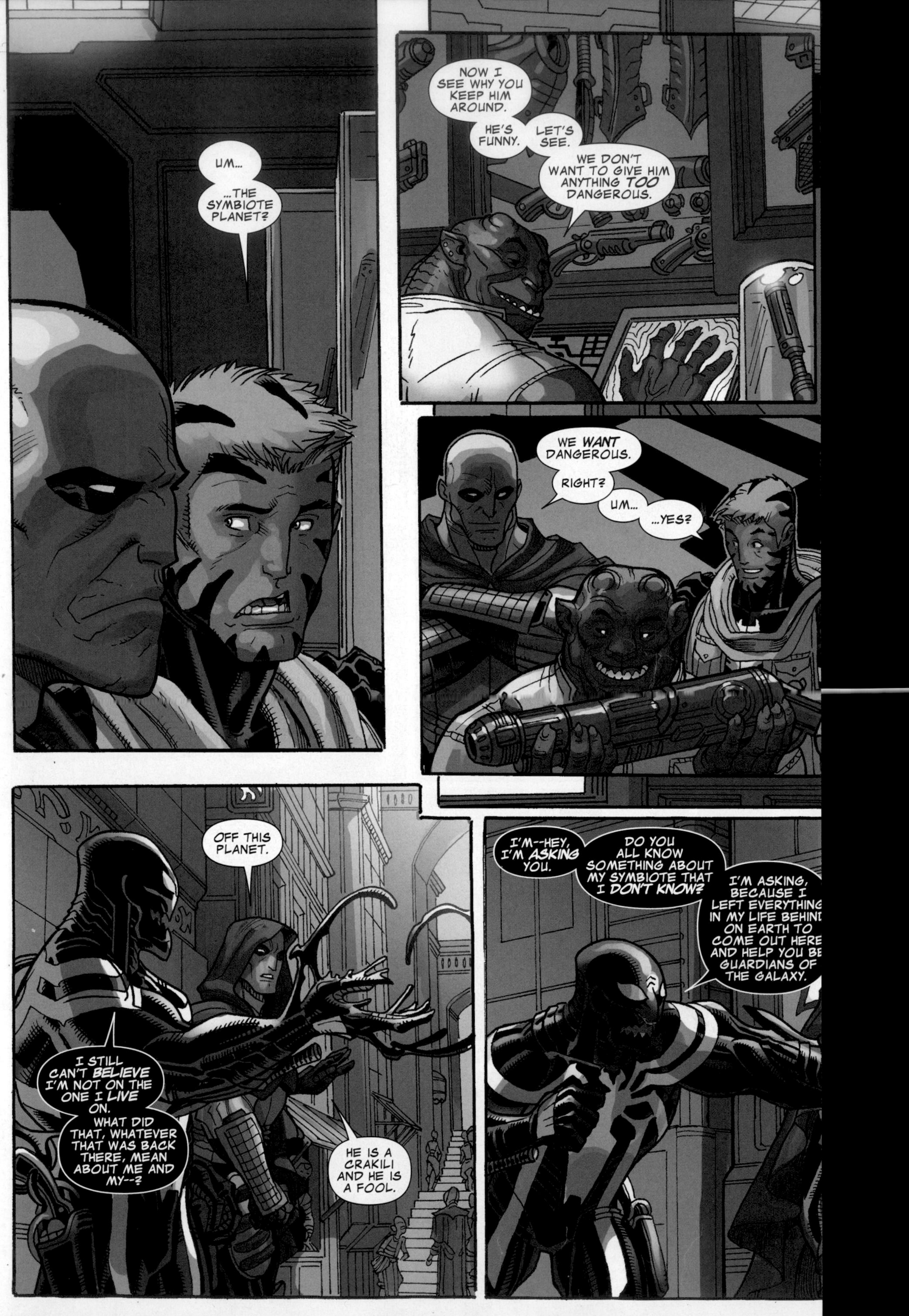
UM...
...THE SYMBIOTE PLANET?
NOW I SEE WHY YOU KEEP HIM AROUND.
HE'S FUNNY.
LET'S SEE.
WE DON'T WANT TO GIVE HIM ANYTHING TOO DANGEROUS.
WE WANT DANGEROUS.
RIGHT?
UM...
...YES?
OFF THIS PLANET.
I STILL CAN'T BELIEVE I'M NOT ON THE ONE I LIVE ON.
WHAT DID THAT, WHATEVER THAT WAS BACK THERE, MEAN ABOUT ME AND MY--?
HE IS A CRAKILI AND HE IS A FOOL.
I'M--HEY, I'M ASKING YOU.
DO YOU ALL KNOW SOMETHING ABOUT MY SYMBIOTE THAT I DON'T KNOW?
I'M ASKING, BECAUSE I LEFT EVERYTHING IN MY LIFE BEHIND ON EARTH TO COME OUT HERE AND HELP YOU BE GUARDIANS OF THE GALAXY.

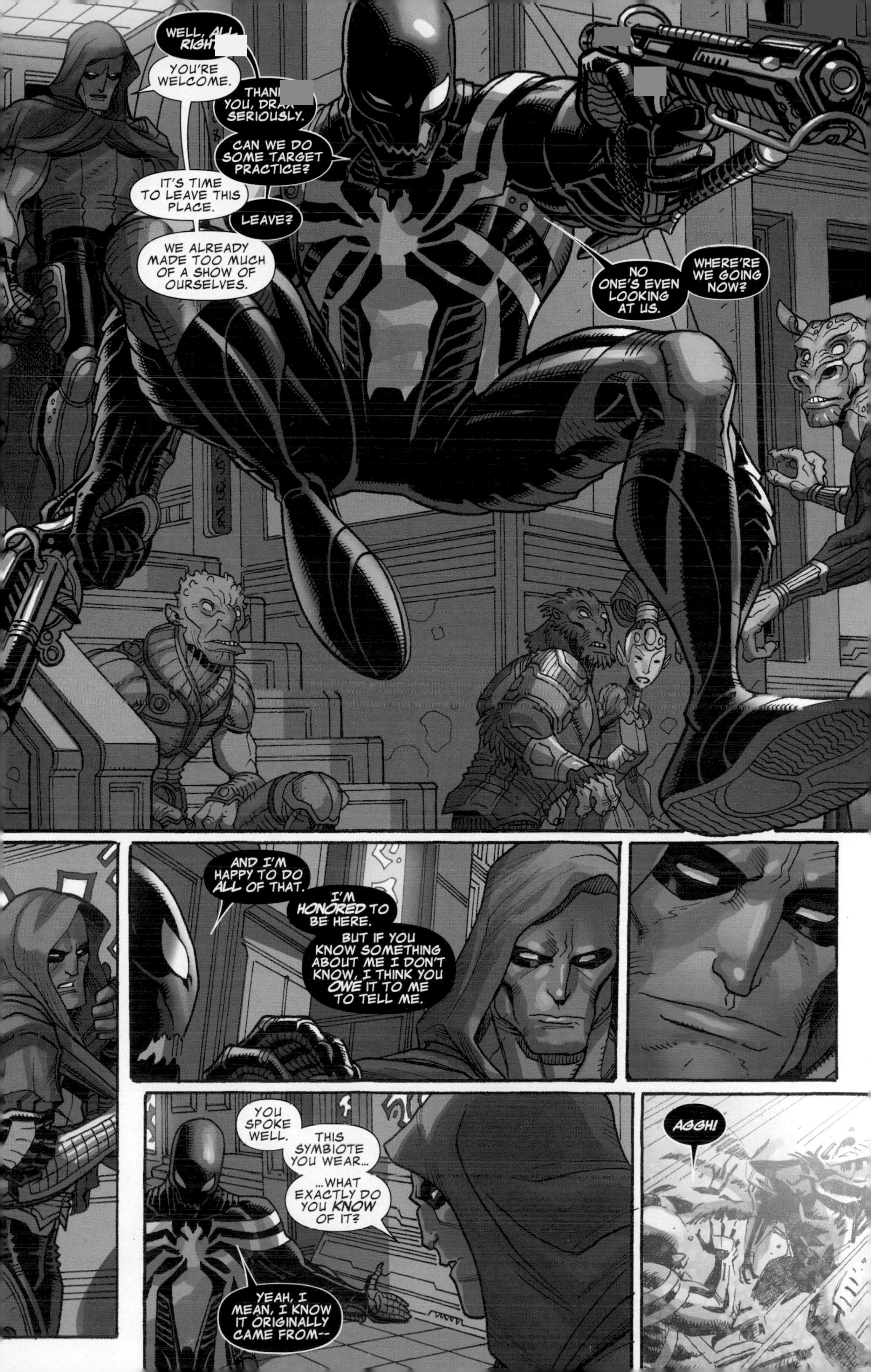
WELL, ALL RIGH
YOU'RE WELCOME.
THANK YOU, DRAX SERIOUSLY.
CAN WE DO SOME TARGET PRACTICE?
IT'S TIME TO LEAVE THIS PLACE.
LEAVE?
WE ALREADY MADE TOO MUCH OF A SHOW OF OURSELVES.
NO ONE'S EVEN LOOKING AT US.
WHERE'RE WE GOING NOW?
AND I'M HAPPY TO DO ALL OF THAT.
I'M HONORED TO BE HERE.
BUT IF YOU KNOW SOMETHING ABOUT ME I DON'T KNOW, I THINK YOU OWE IT TO ME TO TELL ME.
YOU SPOKE WELL.
THIS SYMBIOTE YOU WEAR...
...WHAT EXACTLY DO YOU KNOW OF IT?
YEAH, I MEAN, I KNOW IT ORIGINALLY CAME FROM--
AGGH!

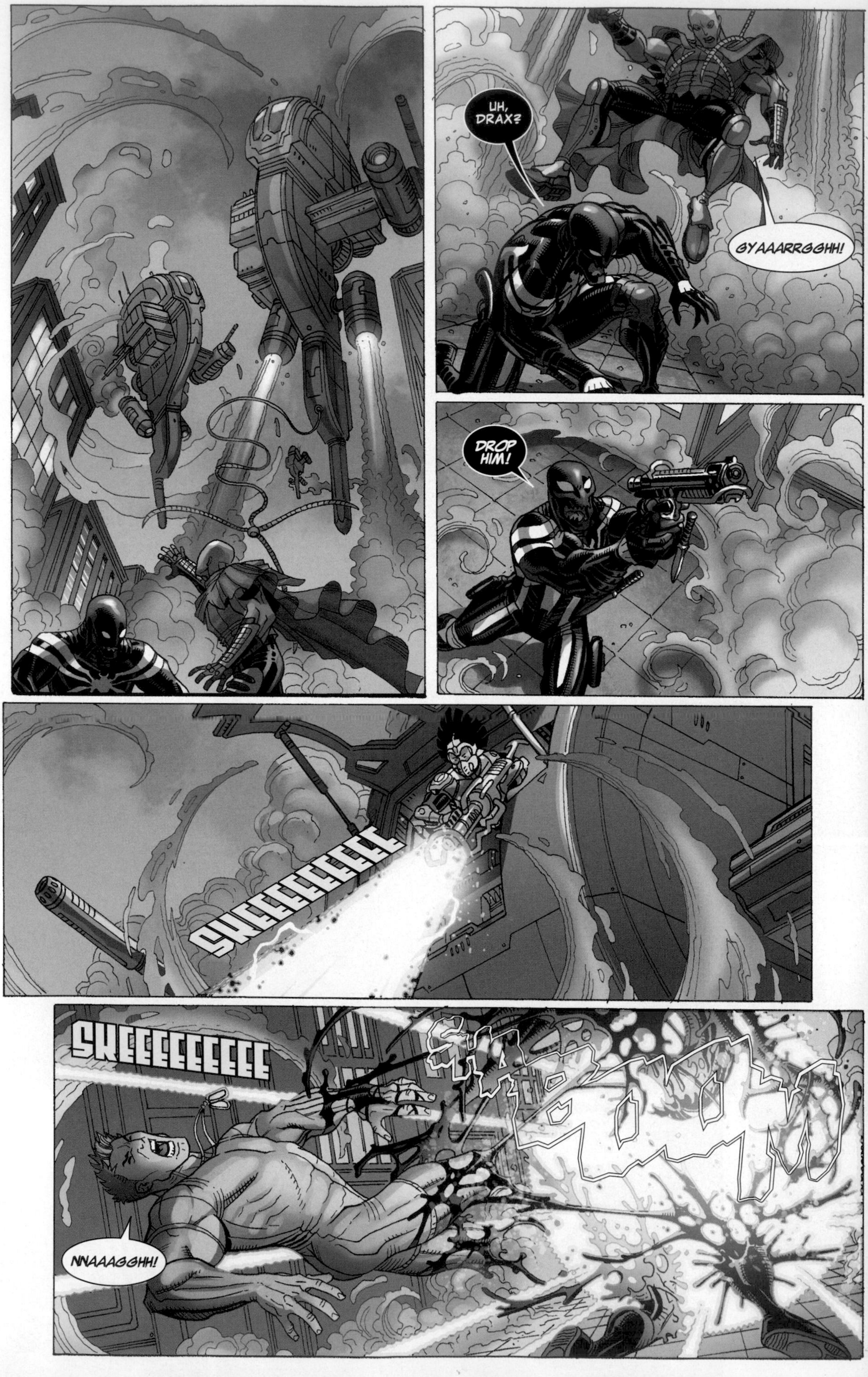
UH, DRAX?
GYAAARRGGHH!
DROP HIM!
SKEEEEEEEEE
SKEEEEEEEEEE
NNAAAGGHH!

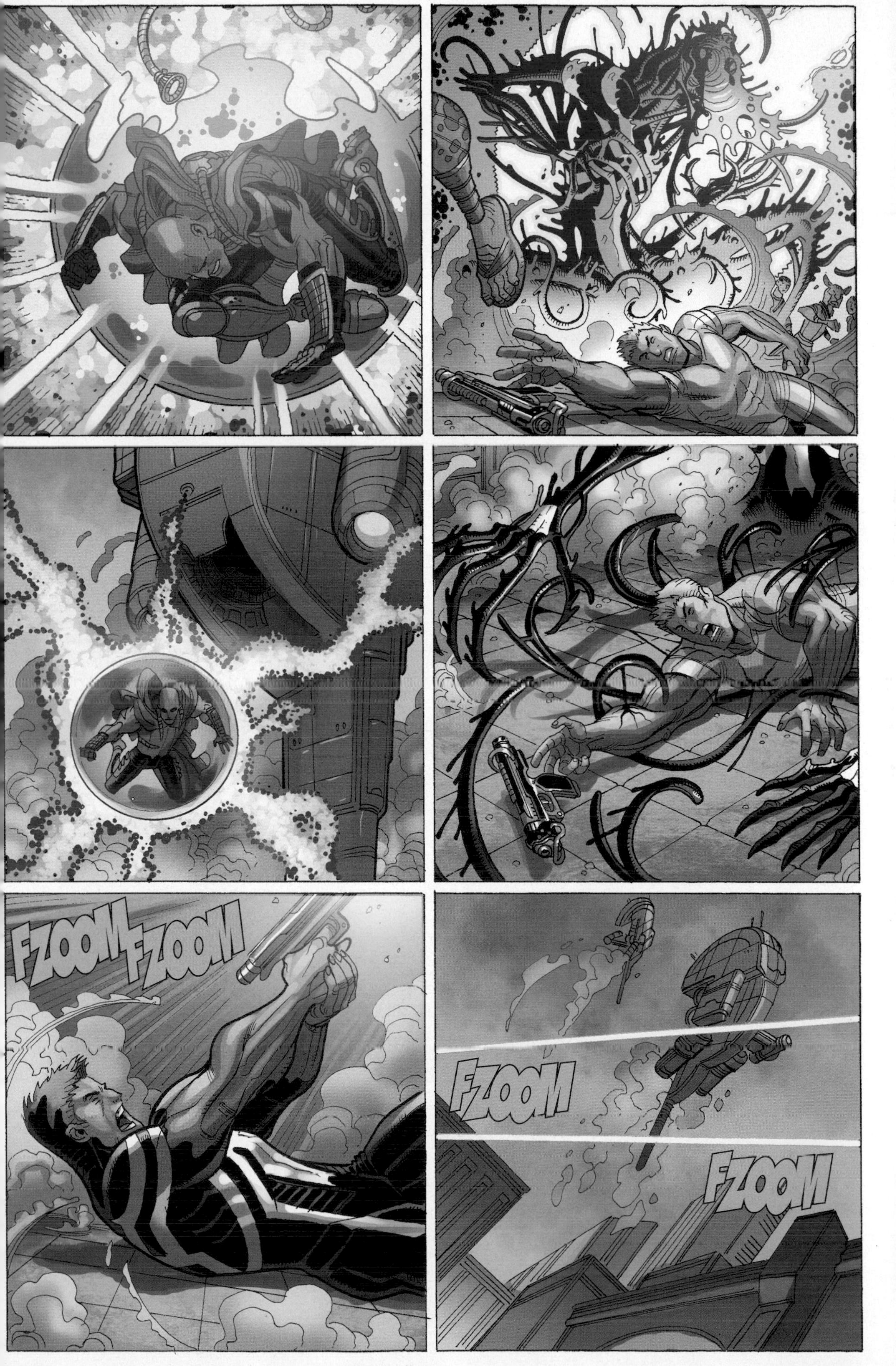
FZOOM FZOOM
FZOOM
FZOOM

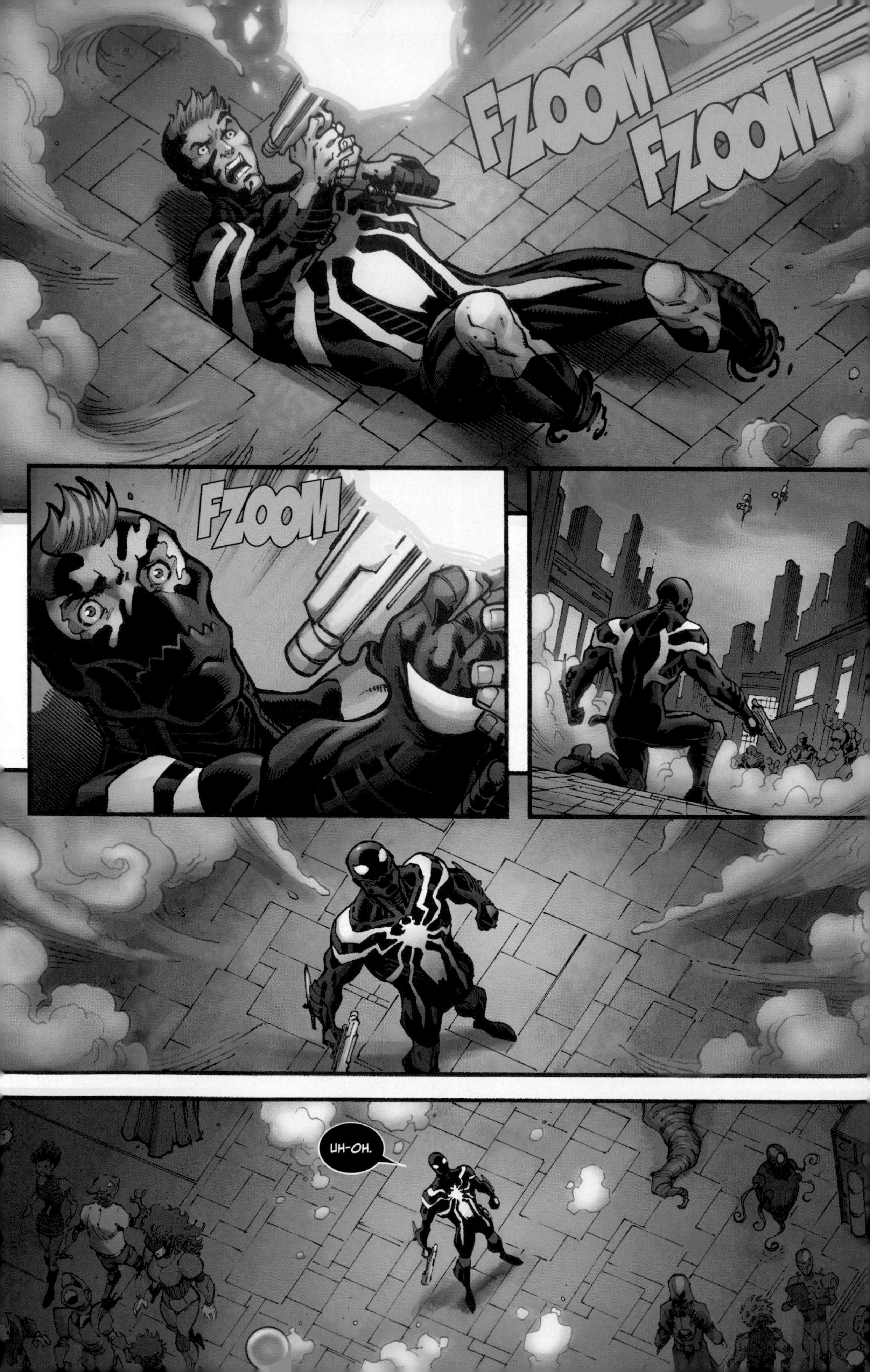
FZOOM
FZOOM
FZOOM
UH-OH.

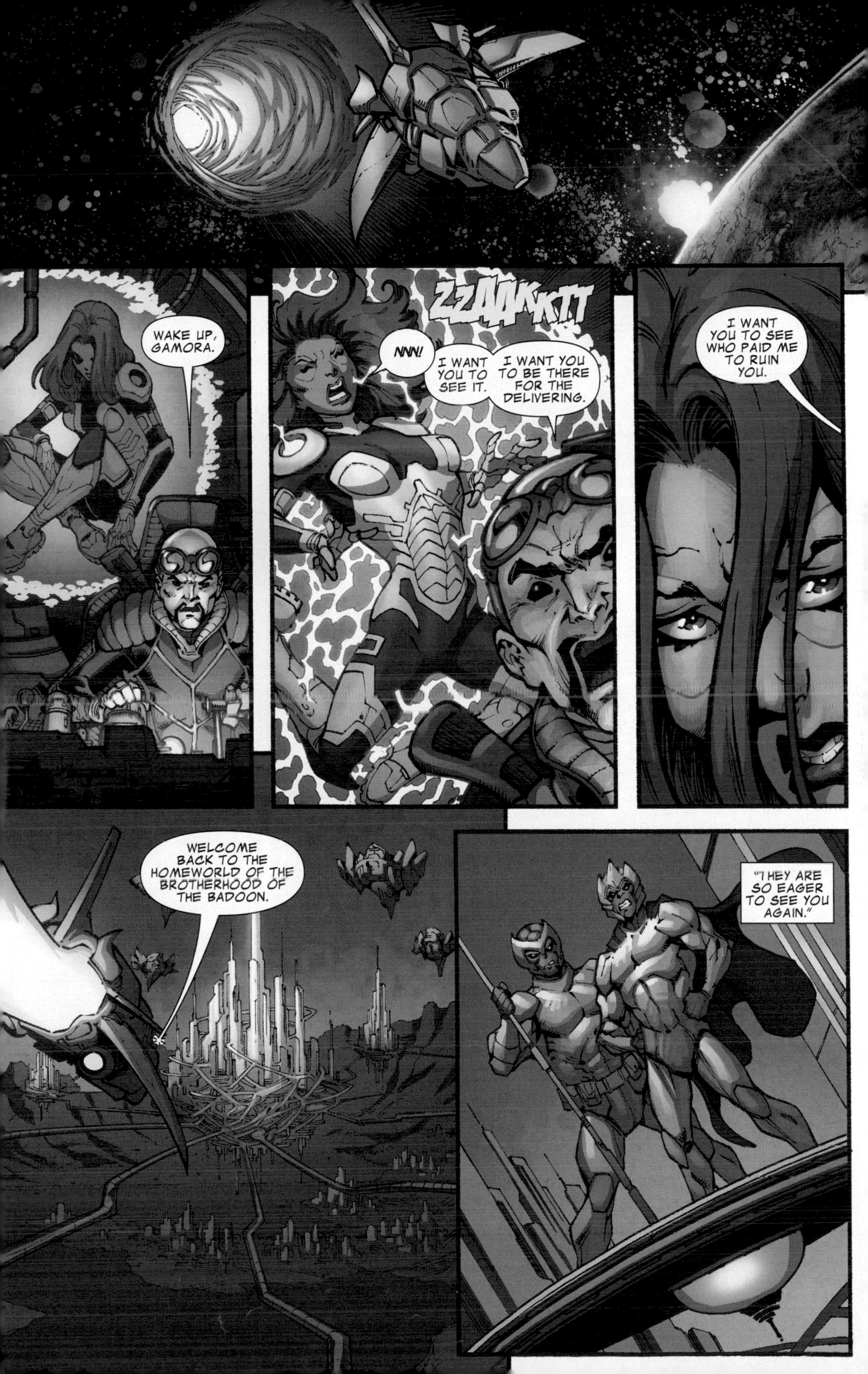
WAKE UP, GAMORA.
ZZAAKKTT
NNN!
I WANT YOU TO SEE IT.
I WANT YOU TO BE THERE FOR THE DELIVERING.
I WANT YOU TO SEE WHO PAID ME TO RUIN YOU.
WELCOME BACK TO THE HOMEWORLD OF THE BROTHERHOOD OF THE BADOON.
"THEY ARE SO EAGER TO SEE YOU AGAIN."

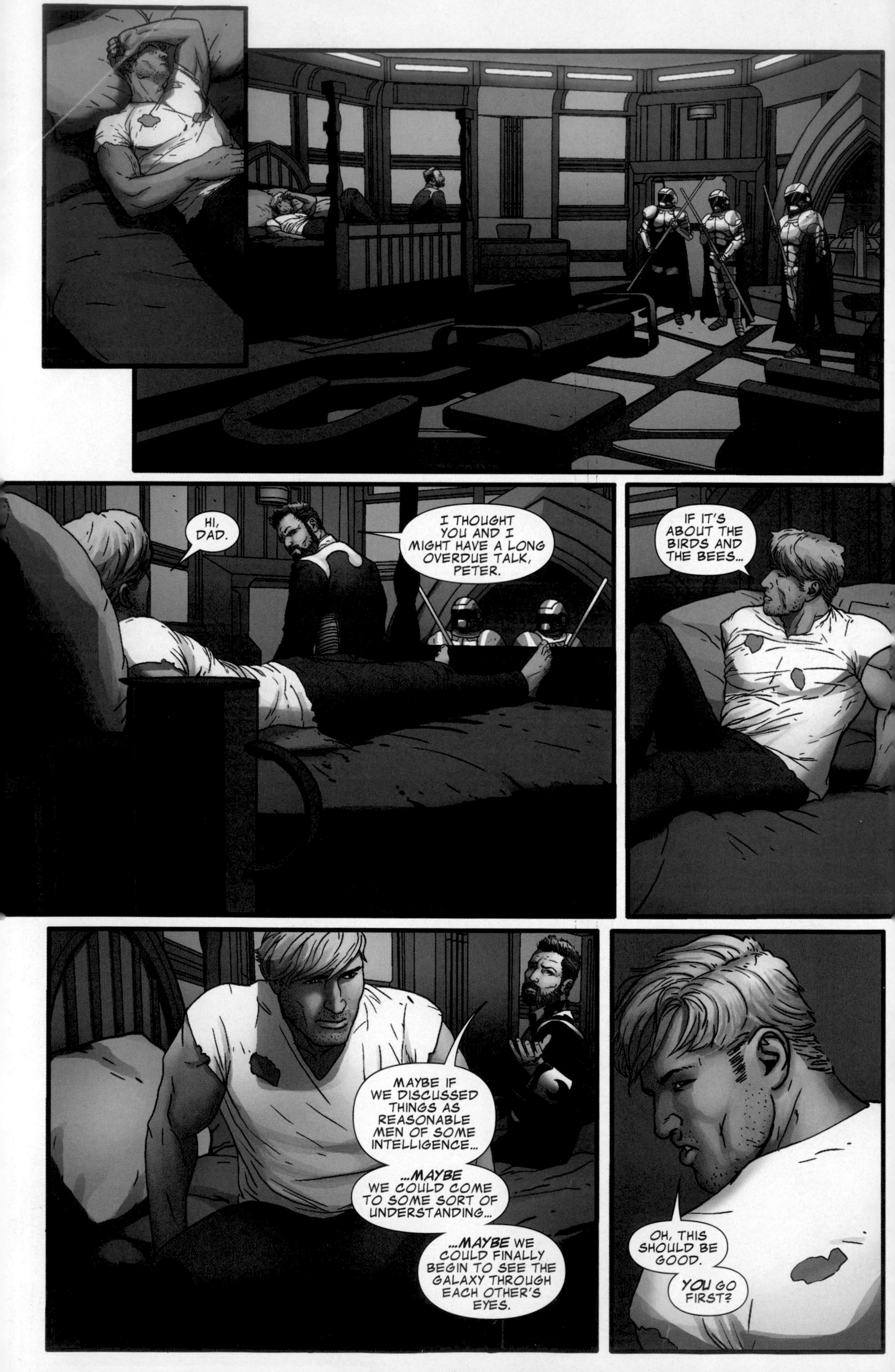
HI, DAD.
I THOUGHT YOU AND I MIGHT HAVE A LONG OVERDUE TALK, PETER.
IF IT'S ABOUT THE BIRDS AND THE BEES...
MAYBE IF WE DISCUSSED THINGS AS REASONABLE MEN OF SOME INTELLIGENCE...
...MAYBE WE COULD COME TO SOME SORT OF UNDERSTANDING...
...MAYBE WE COULD FINALLY BEGIN TO SEE THE GALAXY THROUGH EACH OTHER'S EYES.
OH, THIS SHOULD BE GOOD.
YOU GO FIRST?

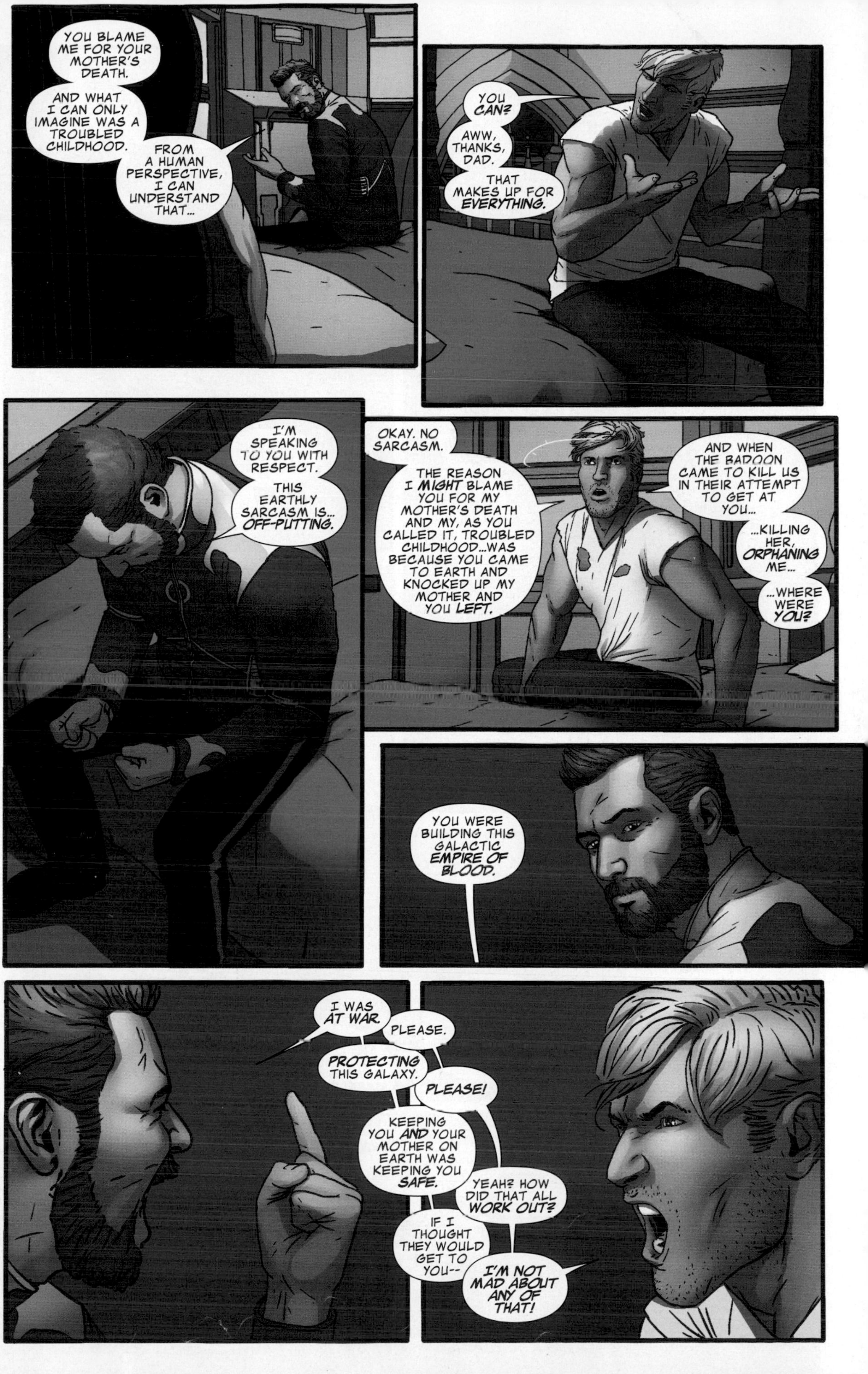
YOU BLAME ME FOR YOUR MOTHER'S DEATH.
AND WHAT I CAN ONLY IMAGINE WAS A TROUBLED CHILDHOOD.
FROM A HUMAN PERSPECTIVE, I CAN UNDERSTAND THAT...
YOU CAN?
AWW, THANKS, DAD.
THAT MAKES UP FOR EVERYTHING.
I'M SPEAKING TO YOU WITH RESPECT.
THIS EARTHLY SARCASM IS... OFF-PUTTING.
OKAY. NO SARCASM.
THE REASON I MIGHT BLAME YOU FOR MY MOTHER'S DEATH AND MY, AS YOU CALLED IT, TROUBLED CHILDHOOD...WAS BECAUSE YOU CAME TO EARTH AND KNOCKED UP MY MOTHER AND YOU LEFT.
AND WHEN THE BADOON CAME TO KILL US IN THEIR ATTEMPT TO GET AT YOU...
...KILLING HER, ORPHANING ME...
...WHERE WERE YOU?
YOU WERE BUILDING THIS GALACTIC EMPIRE OF BLOOD.
I WAS AT WAR.
PLEASE.
PROTECTING THIS GALAXY.
PLEASE!
KEEPING YOU AND YOUR MOTHER ON EARTH WAS KEEPING YOU SAFE.
YEAH? HOW DID THAT ALL WORK OUT?
IF I THOUGHT THEY WOULD GET TO YOU--
I'M NOT MAD ABOUT ANY OF THAT!

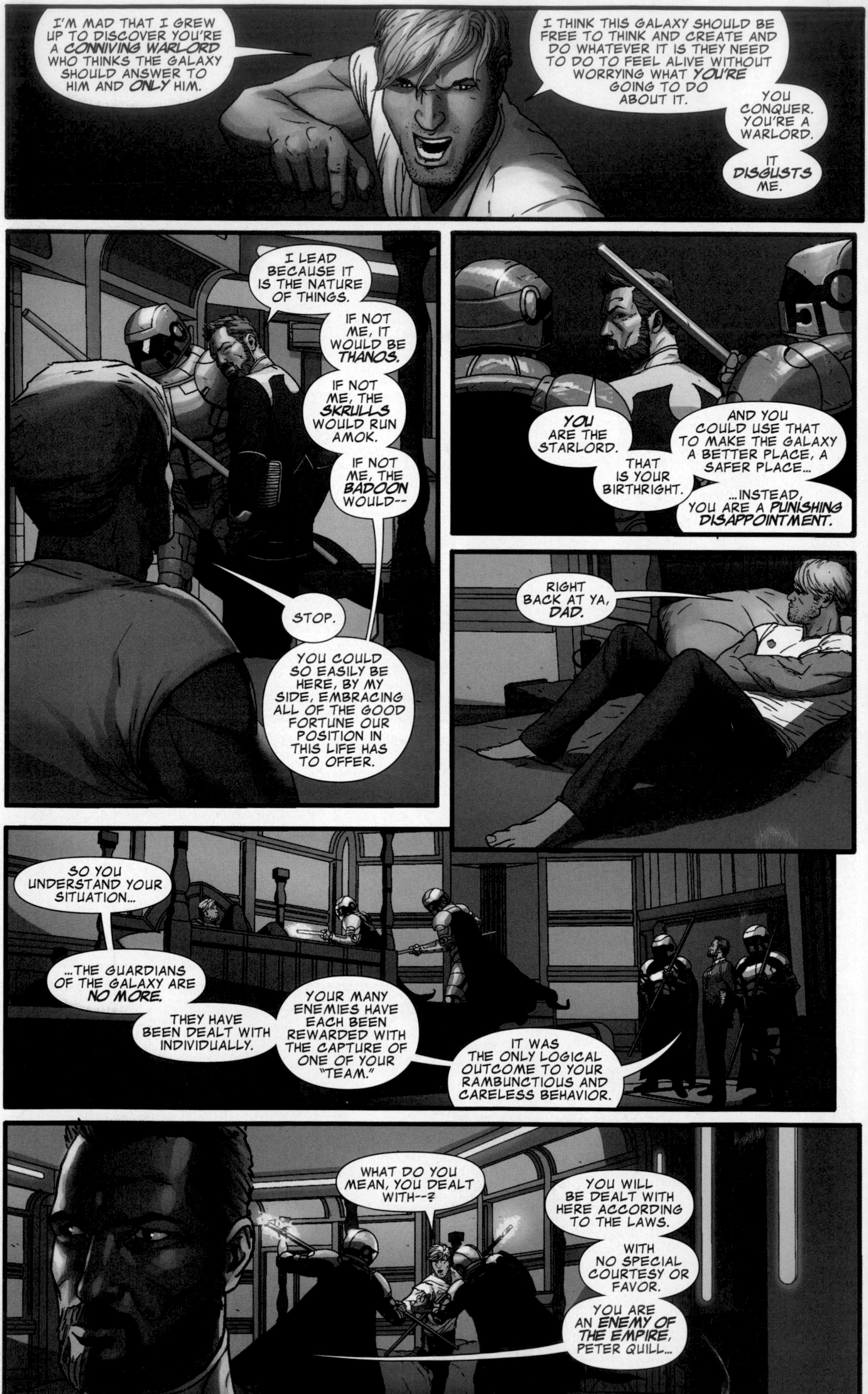

I'M MAD THAT I GREW UP TO DISCOVER YOU'RE A CONNIVING WARLORD WHO THINKS THE GALAXY SHOULD ANSWER TO HIM AND ONLY HIM.
I THINK THIS GALAXY SHOULD BE FREE TO THINK AND CREATE AND DO WHATEVER IT IS THEY NEED TO DO TO FEEL ALIVE WITHOUT WORRYING WHAT YOU'RE GOING TO DO ABOUT IT.
YOU CONQUER. YOU'RE A WARLORD.
IT DISGUSTS ME.
I LEAD BECAUSE IT IS THE NATURE OF THINGS.
IF NOT ME, IT WOULD BE THANOS.
IF NOT ME, THE SKRULLS WOULD RUN AMOK.
IF NOT ME, THE BADOON WOULD--
STOP.
YOU COULD SO EASILY BE HERE, BY MY SIDE, EMBRACING ALL OF THE GOOD FORTUNE OUR POSITION IN THIS LIFE HAS TO OFFER.
YOU ARE THE STARLORD.
THAT IS YOUR BIRTHRIGHT.
AND YOU COULD USE THAT TO MAKE THE GALAXY A BETTER PLACE, A SAFER PLACE...
...INSTEAD, YOU ARE A PUNISHING DISAPPOINTMENT.
RIGHT BACK AT YA, DAD.
SO YOU UNDERSTAND YOUR SITUATION...
...THE GUARDIANS OF THE GALAXY ARE NO MORE.
THEY HAVE BEEN DEALT WITH INDIVIDUALLY.
YOUR MANY ENEMIES HAVE EACH BEEN REWARDED WITH THE CAPTURE OF ONE OF YOUR "TEAM."
IT WAS THE ONLY LOGICAL OUTCOME TO YOUR RAMBUNCTIOUS AND CARELESS BEHAVIOR.
WHAT DO YOU MEAN, YOU DEALT WITH--?
YOU WILL BE DEALT WITH HERE ACCORDING TO THE LAWS.
WITH NO SPECIAL COURTESY OR FAVOR.
YOU ARE AN ENEMY OF THE EMPIRE, PETER QUILL...

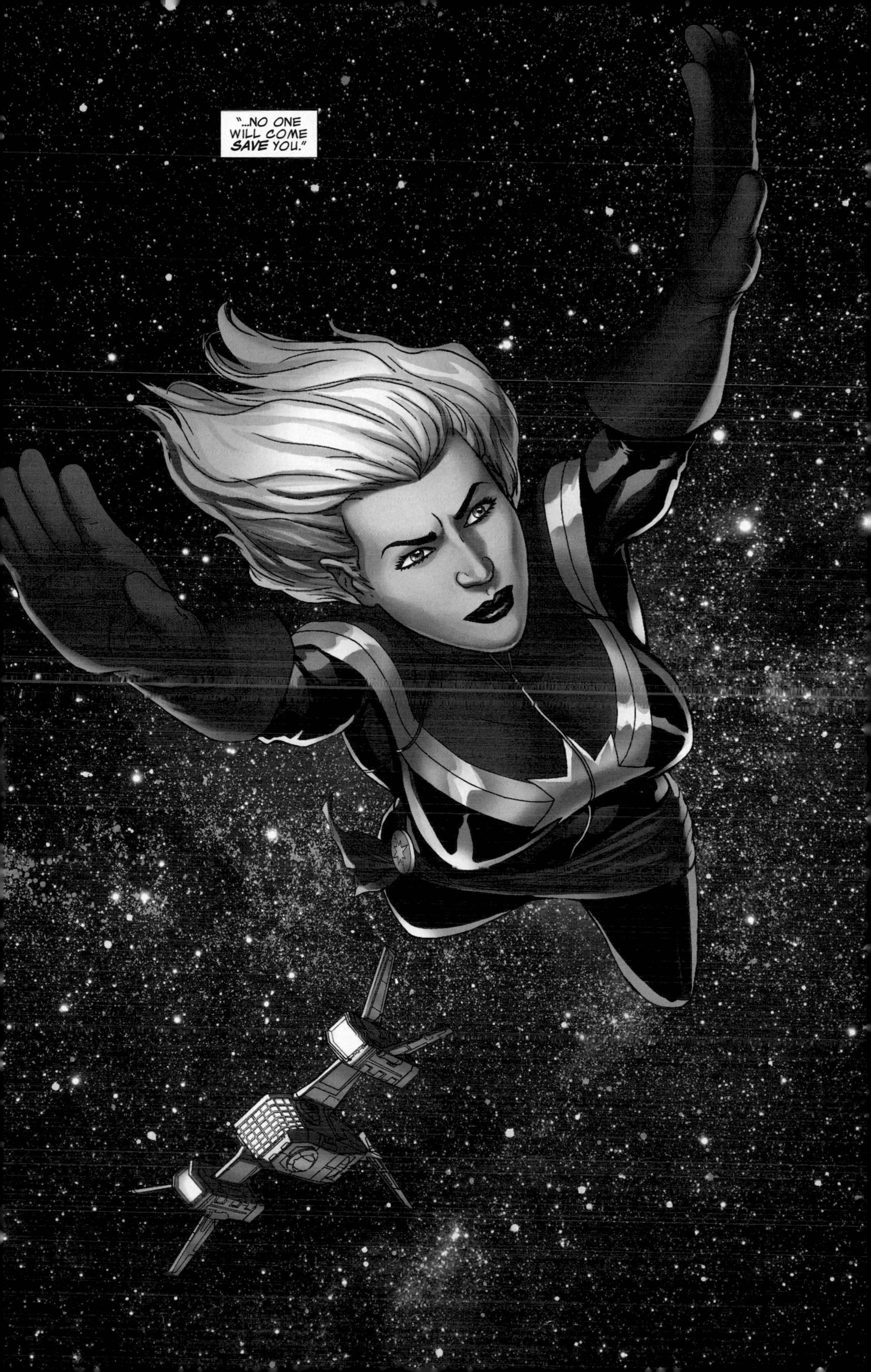
"...NO ONE WILL COME SAVE YOU."

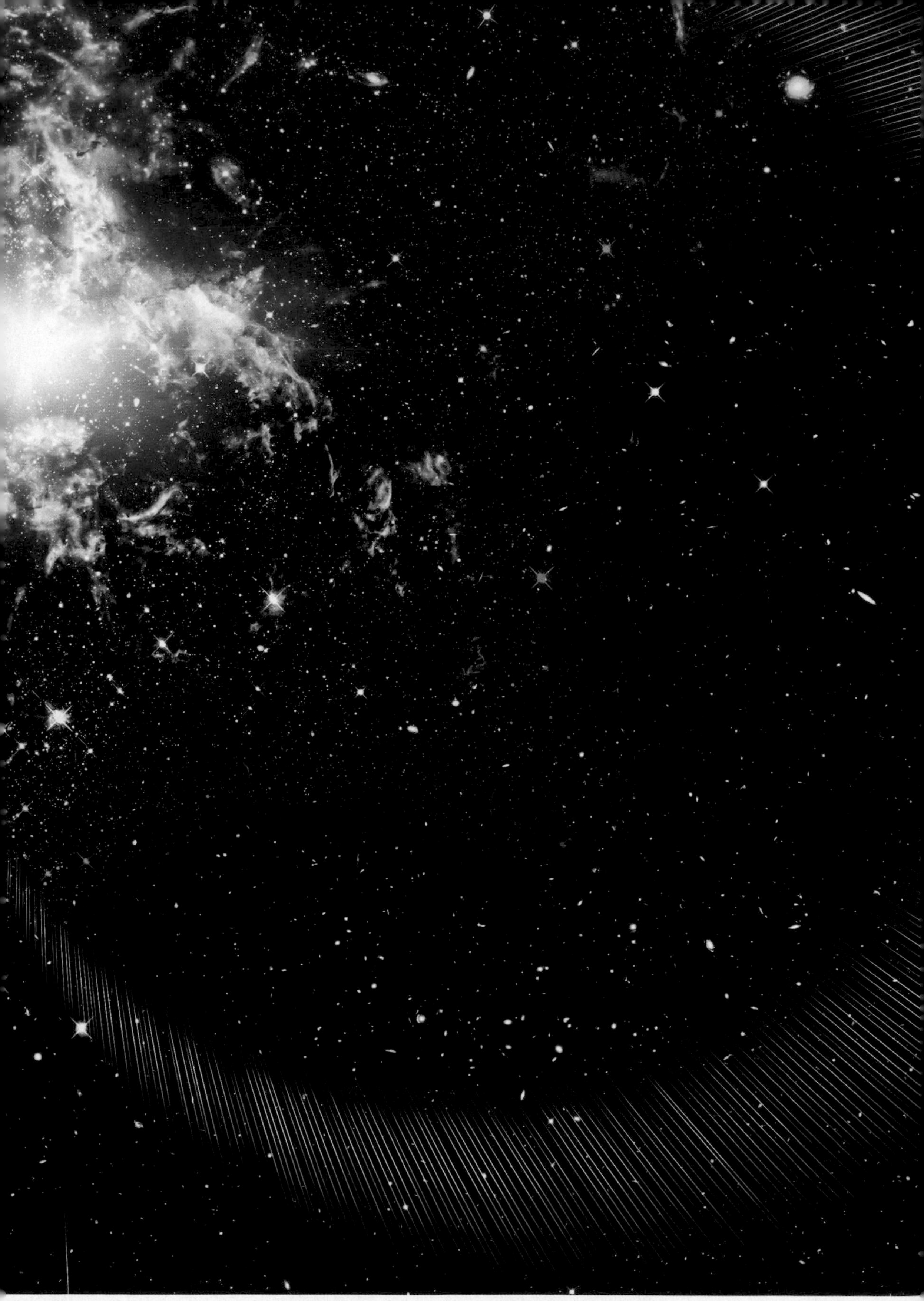

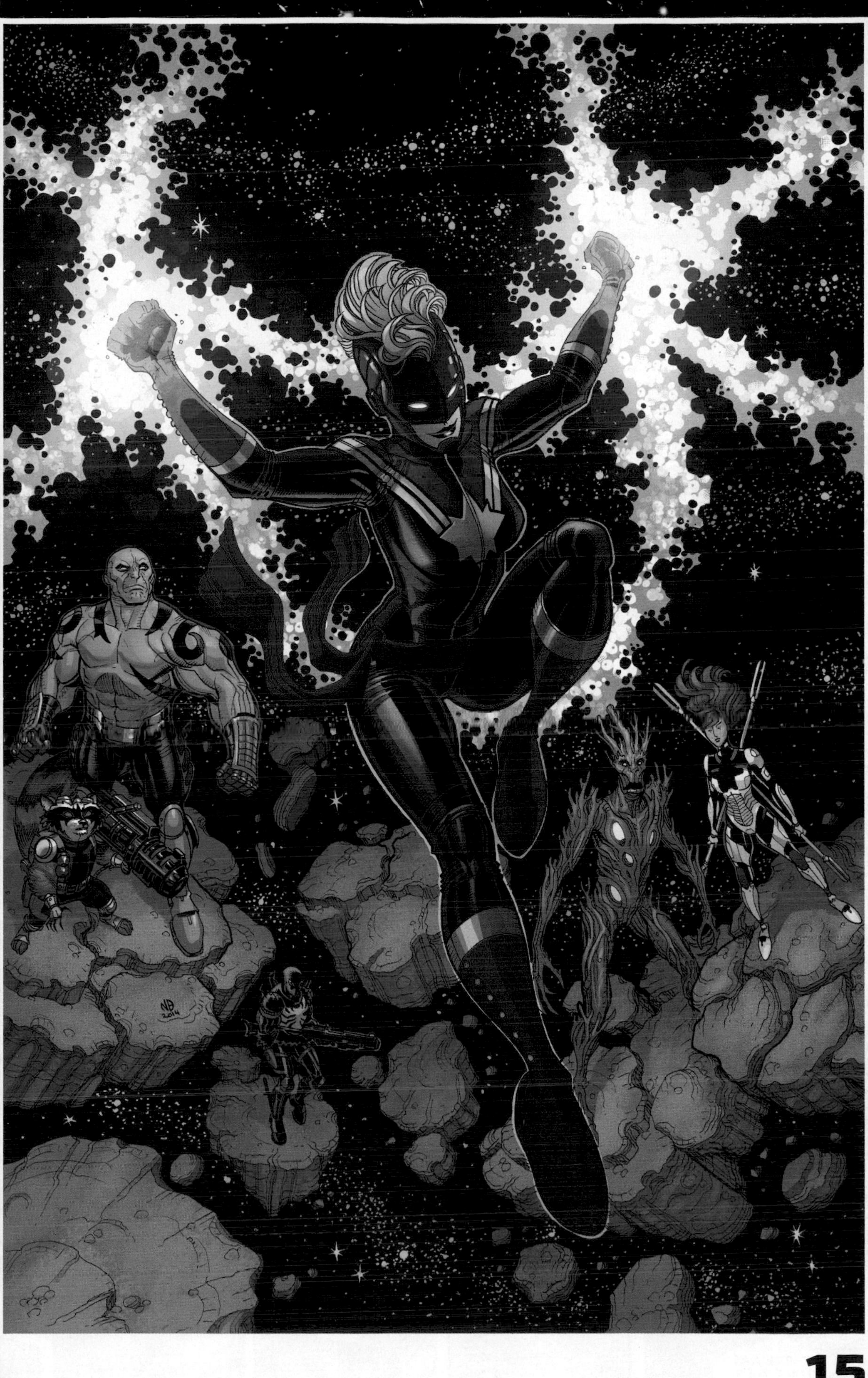

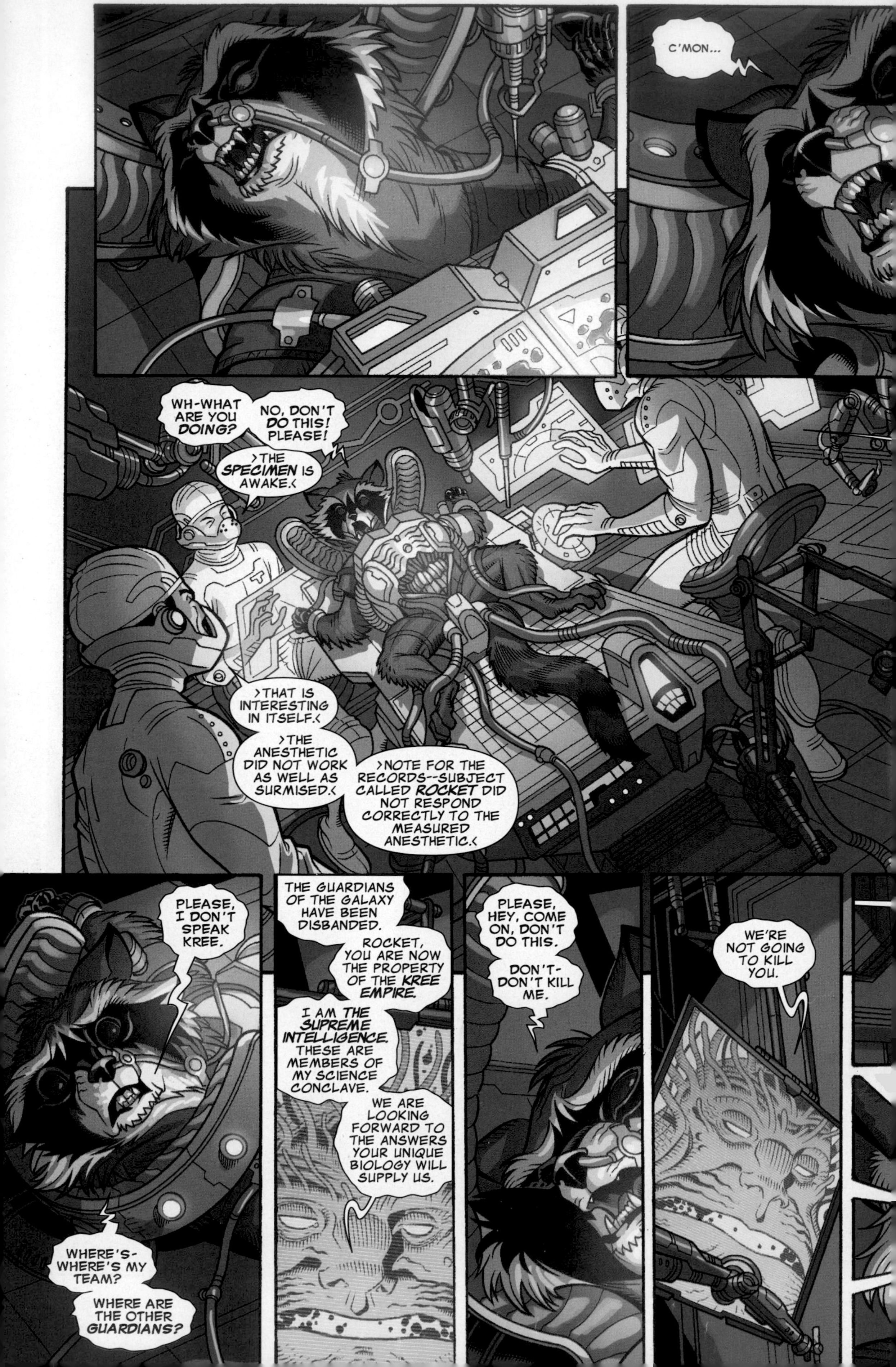
C'MON...
WH-WHAT ARE YOU DOING?
NO, DON'T DO THIS! PLEASE!
>THE SPECIMEN IS AWAKE.<
>THAT IS INTERESTING IN ITSELF.<
>THE ANESTHETIC DID NOT WORK AS WELL AS SURMISED.<
>NOTE FOR THE RECORDS--SUBJECT CALLED ROCKET DID NOT RESPOND CORRECTLY TO THE MEASURED ANESTHETIC.<
PLEASE, I DON'T SPEAK KREE.
WHERE'S- WHERE'S MY TEAM?
WHERE ARE THE OTHER GUARDIANS?
THE GUARDIANS OF THE GALAXY HAVE BEEN DISBANDED.
ROCKET, YOU ARE NOW THE PROPERTY OF THE KREE EMPIRE.
I AM THE SUPREME INTELLIGENCE. THESE ARE MEMBERS OF MY SCIENCE CONCLAVE.
WE ARE LOOKING FORWARD TO THE ANSWERS YOUR UNIQUE BIOLOGY WILL SUPPLY US.
PLEASE, HEY, COME ON, DON'T DO THIS.
DON'T- DON'T KILL ME.
WE'RE NOT GOING TO KILL YOU.

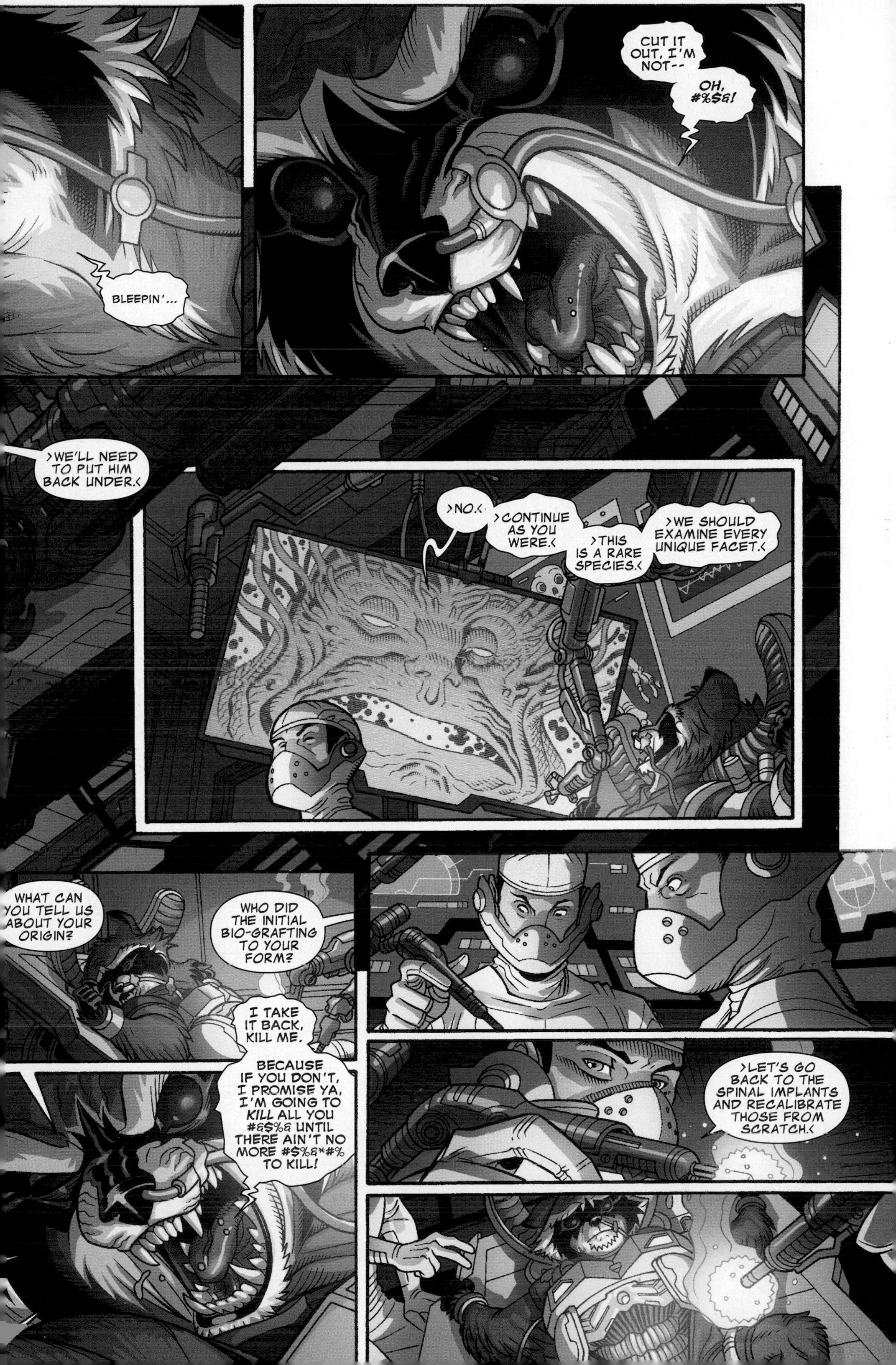
CUT IT OUT, I'M NOT--
OH, #%$&!
BLEEPIN'...
>WE'LL NEED TO PUT HIM BACK UNDER.<
>NO.<
>CONTINUE AS YOU WERE.<
>THIS IS A RARE SPECIES.<
>WE SHOULD EXAMINE EVERY UNIQUE FACET.<
WHAT CAN YOU TELL US ABOUT YOUR ORIGIN?
WHO DID THE INITIAL BIO-GRAFTING TO YOUR FORM?
I TAKE IT BACK, KILL ME.
BECAUSE IF YOU DON'T, I PROMISE YA, I'M GOING TO KILL ALL YOU #&$%& UNTIL THERE AIN'T NO MORE #$%&*#% TO KILL!
>LET'S GO BACK TO THE SPINAL IMPLANTS AND RECALIBRATE THOSE FROM SCRATCH.<

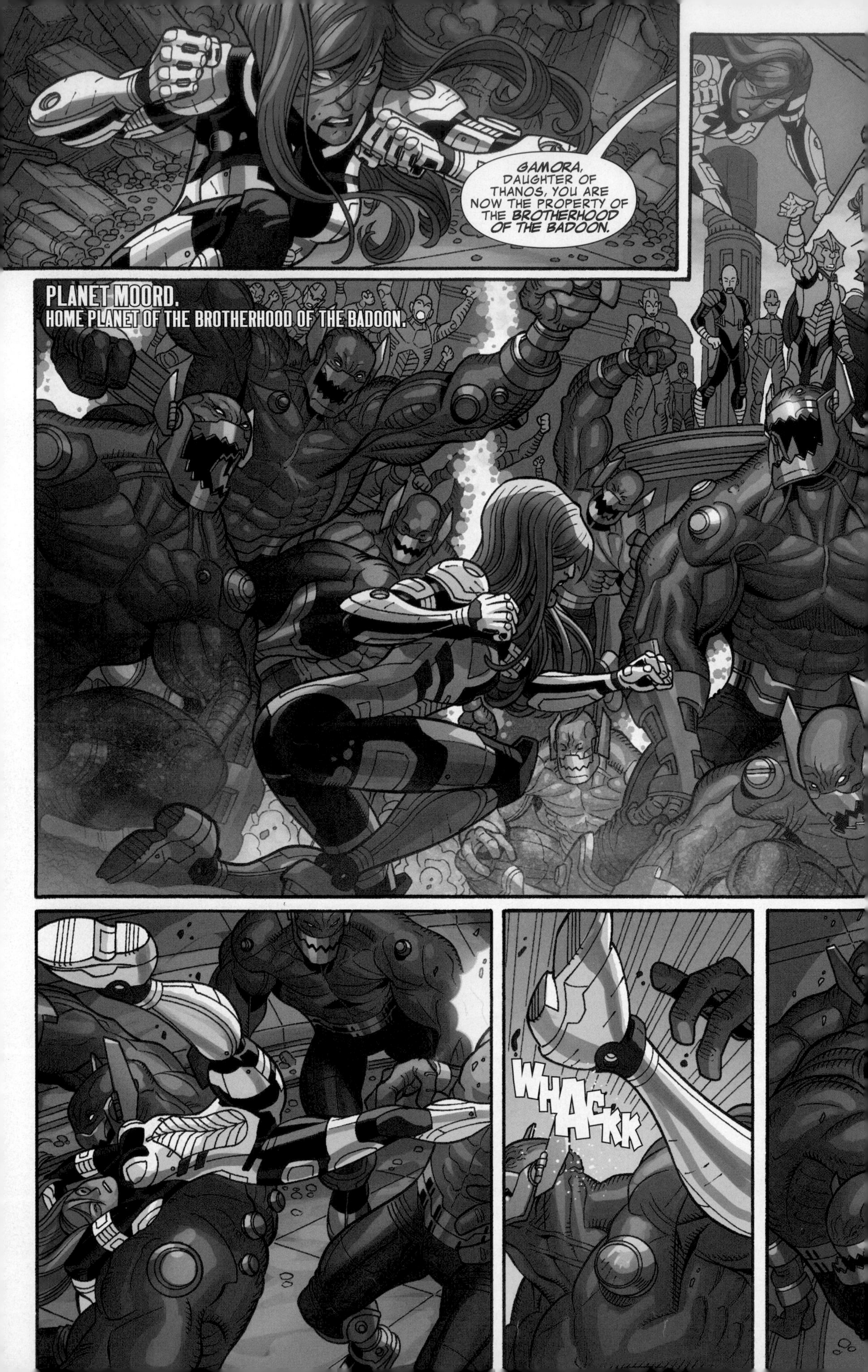
GAMORA, DAUGHTER OF THANOS, YOU ARE NOW THE PROPERTY OF THE BROTHERHOOD OF THE BADOON.
PLANET MOORD.
HOME PLANET OF THE BROTHERHOOD OF THE BADOON.
WHACKK

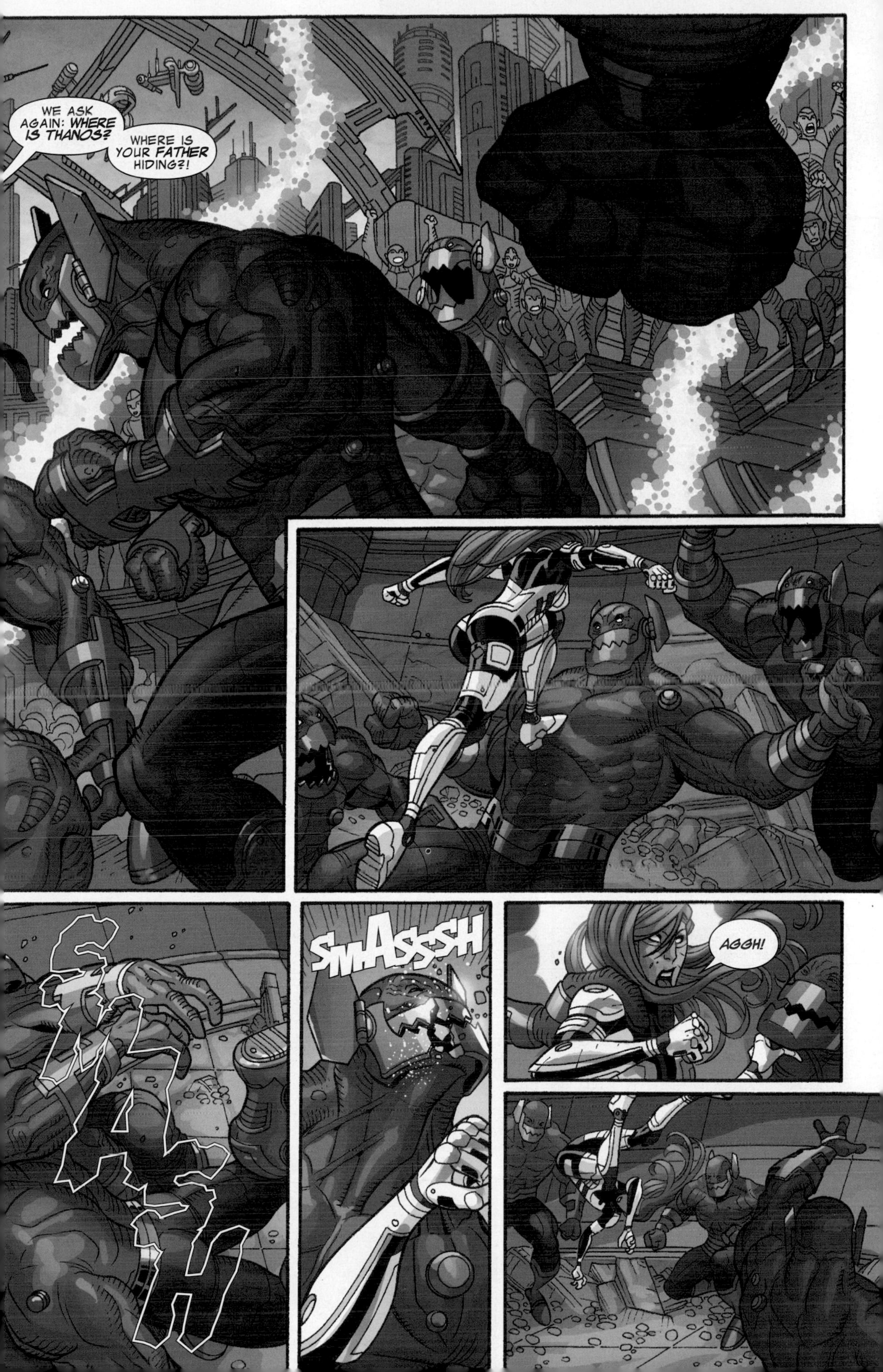

WE ASK AGAIN: WHERE IS THANOS?
WHERE IS YOUR FATHER HIDING?!
SMASSSH
AGGH!

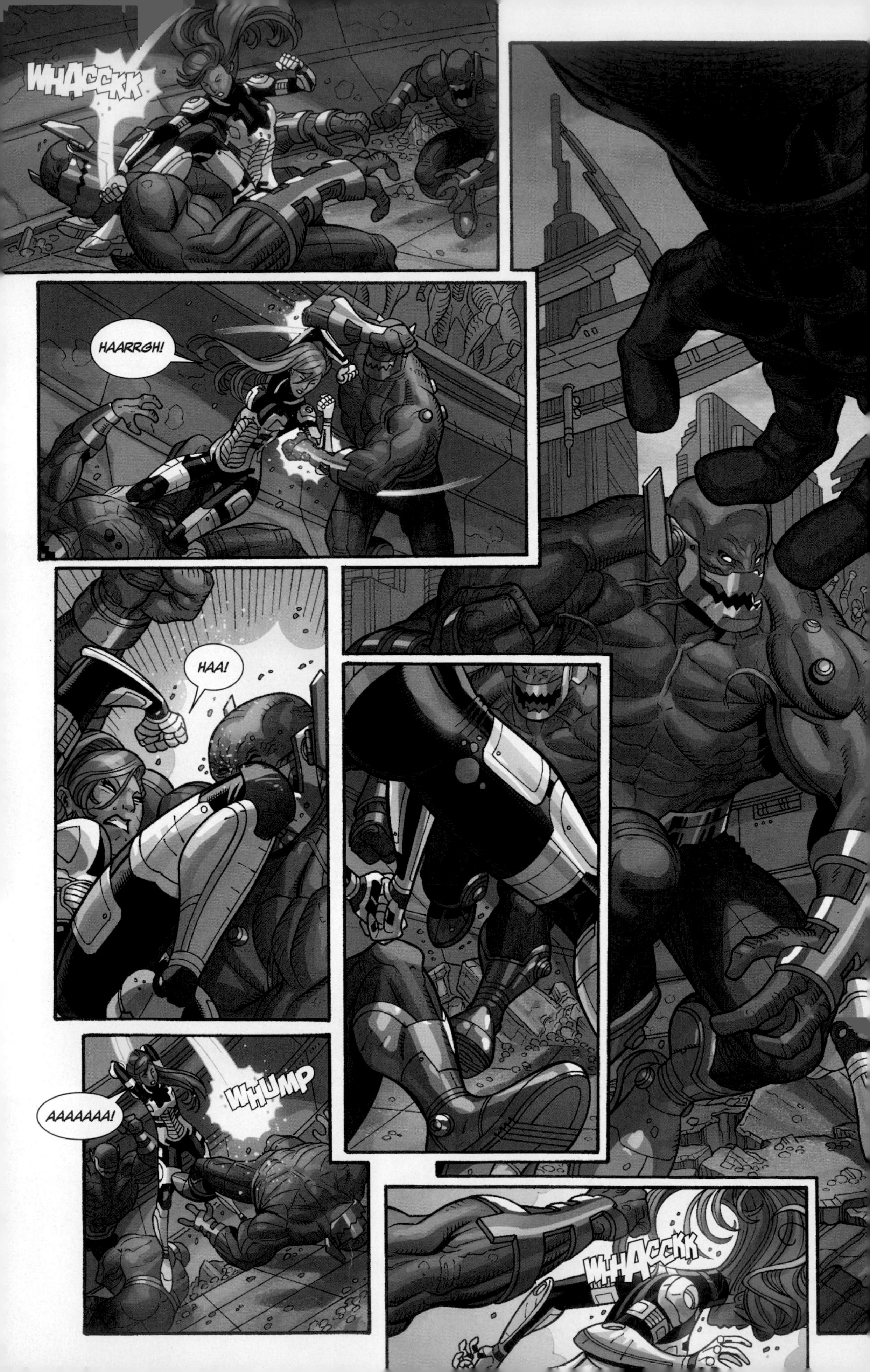
WHACCKK
HAARRGH!
HAA!
AAAAAAA!
WHUMP
WHACCKK

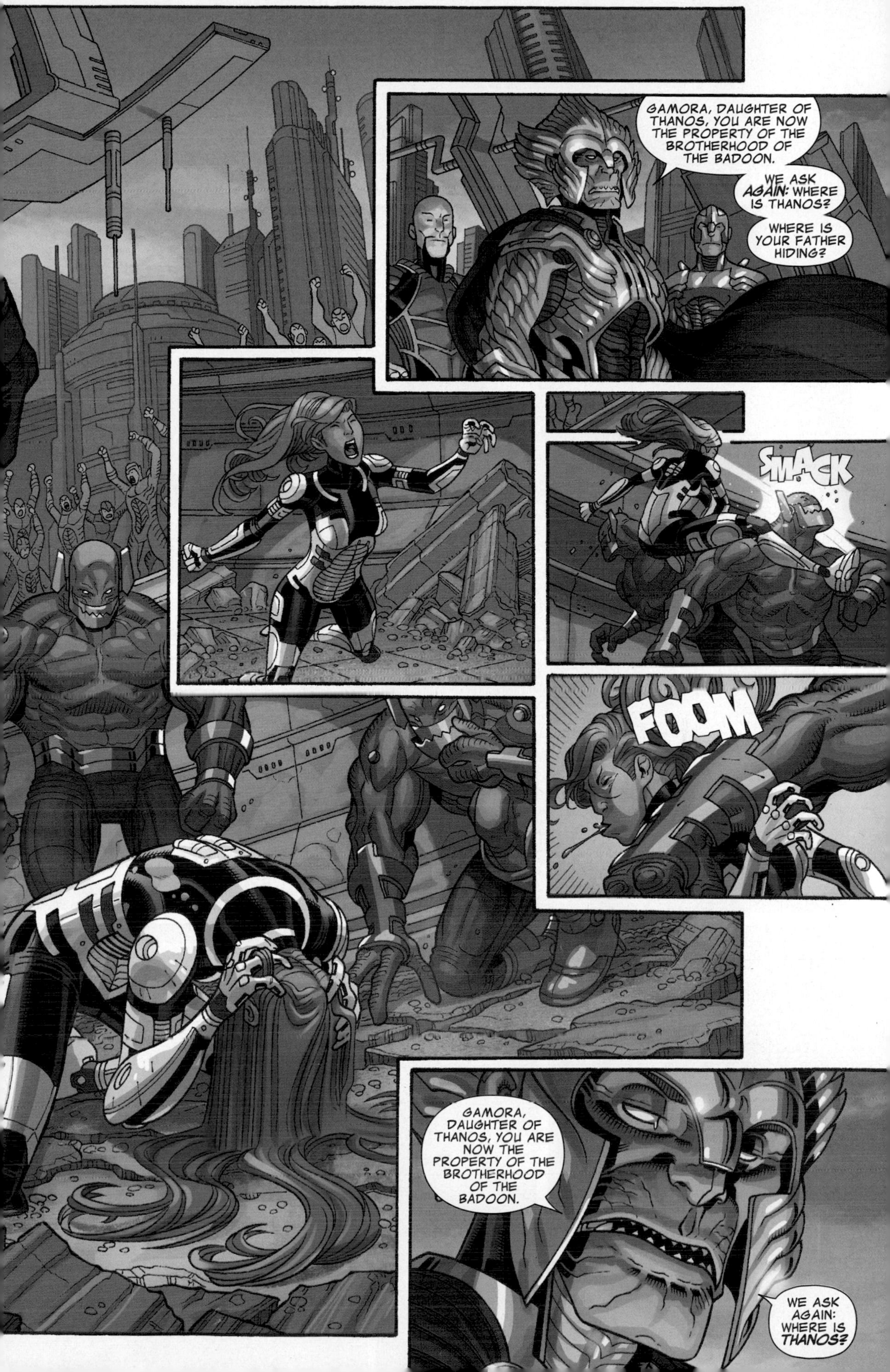
GAMORA, DAUGHTER OF THANOS, YOU ARE NOW THE PROPERTY OF THE BROTHERHOOD OF THE BADOON.
WE ASK AGAIN: WHERE IS THANOS?
WHERE IS YOUR FATHER HIDING?
SMACK
FOOM
GAMORA, DAUGHTER OF THANOS, YOU ARE NOW THE PROPERTY OF THE BROTHERHOOD OF THE BADOON.
WE ASK AGAIN: WHERE IS THANOS?

I AM *MANTA* OF THE SHI'AR IMPERIAL GUARD.

I SPEAK NOW FOR THE LEADER AND CHOSEN PRAETOR, GLADIATOR.

ARTHUR SAMPSON DOUGLAS, A.K.A. *DRAX THE DESTROYER*, YOU ARE NOW A PRISONER OF THE SHI'AR EMPIRE.

YOU WILL ANSWER FOR YOUR CRIMES AGAINST THE GALAXY.

YOU WILL ANSWER FOR YOUR NUMEROUS COUNTS OF PIRACY, MURDER, CONSPIRACY...

THAT IS NOT AN APPROPRIATE RESPONSE TO YOUR SITUATION.

YOU ARE A COWARD.

YOU ARE TO BE HELD UNTIL A PROPER TRIAL IS SCHEDULED FOR YOU.

THIS IS ILL-THOUGHT-OUT RETALIATION FOR THE GUARDIANS STOPPING YOUR ILL-THOUGHT-OUT SCHEME TO PUNISH THE EARTH FOR YOUR FAILINGS AS A LEADER.

THE GUARDIANS ARE *NO MORE*.

YOU WILL BE *PUNISHED* FOR YOUR CRIMES.

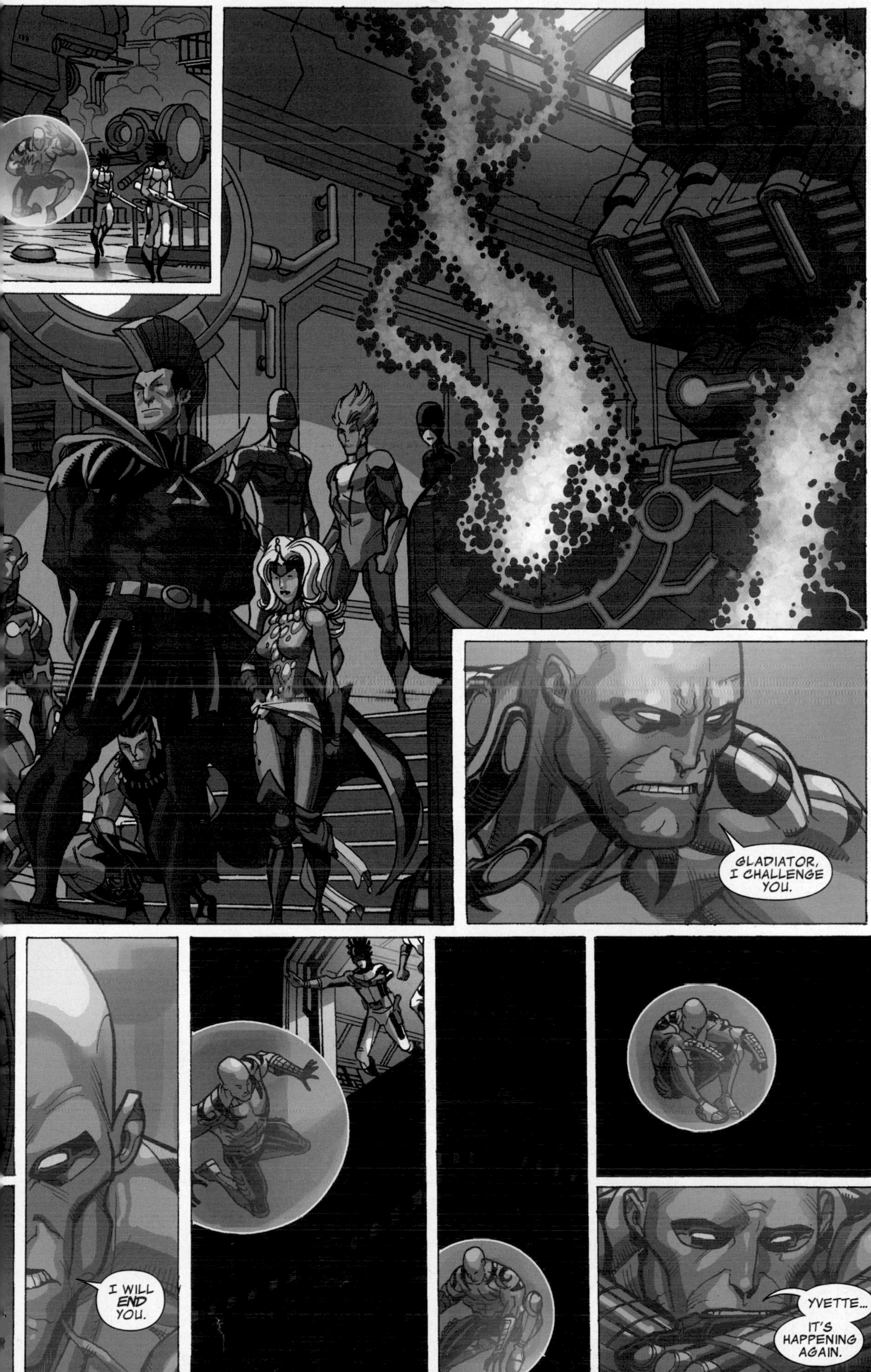
GLADIATOR, I CHALLENGE YOU.
I WILL END YOU.
YVETTE...
IT'S HAPPENING AGAIN.

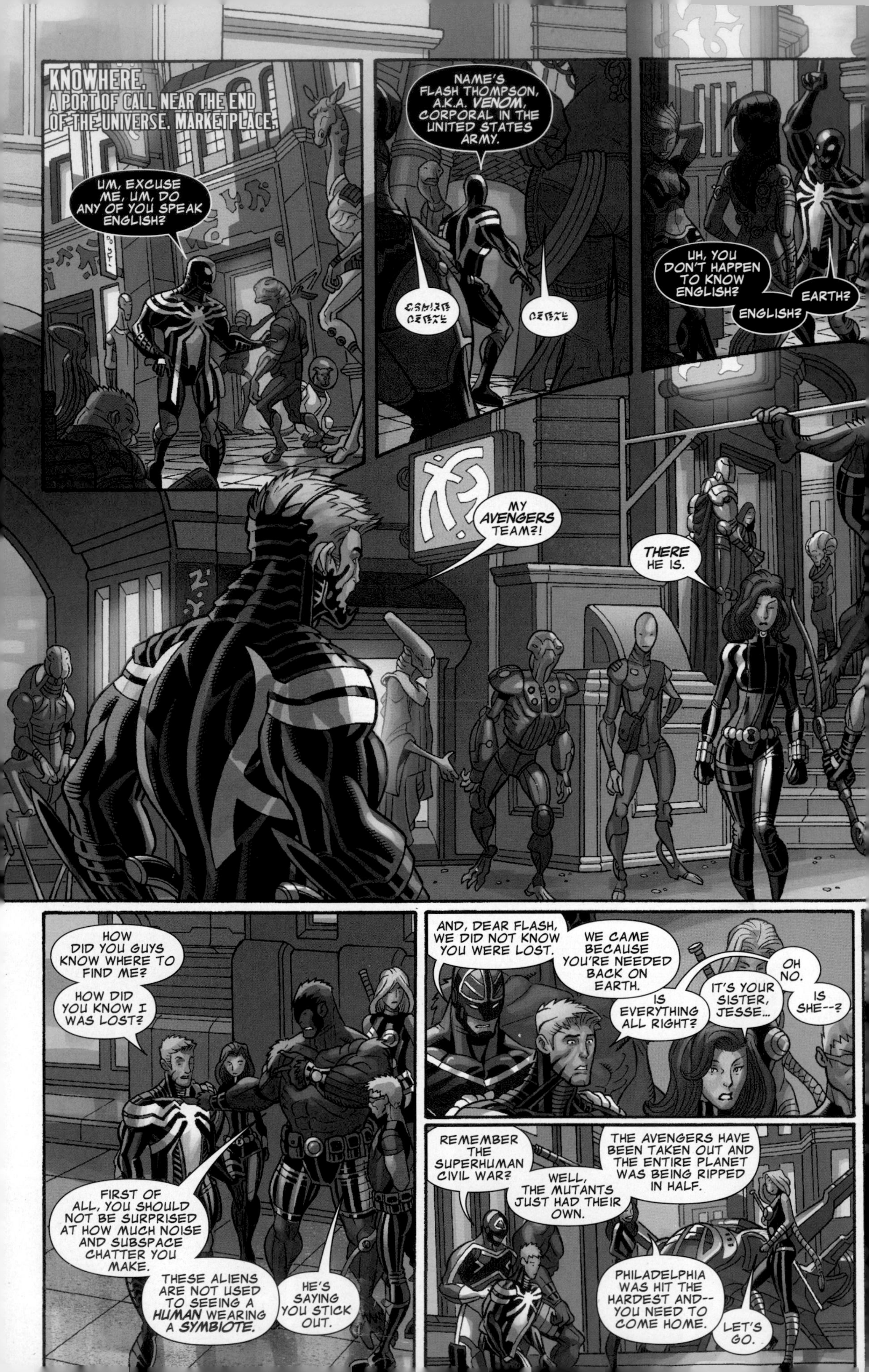
KNOWHERE.
A PORT OF CALL NEAR THE END OF THE UNIVERSE. MARKETPLACE.
UM, EXCUSE ME, UM, DO ANY OF YOU SPEAK ENGLISH?
NAME'S FLASH THOMPSON, A.K.A. VENOM, CORPORAL IN THE UNITED STATES ARMY.
UH, YOU DON'T HAPPEN TO KNOW ENGLISH?
EARTH?
ENGLISH?
MY AVENGERS TEAM?!
THERE HE IS.
HOW DID YOU GUYS KNOW WHERE TO FIND ME?
HOW DID YOU KNOW I WAS LOST?
FIRST OF ALL, YOU SHOULD NOT BE SURPRISED AT HOW MUCH NOISE AND SUBSPACE CHATTER YOU MAKE.
THESE ALIENS ARE NOT USED TO SEEING A HUMAN WEARING A SYMBIOTE.
HE'S SAYING YOU STICK OUT.
AND, DEAR FLASH, WE DID NOT KNOW YOU WERE LOST.
WE CAME BECAUSE YOU'RE NEEDED BACK ON EARTH.
IS EVERYTHING ALL RIGHT?
IT'S YOUR SISTER, JESSE...
OH NO.
IS SHE--?
REMEMBER THE SUPERHUMAN CIVIL WAR?
WELL, THE MUTANTS JUST HAD THEIR OWN.
THE AVENGERS HAVE BEEN TAKEN OUT AND THE ENTIRE PLANET WAS BEING RIPPED IN HALF.
PHILADELPHIA WAS HIT THE HARDEST AND-- YOU NEED TO COME HOME.
LET'S GO.

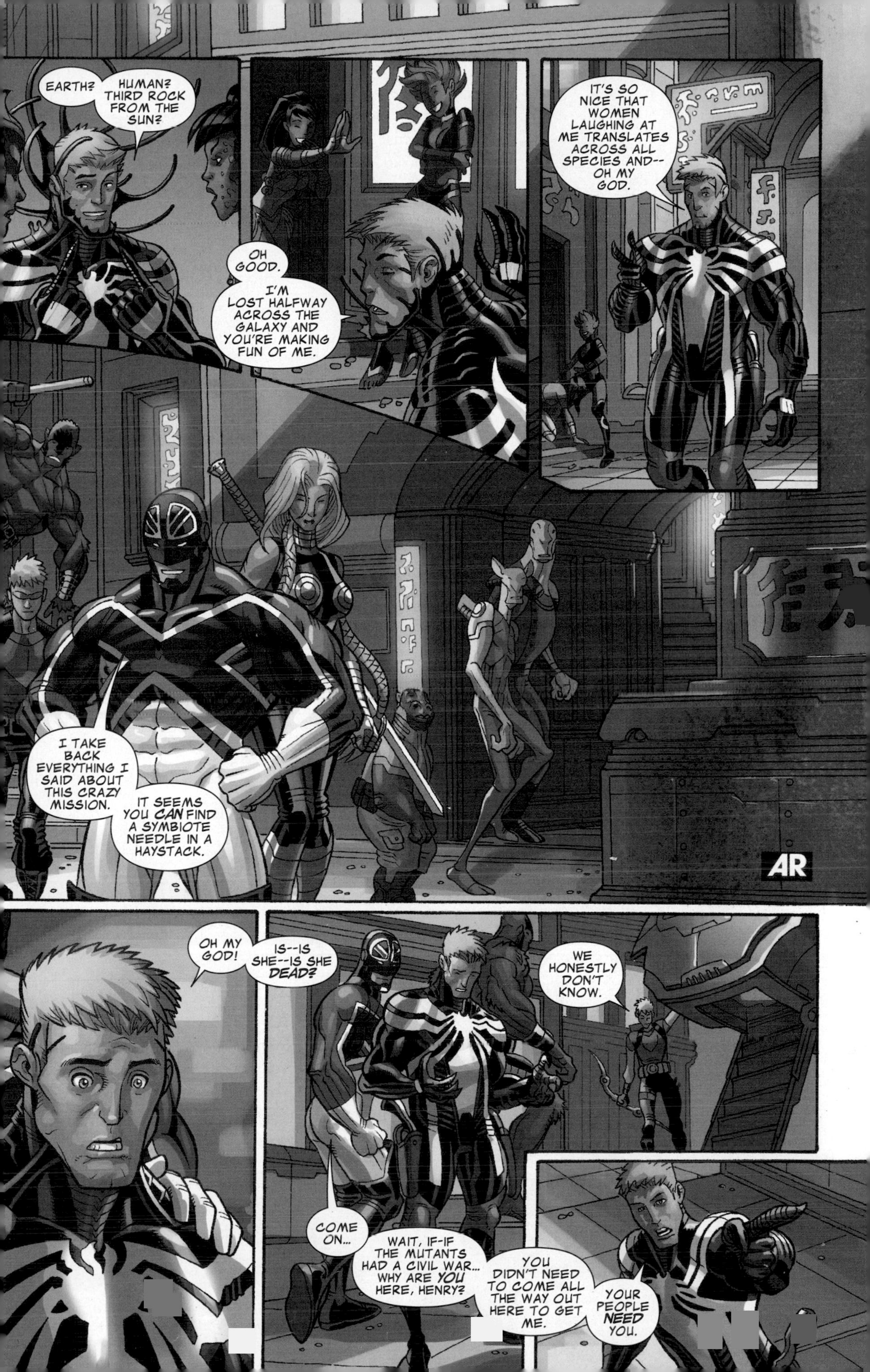
EARTH?
HUMAN? THIRD ROCK FROM THE SUN?
OH GOOD.
I'M LOST HALFWAY ACROSS THE GALAXY AND YOU'RE MAKING FUN OF ME.
IT'S SO NICE THAT WOMEN LAUGHING AT ME TRANSLATES ACROSS ALL SPECIES AND-- OH MY GOD.
I TAKE BACK EVERYTHING I SAID ABOUT THIS CRAZY MISSION.
IT SEEMS YOU CAN FIND A SYMBIOTE NEEDLE IN A HAYSTACK.
AR
OH MY GOD!
IS--IS SHE--IS SHE DEAD?
WE HONESTLY DON'T KNOW.
COME ON...
WAIT, IF-IF THE MUTANTS HAD A CIVIL WAR... WHY ARE YOU HERE, HENRY?
YOU DIDN'T NEED TO COME ALL THE WAY OUT HERE TO GET ME.
YOUR PEOPLE NEED YOU.

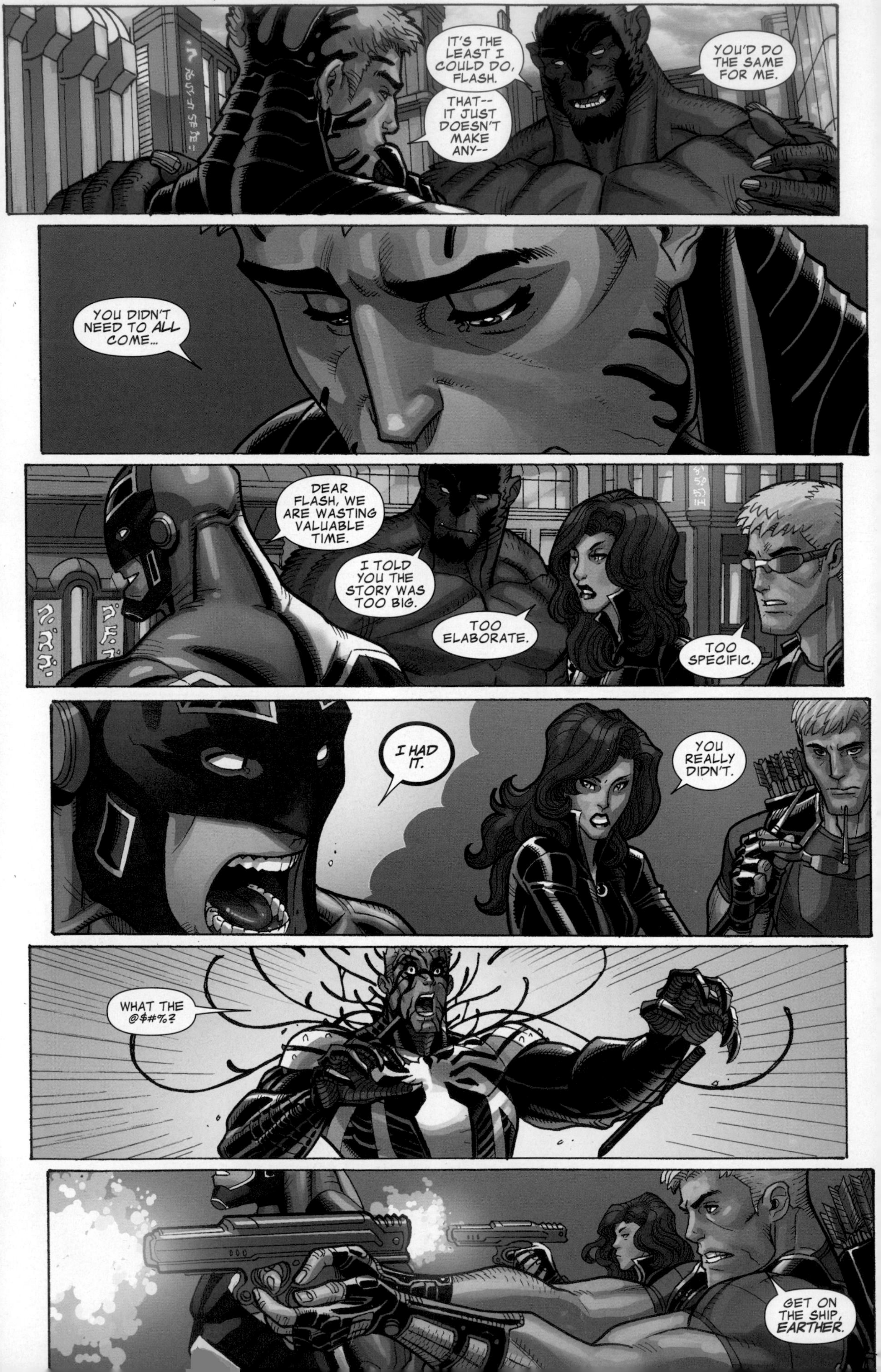
IT'S THE LEAST I COULD DO, FLASH.
THAT-- IT JUST DOESN'T MAKE ANY--
YOU'D DO THE SAME FOR ME.
YOU DIDN'T NEED TO ALL COME...
DEAR FLASH, WE ARE WASTING VALUABLE TIME.
I TOLD YOU THE STORY WAS TOO BIG.
TOO ELABORATE.
TOO SPECIFIC.
I HAD IT.
YOU REALLY DIDN'T.
WHAT THE @$#%?
GET ON THE SHIP, EARTHER.

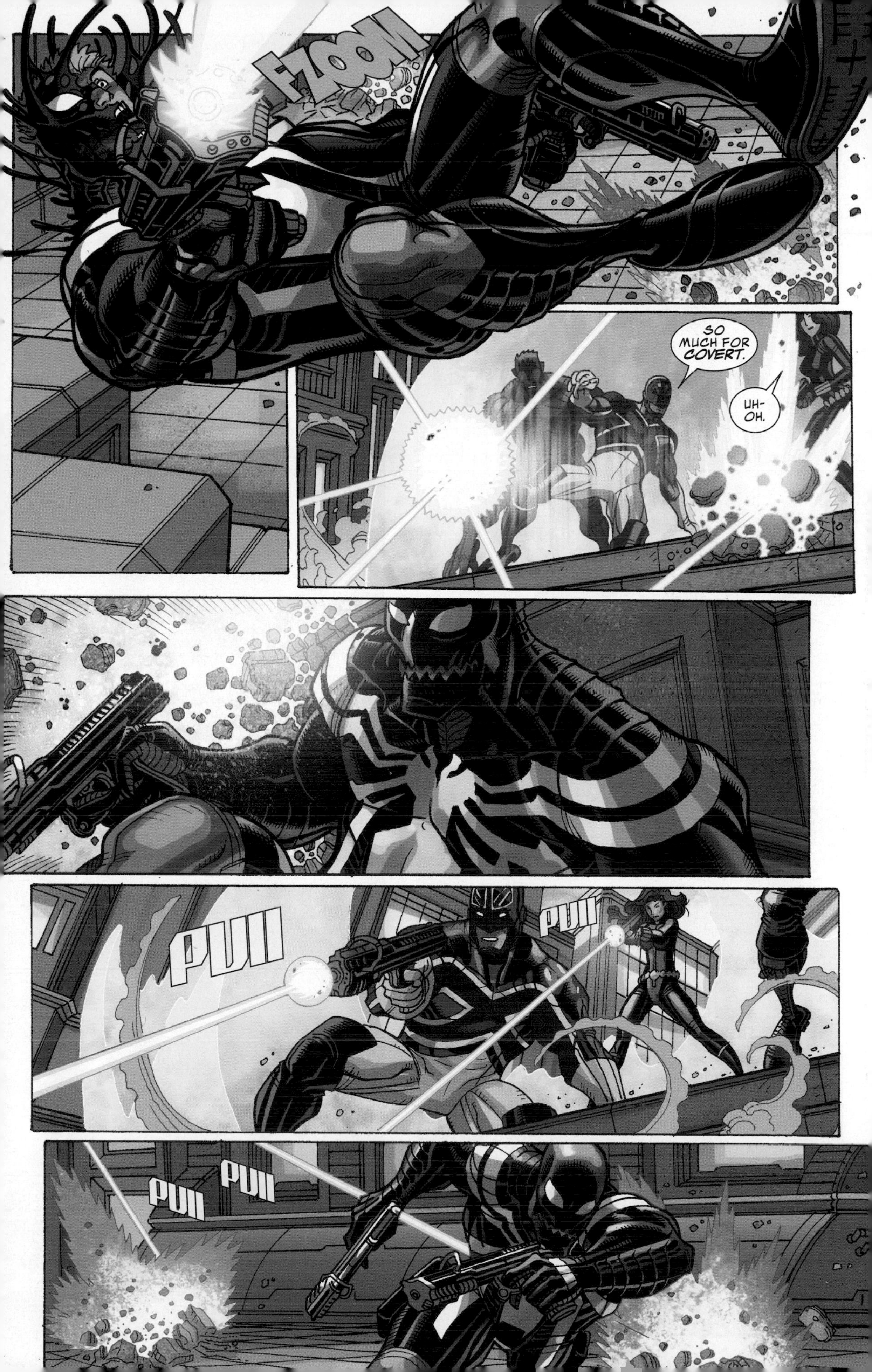
FZOOM
SO MUCH FOR COVERT.
UH-OH.
PUII
PUII
PUII
PUII

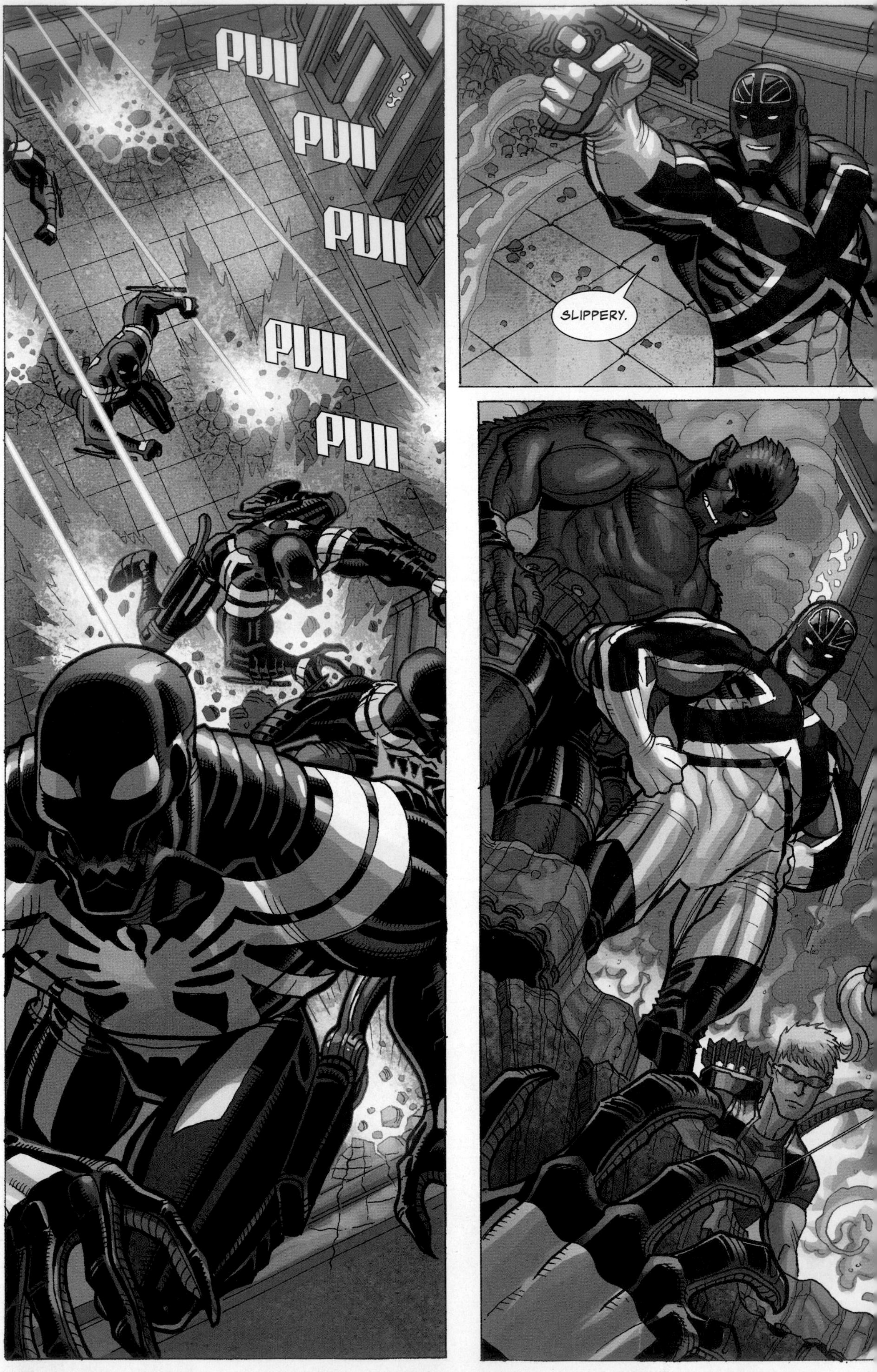
PVII
PVII
PVII
PVII
PVII
SLIPPERY.

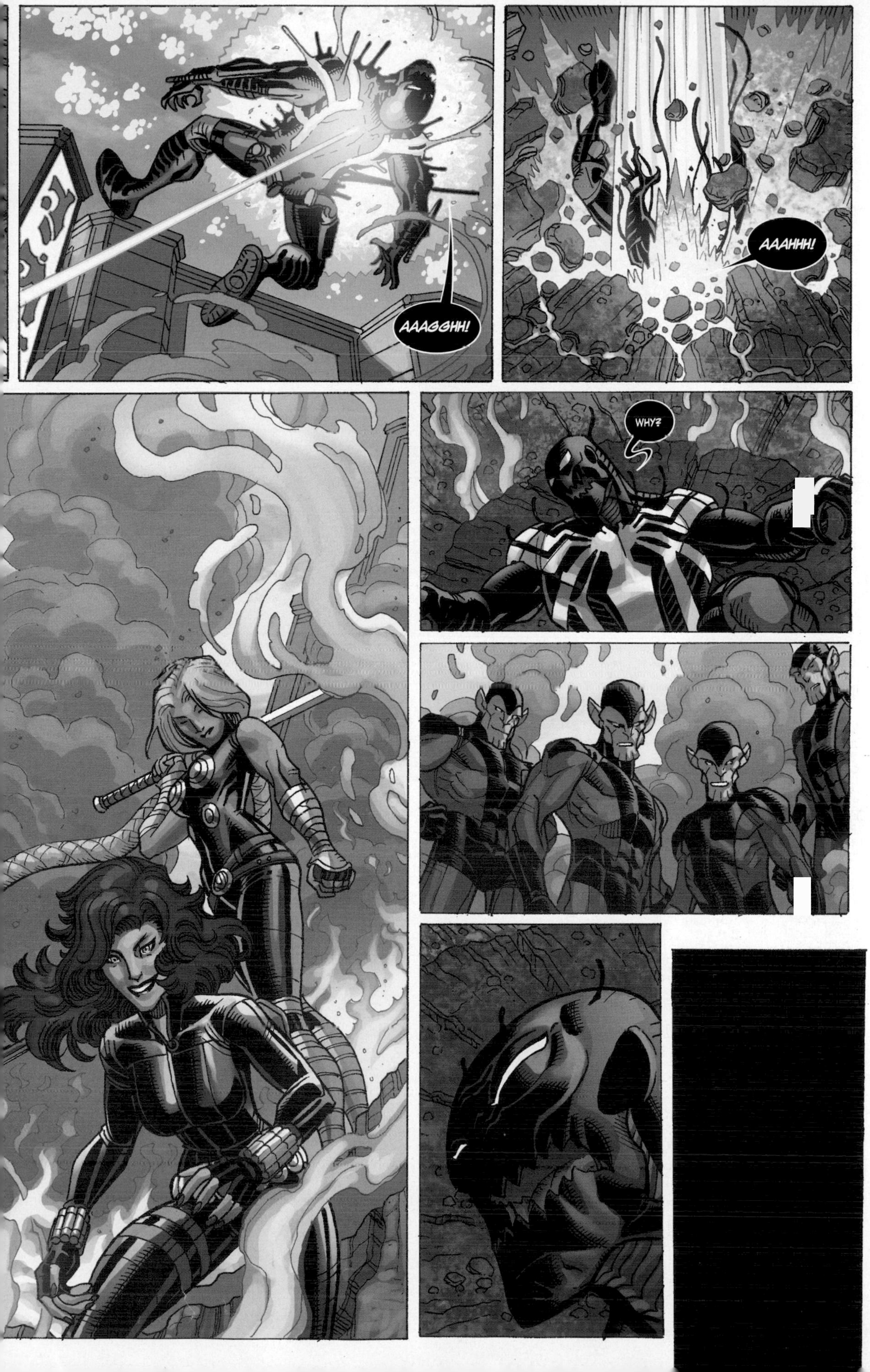
AAAGGHH!
AAAHHH!
WHY?

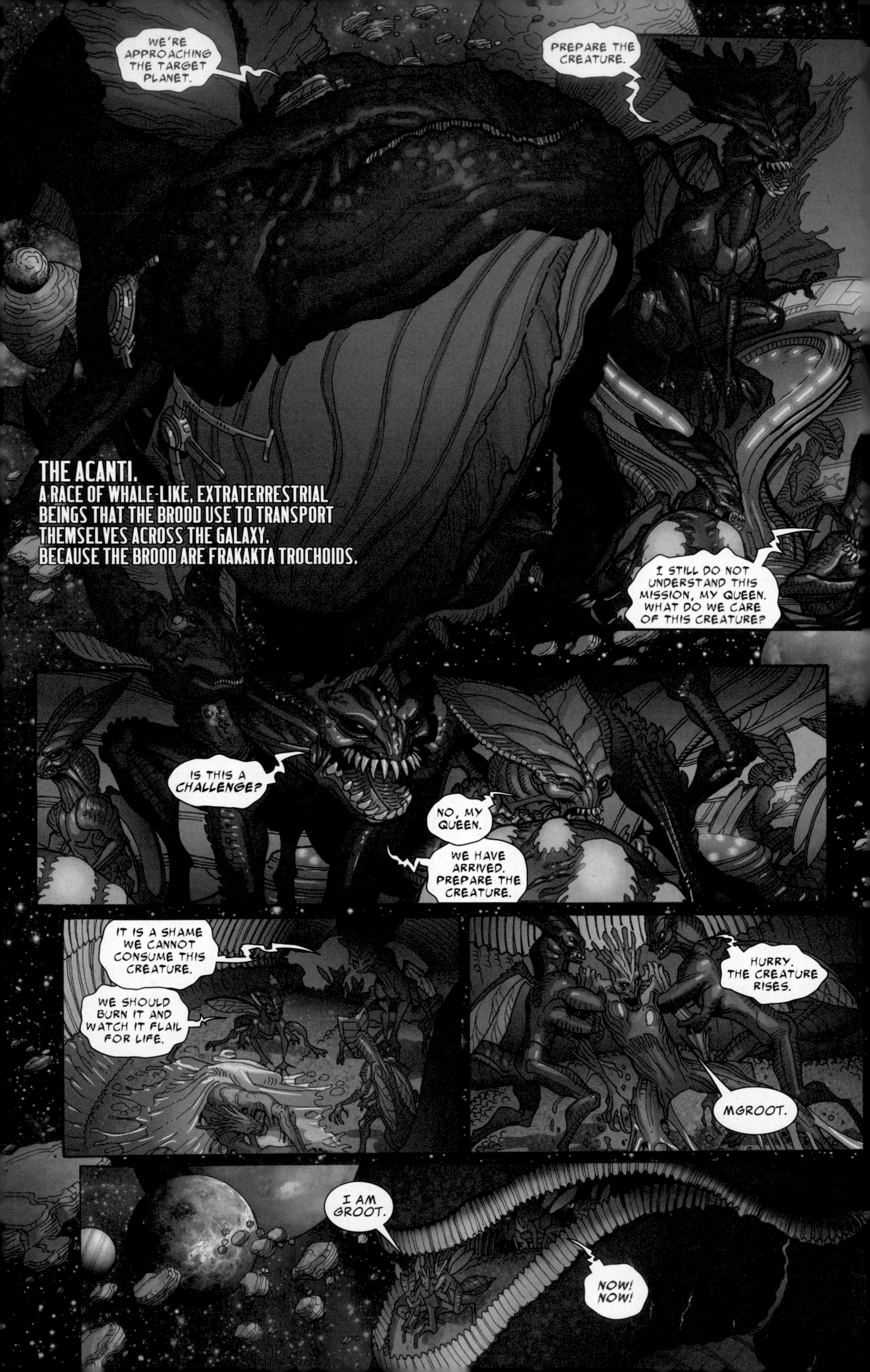
WE'RE APPROACHING THE TARGET PLANET.
PREPARE THE CREATURE.
THE ACANTI.
A RACE OF WHALE-LIKE, EXTRATERRESTRIAL BEINGS THAT THE BROOD USE TO TRANSPORT THEMSELVES ACROSS THE GALAXY.
BECAUSE THE BROOD ARE FRAKAKTA TROCHOIDS.
I STILL DO NOT UNDERSTAND THIS MISSION, MY QUEEN. WHAT DO WE CARE OF THIS CREATURE?
IS THIS A CHALLENGE?
NO, MY QUEEN.
WE HAVE ARRIVED. PREPARE THE CREATURE.
IT IS A SHAME WE CANNOT CONSUME THIS CREATURE.
WE SHOULD BURN IT AND WATCH IT FLAIL FOR LIFE.
HURRY. THE CREATURE RISES.
MGROOT.
I AM GROOT.
NOW! NOW!

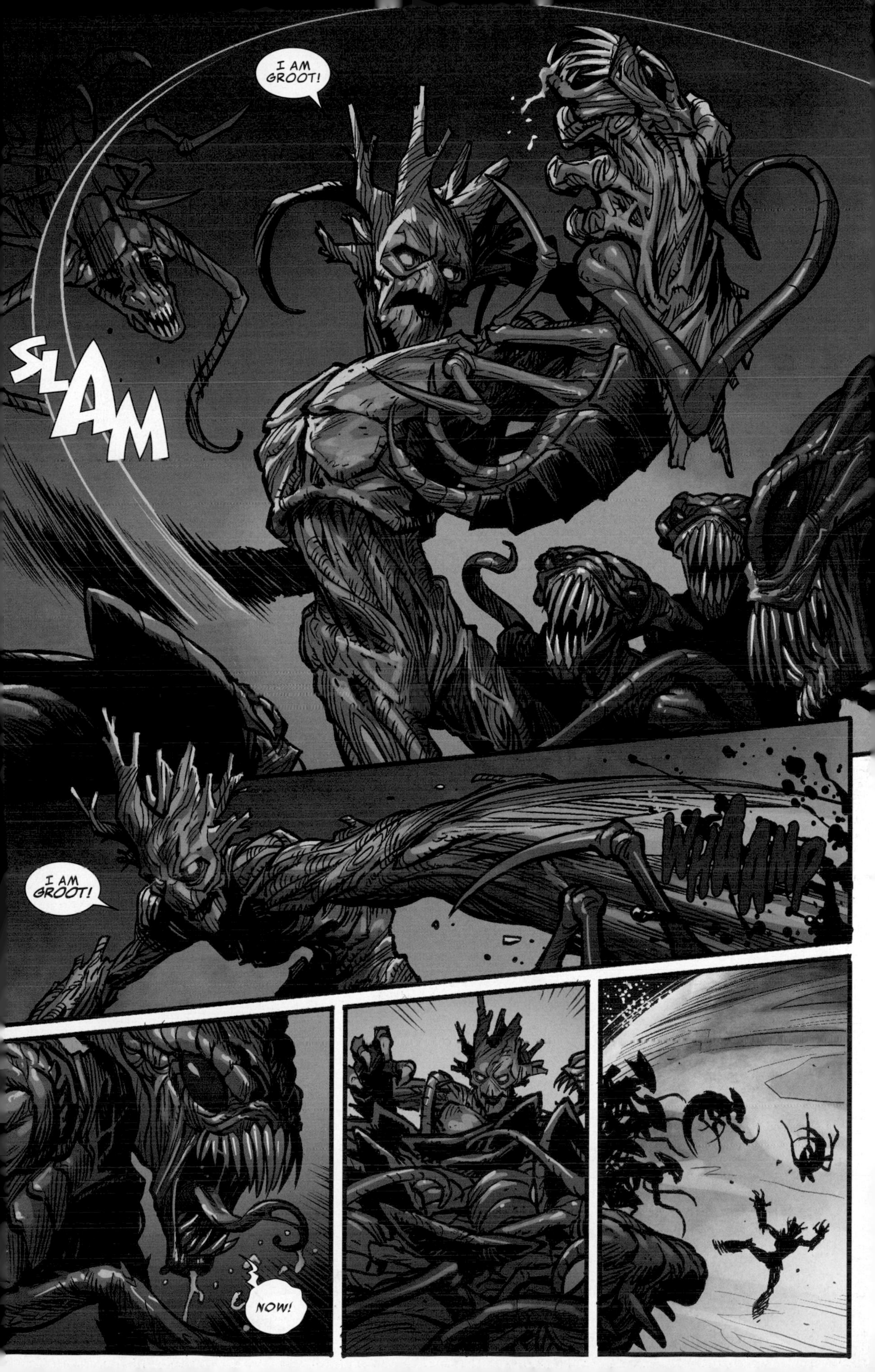

I AM GROOT!
SLAM
WHAAMP!
I AM GROOT!
NOW!

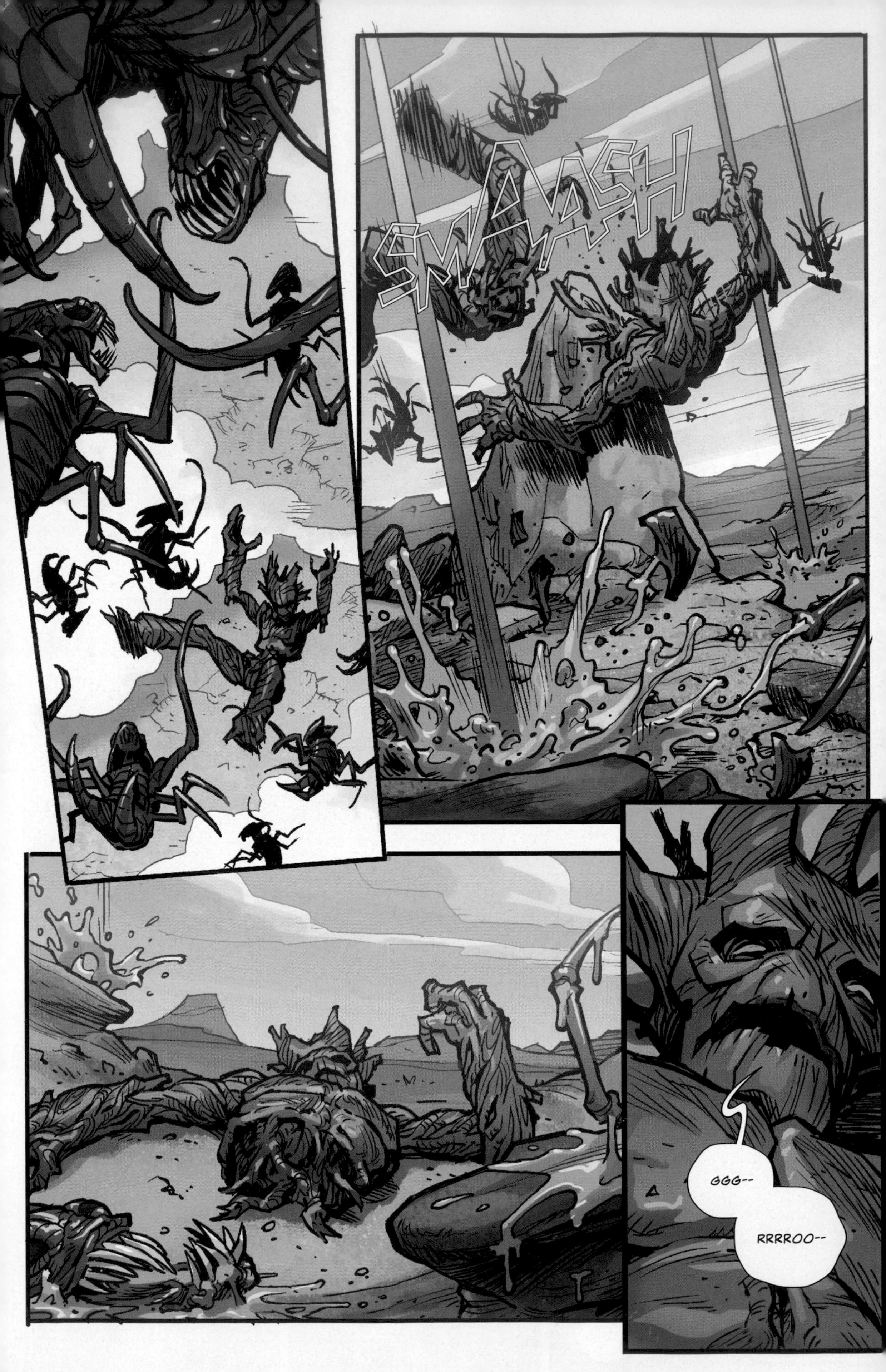
SWAASH
GGG--
RRRROO--

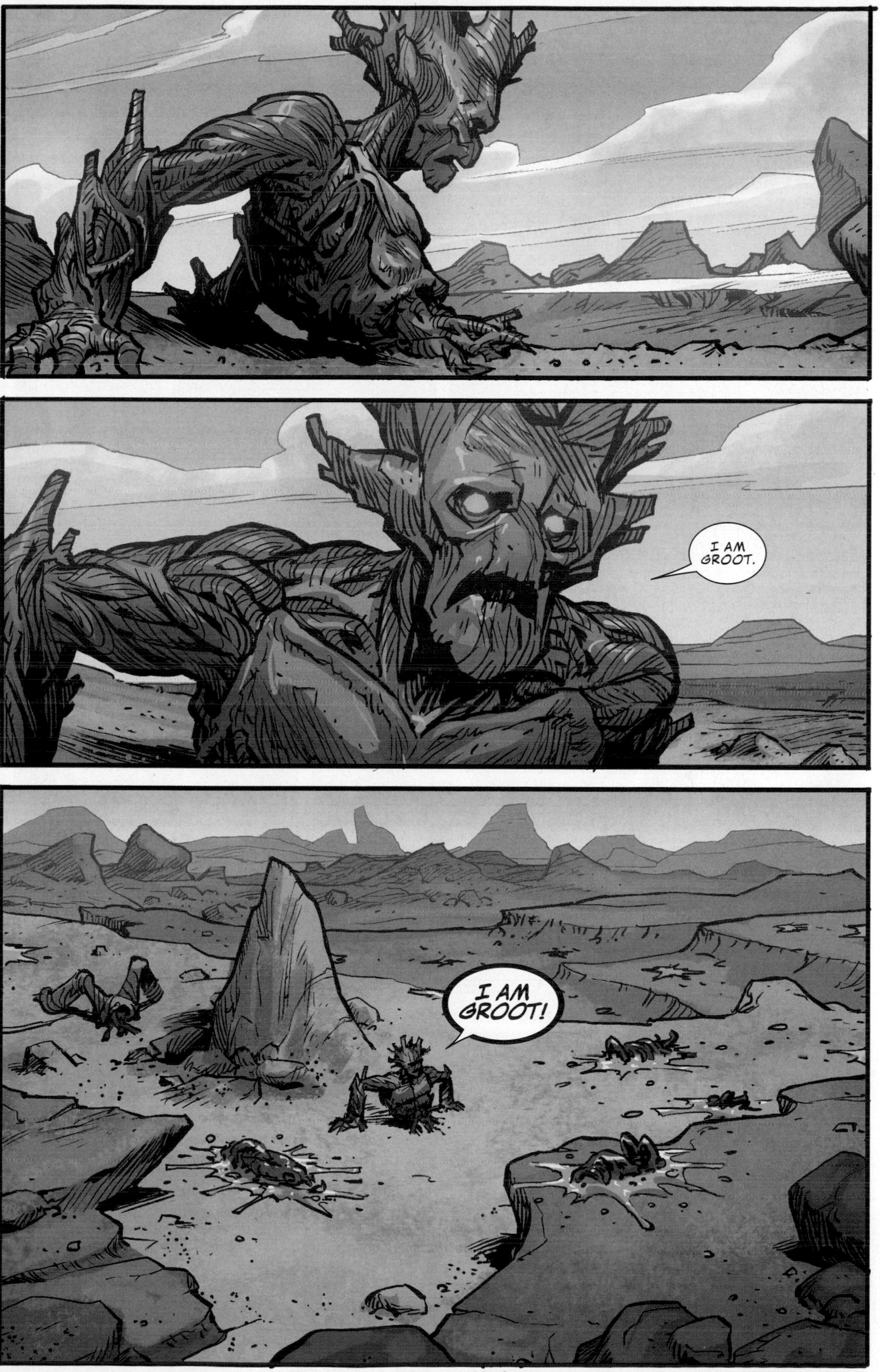
I AM GROOT.
I AM GROOT!

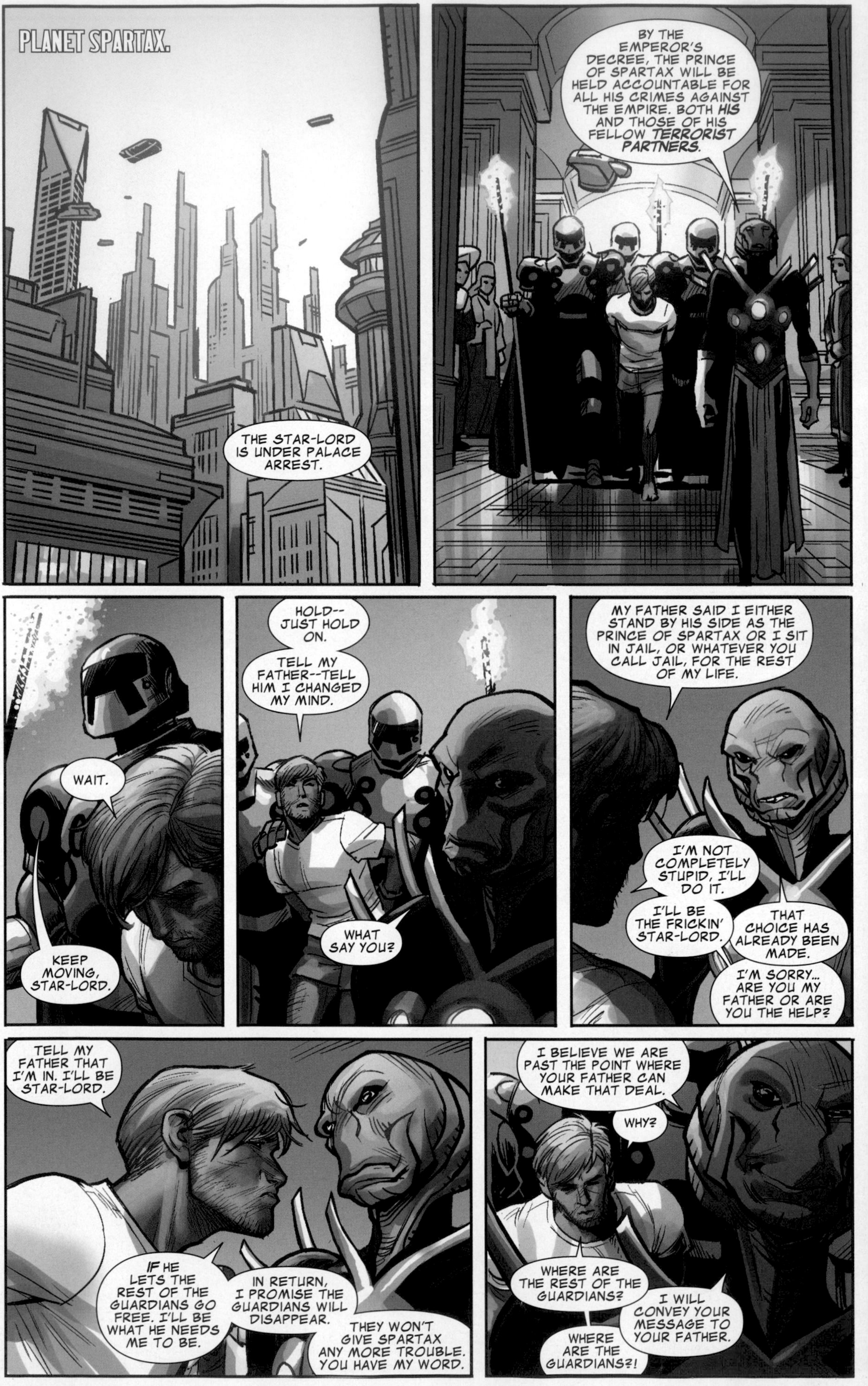
PLANET SPARTAX.
THE STAR-LORD IS UNDER PALACE ARREST.
BY THE EMPEROR'S DECREE, THE PRINCE OF SPARTAX WILL BE HELD ACCOUNTABLE FOR ALL HIS CRIMES AGAINST THE EMPIRE. BOTH HIS AND THOSE OF HIS FELLOW TERRORIST PARTNERS.
WAIT.
KEEP MOVING, STAR-LORD.
HOLD-- JUST HOLD ON.
TELL MY FATHER--TELL HIM I CHANGED MY MIND.
WHAT SAY YOU?
MY FATHER SAID I EITHER STAND BY HIS SIDE AS THE PRINCE OF SPARTAX OR I SIT IN JAIL, OR WHATEVER YOU CALL JAIL, FOR THE REST OF MY LIFE.
I'M NOT COMPLETELY STUPID, I'LL DO IT.
I'LL BE THE FRICKIN' STAR-LORD.
THAT CHOICE HAS ALREADY BEEN MADE.
I'M SORRY... ARE YOU MY FATHER OR ARE YOU THE HELP?
TELL MY FATHER THAT I'M IN. I'LL BE STAR-LORD.
IF HE LETS THE REST OF THE GUARDIANS GO FREE. I'LL BE WHAT HE NEEDS ME TO BE.
IN RETURN, I PROMISE THE GUARDIANS WILL DISAPPEAR.
THEY WON'T GIVE SPARTAX ANY MORE TROUBLE. YOU HAVE MY WORD.
I BELIEVE WE ARE PAST THE POINT WHERE YOUR FATHER CAN MAKE THAT DEAL.
WHY?
WHERE ARE THE REST OF THE GUARDIANS?
WHERE ARE THE GUARDIANS?!
I WILL CONVEY YOUR MESSAGE TO YOUR FATHER.

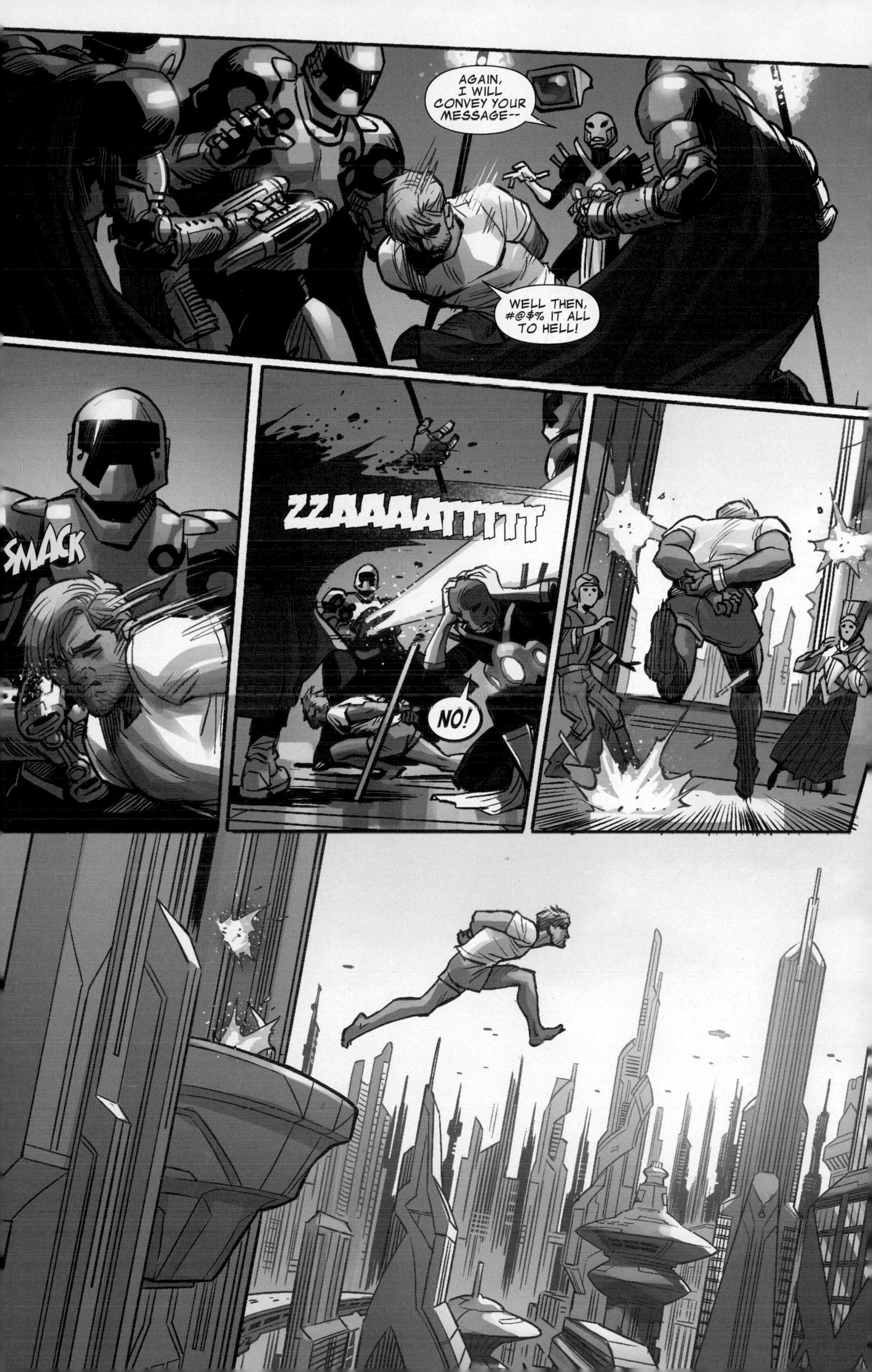
AGAIN, I WILL CONVEY YOUR MESSAGE--
WELL THEN, #@$% IT ALL TO HELL!
SMACK
ZZAAAAATTTTT
NO!

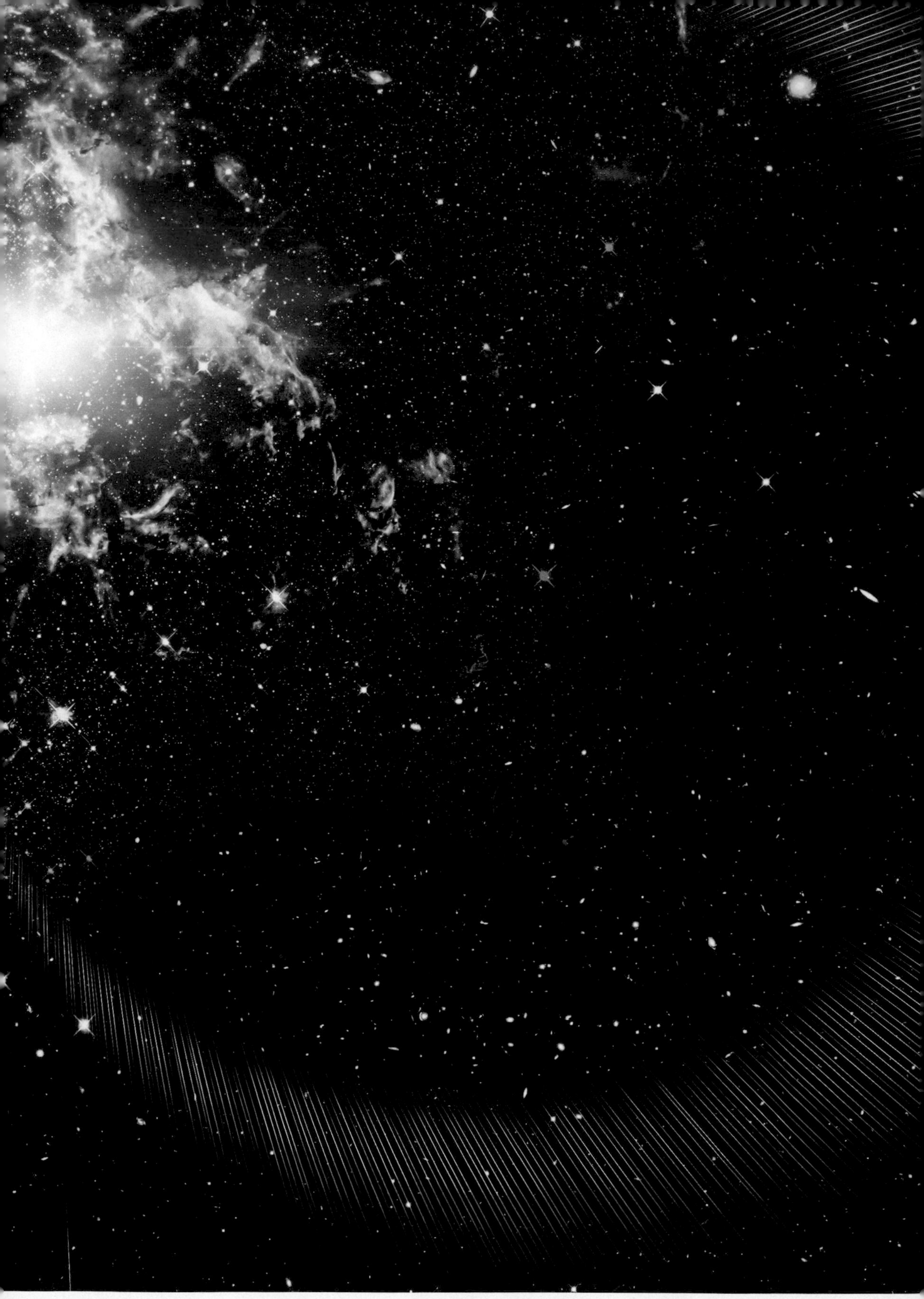

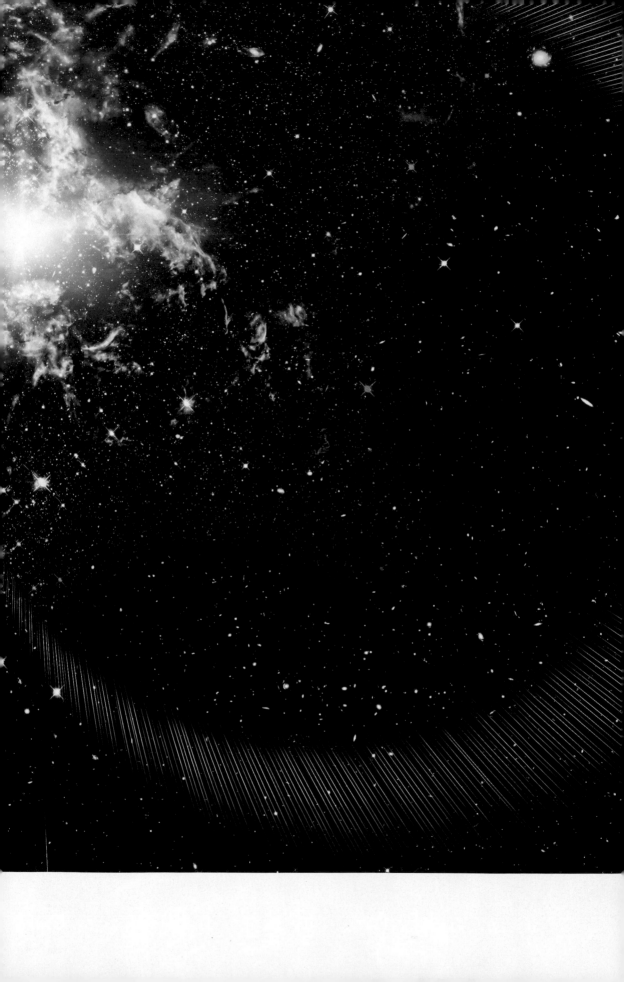

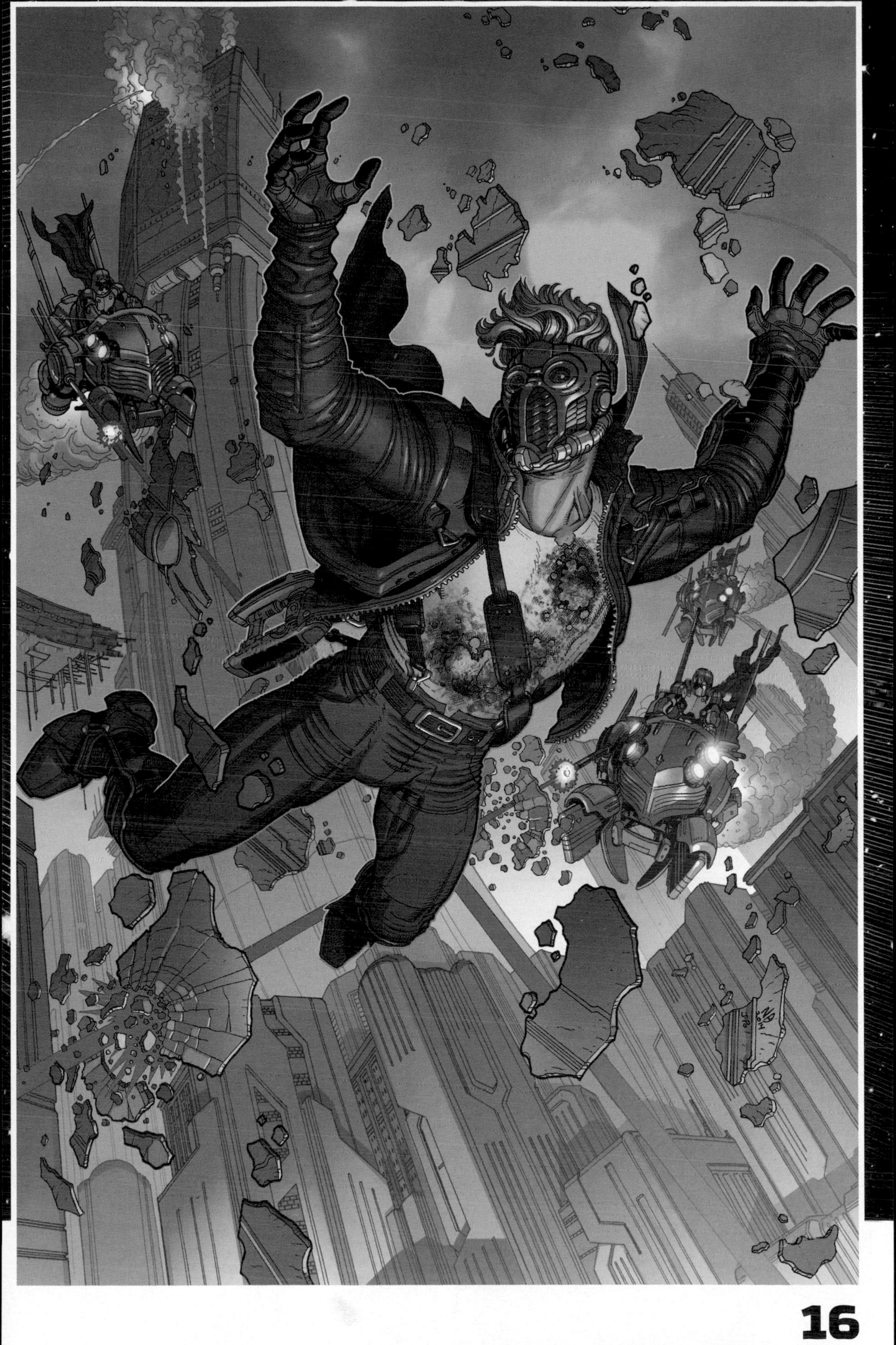

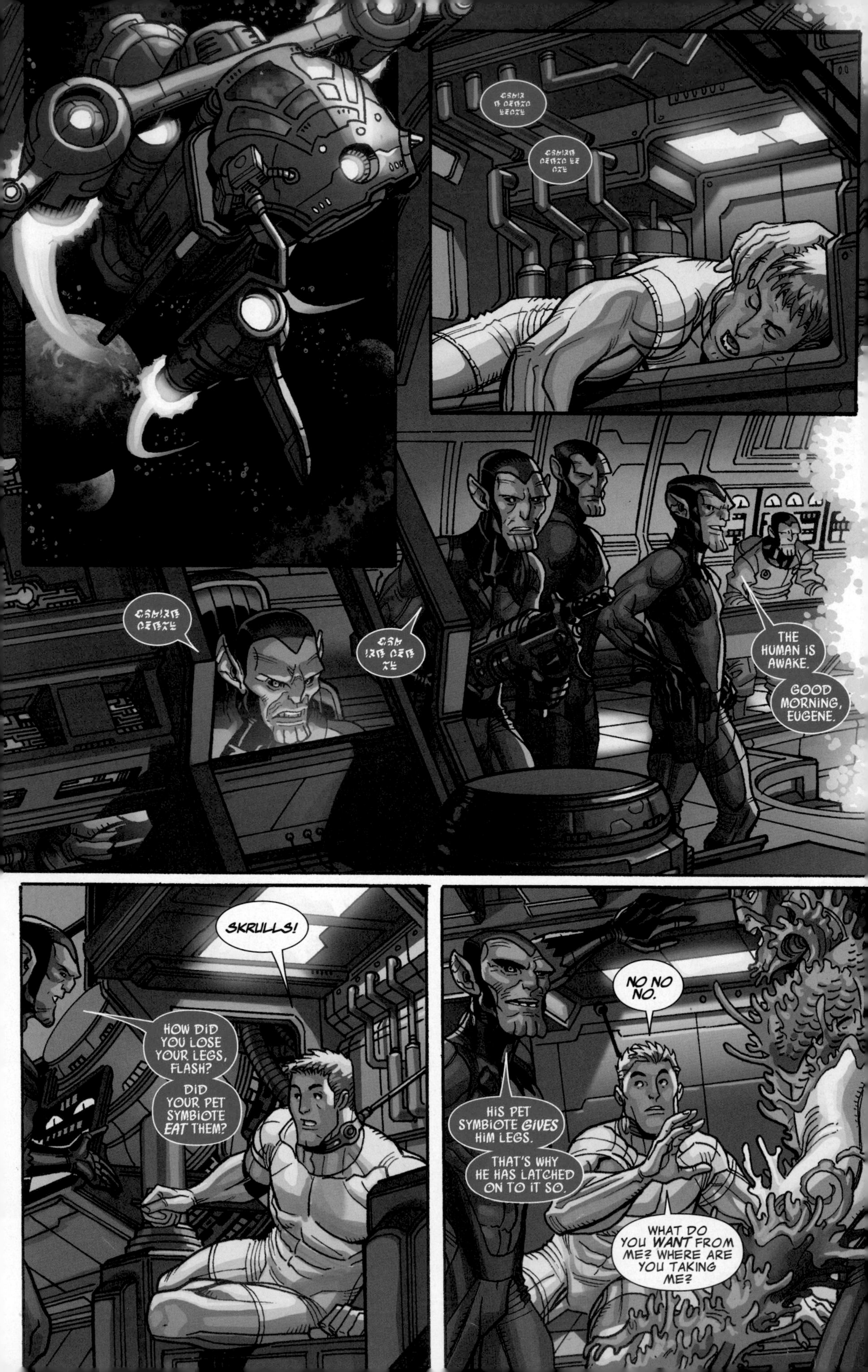
THE HUMAN IS AWAKE.
GOOD MORNING, EUGENE.
SKRULLS!
HOW DID YOU LOSE YOUR LEGS, FLASH?
DID YOUR PET SYMBIOTE EAT THEM?
NO NO NO.
HIS PET SYMBIOTE GIVES HIM LEGS.
THAT'S WHY HE HAS LATCHED ON TO IT SO.
WHAT DO YOU WANT FROM ME? WHERE ARE YOU TAKING ME?

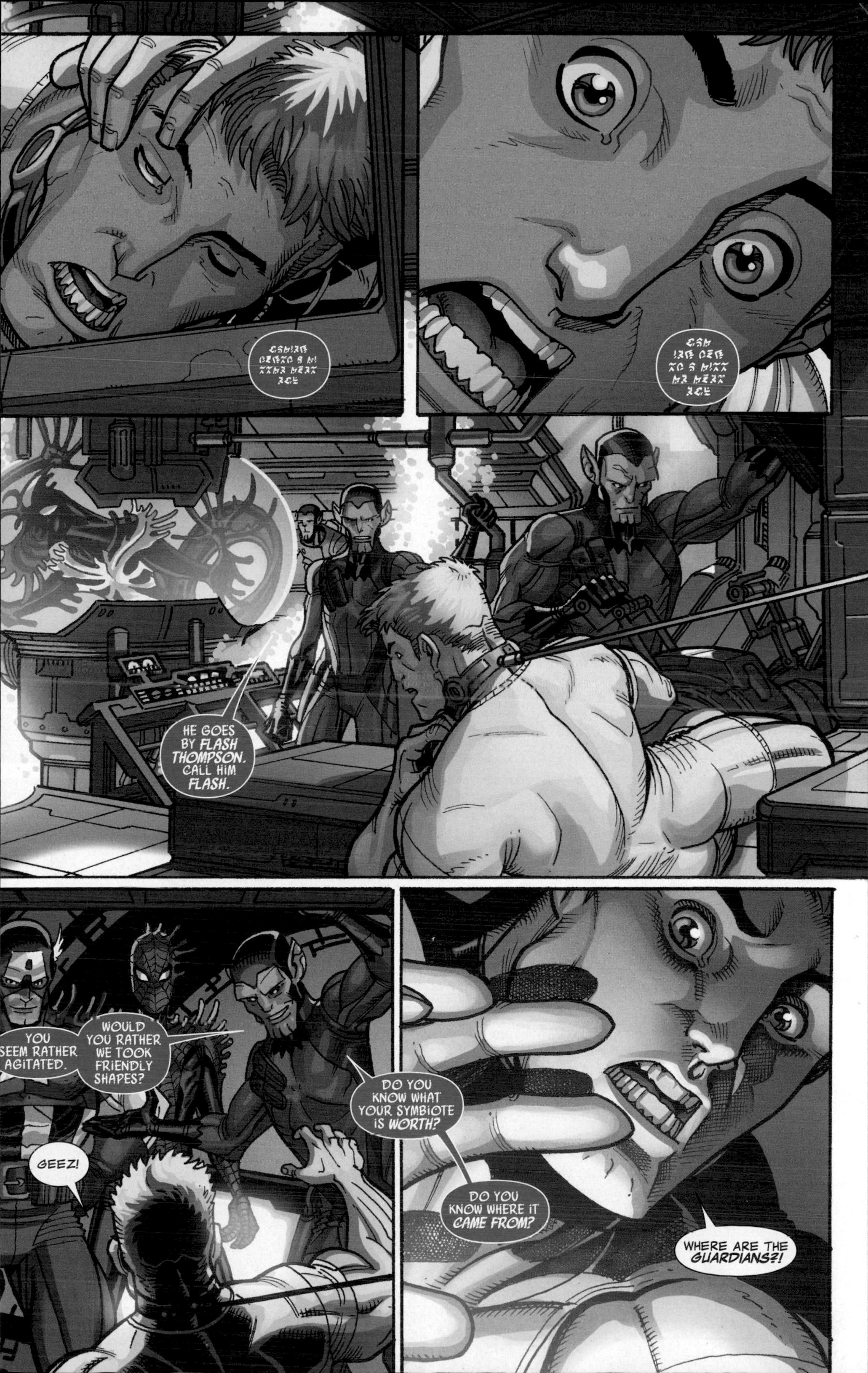
HE GOES BY FLASH THOMPSON. CALL HIM FLASH.
YOU SEEM RATHER AGITATED.
WOULD YOU RATHER WE TOOK FRIENDLY SHAPES?
DO YOU KNOW WHAT YOUR SYMBIOTE IS WORTH?
GEEZ!
DO YOU KNOW WHERE IT CAME FROM?
WHERE ARE THE GUARDIANS?!

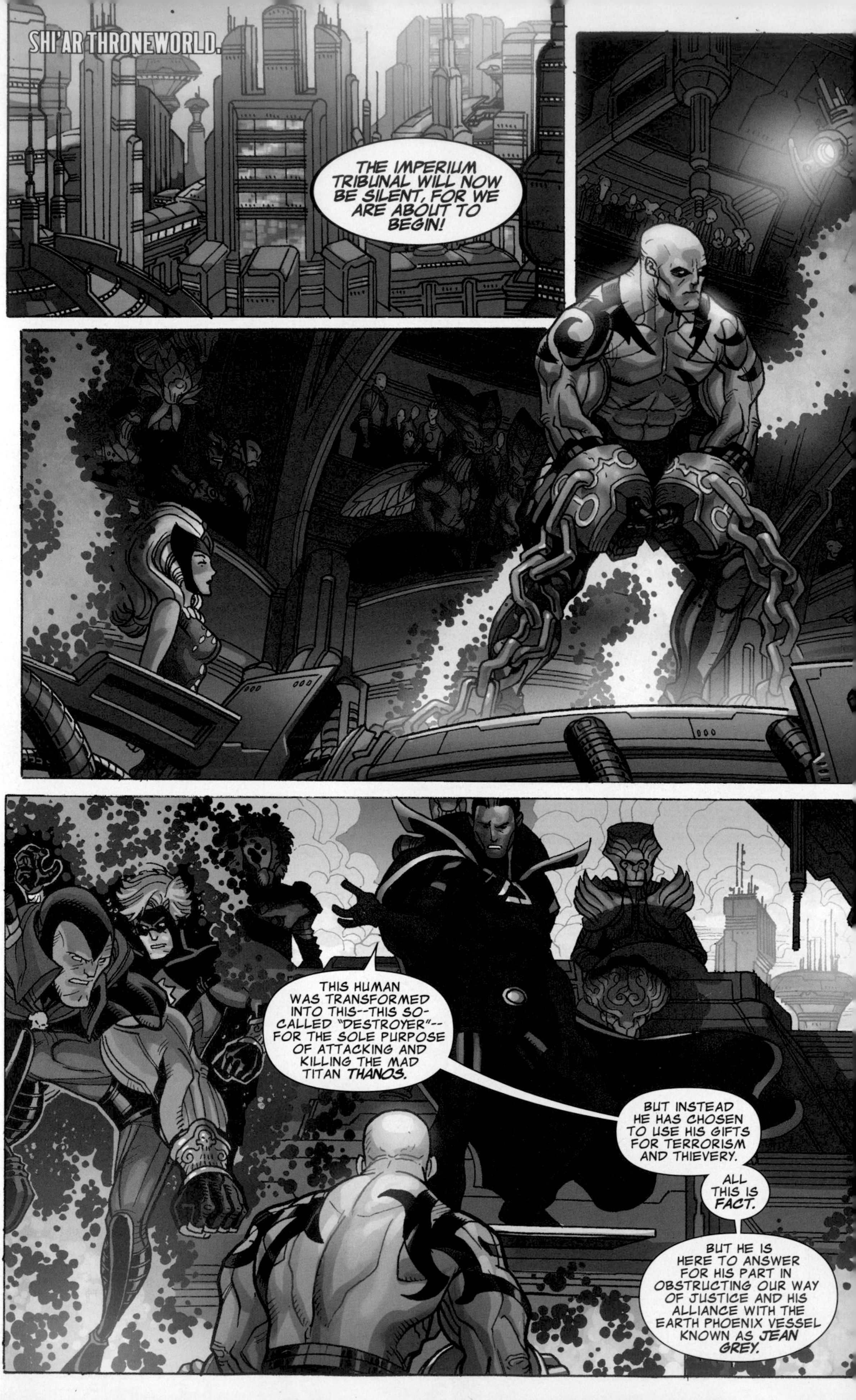
SHI'AR THRONEWORLD.
THE IMPERIUM TRIBUNAL WILL NOW BE SILENT, FOR WE ARE ABOUT TO BEGIN!
THIS HUMAN WAS TRANSFORMED INTO THIS--THIS SO-CALLED "DESTROYER"--FOR THE SOLE PURPOSE OF ATTACKING AND KILLING THE MAD TITAN THANOS.
BUT INSTEAD HE HAS CHOSEN TO USE HIS GIFTS FOR TERRORISM AND THIEVERY.
ALL THIS IS FACT.
BUT HE IS HERE TO ANSWER FOR HIS PART IN OBSTRUCTING OUR WAY OF JUSTICE AND HIS ALLIANCE WITH THE EARTH PHOENIX VESSEL KNOWN AS JEAN GREY.

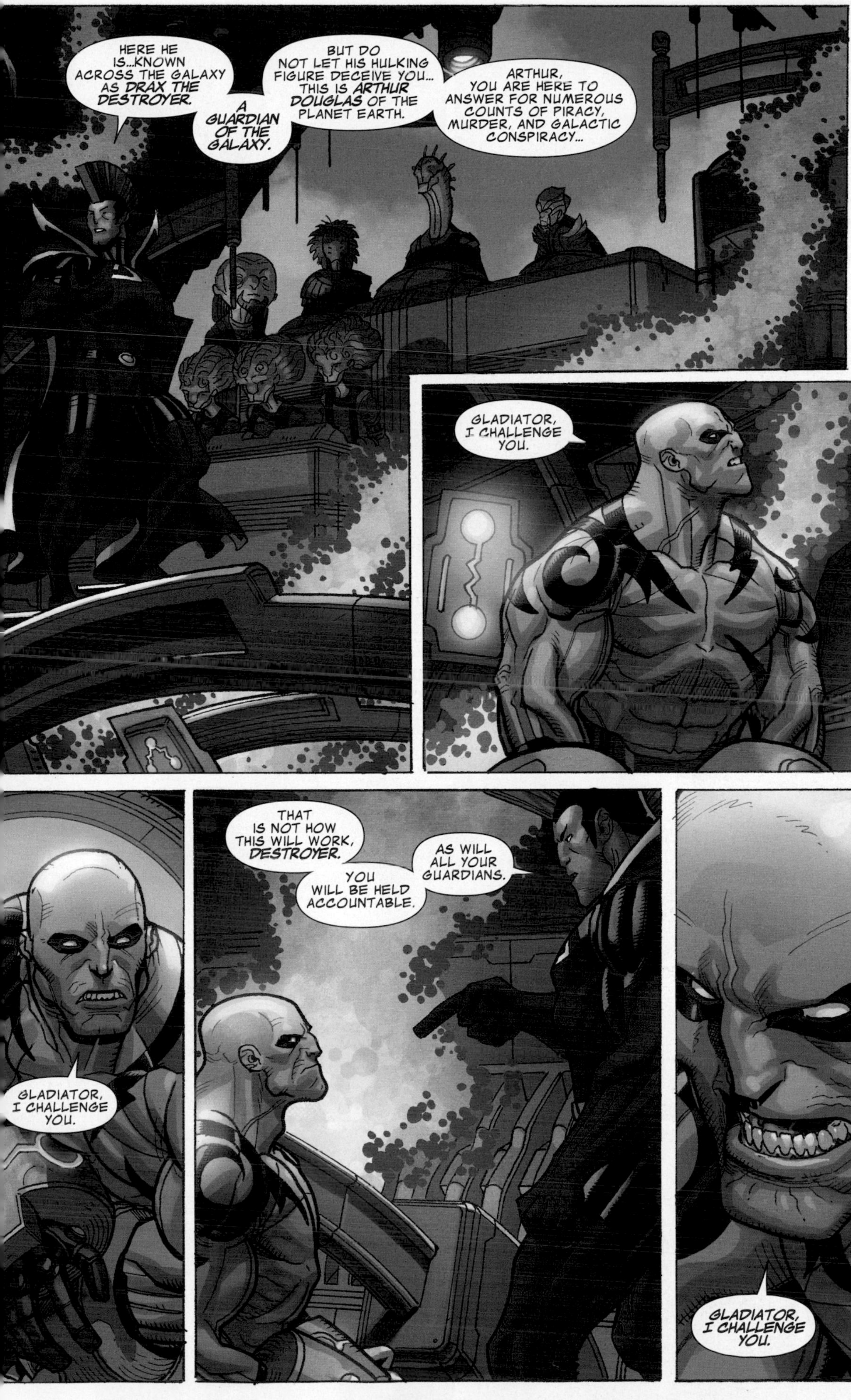
HERE HE IS...KNOWN ACROSS THE GALAXY AS DRAX THE DESTROYER.
A GUARDIAN OF THE GALAXY.
BUT DO NOT LET HIS HULKING FIGURE DECEIVE YOU... THIS IS ARTHUR DOUGLAS OF THE PLANET EARTH.
ARTHUR, YOU ARE HERE TO ANSWER FOR NUMEROUS COUNTS OF PIRACY, MURDER, AND GALACTIC CONSPIRACY...
GLADIATOR, I CHALLENGE YOU.
GLADIATOR, I CHALLENGE YOU.
THAT IS NOT HOW THIS WILL WORK, DESTROYER.
YOU WILL BE HELD ACCOUNTABLE.
AS WILL ALL YOUR GUARDIANS.
GLADIATOR, I CHALLENGE YOU.

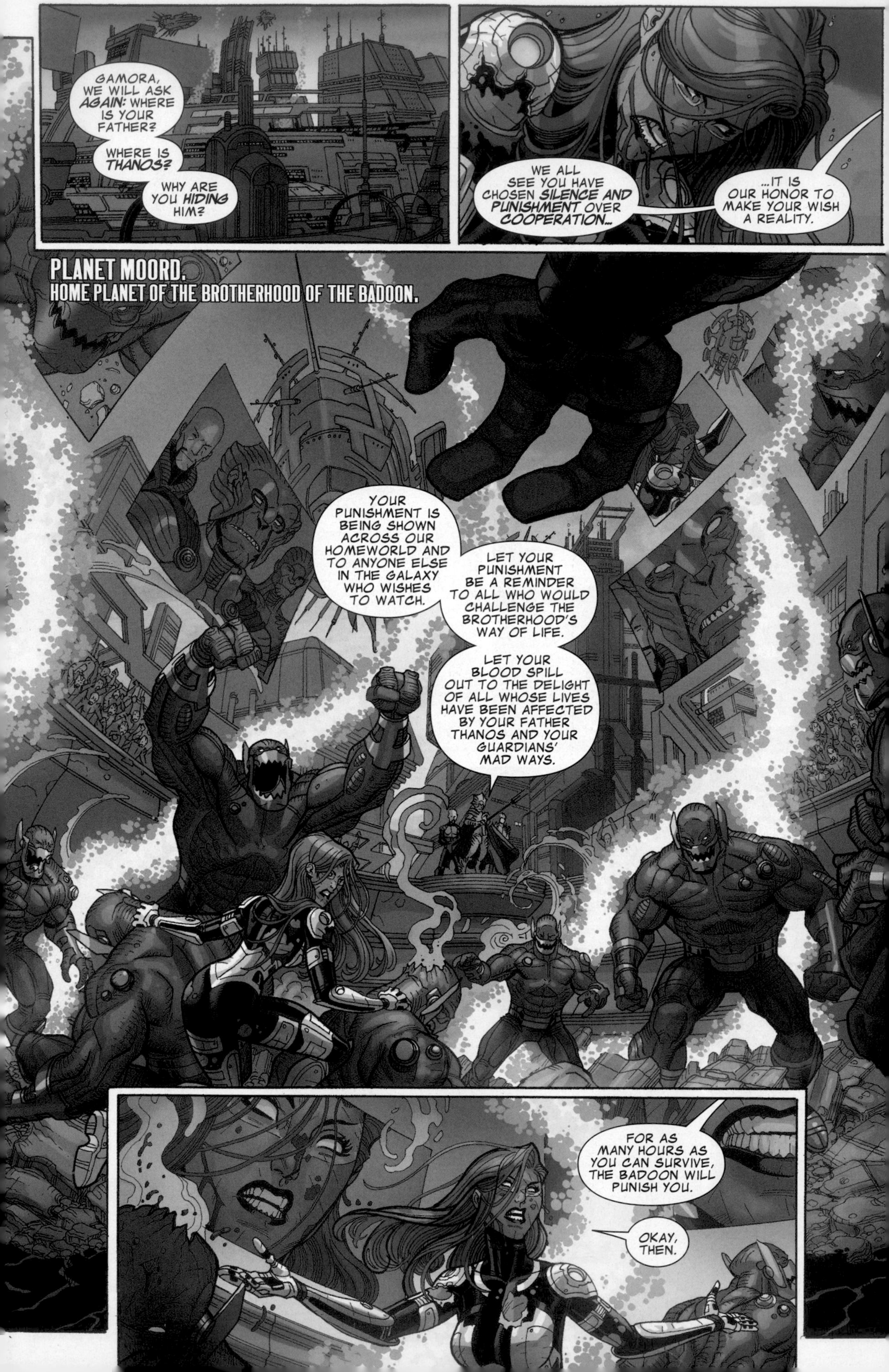
GAMORA, WE WILL ASK AGAIN: WHERE IS YOUR FATHER?
WHERE IS THANOS?
WHY ARE YOU HIDING HIM?
WE ALL SEE YOU HAVE CHOSEN SILENCE AND PUNISHMENT OVER COOPERATION...
...IT IS OUR HONOR TO MAKE YOUR WISH A REALITY.
PLANET MOORD.
HOME PLANET OF THE BROTHERHOOD OF THE BADOON.
YOUR PUNISHMENT IS BEING SHOWN ACROSS OUR HOMEWORLD AND TO ANYONE ELSE IN THE GALAXY WHO WISHES TO WATCH.
LET YOUR PUNISHMENT BE A REMINDER TO ALL WHO WOULD CHALLENGE THE BROTHERHOOD'S WAY OF LIFE.
LET YOUR BLOOD SPILL OUT TO THE DELIGHT OF ALL WHOSE LIVES HAVE BEEN AFFECTED BY YOUR FATHER THANOS AND YOUR GUARDIANS' MAD WAYS.
FOR AS MANY HOURS AS YOU CAN SURVIVE, THE BADOON WILL PUNISH YOU.
OKAY, THEN.

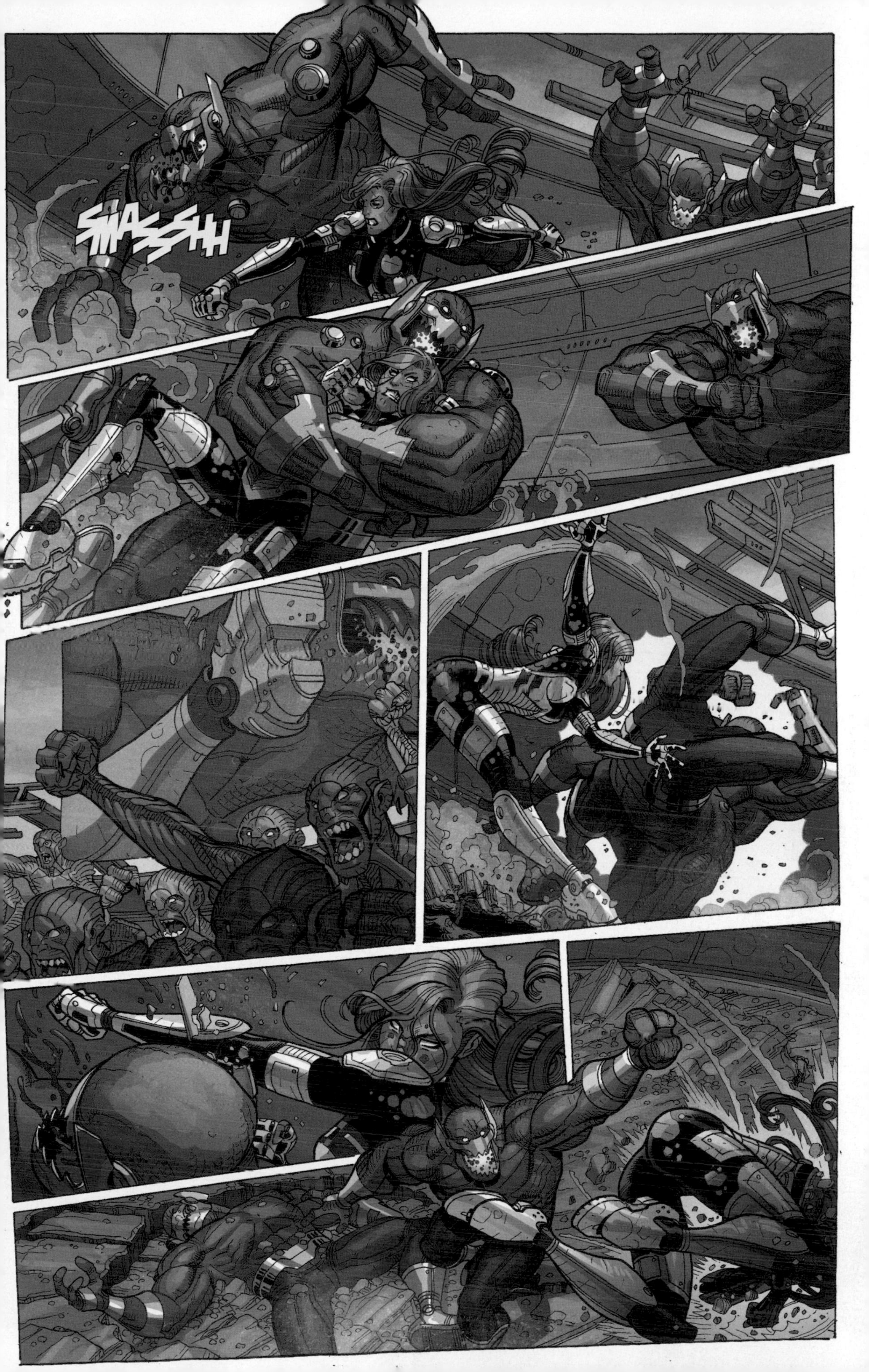
SMASSHH

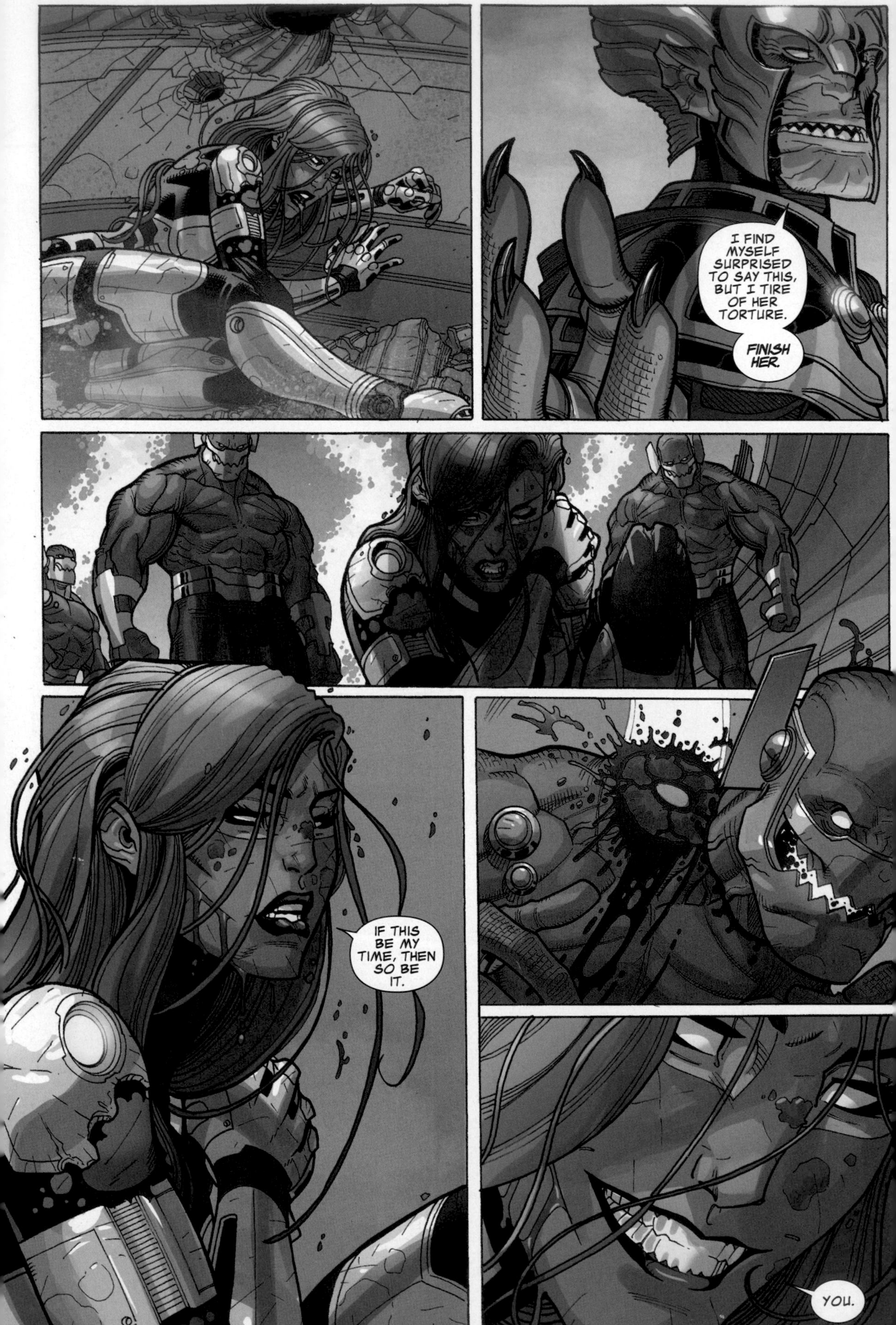

I FIND MYSELF SURPRISED TO SAY THIS, BUT I TIRE OF HER TORTURE.
FINISH HER.
IF THIS BE MY TIME, THEN SO BE IT.
YOU.

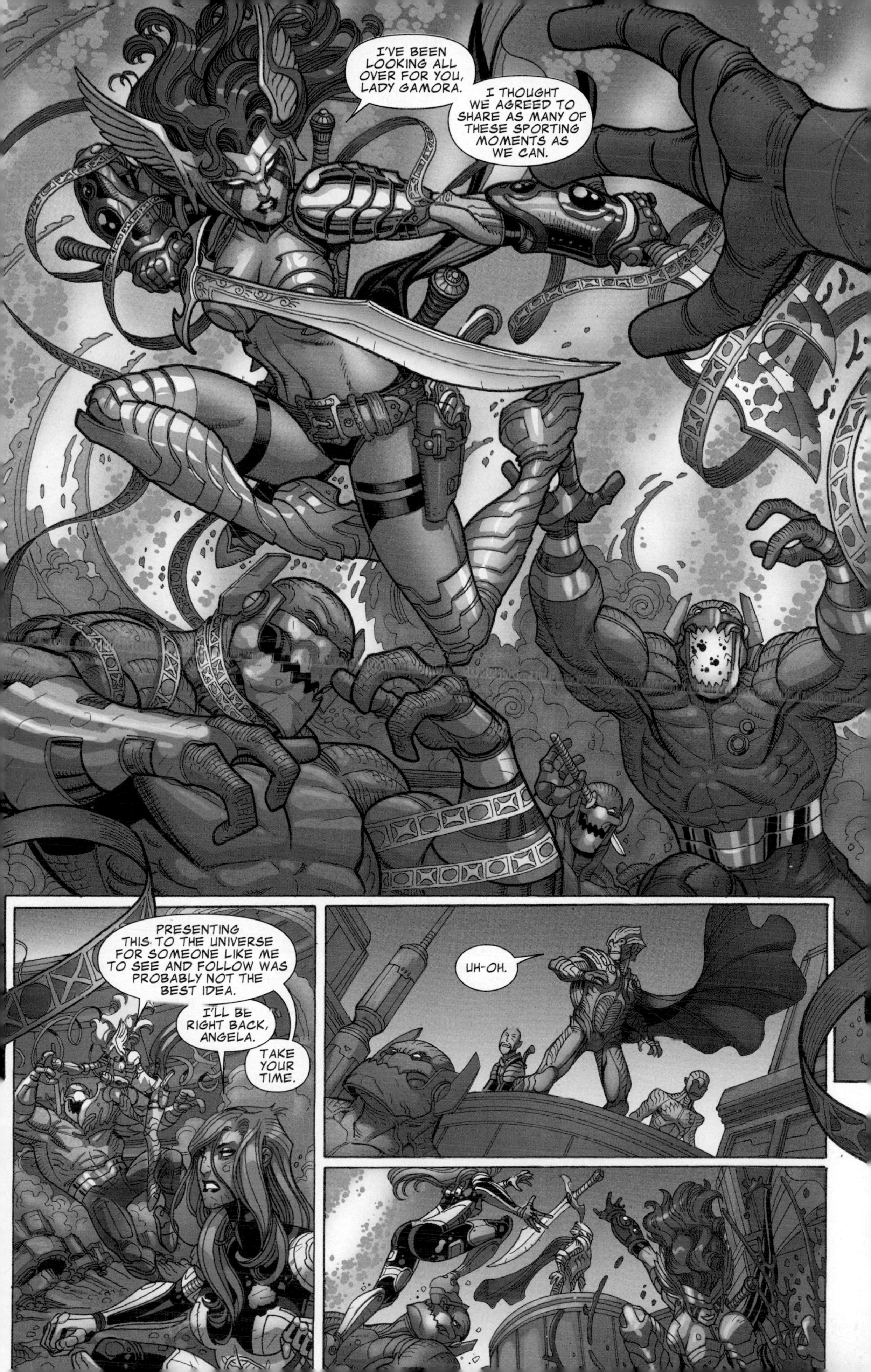
I'VE BEEN LOOKING ALL OVER FOR YOU, LADY GAMORA.
I THOUGHT WE AGREED TO SHARE AS MANY OF THESE SPORTING MOMENTS AS WE CAN.
PRESENTING THIS TO THE UNIVERSE FOR SOMEONE LIKE ME TO SEE AND FOLLOW WAS PROBABLY NOT THE BEST IDEA.
I'LL BE RIGHT BACK, ANGELA.
TAKE YOUR TIME.
UH-OH.

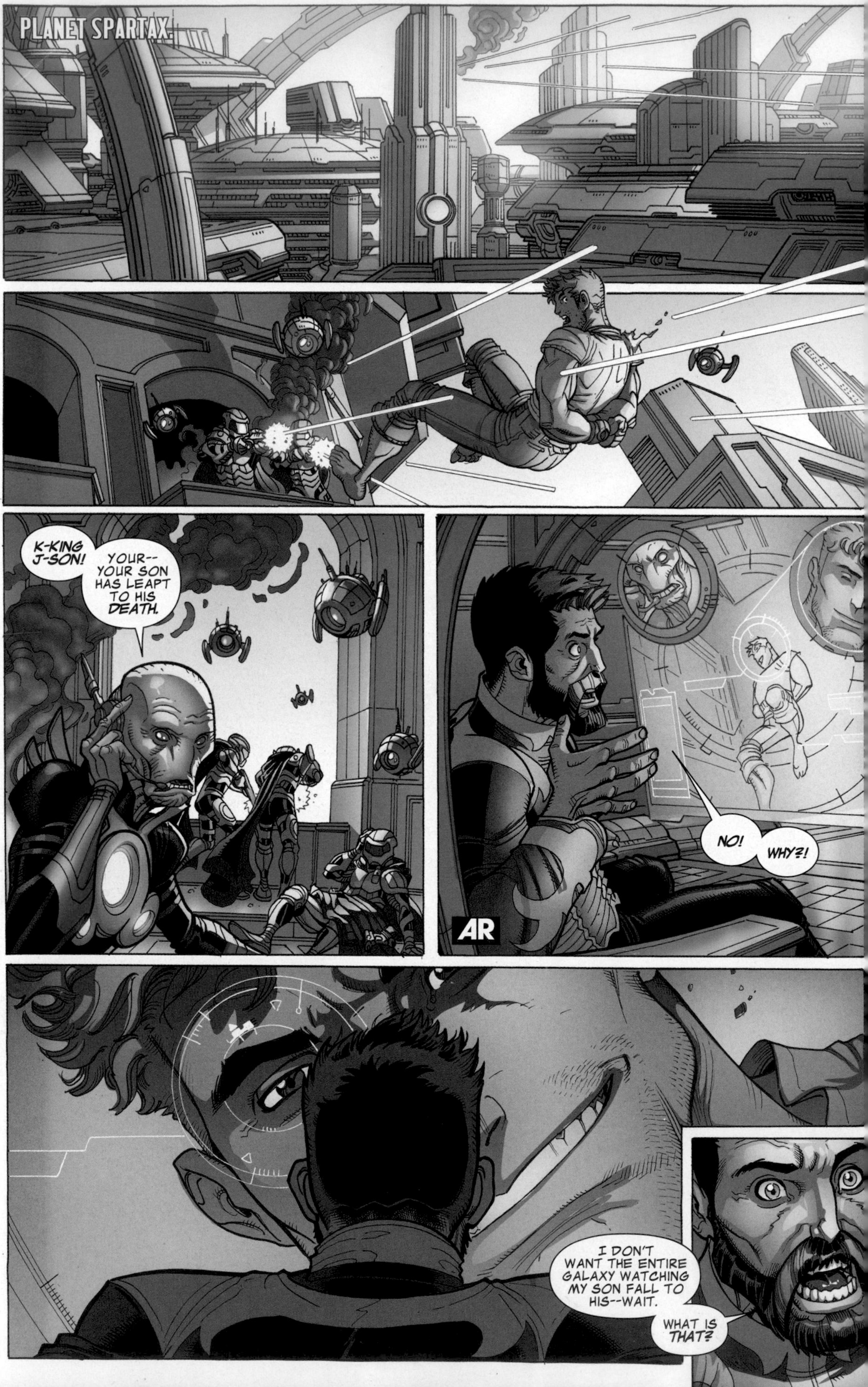
PLANET SPARTAX.
K-KING J-SON!
YOUR-- YOUR SON HAS LEAPT TO HIS DEATH.
NO!
WHY?!
AR
I DON'T WANT THE ENTIRE GALAXY WATCHING MY SON FALL TO HIS--WAIT.
WHAT IS THAT?

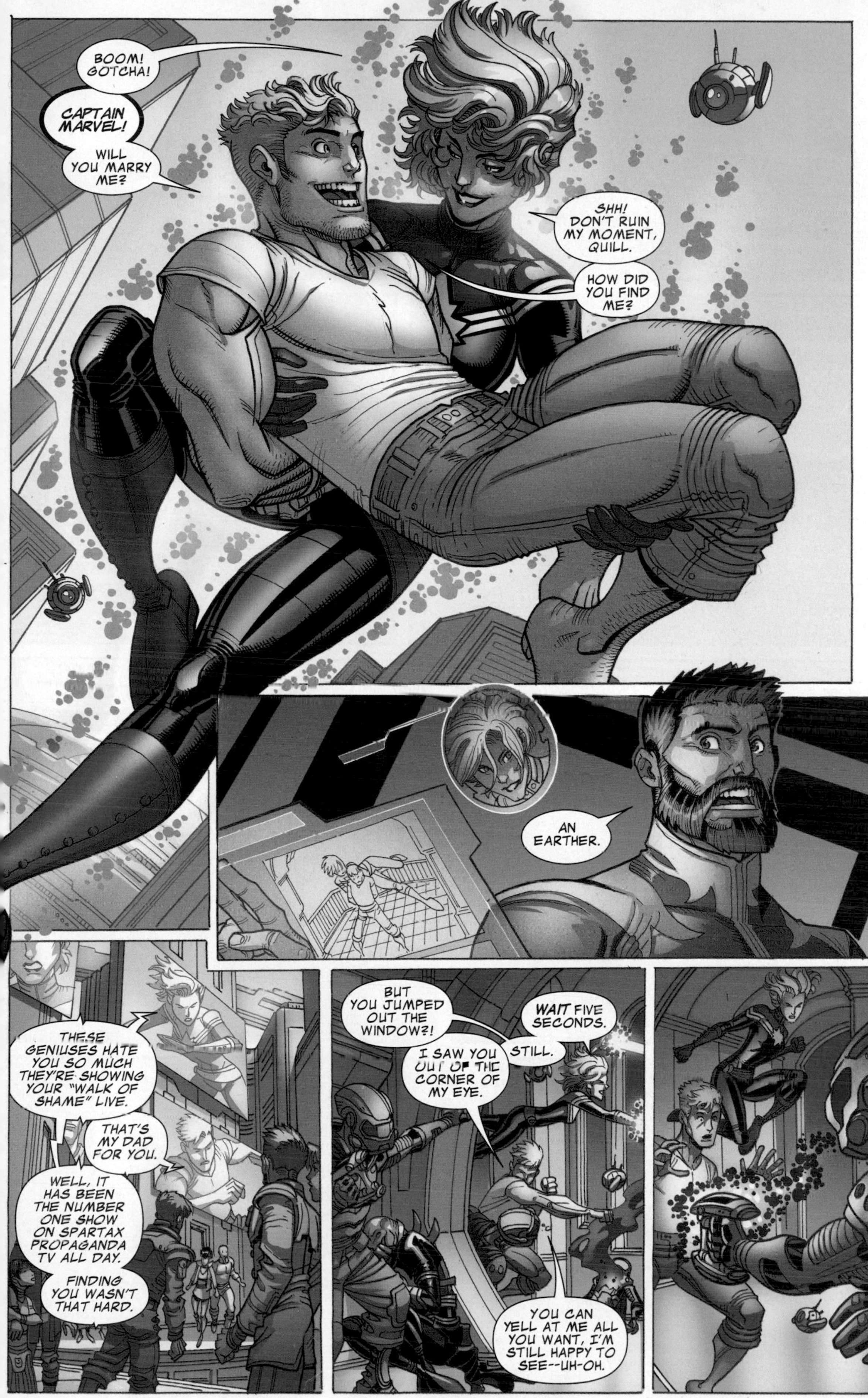
BOOM! GOTCHA!
CAPTAIN MARVEL!
WILL YOU MARRY ME?
SHH! DON'T RUIN MY MOMENT, QUILL.
HOW DID YOU FIND ME?
AN EARTHER.
THESE GENIUSES HATE YOU SO MUCH THEY'RE SHOWING YOUR "WALK OF SHAME" LIVE.
THAT'S MY DAD FOR YOU.
WELL, IT HAS BEEN THE NUMBER ONE SHOW ON SPARTAX PROPAGANDA TV ALL DAY.
FINDING YOU WASN'T THAT HARD.
BUT YOU JUMPED OUT THE WINDOW?!
WAIT FIVE SECONDS.
STILL.
I SAW YOU OUT OF THE CORNER OF MY EYE.
YOU CAN YELL AT ME ALL YOU WANT, I'M STILL HAPPY TO SEE--UH-OH.

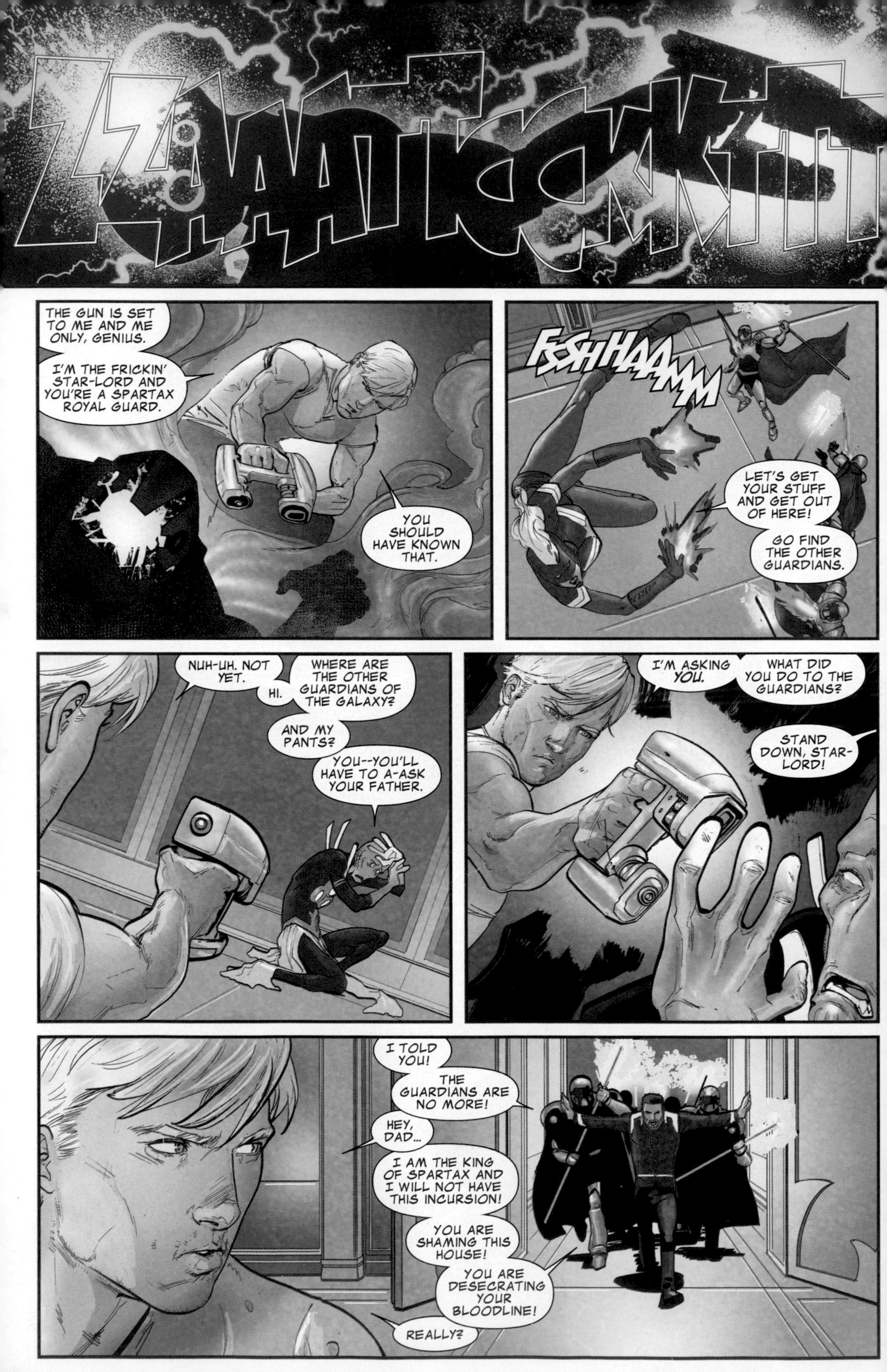
ZZAAATKCKKTTT
THE GUN IS SET TO ME AND ME ONLY, GENIUS.
I'M THE FRICKIN' STAR-LORD AND YOU'RE A SPARTAX ROYAL GUARD.
YOU SHOULD HAVE KNOWN THAT.
FSSHHAAMM
LET'S GET YOUR STUFF AND GET OUT OF HERE!
GO FIND THE OTHER GUARDIANS.
NUH-UH. NOT YET.
HI.
WHERE ARE THE OTHER GUARDIANS OF THE GALAXY?
AND MY PANTS?
YOU--YOU'LL HAVE TO A-ASK YOUR FATHER.
I'M ASKING YOU.
WHAT DID YOU DO TO THE GUARDIANS?
STAND DOWN, STAR-LORD!
I TOLD YOU!
THE GUARDIANS ARE NO MORE!
HEY, DAD...
I AM THE KING OF SPARTAX AND I WILL NOT HAVE THIS INCURSION!
YOU ARE SHAMING THIS HOUSE!
YOU ARE DESECRATING YOUR BLOODLINE!
REALLY?

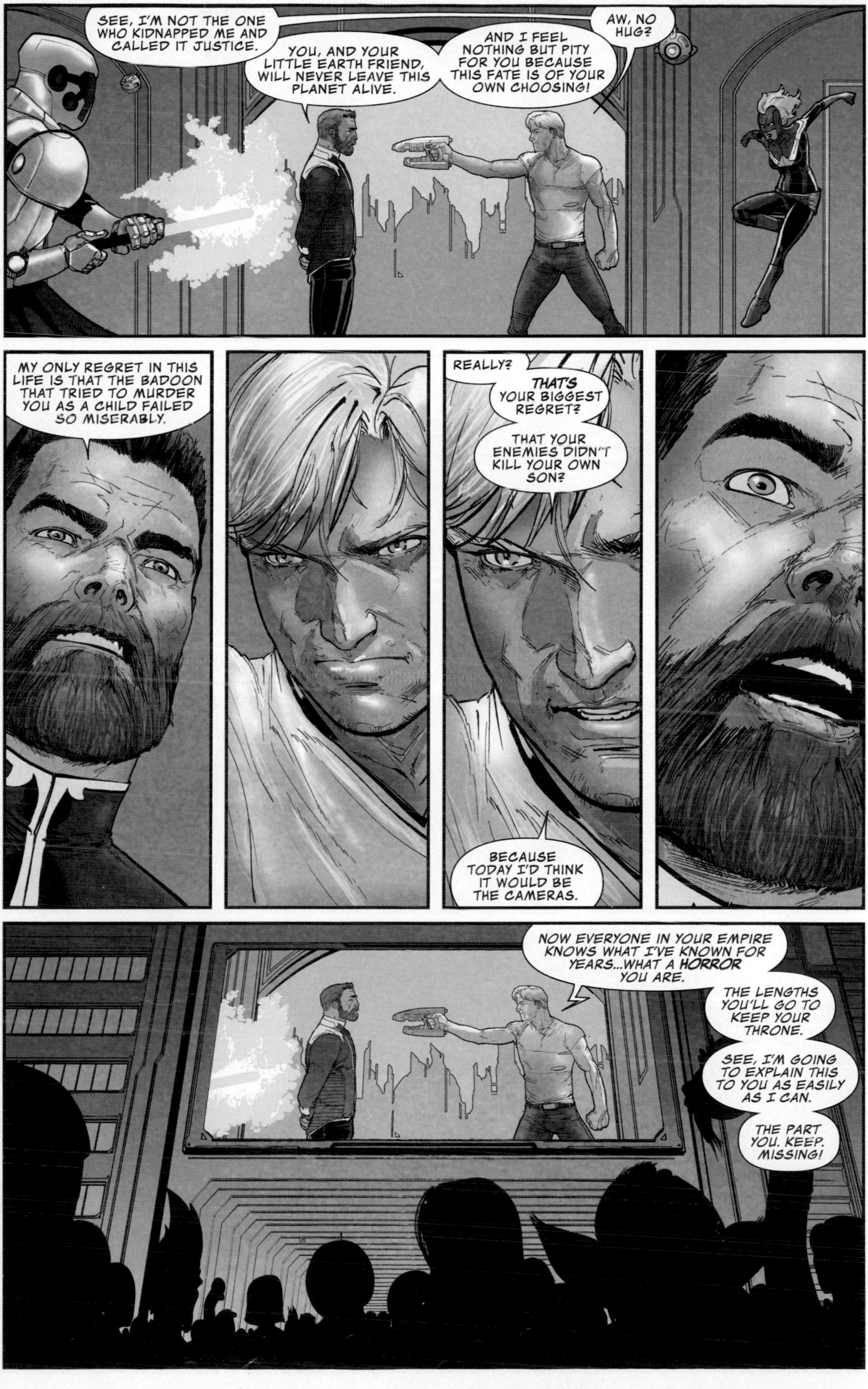

SEE, I'M NOT THE ONE WHO KIDNAPPED ME AND CALLED IT JUSTICE.
YOU, AND YOUR LITTLE EARTH FRIEND, WILL NEVER LEAVE THIS PLANET ALIVE.
AND I FEEL NOTHING BUT PITY FOR YOU BECAUSE THIS FATE IS OF YOUR OWN CHOOSING!
AW, NO HUG?
MY ONLY REGRET IN THIS LIFE IS THAT THE BADOON THAT TRIED TO MURDER YOU AS A CHILD FAILED SO MISERABLY.
REALLY?
THAT'S YOUR BIGGEST REGRET?
THAT YOUR ENEMIES DIDN'T KILL YOUR OWN SON?
BECAUSE TODAY I'D THINK IT WOULD BE THE CAMERAS.
NOW EVERYONE IN YOUR EMPIRE KNOWS WHAT I'VE KNOWN FOR YEARS...WHAT A HORROR YOU ARE.
THE LENGTHS YOU'LL GO TO KEEP YOUR THRONE.
SEE, I'M GOING TO EXPLAIN THIS TO YOU AS EASILY AS I CAN.
THE PART YOU. KEEP. MISSING!

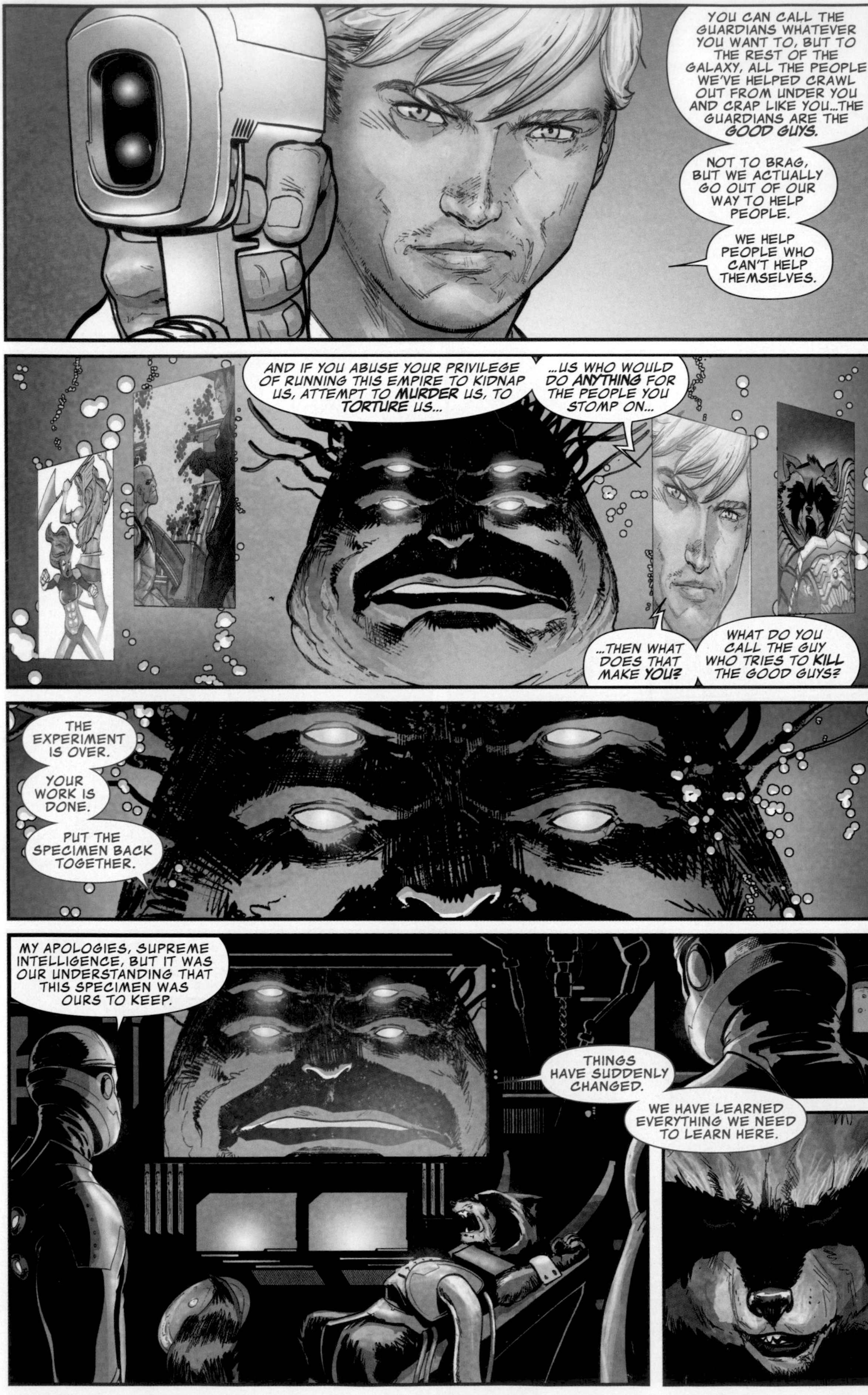
YOU CAN CALL THE GUARDIANS WHATEVER YOU WANT TO, BUT TO THE REST OF THE GALAXY, ALL THE PEOPLE WE'VE HELPED CRAWL OUT FROM UNDER YOU AND CRAP LIKE YOU...THE GUARDIANS ARE THE GOOD GUYS.
NOT TO BRAG, BUT WE ACTUALLY GO OUT OF OUR WAY TO HELP PEOPLE.
WE HELP PEOPLE WHO CAN'T HELP THEMSELVES.
AND IF YOU ABUSE YOUR PRIVILEGE OF RUNNING THIS EMPIRE TO KIDNAP US, ATTEMPT TO MURDER US, TO TORTURE US...
...US WHO WOULD DO ANYTHING FOR THE PEOPLE YOU STOMP ON...
...THEN WHAT DOES THAT MAKE YOU?
WHAT DO YOU CALL THE GUY WHO TRIES TO KILL THE GOOD GUYS?
THE EXPERIMENT IS OVER.
YOUR WORK IS DONE.
PUT THE SPECIMEN BACK TOGETHER.
MY APOLOGIES, SUPREME INTELLIGENCE, BUT IT WAS OUR UNDERSTANDING THAT THIS SPECIMEN WAS OURS TO KEEP.
THINGS HAVE SUDDENLY CHANGED.
WE HAVE LEARNED EVERYTHING WE NEED TO LEARN HERE.

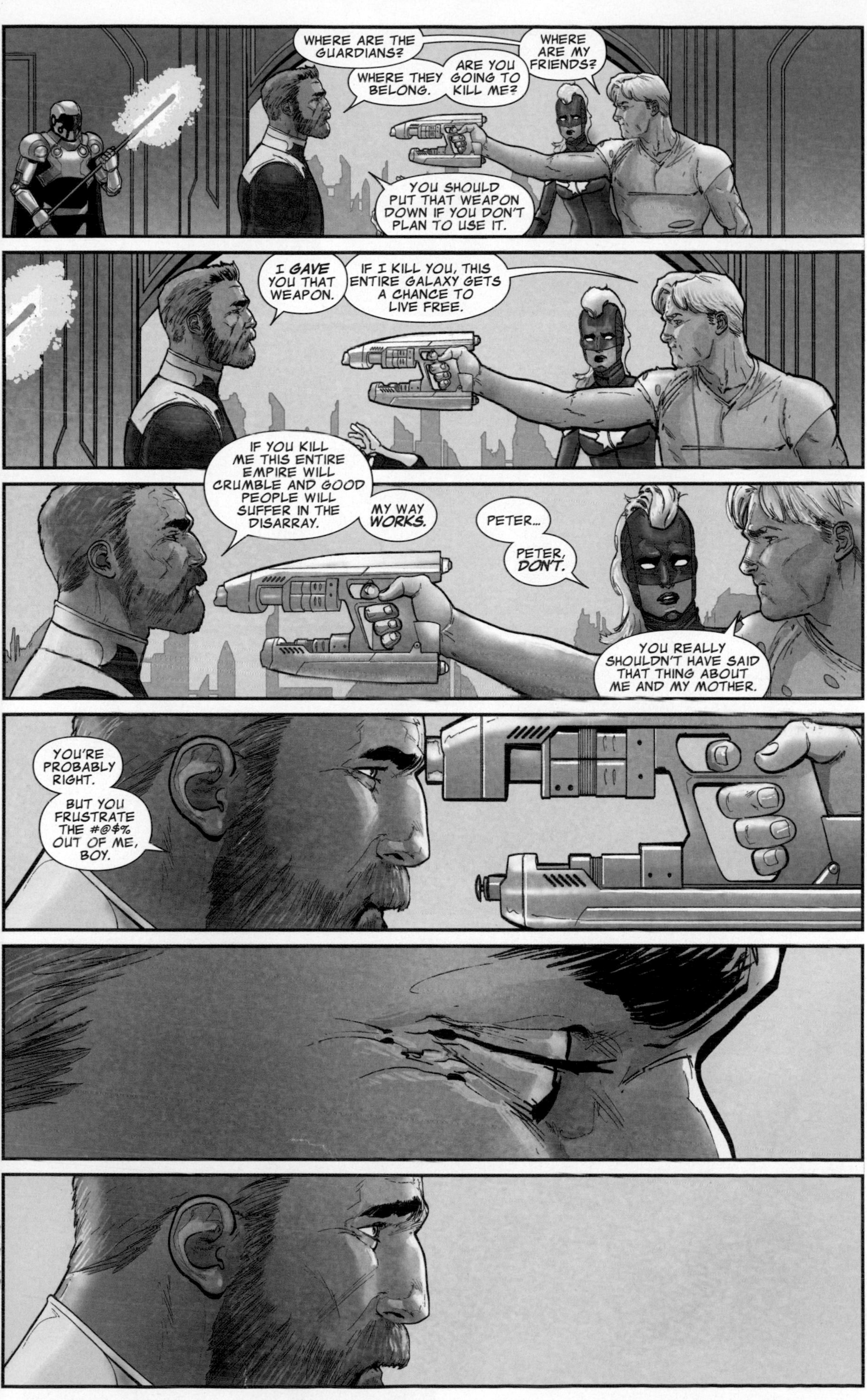
WHERE ARE THE GUARDIANS?
WHERE ARE MY FRIENDS?
WHERE THEY BELONG.
ARE YOU GOING TO KILL ME?
YOU SHOULD PUT THAT WEAPON DOWN IF YOU DON'T PLAN TO USE IT.
I GAVE YOU THAT WEAPON.
IF I KILL YOU, THIS ENTIRE GALAXY GETS A CHANCE TO LIVE FREE.
IF YOU KILL ME THIS ENTIRE EMPIRE WILL CRUMBLE AND GOOD PEOPLE WILL SUFFER IN THE DISARRAY.
MY WAY WORKS.
PETER...
PETER, DON'T.
YOU REALLY SHOULDN'T HAVE SAID THAT THING ABOUT ME AND MY MOTHER.
YOU'RE PROBABLY RIGHT.
BUT YOU FRUSTRATE THE #@$% OUT OF ME, BOY.

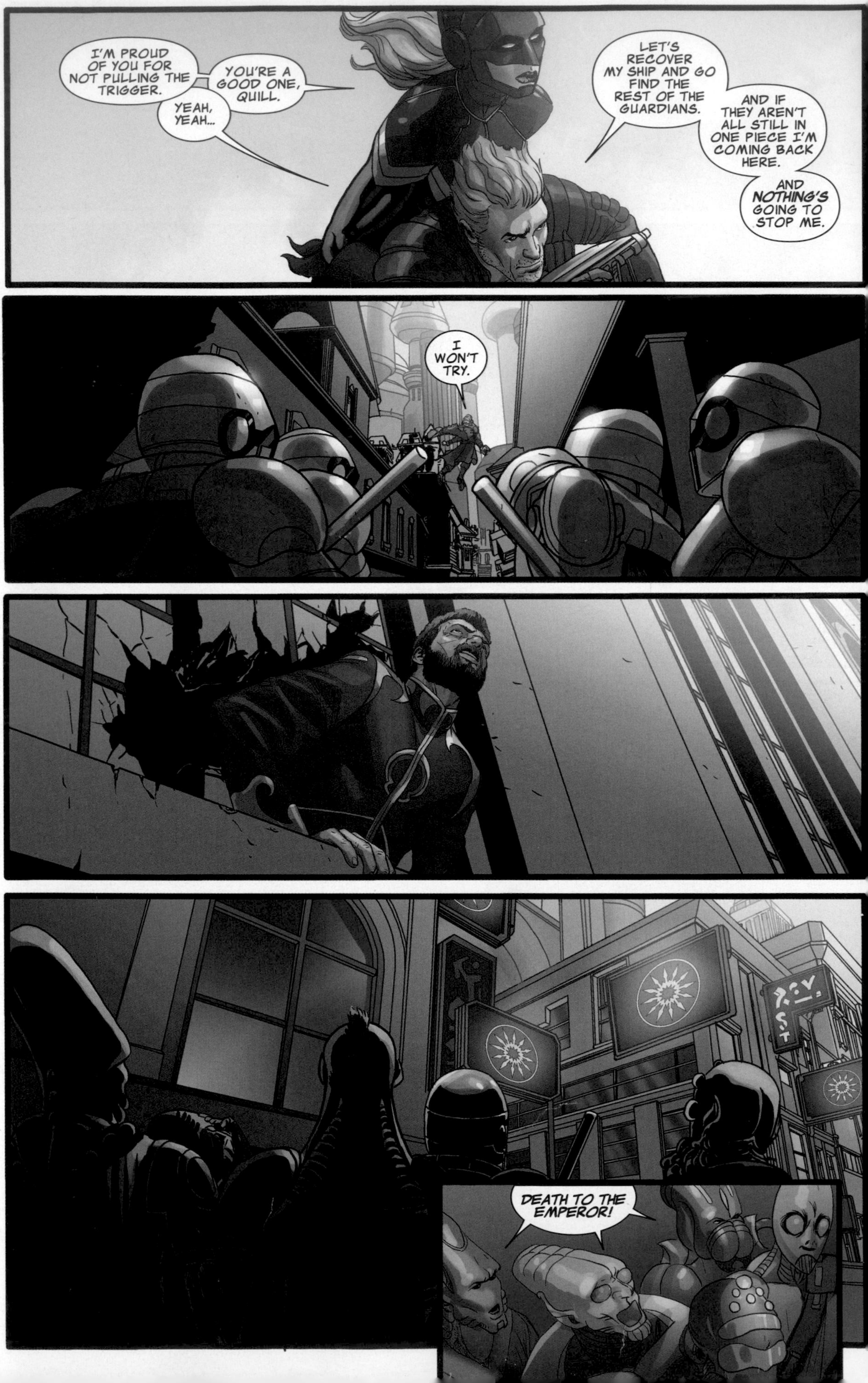
I'M PROUD OF YOU FOR NOT PULLING THE TRIGGER.
YOU'RE A GOOD ONE, QUILL.
YEAH, YEAH...
LET'S RECOVER MY SHIP AND GO FIND THE REST OF THE GUARDIANS.
AND IF THEY AREN'T ALL STILL IN ONE PIECE I'M COMING BACK HERE.
AND NOTHING'S GOING TO STOP ME.
I WON'T TRY.
DEATH TO THE EMPEROR!

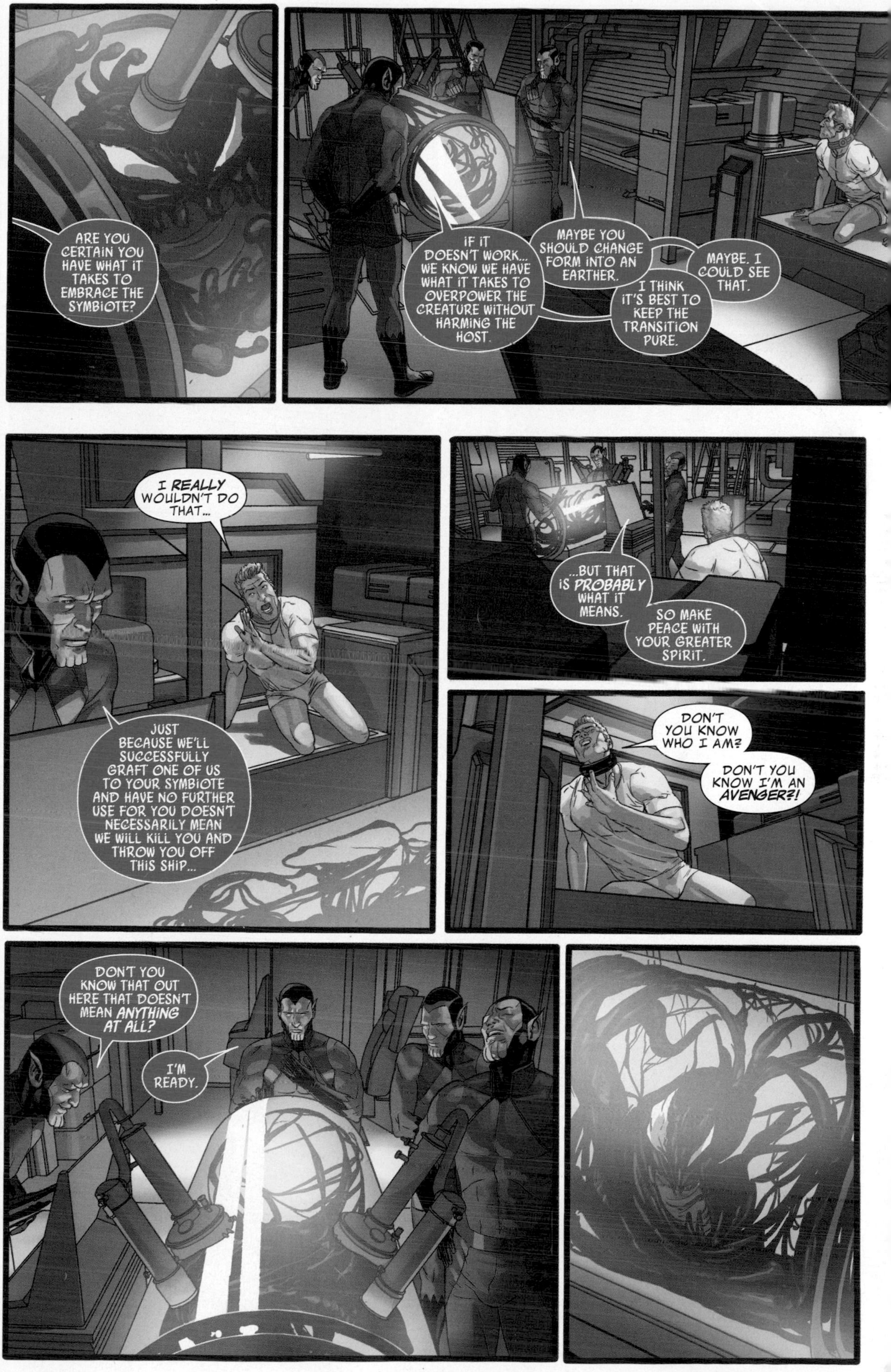
ARE YOU CERTAIN YOU HAVE WHAT IT TAKES TO EMBRACE THE SYMBIOTE?
IF IT DOESN'T WORK... WE KNOW WE HAVE WHAT IT TAKES TO OVERPOWER THE CREATURE WITHOUT HARMING THE HOST.
MAYBE YOU SHOULD CHANGE FORM INTO AN EARTHER.
I THINK IT'S BEST TO KEEP THE TRANSITION PURE.
MAYBE. I COULD SEE THAT.
I REALLY WOULDN'T DO THAT...
JUST BECAUSE WE'LL SUCCESSFULLY GRAFT ONE OF US TO YOUR SYMBIOTE AND HAVE NO FURTHER USE FOR YOU DOESN'T NECESSARILY MEAN WE WILL KILL YOU AND THROW YOU OFF THIS SHIP...
...BUT THAT IS PROBABLY WHAT IT MEANS.
SO MAKE PEACE WITH YOUR GREATER SPIRIT.
DON'T YOU KNOW WHO I AM?
DON'T YOU KNOW I'M AN AVENGER?!
DON'T YOU KNOW THAT OUT HERE THAT DOESN'T MEAN ANYTHING AT ALL?
I'M READY.

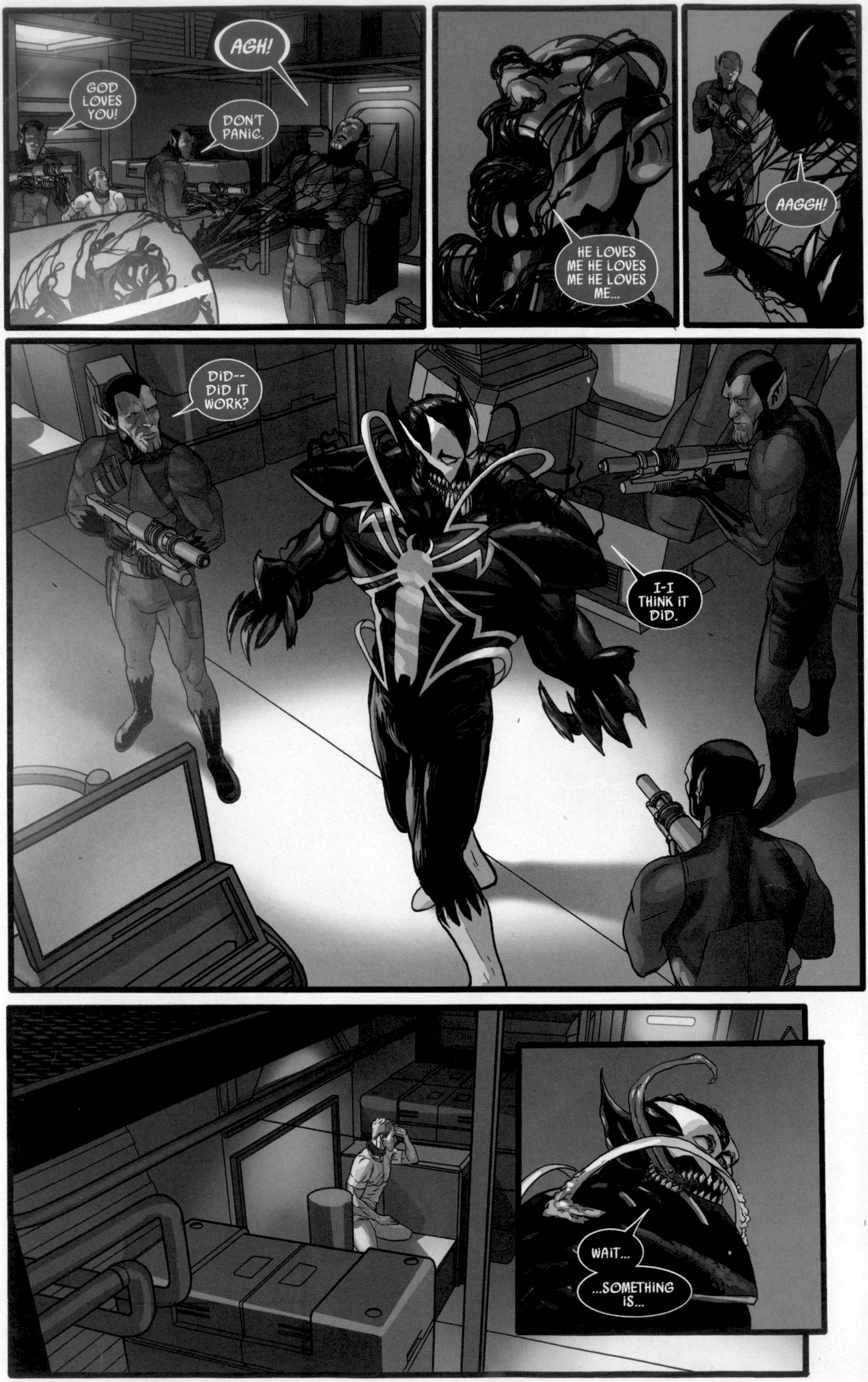
AGH!
GOD LOVES YOU!
DON'T PANIC.
HE LOVES ME HE LOVES ME HE LOVES ME...
AAGGH!
DID-- DID IT WORK?
I-I THINK IT DID.
WAIT...
...SOMETHING IS...

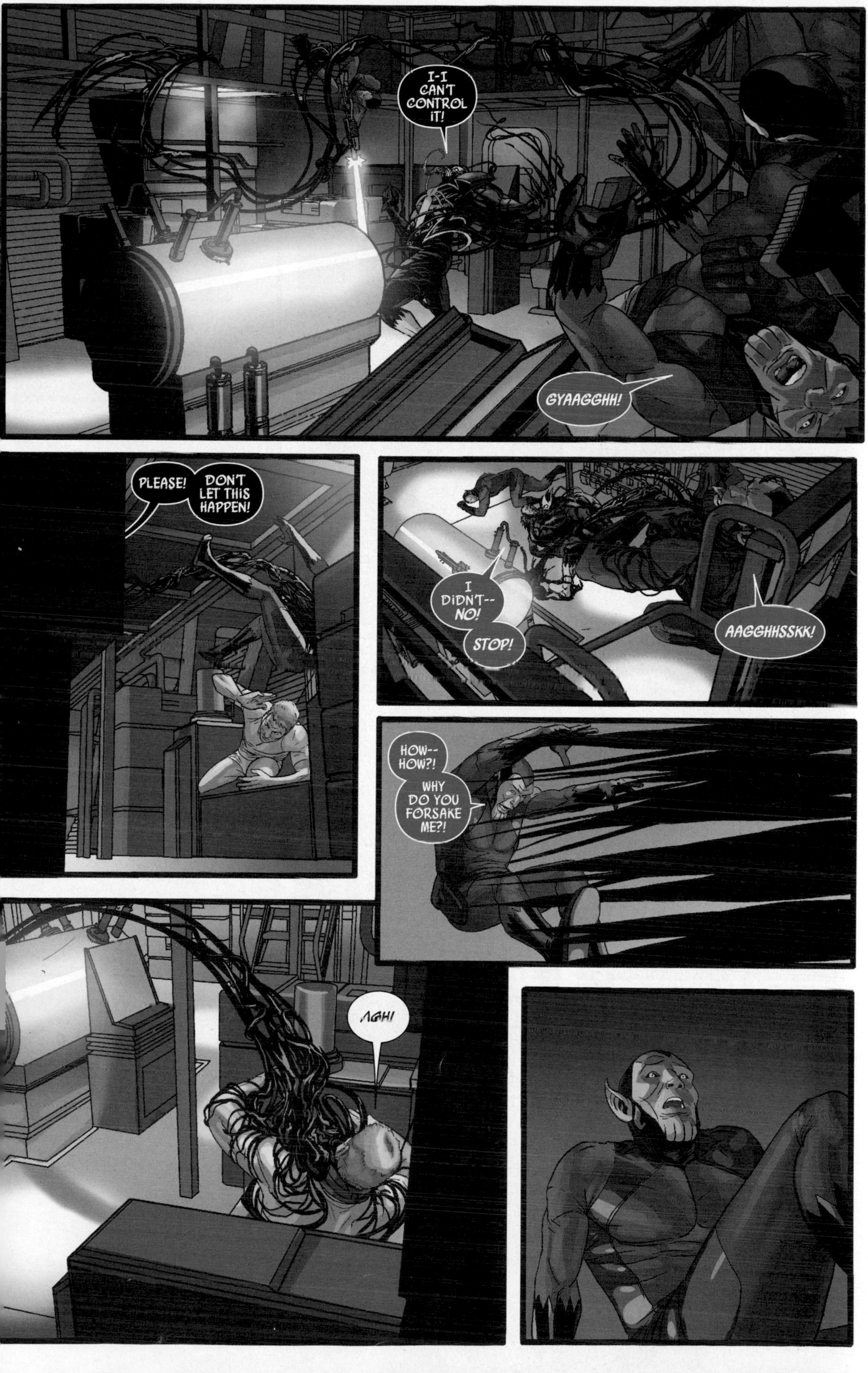
I-I CAN'T CONTROL IT!
GYAAGGHH!
PLEASE!
DON'T LET THIS HAPPEN!
I DIDN'T-- NO!
STOP!
AAGGHHSSKK!
HOW-- HOW?!
WHY DO YOU FORSAKE ME?!
AGH!

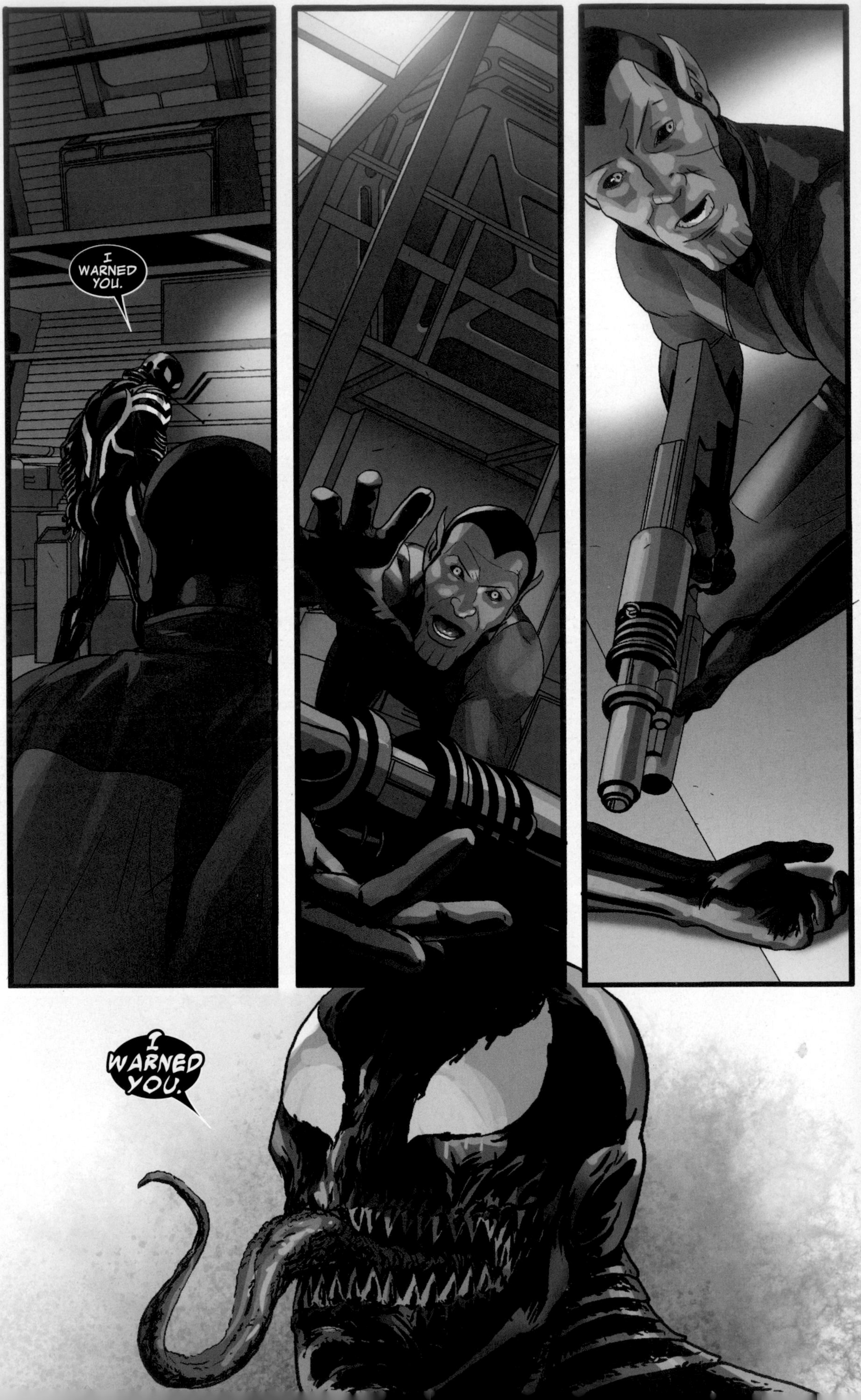

I WARNED YOU.
I WARNED YOU.

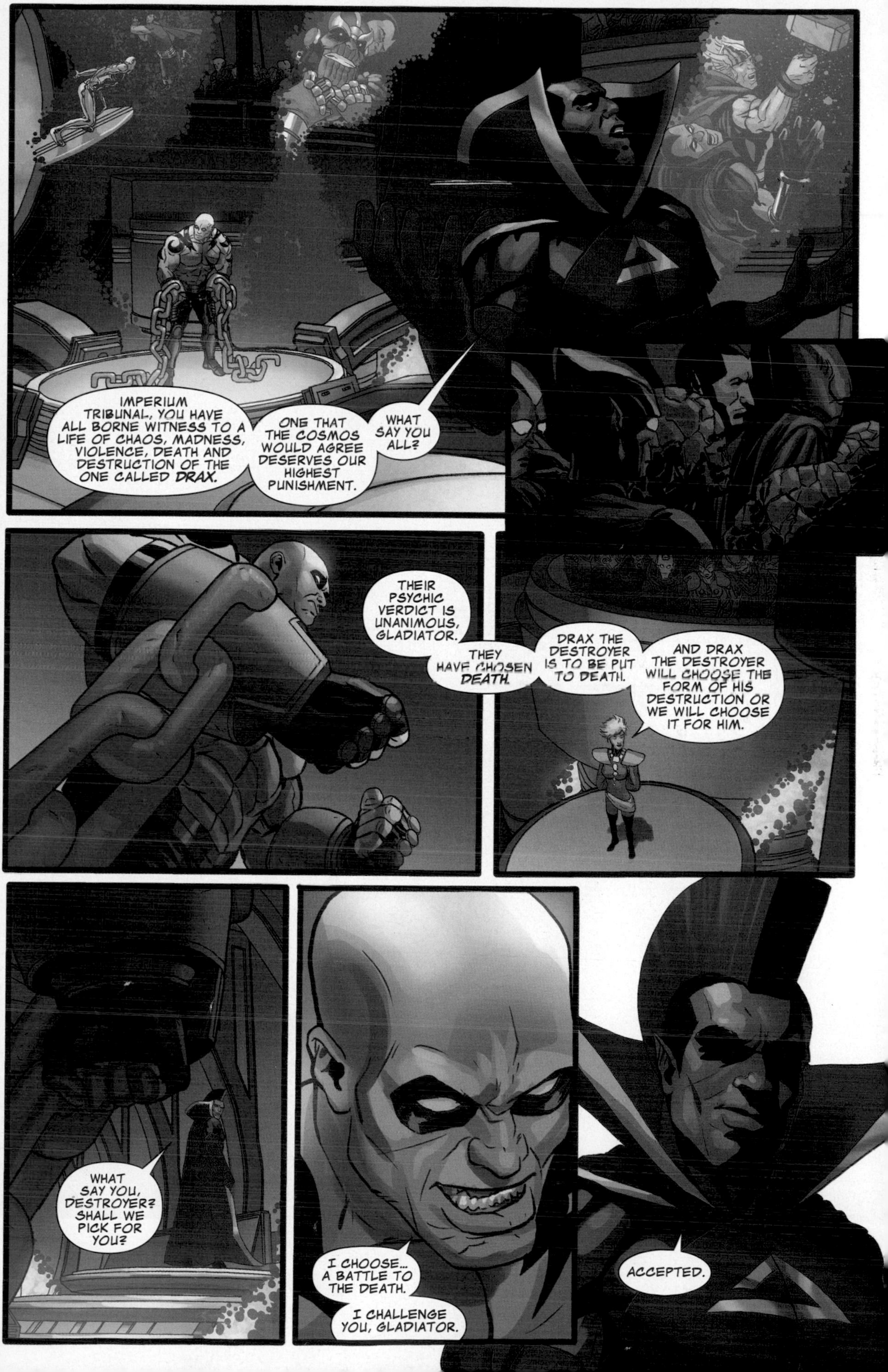
IMPERIUM TRIBUNAL, YOU HAVE ALL BORNE WITNESS TO A LIFE OF CHAOS, MADNESS, VIOLENCE, DEATH AND DESTRUCTION OF THE ONE CALLED DRAX.
ONE THAT THE COSMOS WOULD AGREE DESERVES OUR HIGHEST PUNISHMENT.
WHAT SAY YOU ALL?
THEIR PSYCHIC VERDICT IS UNANIMOUS, GLADIATOR.
THEY HAVE CHOSEN DEATH.
DRAX THE DESTROYER IS TO BE PUT TO DEATH.
AND DRAX THE DESTROYER WILL CHOOSE THE FORM OF HIS DESTRUCTION OR WE WILL CHOOSE IT FOR HIM.
WHAT SAY YOU, DESTROYER? SHALL WE PICK FOR YOU?
I CHOOSE... A BATTLE TO THE DEATH.
I CHALLENGE YOU, GLADIATOR.
ACCEPTED.

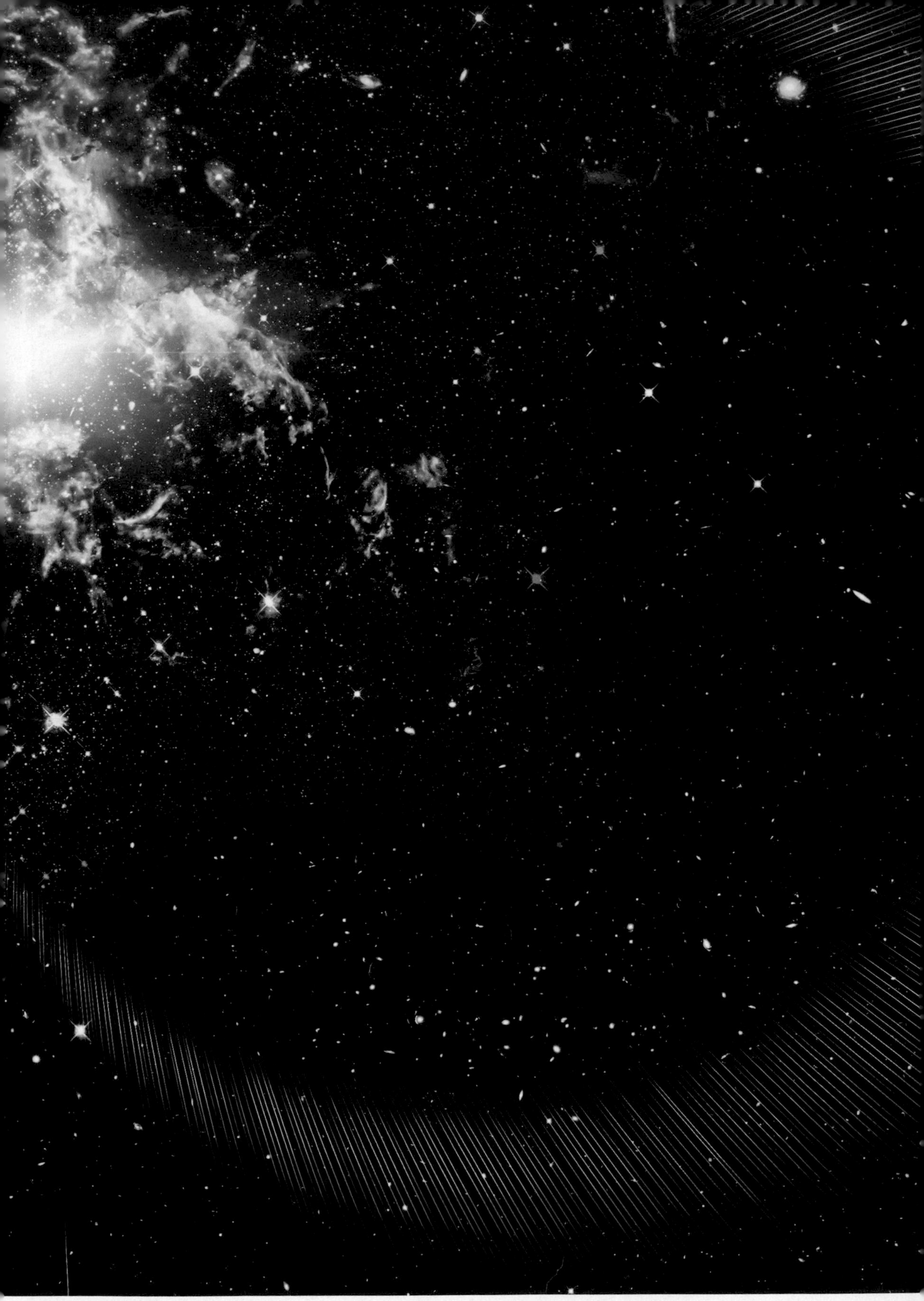

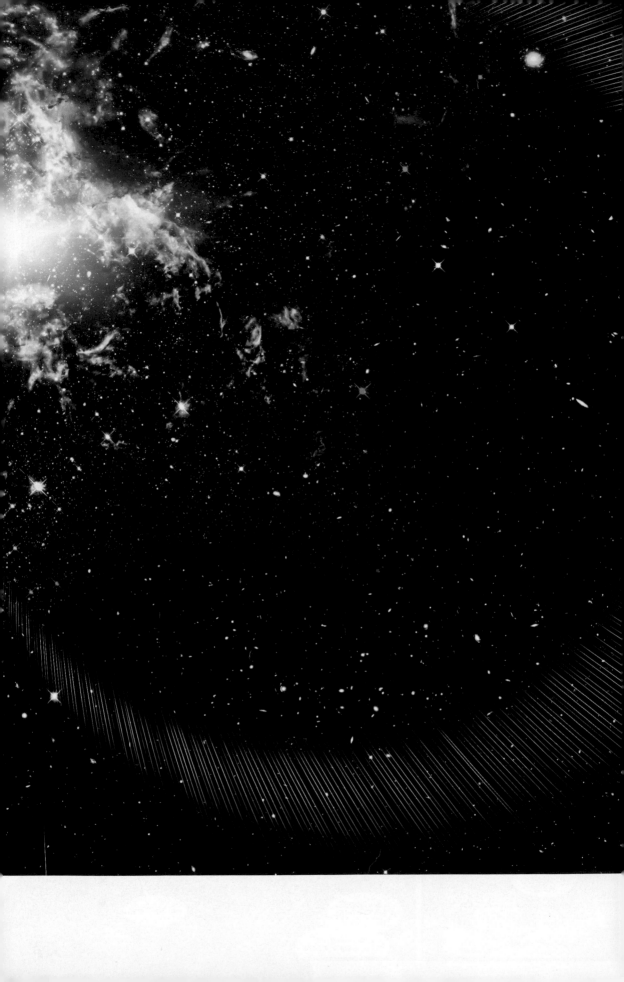

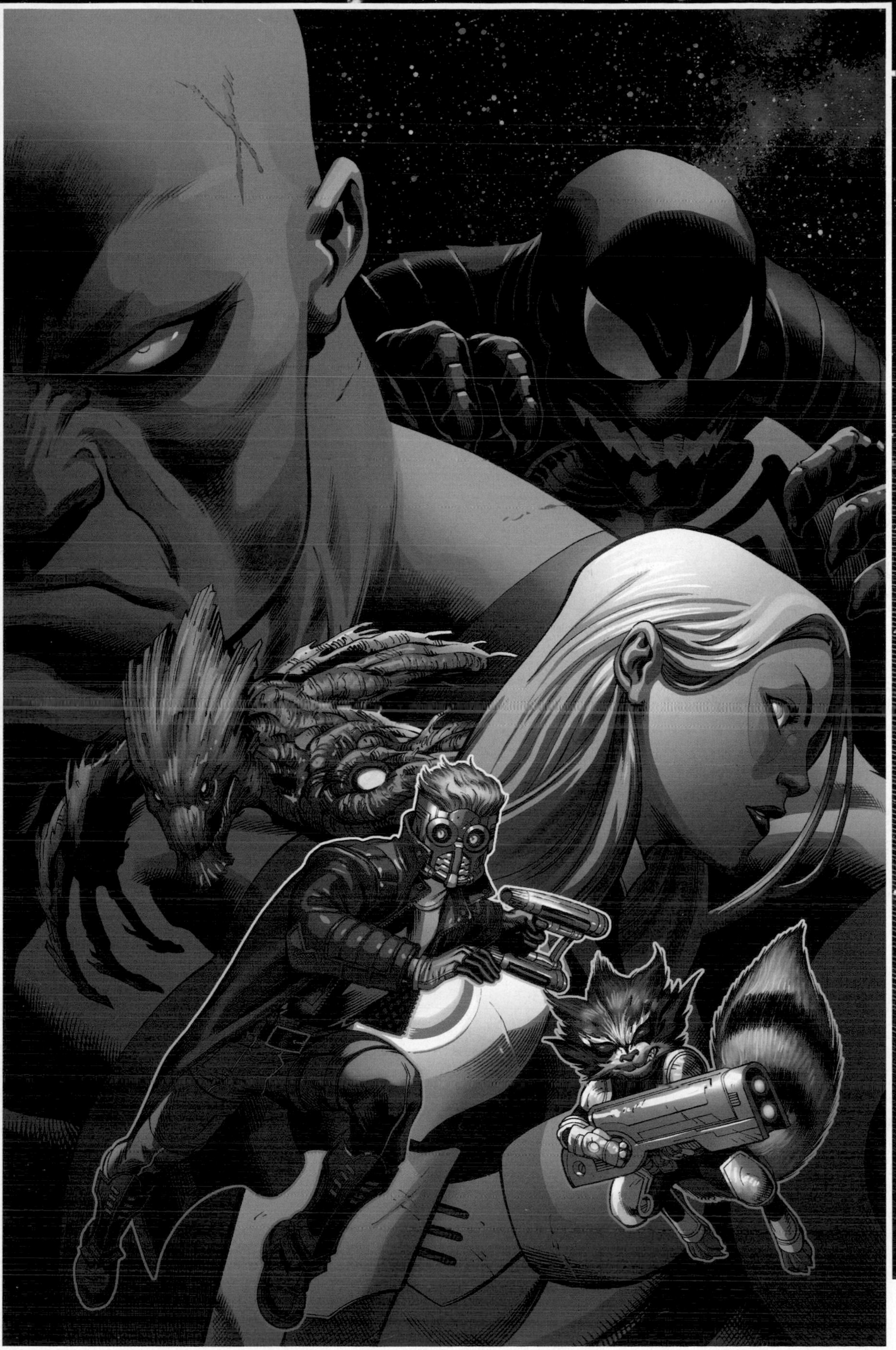

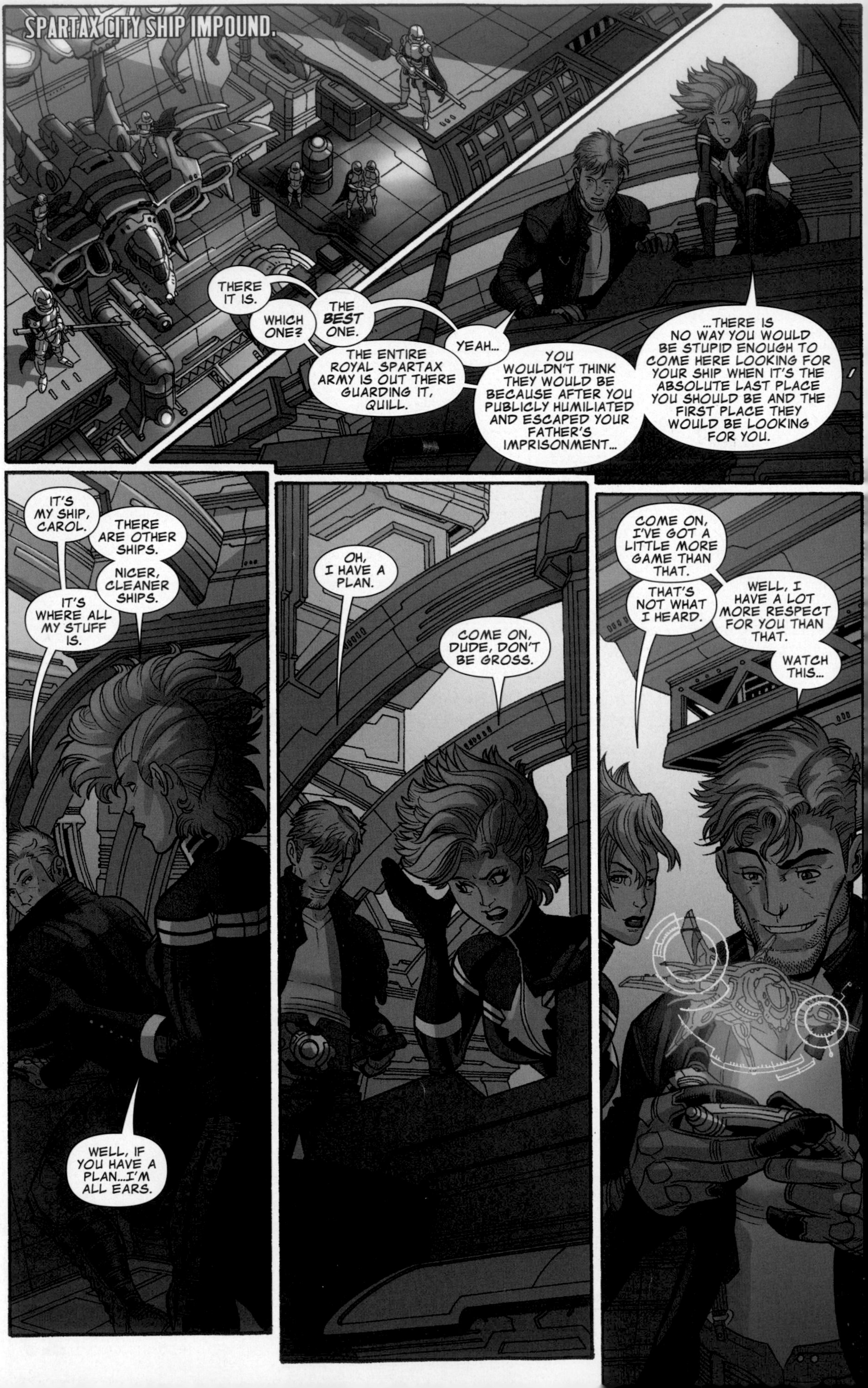
SPARTAX CITY SHIP IMPOUND.
THERE IT IS.
WHICH ONE?
THE BEST ONE.
THE ENTIRE ROYAL SPARTAX ARMY IS OUT THERE GUARDING IT, QUILL.
YEAH...
YOU WOULDN'T THINK THEY WOULD BE BECAUSE AFTER YOU PUBLICLY HUMILIATED AND ESCAPED YOUR FATHER'S IMPRISONMENT...
...THERE IS NO WAY YOU WOULD BE STUPID ENOUGH TO COME HERE LOOKING FOR YOUR SHIP WHEN IT'S THE ABSOLUTE LAST PLACE YOU SHOULD BE AND THE FIRST PLACE THEY WOULD BE LOOKING FOR YOU.
IT'S MY SHIP, CAROL.
THERE ARE OTHER SHIPS.
NICER, CLEANER SHIPS.
IT'S WHERE ALL MY STUFF IS.
WELL, IF YOU HAVE A PLAN...I'M ALL EARS.
OH, I HAVE A PLAN.
COME ON, DUDE, DON'T BE GROSS.
COME ON, I'VE GOT A LITTLE MORE GAME THAN THAT.
THAT'S NOT WHAT I HEARD.
WELL, I HAVE A LOT MORE RESPECT FOR YOU THAN THAT.
WATCH THIS...

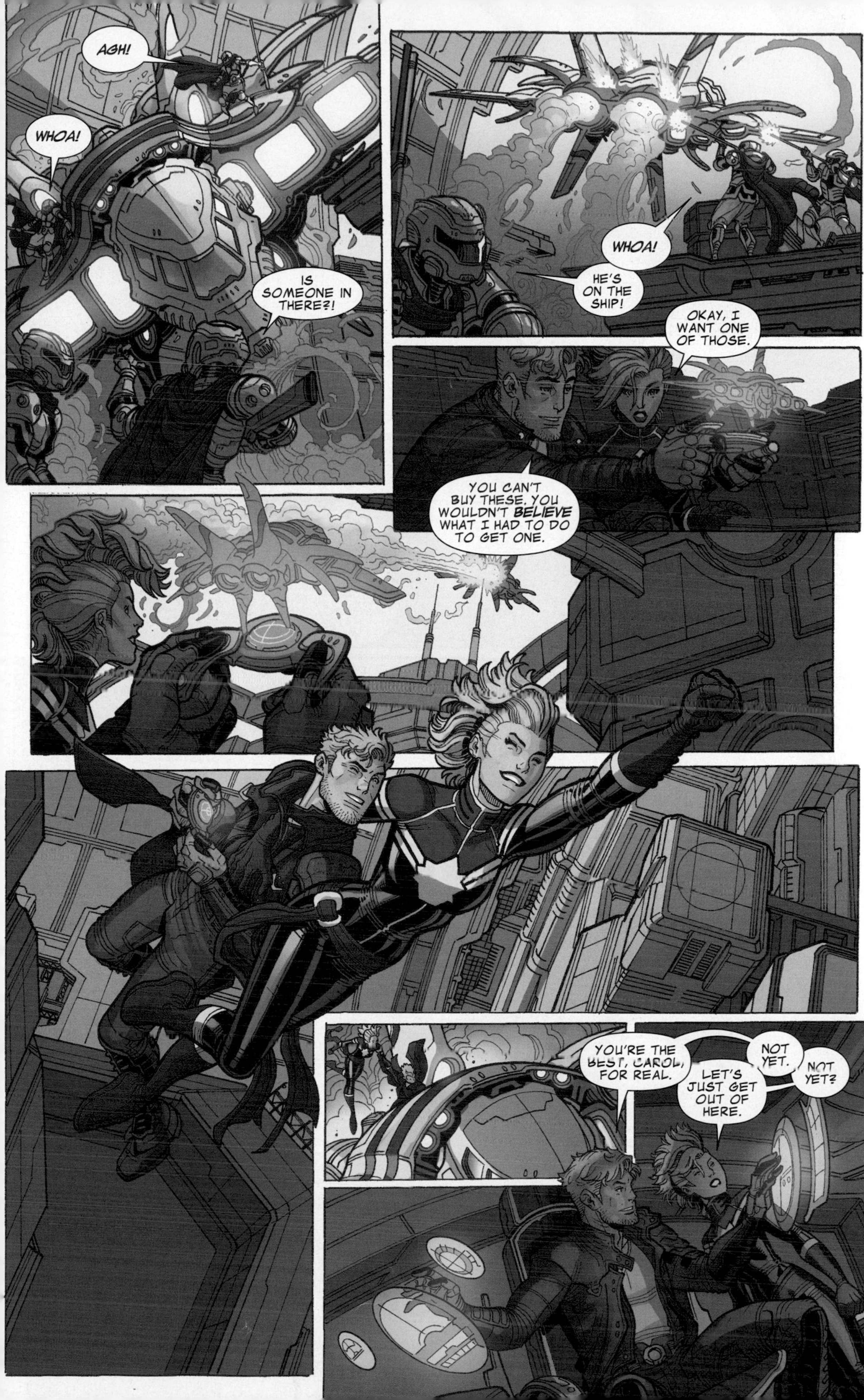
AGH!
WHOA!
IS SOMEONE IN THERE?!
WHOA!
HE'S ON THE SHIP!
OKAY, I WANT ONE OF THOSE.
YOU CAN'T BUY THESE. YOU WOULDN'T BELIEVE WHAT I HAD TO DO TO GET ONE.
YOU'RE THE BEST, CAROL, FOR REAL.
NOT YET.
NOT YET?
LET'S JUST GET OUT OF HERE.

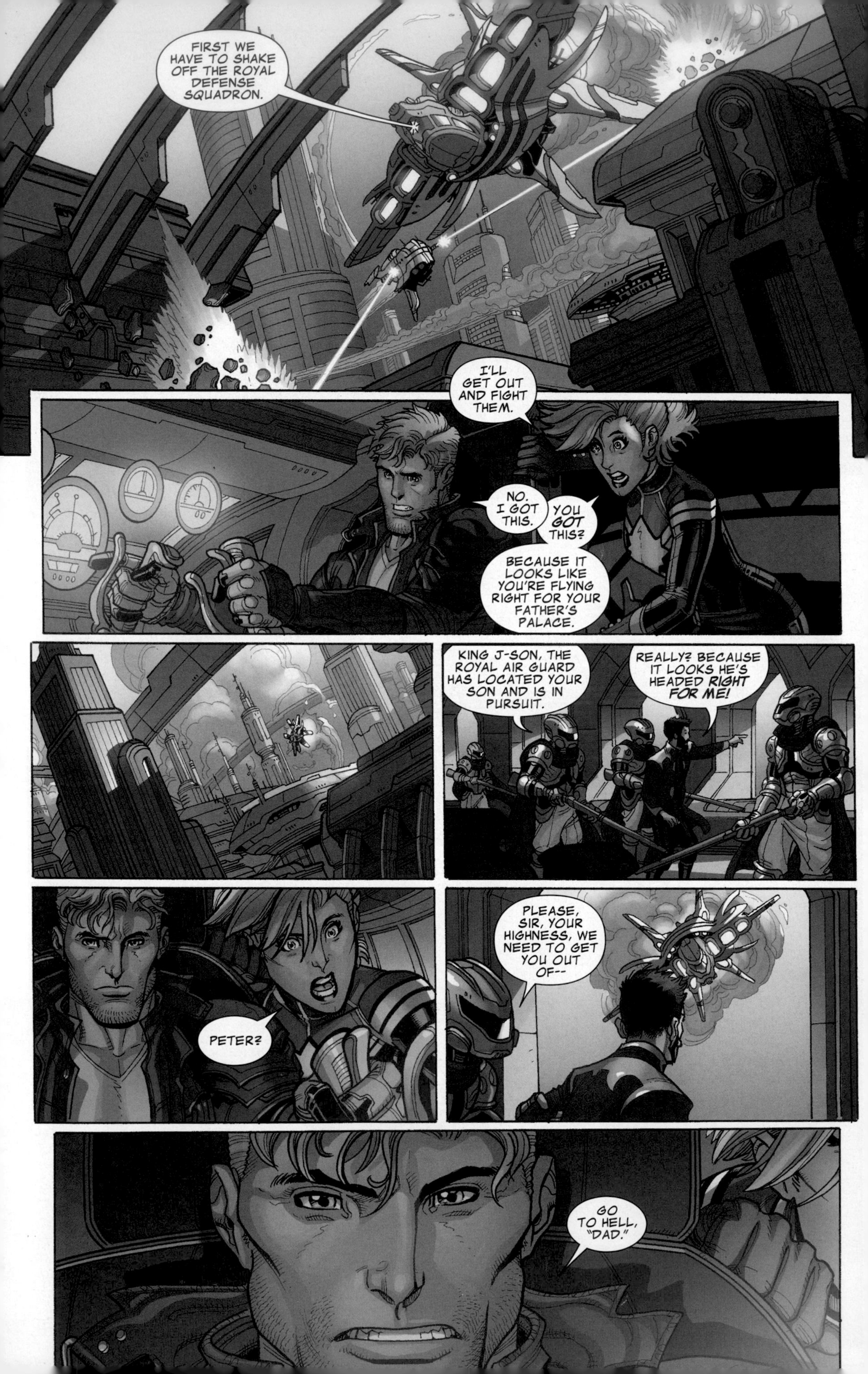
FIRST WE HAVE TO SHAKE OFF THE ROYAL DEFENSE SQUADRON.
I'LL GET OUT AND FIGHT THEM.
NO. I GOT THIS.
YOU GOT THIS?
BECAUSE IT LOOKS LIKE YOU'RE FLYING RIGHT FOR YOUR FATHER'S PALACE.
KING J-SON, THE ROYAL AIR GUARD HAS LOCATED YOUR SON AND IS IN PURSUIT.
REALLY? BECAUSE IT LOOKS HE'S HEADED RIGHT FOR ME!
PETER?
PLEASE, SIR, YOUR HIGHNESS, WE NEED TO GET YOU OUT OF--
GO TO HELL, "DAD."

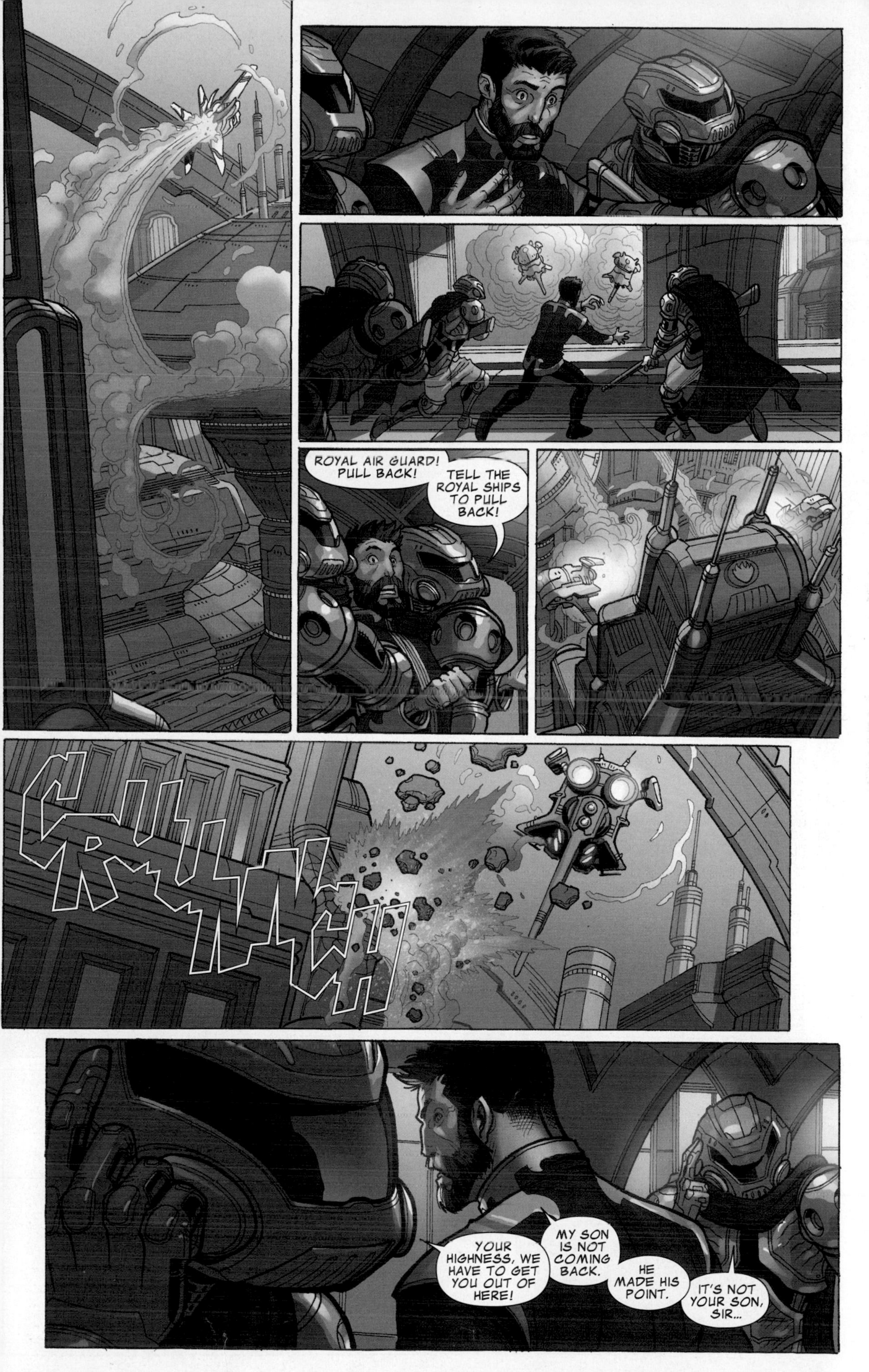
ROYAL AIR GUARD! PULL BACK!
TELL THE ROYAL SHIPS TO PULL BACK!
CRUNCH
YOUR HIGHNESS, WE HAVE TO GET YOU OUT OF HERE!
MY SON IS NOT COMING BACK.
HE MADE HIS POINT.
IT'S NOT YOUR SON, SIR...

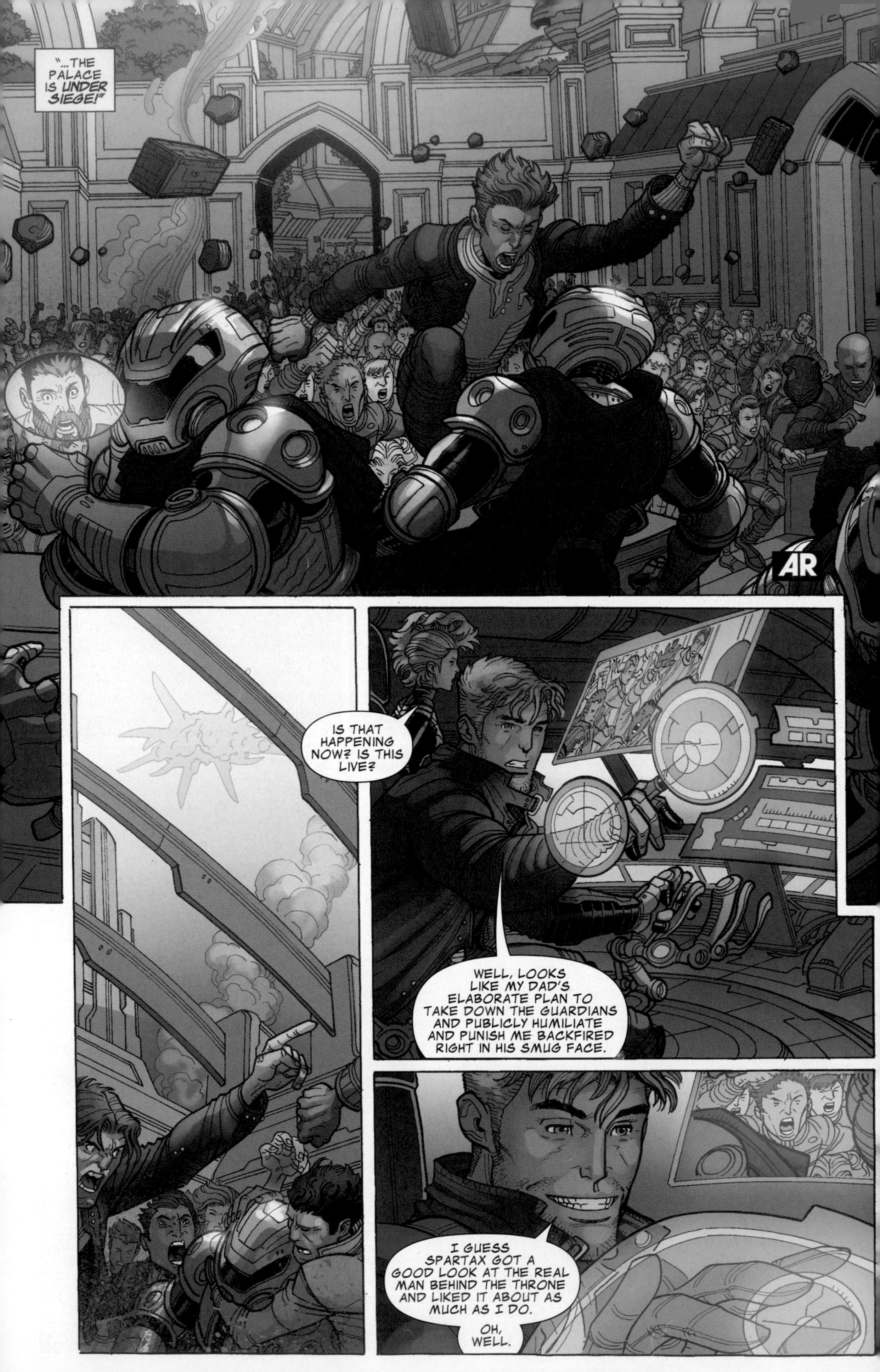
"...THE PALACE IS UNDER SIEGE!"
AR
IS THAT HAPPENING NOW? IS THIS LIVE?
WELL, LOOKS LIKE MY DAD'S ELABORATE PLAN TO TAKE DOWN THE GUARDIANS AND PUBLICLY HUMILIATE AND PUNISH ME BACKFIRED RIGHT IN HIS SMUG FACE.
I GUESS SPARTAX GOT A GOOD LOOK AT THE REAL MAN BEHIND THE THRONE AND LIKED IT ABOUT AS MUCH AS I DO.
OH, WELL.

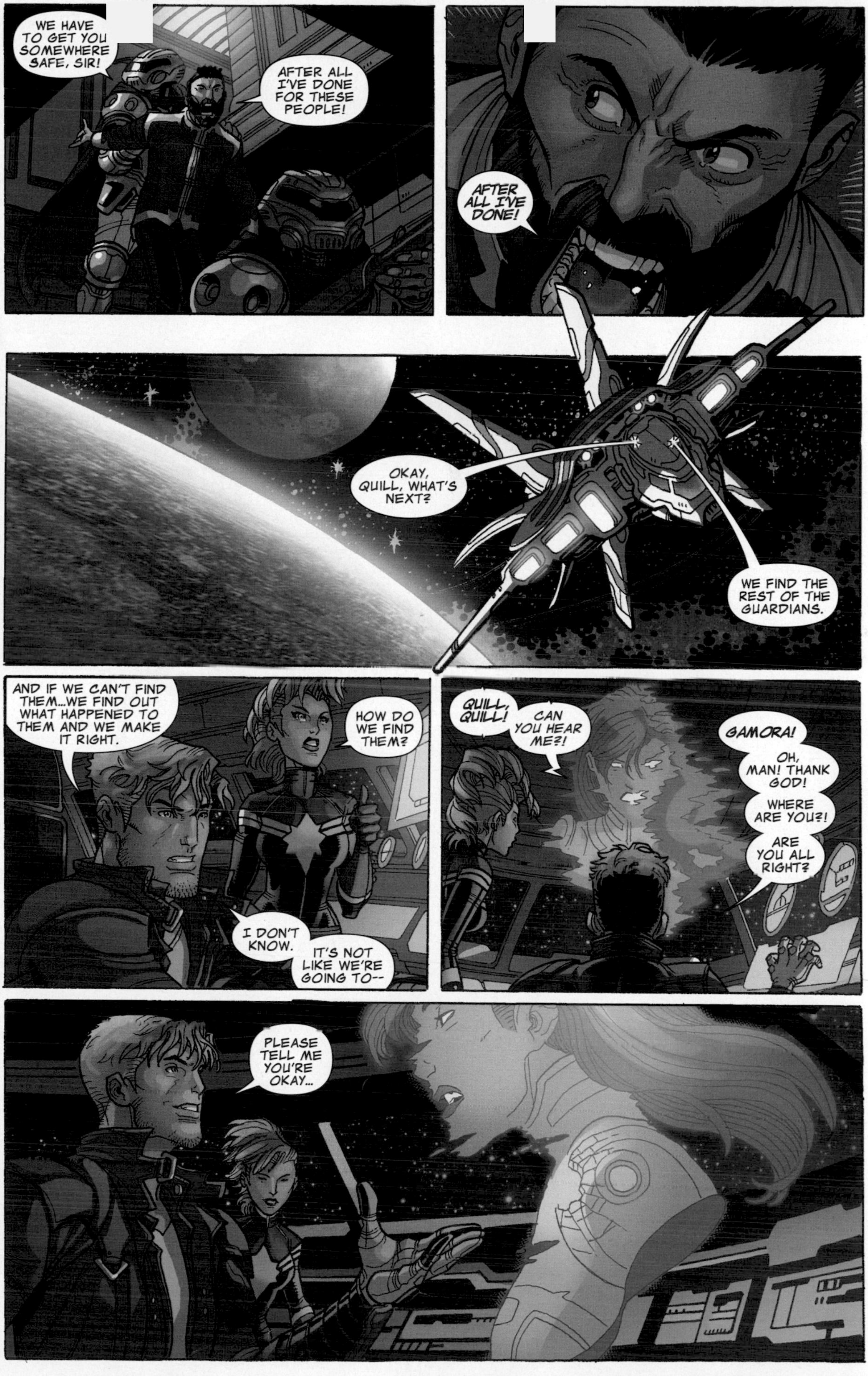
WE HAVE TO GET YOU SOMEWHERE SAFE, SIR!
AFTER ALL I'VE DONE FOR THESE PEOPLE!
AFTER ALL I'VE DONE!
OKAY, QUILL, WHAT'S NEXT?
WE FIND THE REST OF THE GUARDIANS.
AND IF WE CAN'T FIND THEM...WE FIND OUT WHAT HAPPENED TO THEM AND WE MAKE IT RIGHT.
HOW DO WE FIND THEM?
I DON'T KNOW.
IT'S NOT LIKE WE'RE GOING TO--
QUILL, QUILL!
CAN YOU HEAR ME?!
GAMORA!
OH, MAN! THANK GOD!
WHERE ARE YOU?!
ARE YOU ALL RIGHT?
PLEASE TELL ME YOU'RE OKAY...

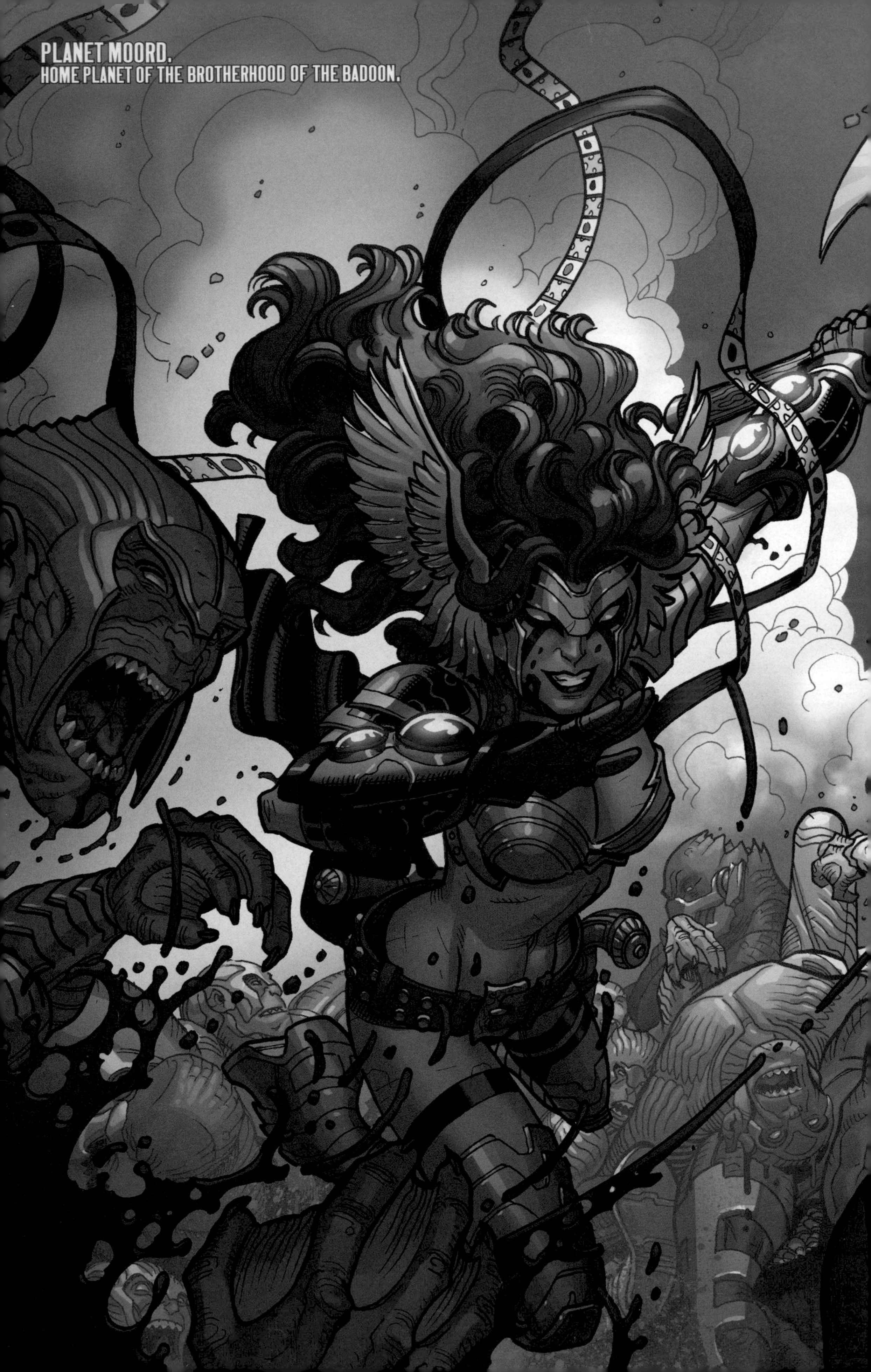
PLANET MOORD.
HOME PLANET OF THE BROTHERHOOD OF THE BADOON.

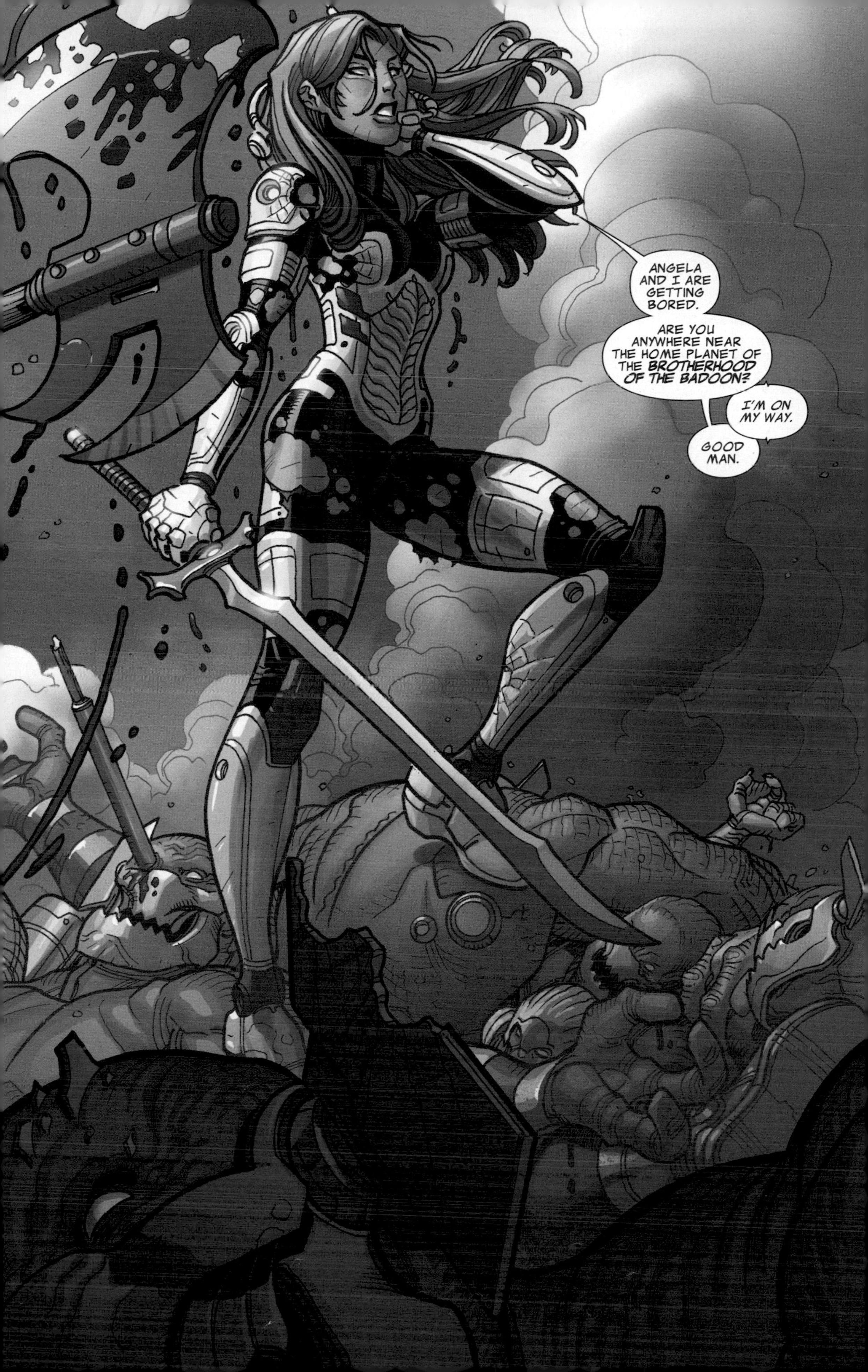
ANGELA AND I ARE GETTING BORED.
ARE YOU ANYWHERE NEAR THE HOME PLANET OF THE BROTHERHOOD OF THE BADOON?
I'M ON MY WAY.
GOOD MAN.

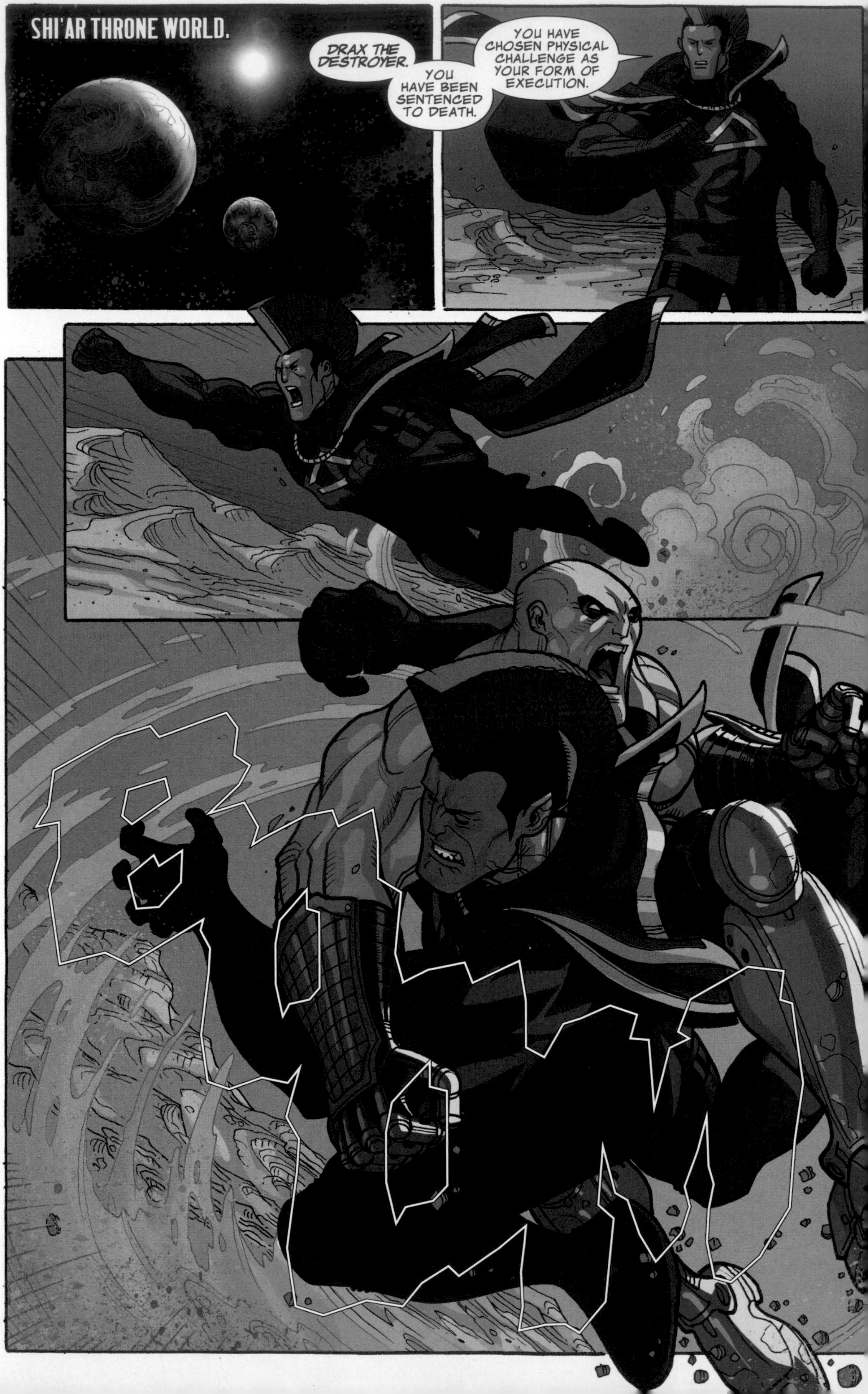
SHI'AR THRONE WORLD.
DRAX THE DESTROYER.
YOU HAVE BEEN SENTENCED TO DEATH.
YOU HAVE CHOSEN PHYSICAL CHALLENGE AS YOUR FORM OF EXECUTION.

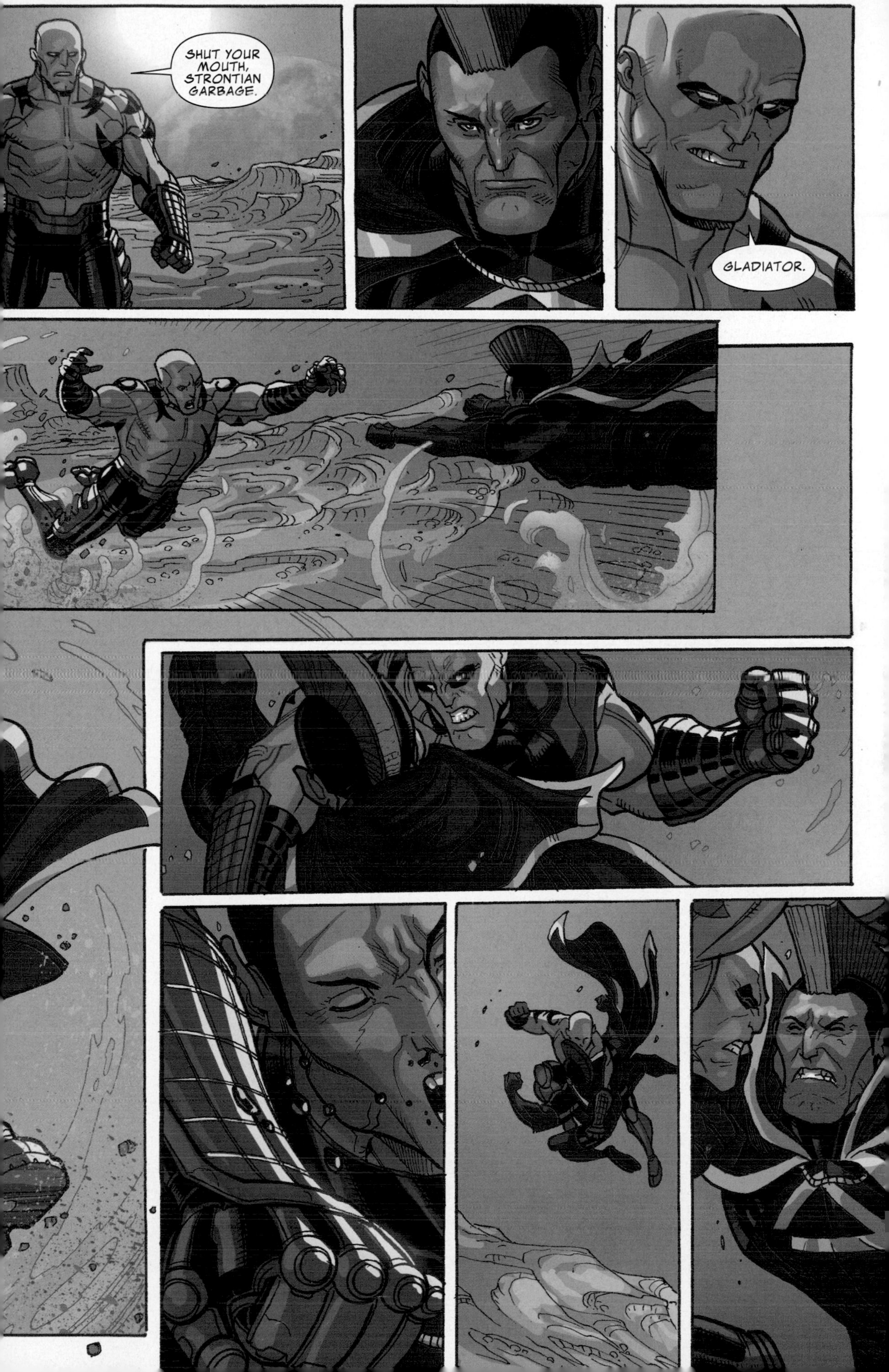
SHUT YOUR MOUTH, STRONTIAN GARBAGE.
GLADIATOR.

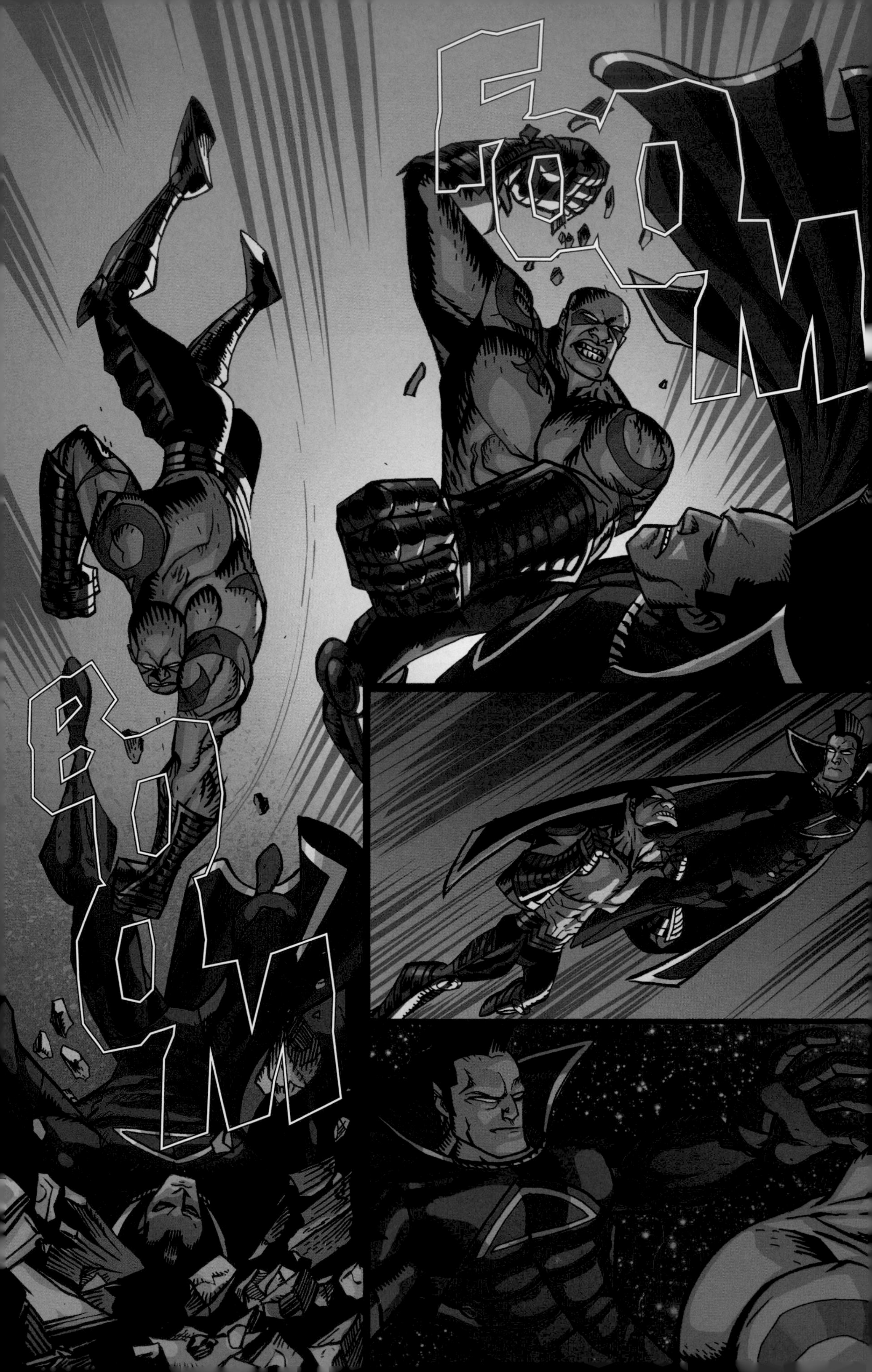
FOOM
BOOM

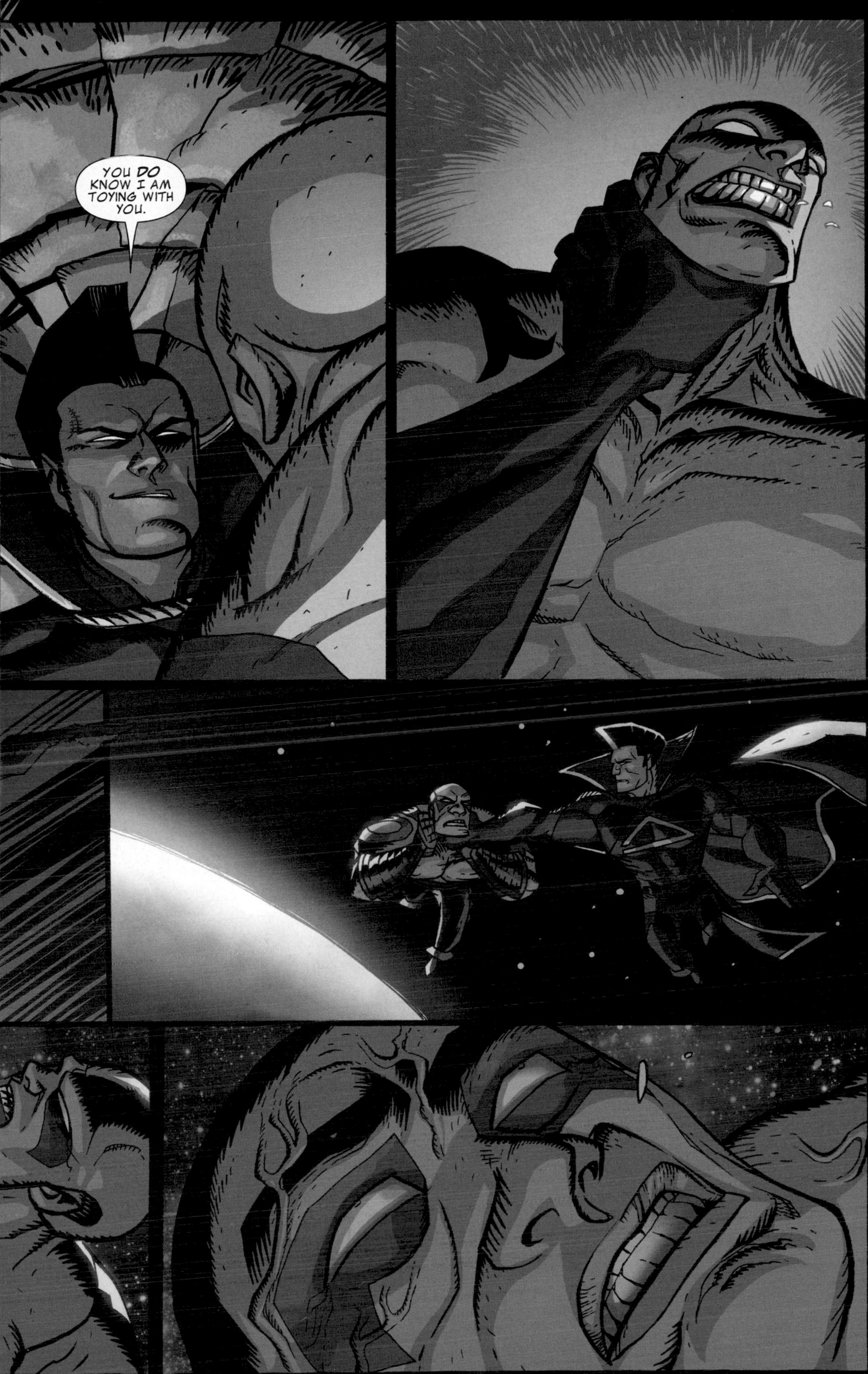
YOU DO KNOW I AM TOYING WITH YOU.

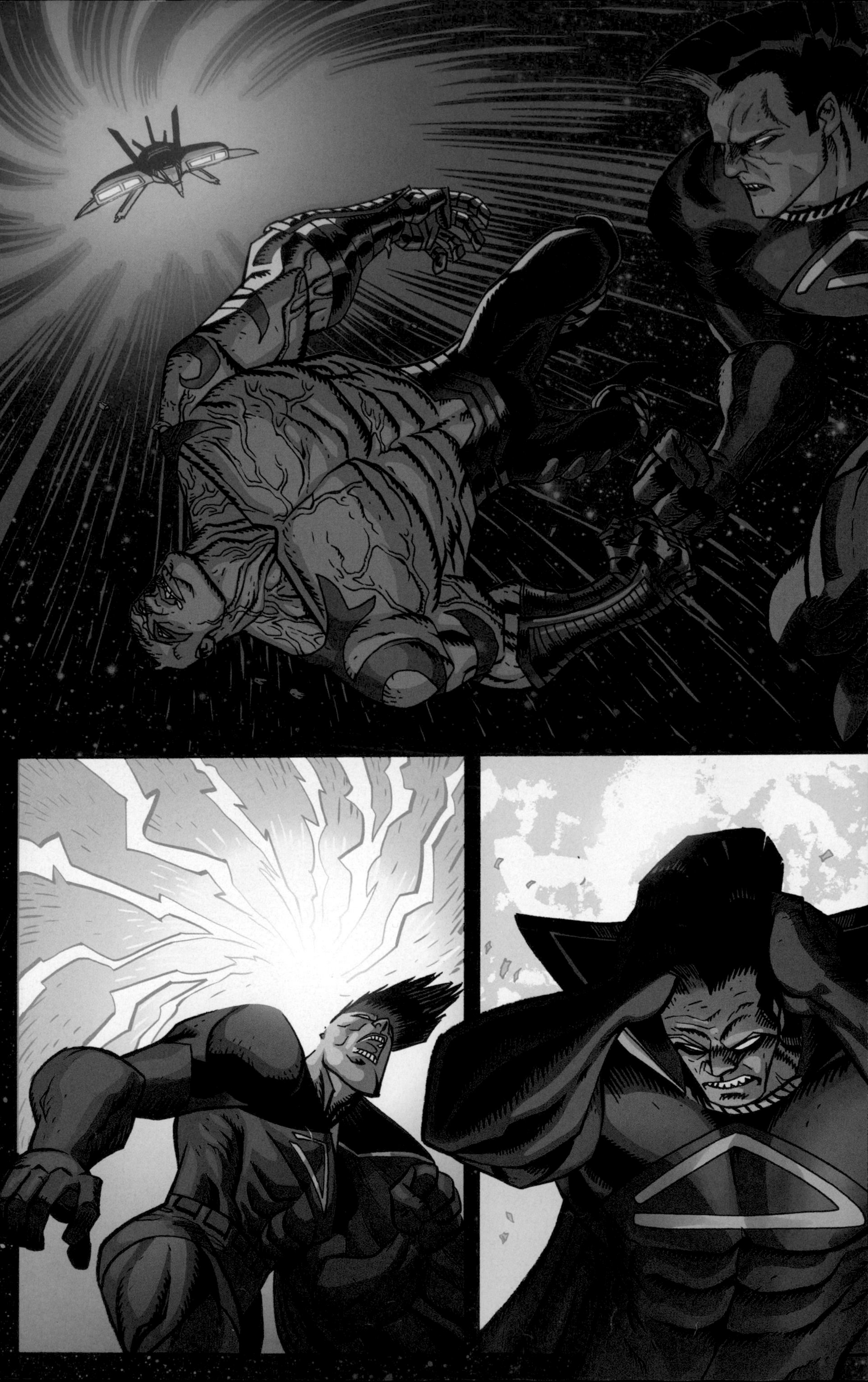

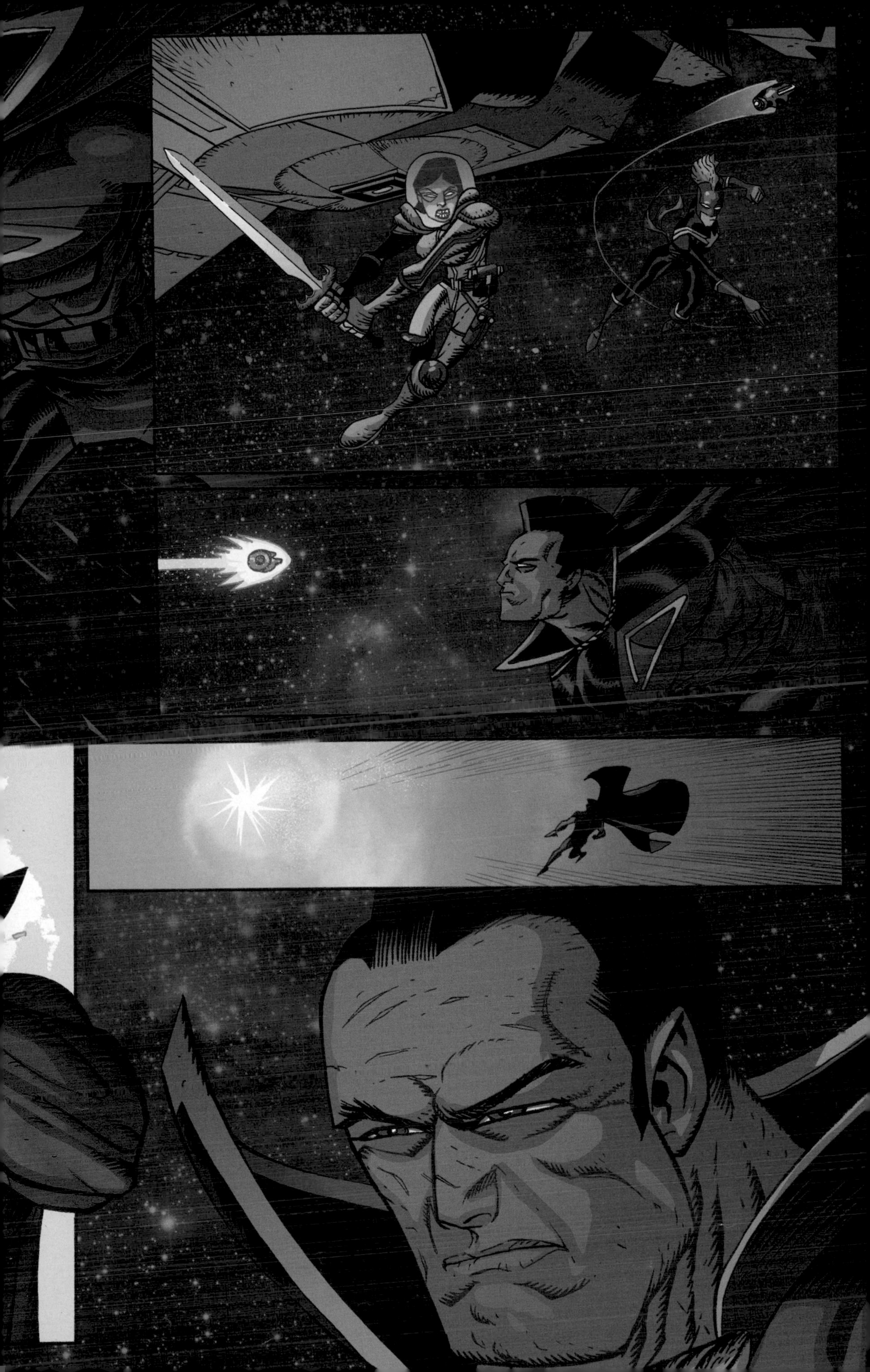

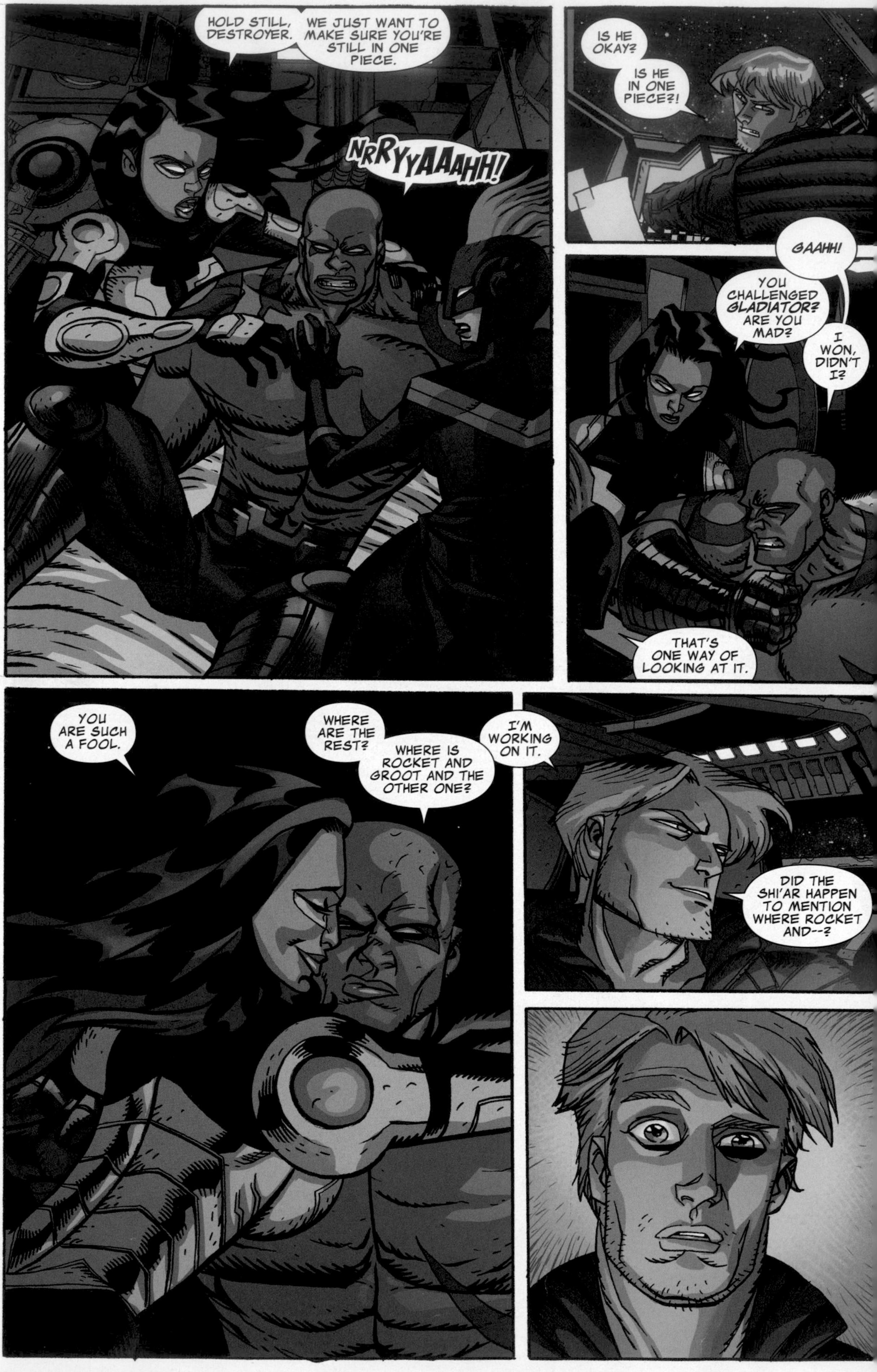
HOLD STILL, DESTROYER.
WE JUST WANT TO MAKE SURE YOU'RE STILL IN ONE PIECE.
NRRYYAAAHH!
IS HE OKAY?
IS HE IN ONE PIECE?!
GAAHH!
YOU CHALLENGED GLADIATOR? ARE YOU MAD?
I WON, DIDN'T I?
THAT'S ONE WAY OF LOOKING AT IT.
YOU ARE SUCH A FOOL.
WHERE ARE THE REST?
WHERE IS ROCKET AND GROOT AND THE OTHER ONE?
I'M WORKING ON IT.
DID THE SHI'AR HAPPEN TO MENTION WHERE ROCKET AND--?

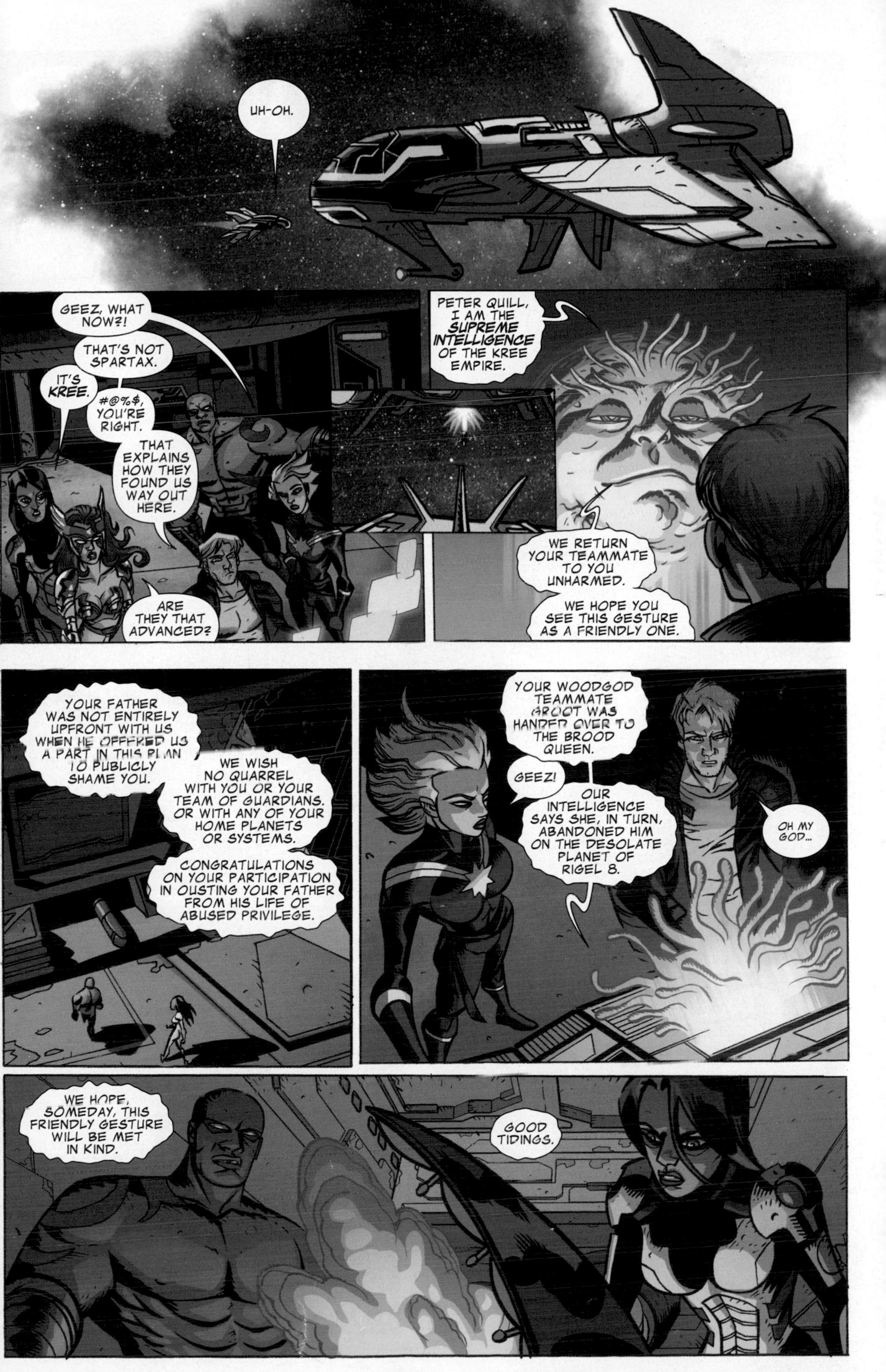

UH-OH.
GEEZ, WHAT NOW?!
THAT'S NOT SPARTAX.
IT'S KREE.
#@%$, YOU'RE RIGHT.
THAT EXPLAINS HOW THEY FOUND US WAY OUT HERE.
ARE THEY THAT ADVANCED?
PETER QUILL, I AM THE SUPREME INTELLIGENCE OF THE KREE EMPIRE.
WE RETURN YOUR TEAMMATE TO YOU UNHARMED.
WE HOPE YOU SEE THIS GESTURE AS A FRIENDLY ONE.
YOUR FATHER WAS NOT ENTIRELY UPFRONT WITH US WHEN HE OFFERED US A PART IN THIS PLAN TO PUBLICLY SHAME YOU.
WE WISH NO QUARREL WITH YOU OR YOUR TEAM OF GUARDIANS. OR WITH ANY OF YOUR HOME PLANETS OR SYSTEMS.
CONGRATULATIONS ON YOUR PARTICIPATION IN OUSTING YOUR FATHER FROM HIS LIFE OF ABUSED PRIVILEGE.
YOUR WOODGOD TEAMMATE GROOT WAS HANDED OVER TO THE BROOD QUEEN.
GEEZ!
OUR INTELLIGENCE SAYS SHE, IN TURN, ABANDONED HIM ON THE DESOLATE PLANET OF RIGEL 8.
OH MY GOD...
WE HOPE, SOMEDAY, THIS FRIENDLY GESTURE WILL BE MET IN KIND.
GOOD TIDINGS.

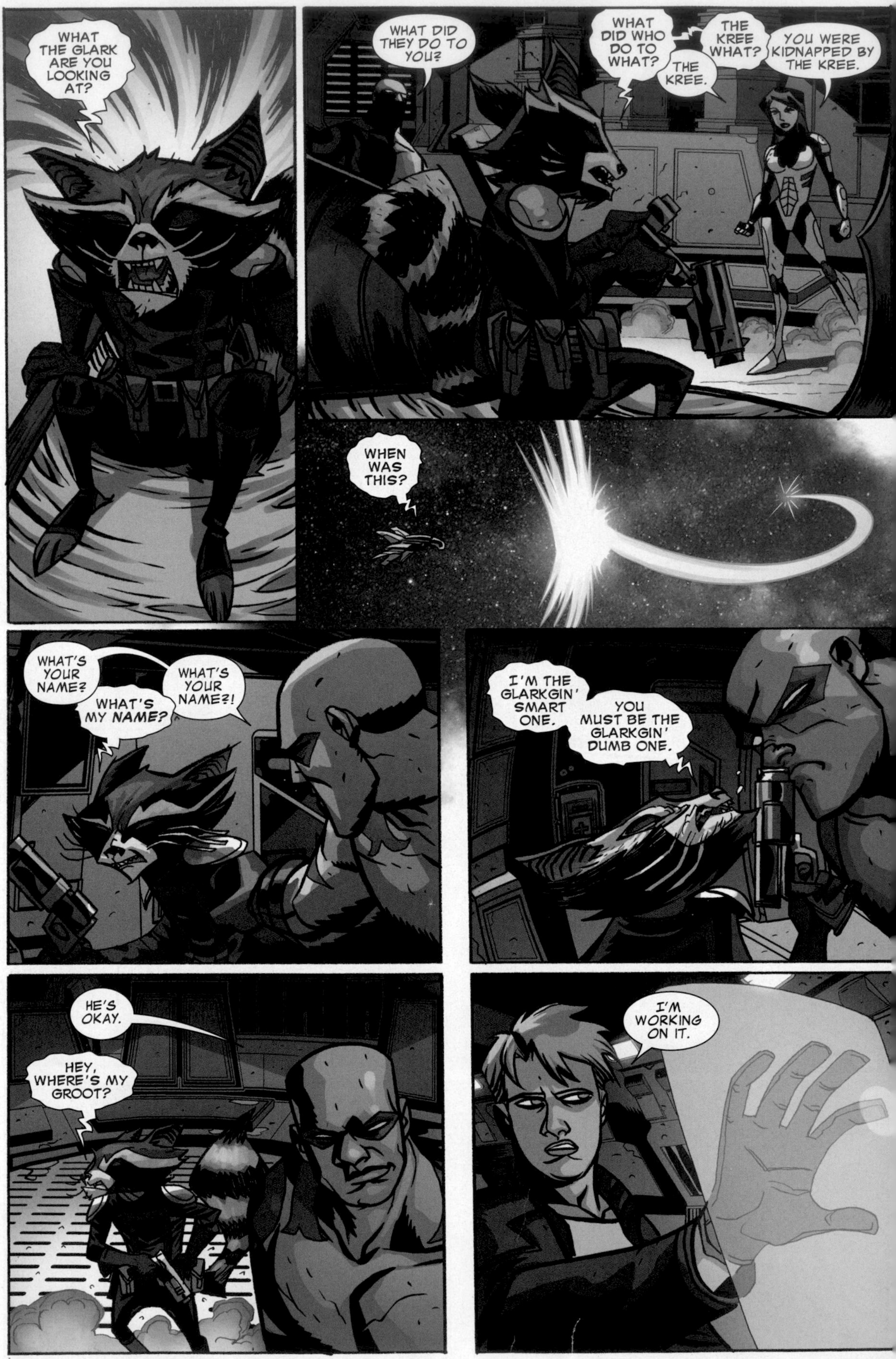
WHAT THE GLARK ARE YOU LOOKING AT?
WHAT DID THEY DO TO YOU?
WHAT DID WHO DO TO WHAT?
THE KREE.
THE KREE WHAT?
YOU WERE KIDNAPPED BY THE KREE.
WHEN WAS THIS?
WHAT'S YOUR NAME?
WHAT'S MY NAME?
WHAT'S YOUR NAME?!
I'M THE GLARKGIN' SMART ONE.
YOU MUST BE THE GLARKGIN' DUMB ONE.
HE'S OKAY.
HEY, WHERE'S MY GROOT?
I'M WORKING ON IT.

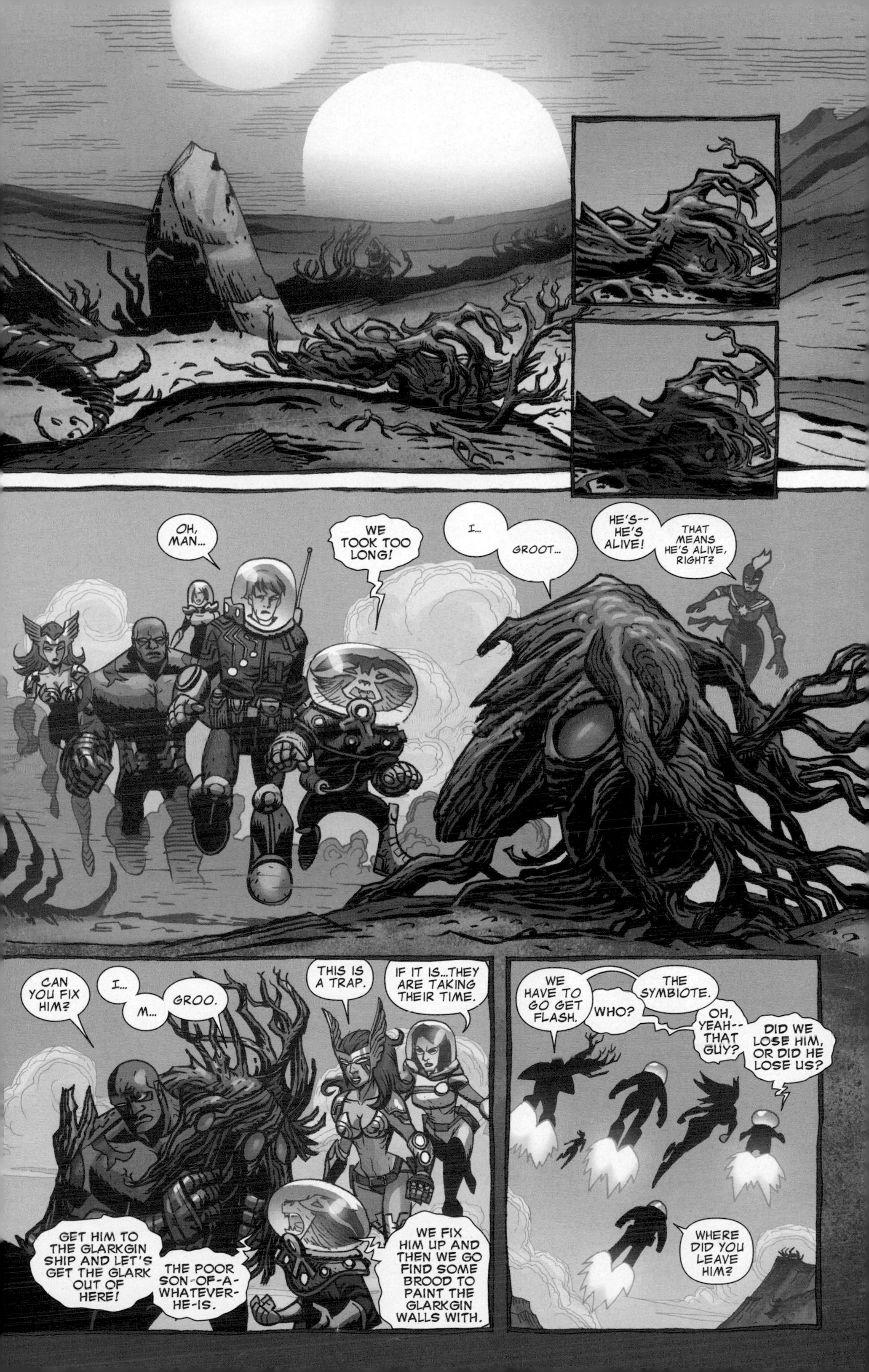

OH, MAN...
WE TOOK TOO LONG!
I...
GROOT...
HE'S-- HE'S ALIVE!
THAT MEANS HE'S ALIVE, RIGHT?
CAN YOU FIX HIM?
I...
M...
GROO.
THIS IS A TRAP.
IF IT IS...THEY ARE TAKING THEIR TIME.
GET HIM TO THE GLARKGIN SHIP AND LET'S GET THE GLARK OUT OF HERE!
THE POOR SON-OF-A-WHATEVER-HE-IS.
WE FIX HIM UP AND THEN WE GO FIND SOME BROOD TO PAINT THE GLARKGIN WALLS WITH.
WE HAVE TO GO GET FLASH.
WHO?
THE SYMBIOTE.
OH, YEAH-- THAT GUY?
DID WE LOSE HIM, OR DID HE LOSE US?
WHERE DID YOU LEAVE HIM?

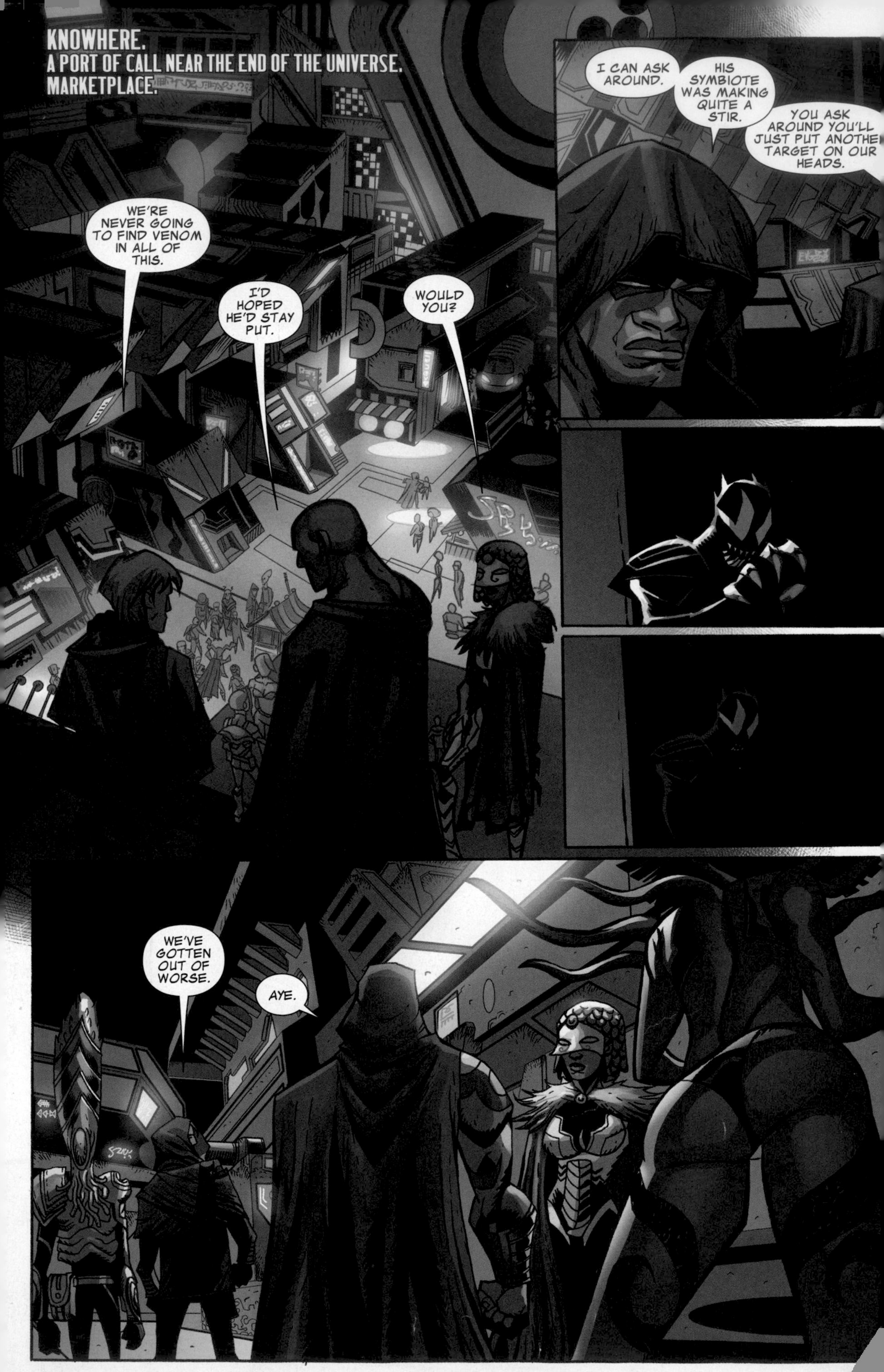
KNOWHERE.
A PORT OF CALL NEAR THE END OF THE UNIVERSE.
MARKETPLACE.
WE'RE NEVER GOING TO FIND VENOM IN ALL OF THIS.
I'D HOPED HE'D STAY PUT.
WOULD YOU?
I CAN ASK AROUND.
HIS SYMBIOTE WAS MAKING QUITE A STIR.
YOU ASK AROUND YOU'LL JUST PUT ANOTHER TARGET ON OUR HEADS.
WE'VE GOTTEN OUT OF WORSE.
AYE.

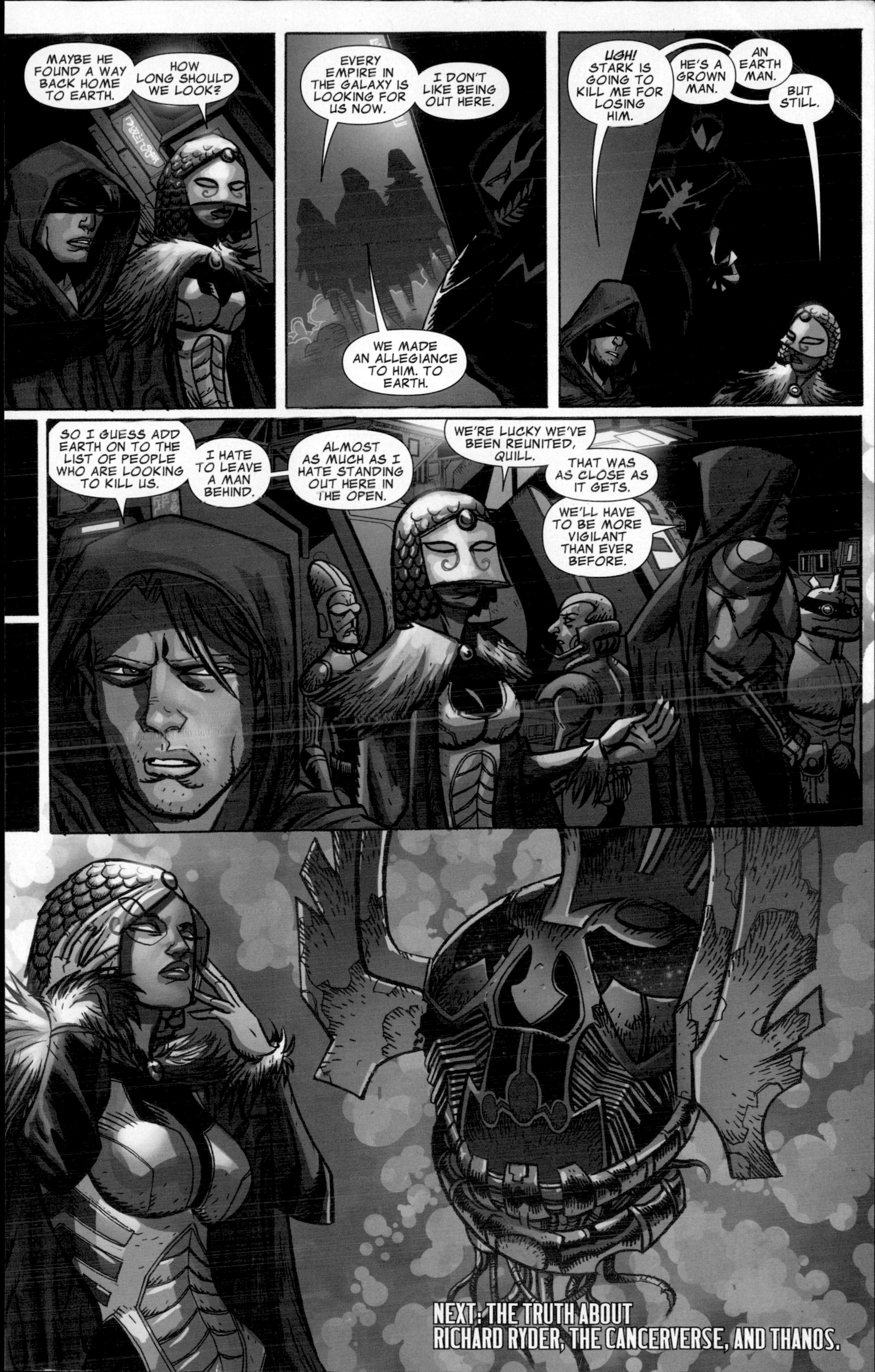
MAYBE HE FOUND A WAY BACK HOME TO EARTH.
HOW LONG SHOULD WE LOOK?
EVERY EMPIRE IN THE GALAXY IS LOOKING FOR US NOW.
I DON'T LIKE BEING OUT HERE.
WE MADE AN ALLEGIANCE TO HIM. TO EARTH.
UGH! STARK IS GOING TO KILL ME FOR LOSING HIM.
HE'S A GROWN MAN.
AN EARTH MAN.
BUT STILL.
SO I GUESS ADD EARTH ON TO THE LIST OF PEOPLE WHO ARE LOOKING TO KILL US.
I HATE TO LEAVE A MAN BEHIND.
ALMOST AS MUCH AS I HATE STANDING OUT HERE IN THE OPEN.
WE'RE LUCKY WE'VE BEEN REUNITED, QUILL.
THAT WAS AS CLOSE AS IT GETS.
WE'LL HAVE TO BE MORE VIGILANT THAN EVER BEFORE.
NEXT: THE TRUTH ABOUT RICHARD RYDER, THE CANCERVERSE, AND THANOS.

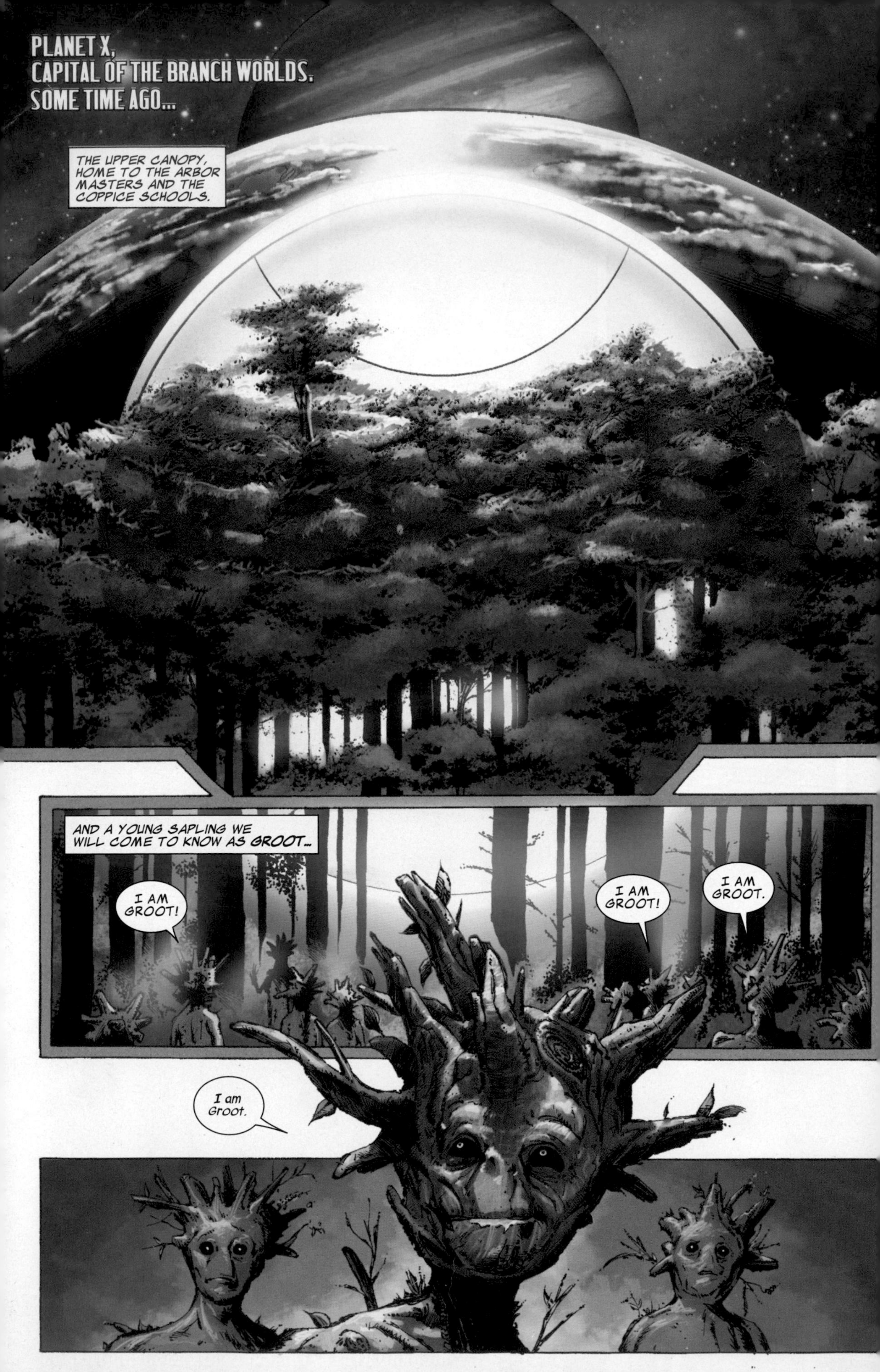
PLANET X,
CAPITAL OF THE BRANCH WORLDS.
SOME TIME AGO...
THE UPPER CANOPY, HOME TO THE ARBOR MASTERS AND THE COPPICE SCHOOLS.
AND A YOUNG SAPLING WE WILL COME TO KNOW AS GROOT...
I AM GROOT!
I AM GROOT!
I AM GROOT.
I am Groot.

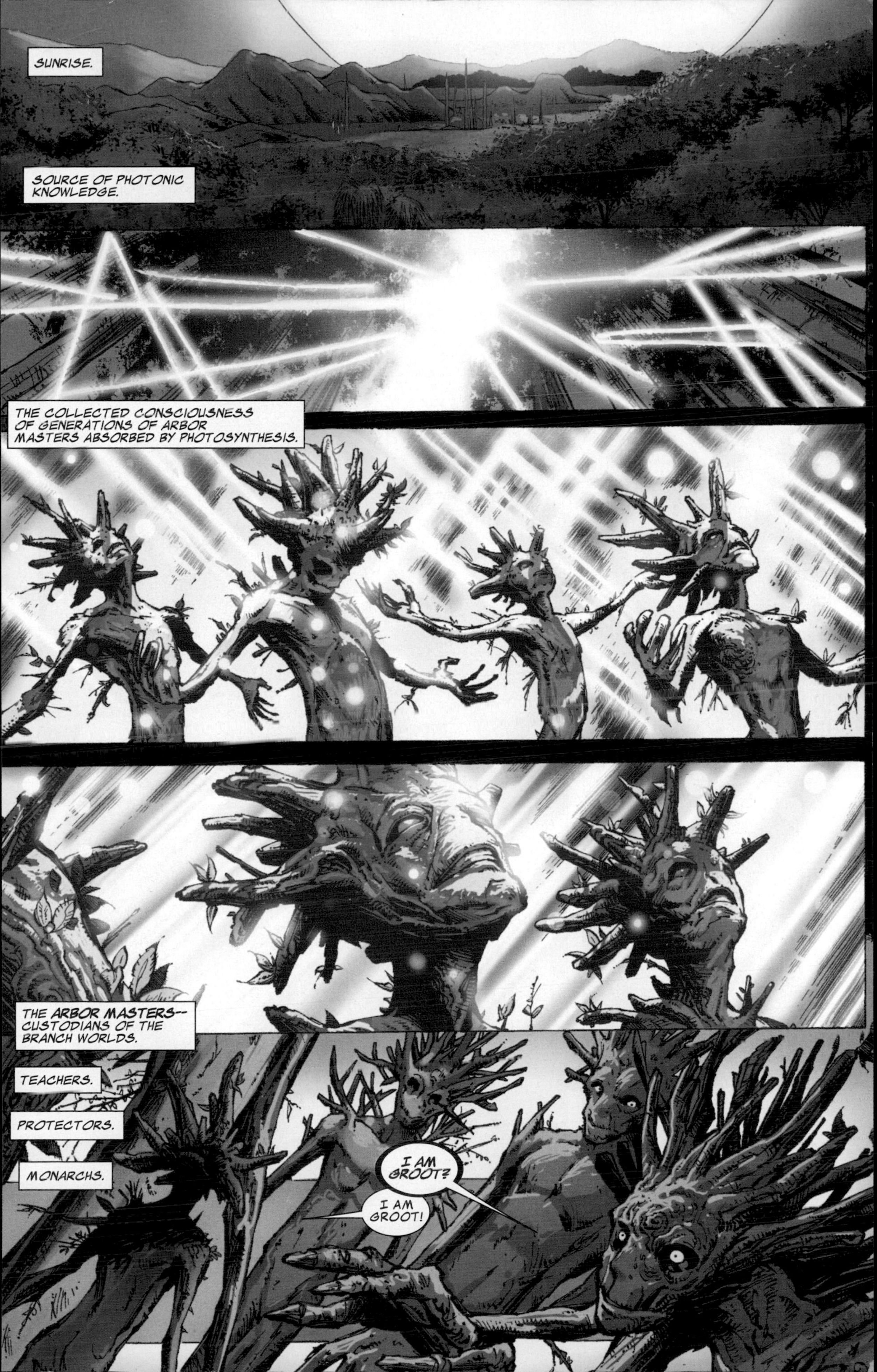
SUNRISE.
SOURCE OF PHOTONIC KNOWLEDGE.
THE COLLECTED CONSCIOUSNESS OF GENERATIONS OF ARBOR MASTERS ABSORBED BY PHOTOSYNTHESIS.
THE ARBOR MASTERS-- CUSTODIANS OF THE BRANCH WORLDS.
TEACHERS.
PROTECTORS.
MONARCHS.
I AM GROOT?
I AM GROOT!

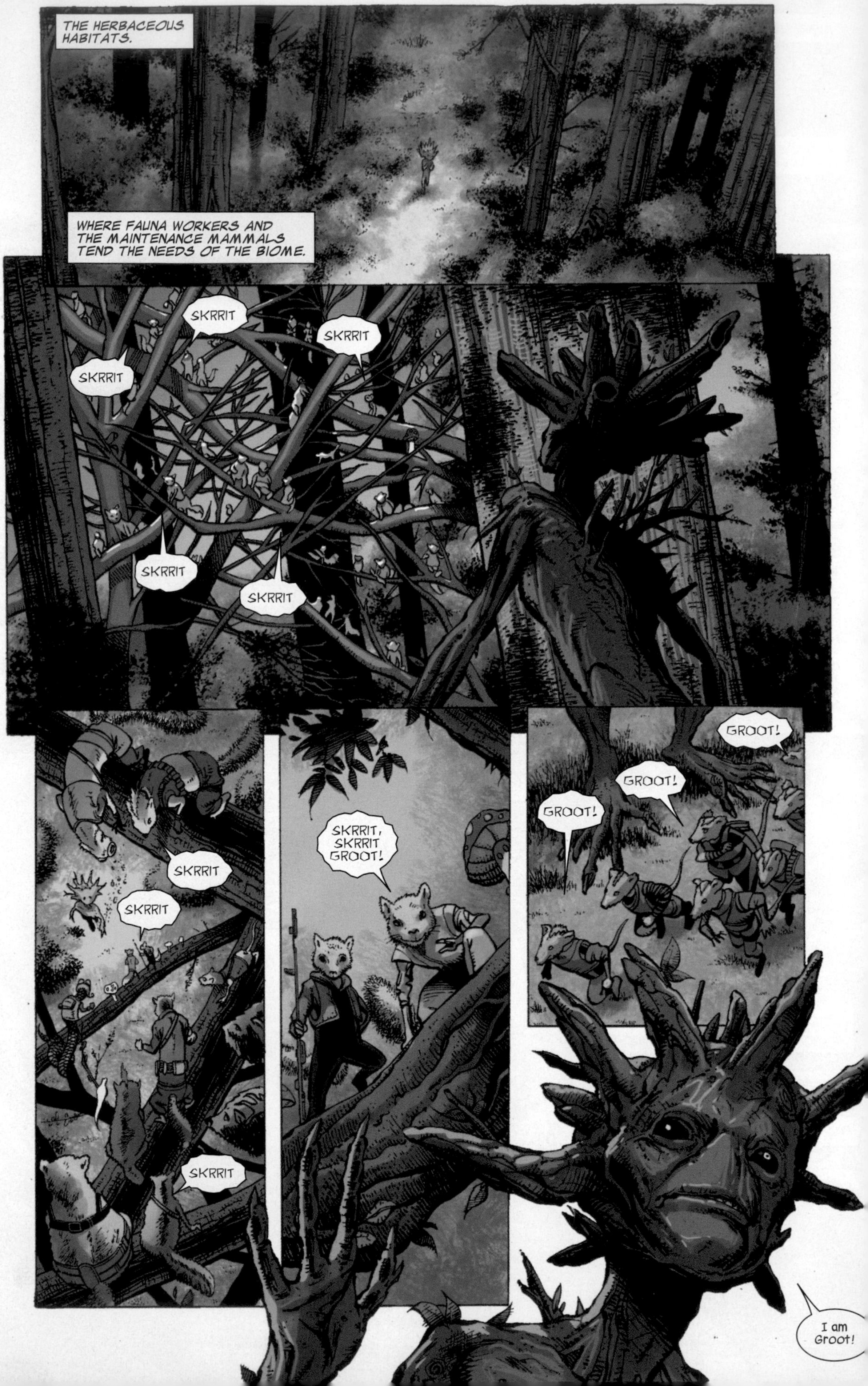
THE HERBACEOUS HABITATS.
WHERE FAUNA WORKERS AND THE MAINTENANCE MAMMALS TEND THE NEEDS OF THE BIOME.
SKRRIT
SKRRIT
SKRRIT
SKRRIT
SKRRIT
SKRRIT
SKRRIT
SKRRIT
SKRRIT, SKRRIT GROOT!
GROOT!
GROOT!
GROOT!
I am Groot!

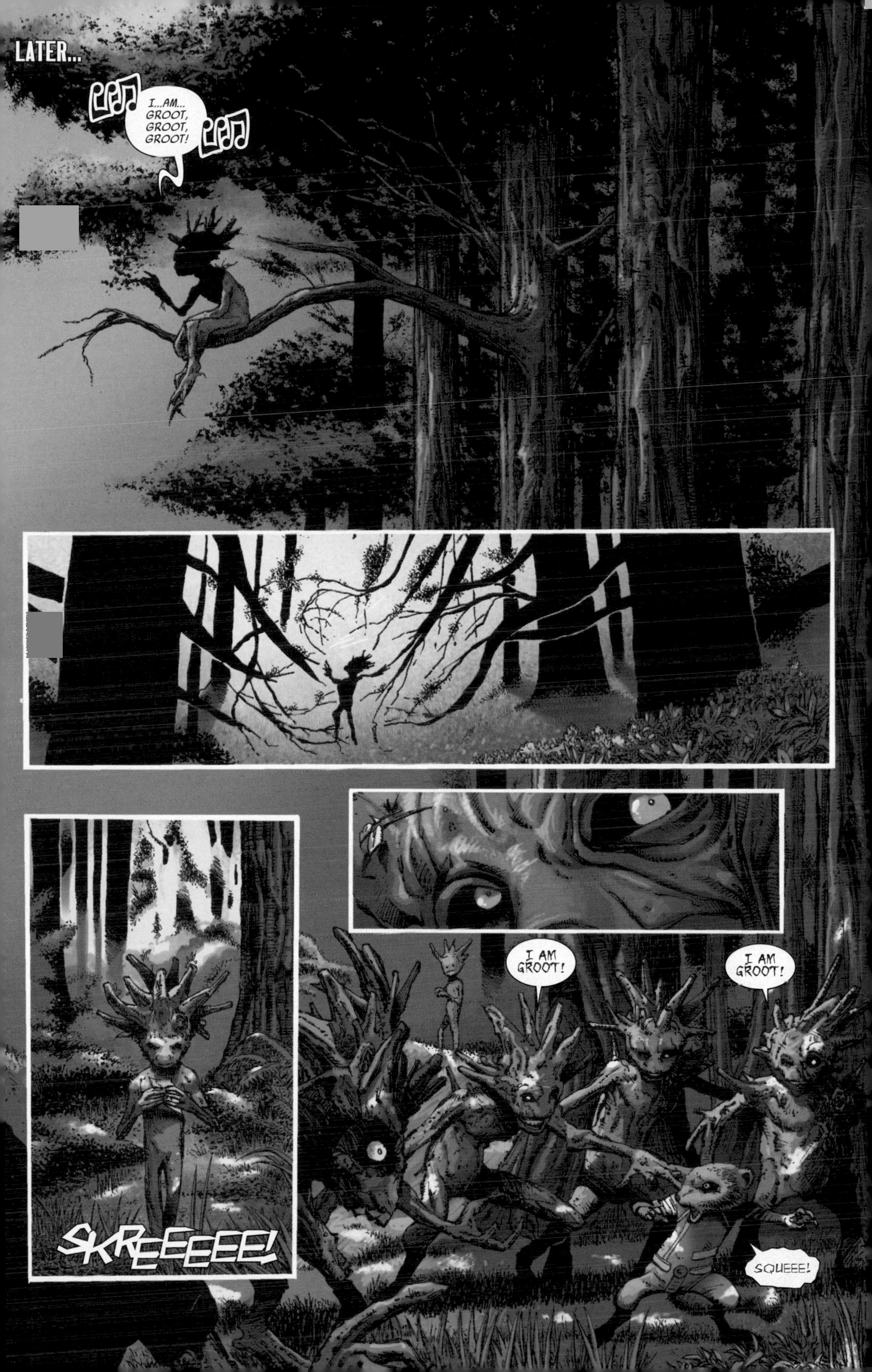
LATER...
I...AM... GROOT, GROOT, GROOT!
SKREEEEEE!
I AM GROOT!
I AM GROOT!
SQUEEE!

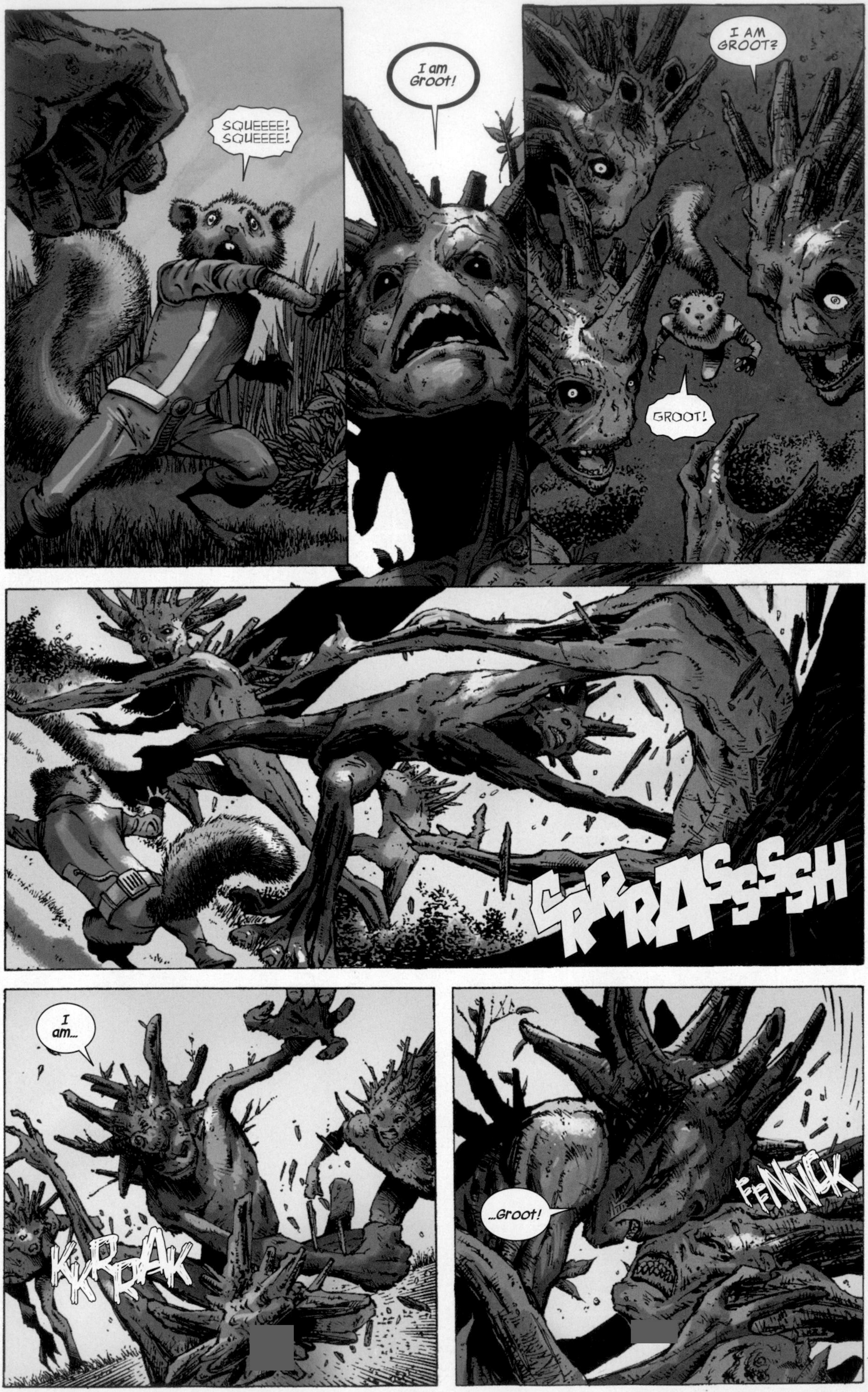
SQUEEEE! SQUEEEE!
I am Groot!
I AM GROOT?
GROOT!
CRRRASSSSH
I am...
KKRRAK
...Groot!
FENNCK

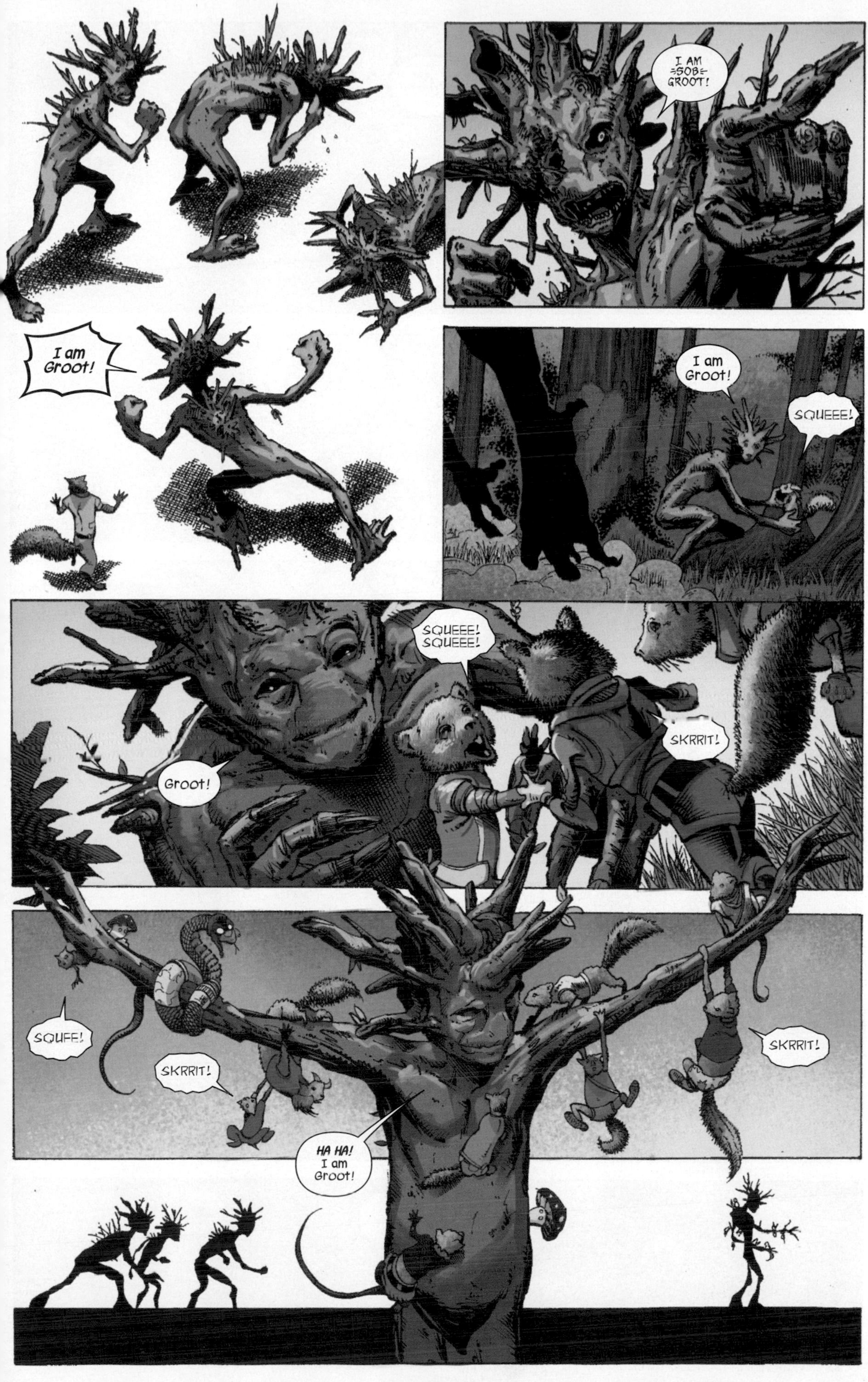
I AM SOB GROOT!
I am Groot!
I am Groot!
SQUEEE!
SQUEEE! SQUEEE!
SKRRIT!
Groot!
SQUFF!
SKRRIT!
SKRRIT!
HA HA! I am Groot!

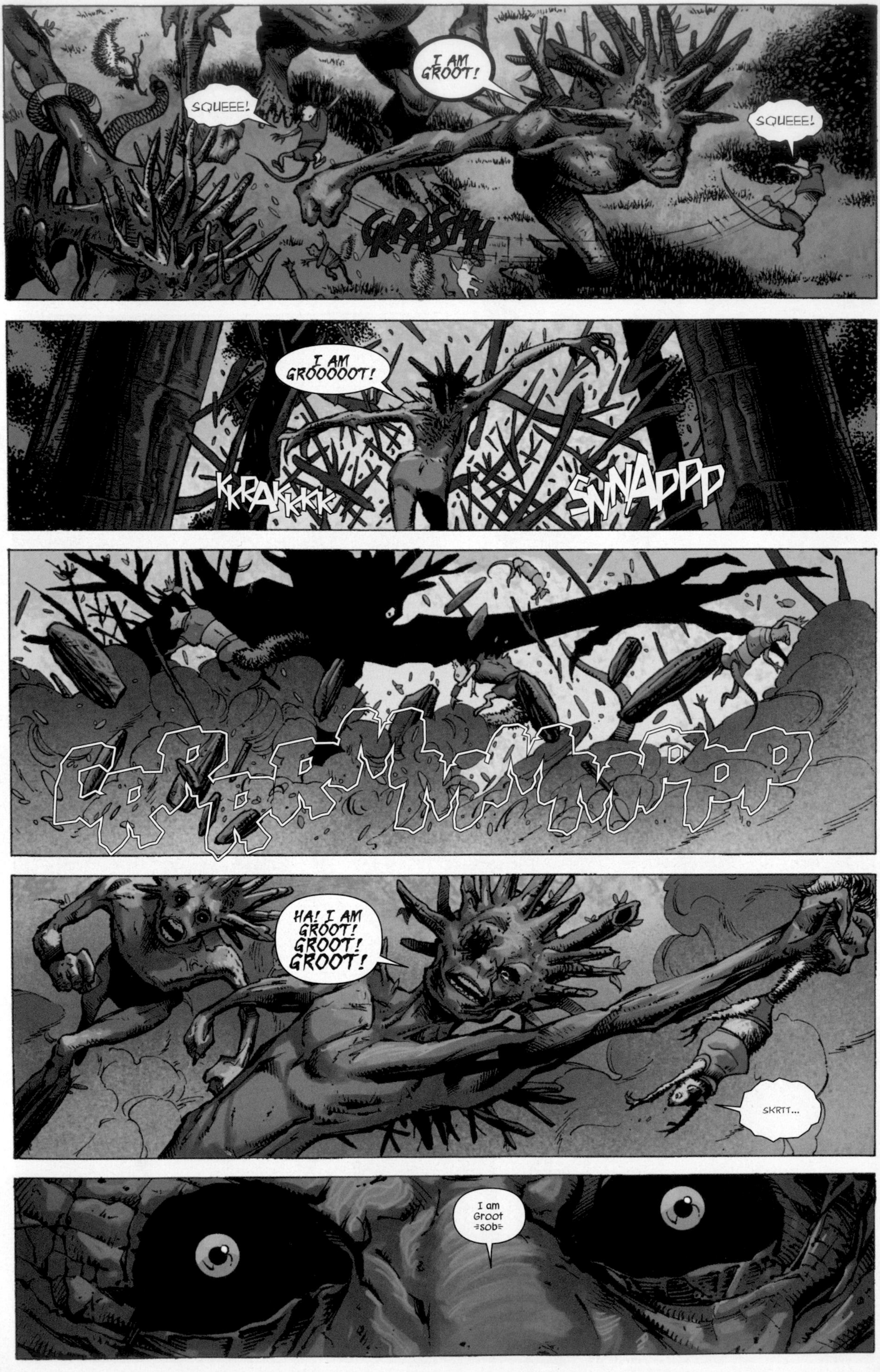
I AM GROOT!
SQUEEE!
SQUEEE!
GRRASHH
I AM GROOOOOT!
KKRAKKKKK
SNNAPPP
CRRRMMMMMPP
HA! I AM GROOT! GROOT! GROOT!
SKRTT...
I am Groot
sob

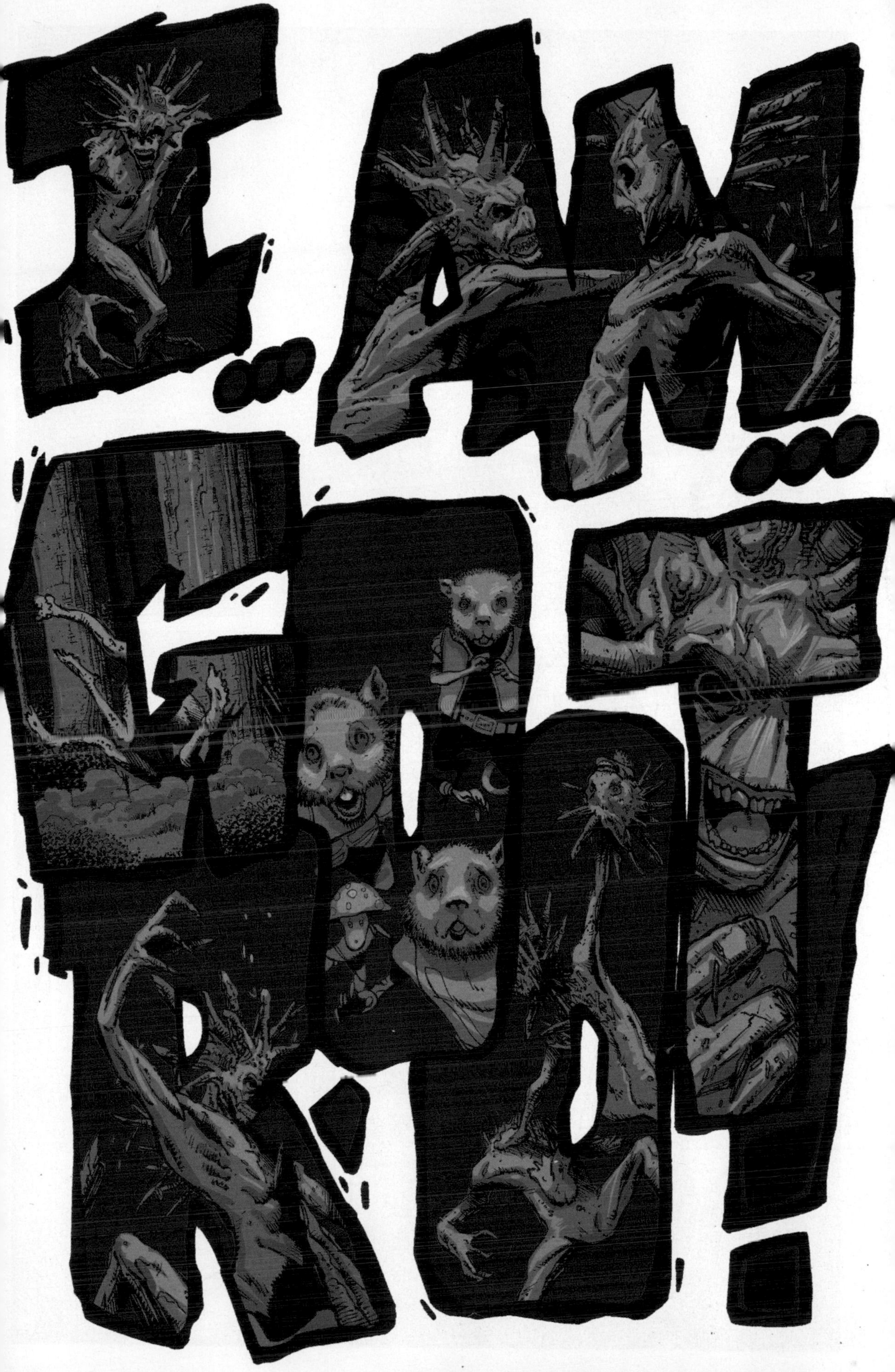
I... AM... GROOT!

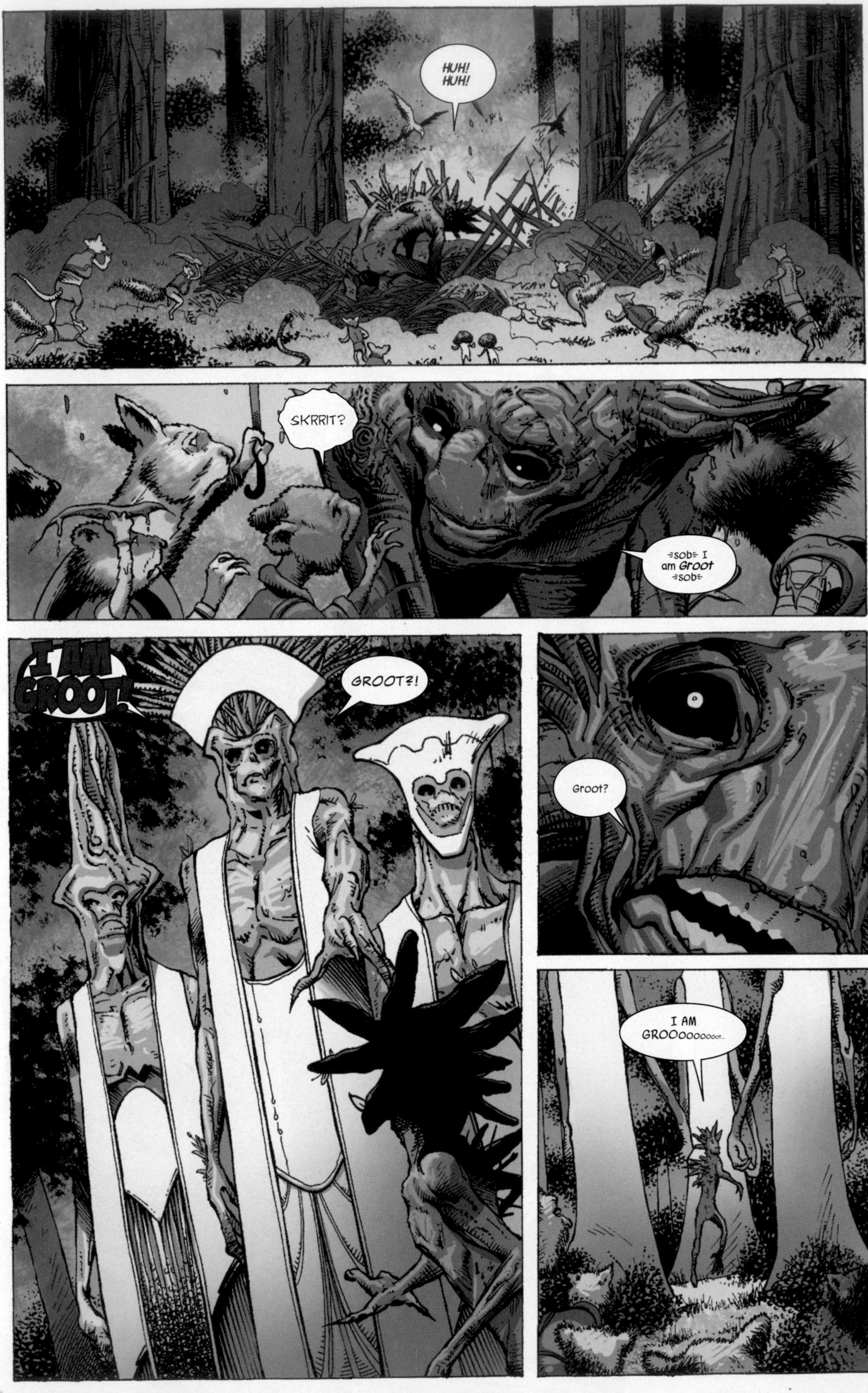
HUH! HUH!
SKRRIT?
=sob= I am Groot =sob=
I AM GROOT!
GROOT?!
Groot?
I AM GROOooooooot...

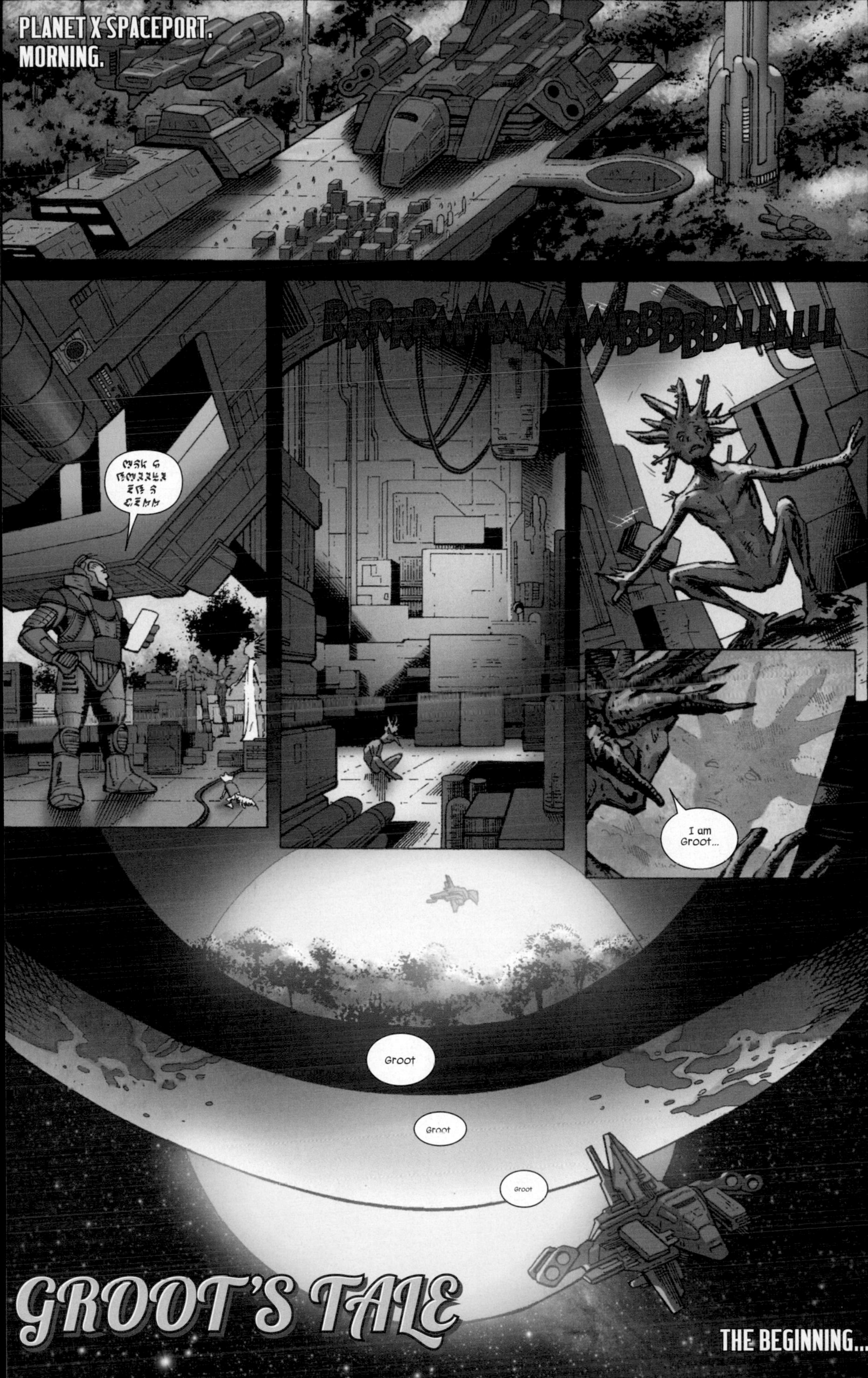
PLANET X SPACEPORT. MORNING.
RRRRRAAAAAAAAAAMBBBBBLLLLLLL
I am Groot...
Groot
Groot
Groot
GROOT'S TALE
THE BEGINNING...

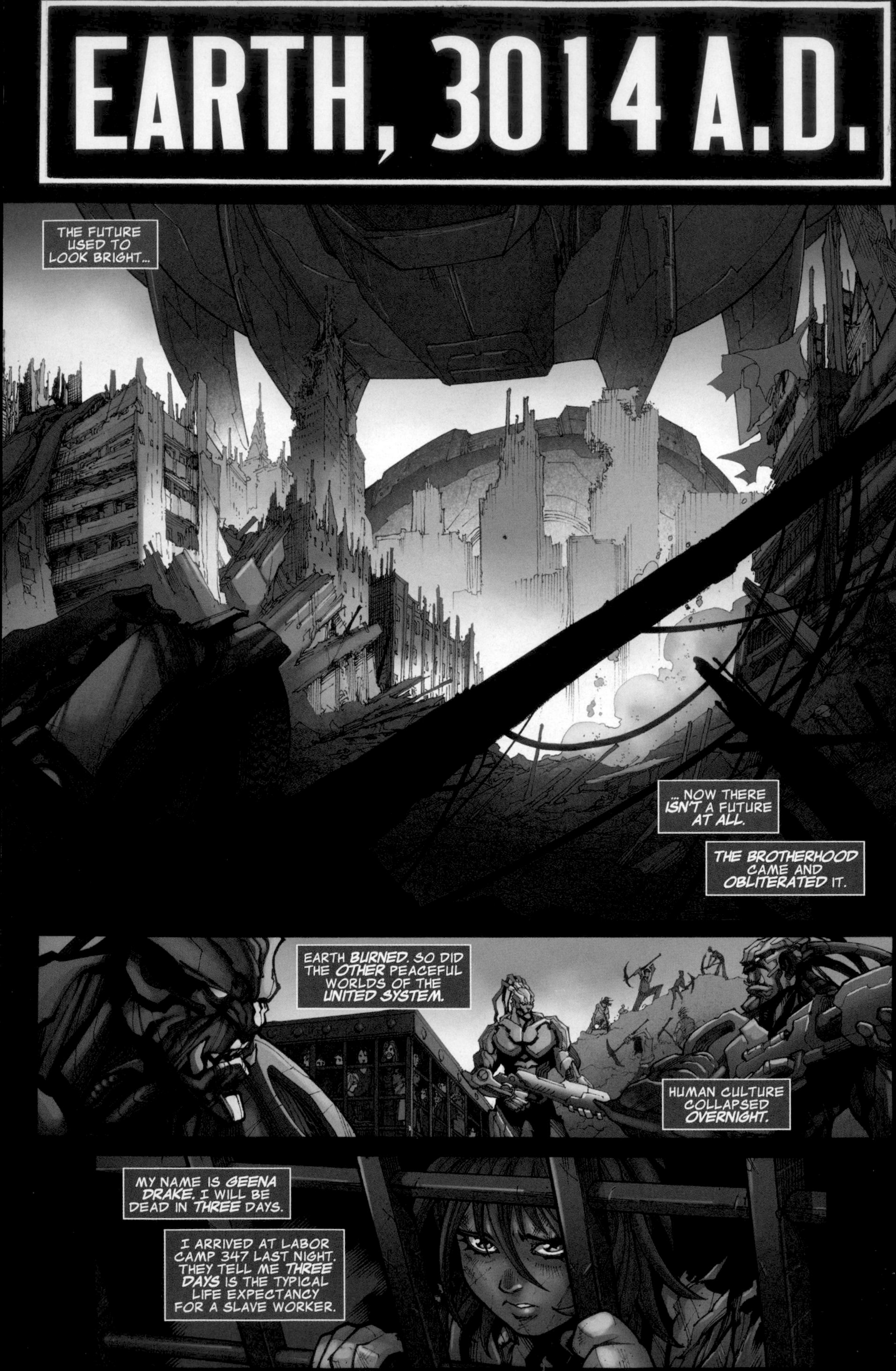
EARTH, 3014 A.D.
THE FUTURE USED TO LOOK BRIGHT...
...NOW THERE ISN'T A FUTURE AT ALL.
THE BROTHERHOOD CAME AND OBLITERATED IT.
EARTH BURNED. SO DID THE OTHER PEACEFUL WORLDS OF THE UNITED SYSTEM.
HUMAN CULTURE COLLAPSED OVERNIGHT.
MY NAME IS GEENA DRAKE. I WILL BE DEAD IN THREE DAYS.
I ARRIVED AT LABOR CAMP 347 LAST NIGHT. THEY TELL ME THREE DAYS IS THE TYPICAL LIFE EXPECTANCY FOR A SLAVE WORKER.

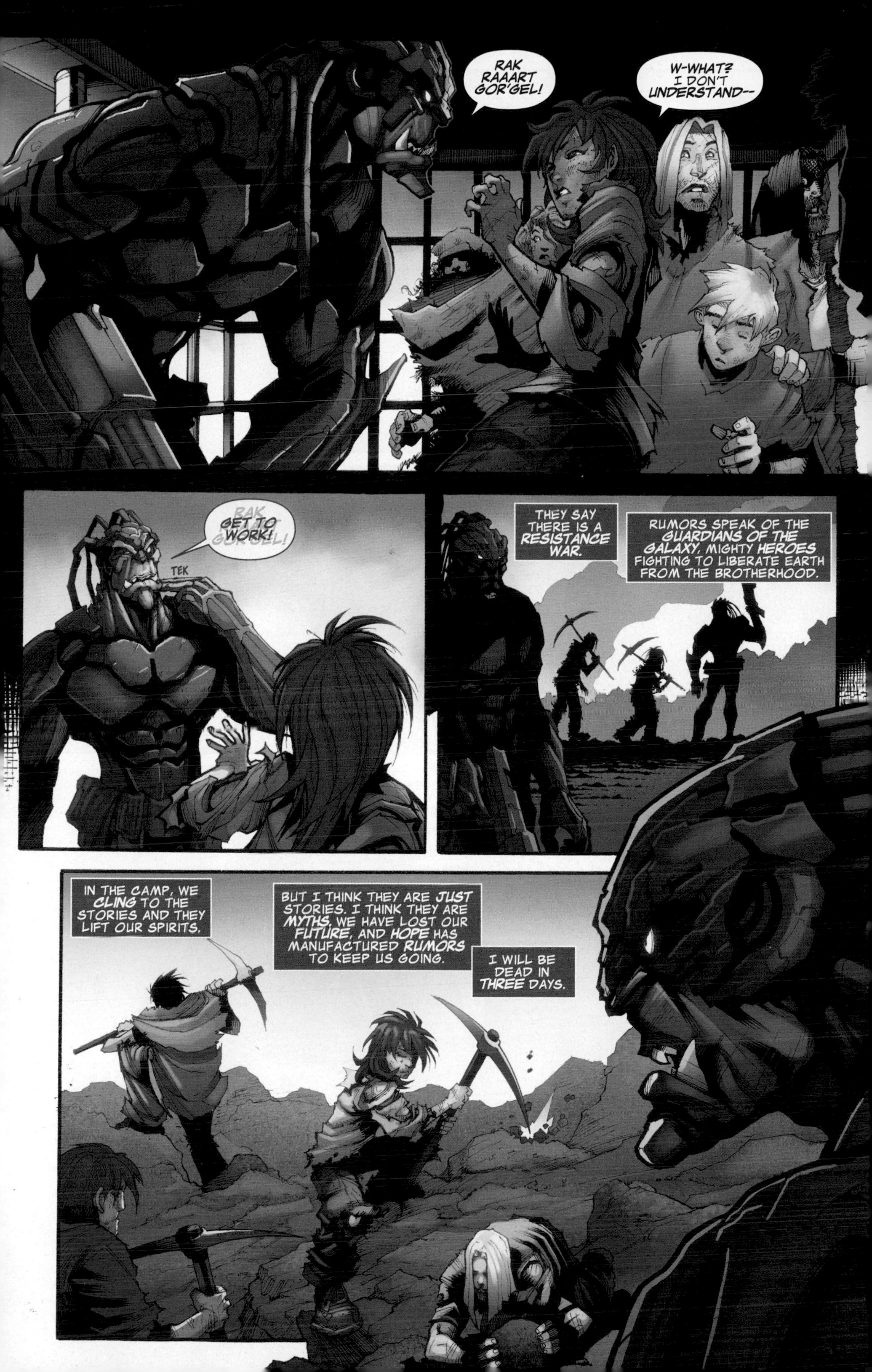
RAK RAAART GOR'GEL!
W-WHAT? I DON'T UNDERSTAND--
RAK RAAART GOR'GEL!
GET TO WORK!
TEK
THEY SAY THERE IS A RESISTANCE WAR.
RUMORS SPEAK OF THE GUARDIANS OF THE GALAXY, MIGHTY HEROES FIGHTING TO LIBERATE EARTH FROM THE BROTHERHOOD.
IN THE CAMP, WE CLING TO THE STORIES AND THEY LIFT OUR SPIRITS.
BUT I THINK THEY ARE JUST STORIES. I THINK THEY ARE MYTHS. WE HAVE LOST OUR FUTURE, AND HOPE HAS MANUFACTURED RUMORS TO KEEP US GOING.
I WILL BE DEAD IN THREE DAYS.

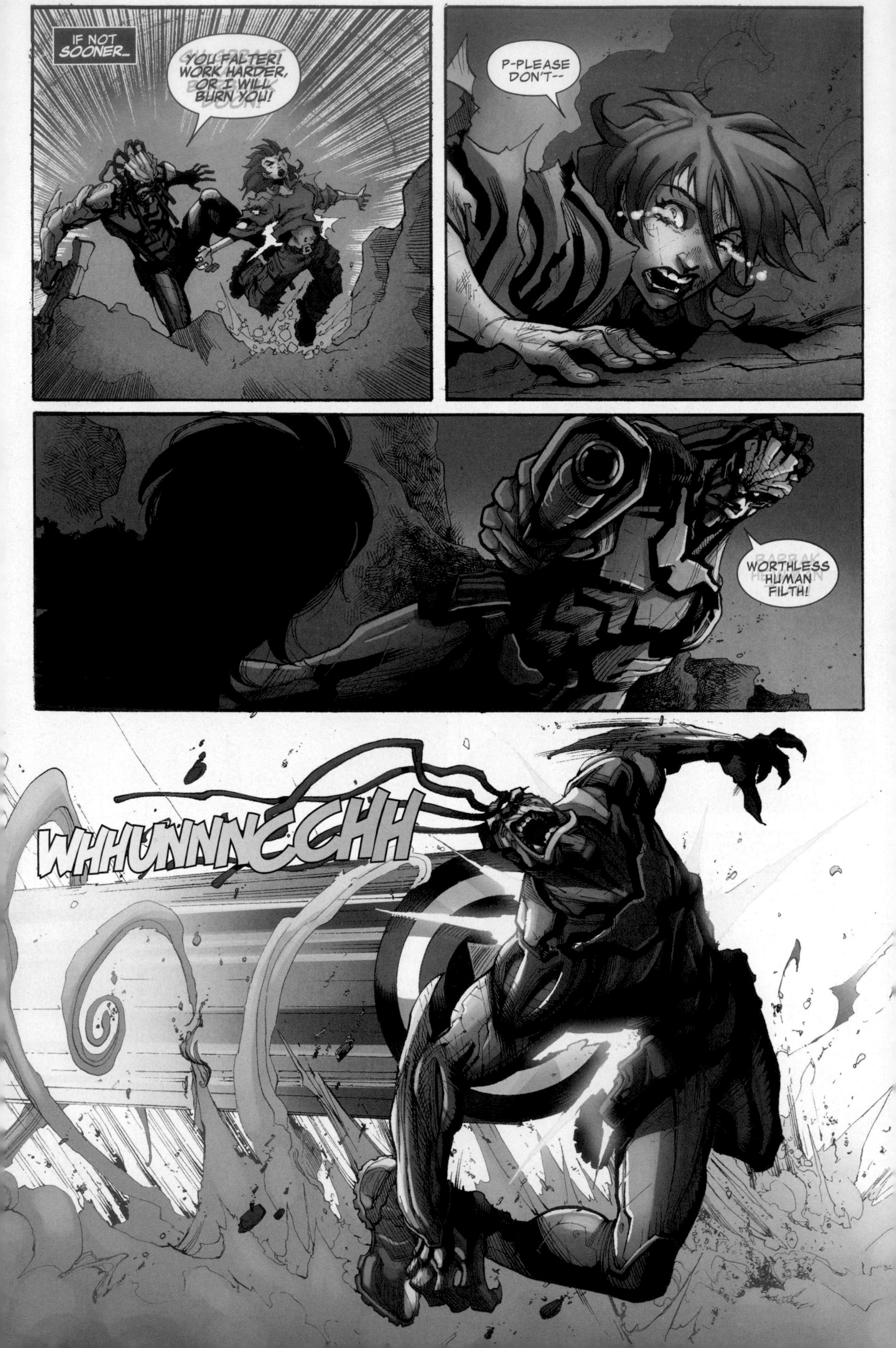

IF NOT SOONER...
YOU FALTER! WORK HARDER, OR I WILL BURN YOU!
P-PLEASE DON'T--
WORTHLESS HUMAN FILTH!
WHHUNNNCCHH

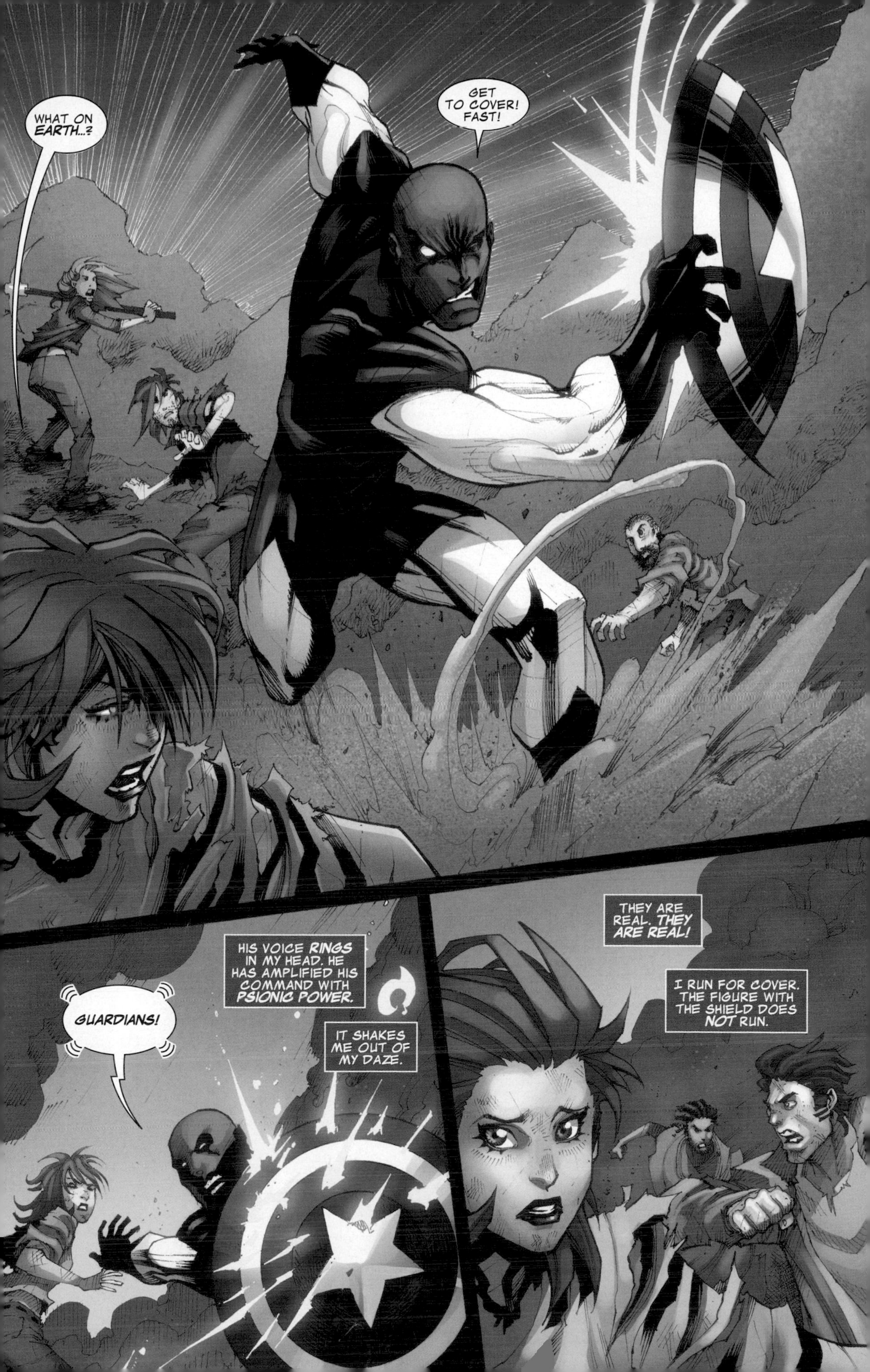
WHAT ON EARTH...?
GET TO COVER! FAST!
GUARDIANS!
HIS VOICE RINGS IN MY HEAD. HE HAS AMPLIFIED HIS COMMAND WITH PSIONIC POWER.
IT SHAKES ME OUT OF MY DAZE.
THEY ARE REAL. THEY ARE REAL!
I RUN FOR COVER. THE FIGURE WITH THE SHIELD DOES NOT RUN.

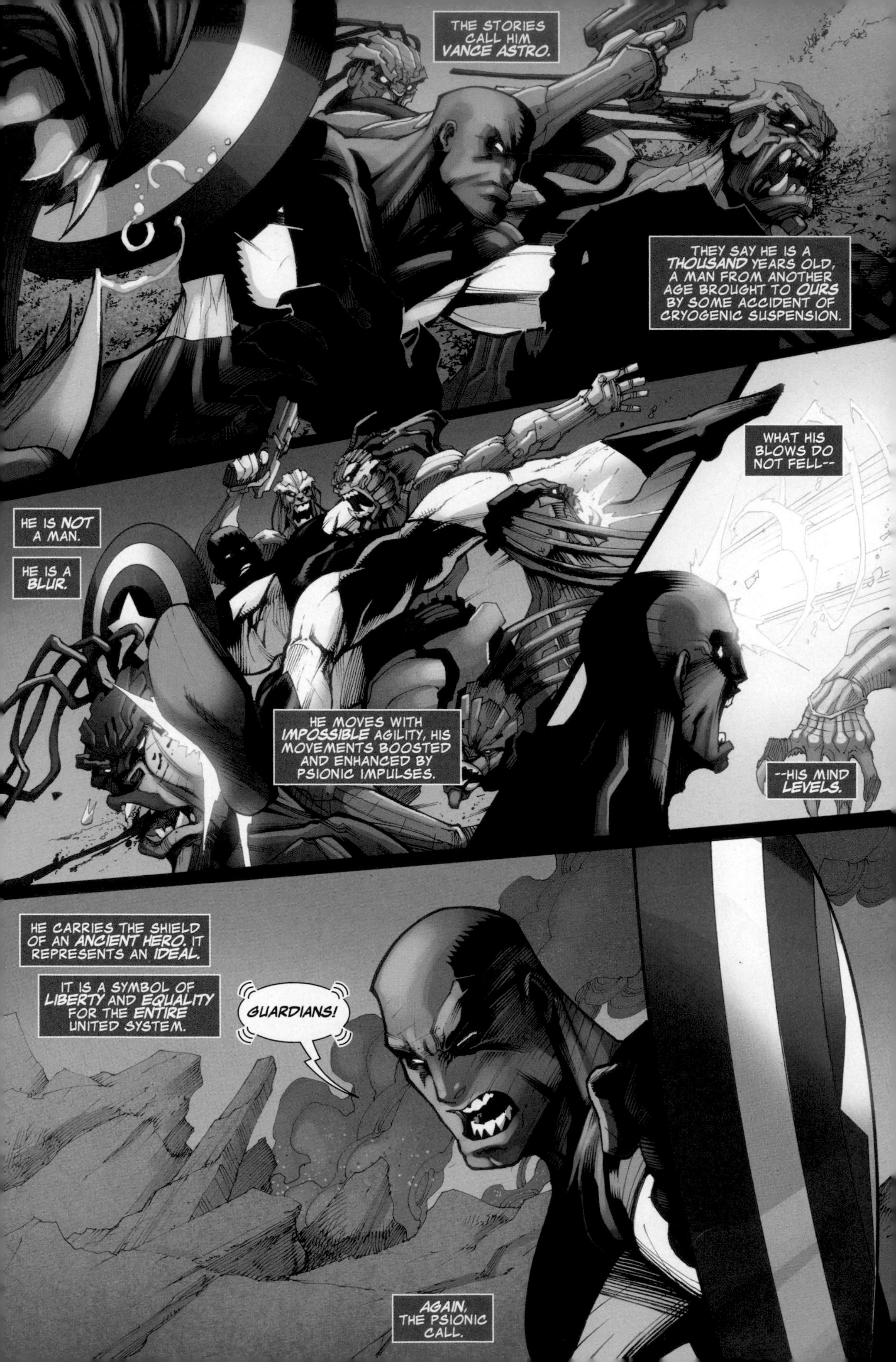
THE STORIES CALL HIM VANCE ASTRO.
THEY SAY HE IS A THOUSAND YEARS OLD, A MAN FROM ANOTHER AGE BROUGHT TO OURS BY SOME ACCIDENT OF CRYOGENIC SUSPENSION.
HE IS NOT A MAN.
HE IS A BLUR.
HE MOVES WITH IMPOSSIBLE AGILITY, HIS MOVEMENTS BOOSTED AND ENHANCED BY PSIONIC IMPULSES.
WHAT HIS BLOWS DO NOT FELL--
--HIS MIND LEVELS.
HE CARRIES THE SHIELD OF AN ANCIENT HERO. IT REPRESENTS AN IDEAL.
IT IS A SYMBOL OF LIBERTY AND EQUALITY FOR THE ENTIRE UNITED SYSTEM.
GUARDIANS!
AGAIN, THE PSIONIC CALL.

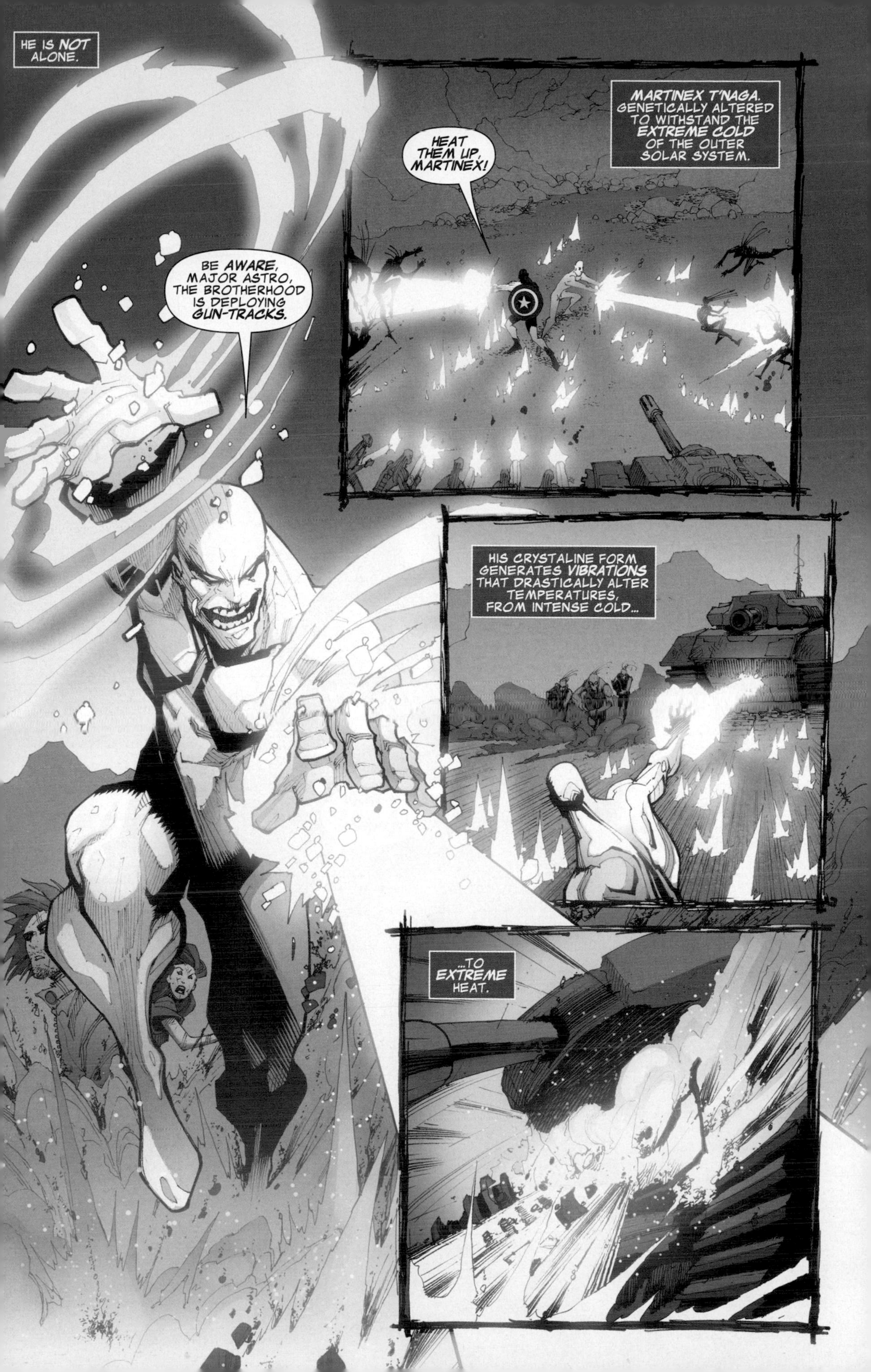
HE IS NOT ALONE.
BE AWARE, MAJOR ASTRO, THE BROTHERHOOD IS DEPLOYING GUN-TRACKS.
HEAT THEM UP, MARTINEX!
MARTINEX T'NAGA. GENETICALLY ALTERED TO WITHSTAND THE EXTREME COLD OF THE OUTER SOLAR SYSTEM.
HIS CRYSTALINE FORM GENERATES VIBRATIONS THAT DRASTICALLY ALTER TEMPERATURES, FROM INTENSE COLD...
...TO EXTREME HEAT.

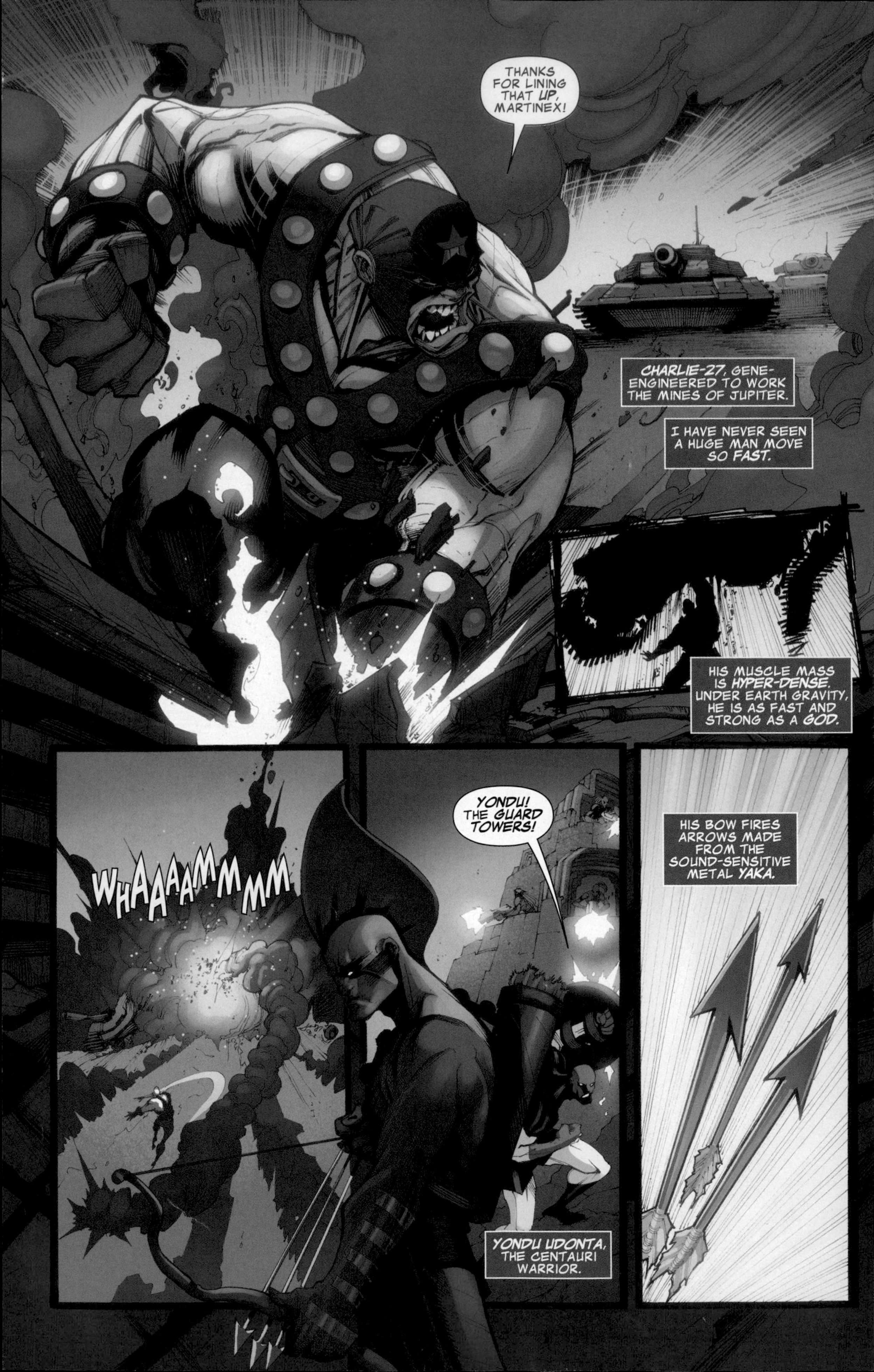
THANKS FOR LINING THAT UP, MARTINEX!
CHARLIE-27, GENE-ENGINEERED TO WORK THE MINES OF JUPITER.
I HAVE NEVER SEEN A HUGE MAN MOVE SO FAST.
HIS MUSCLE MASS IS HYPER-DENSE. UNDER EARTH GRAVITY, HE IS AS FAST AND STRONG AS A GOD.
WHAAAAMMMMM
YONDU! THE GUARD TOWERS!
YONDU UDONTA, THE CENTAURI WARRIOR.
HIS BOW FIRES ARROWS MADE FROM THE SOUND-SENSITIVE METAL YAKA.

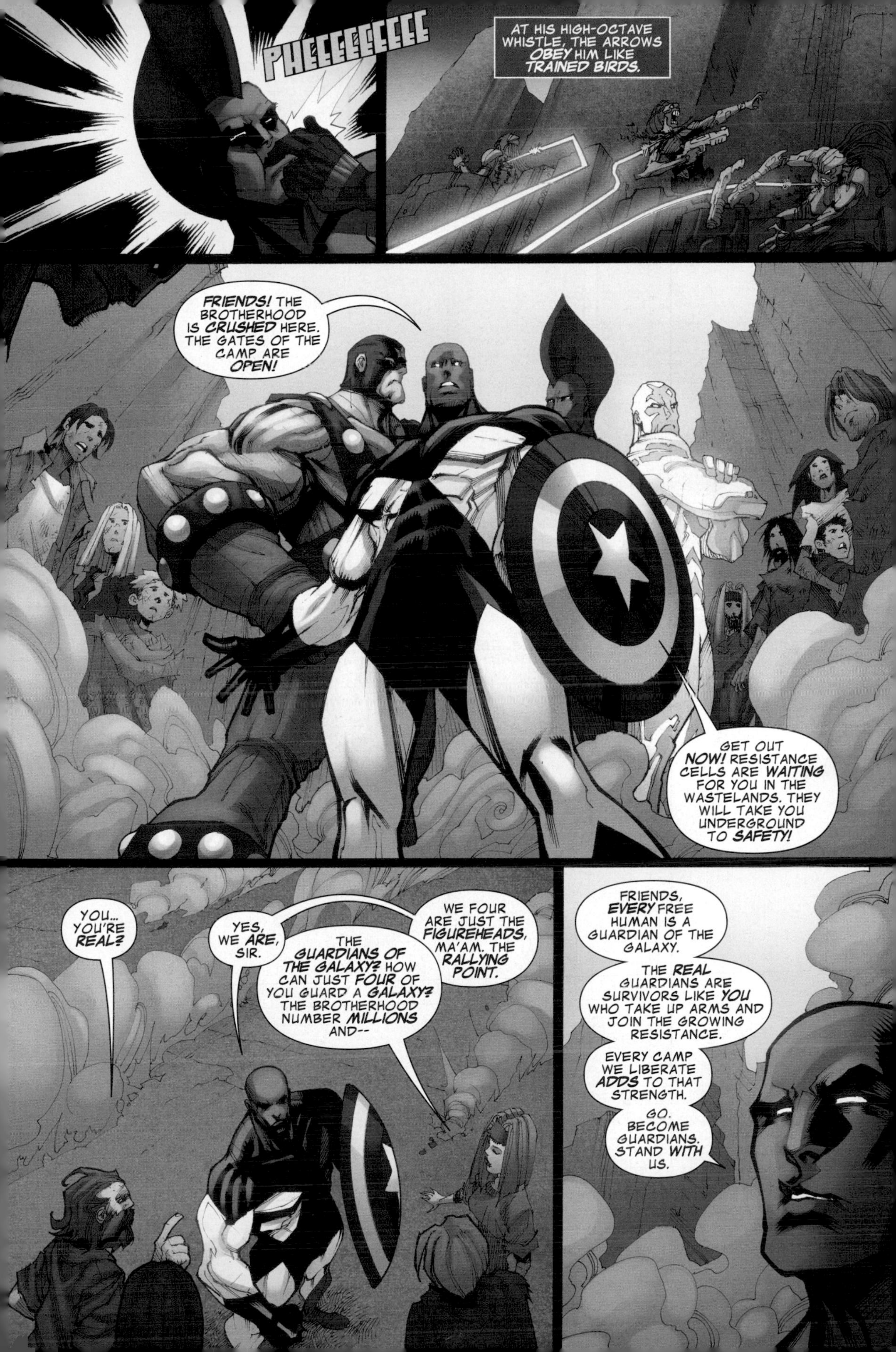
PHEEEEEEEEEE
AT HIS HIGH-OCTAVE WHISTLE, THE ARROWS OBEY HIM LIKE TRAINED BIRDS.
FRIENDS! THE BROTHERHOOD IS CRUSHED HERE. THE GATES OF THE CAMP ARE OPEN!
GET OUT NOW! RESISTANCE CELLS ARE WAITING FOR YOU IN THE WASTELANDS. THEY WILL TAKE YOU UNDERGROUND TO SAFETY!
YOU... YOU'RE REAL?
YES, WE ARE, SIR.
THE GUARDIANS OF THE GALAXY? HOW CAN JUST FOUR OF YOU GUARD A GALAXY? THE BROTHERHOOD NUMBER MILLIONS AND--
WE FOUR ARE JUST THE FIGUREHEADS, MA'AM. THE RALLYING POINT.
FRIENDS, EVERY FREE HUMAN IS A GUARDIAN OF THE GALAXY.
THE REAL GUARDIANS ARE SURVIVORS LIKE YOU WHO TAKE UP ARMS AND JOIN THE GROWING RESISTANCE.
EVERY CAMP WE LIBERATE ADDS TO THAT STRENGTH.
GO. BECOME GUARDIANS. STAND WITH US.

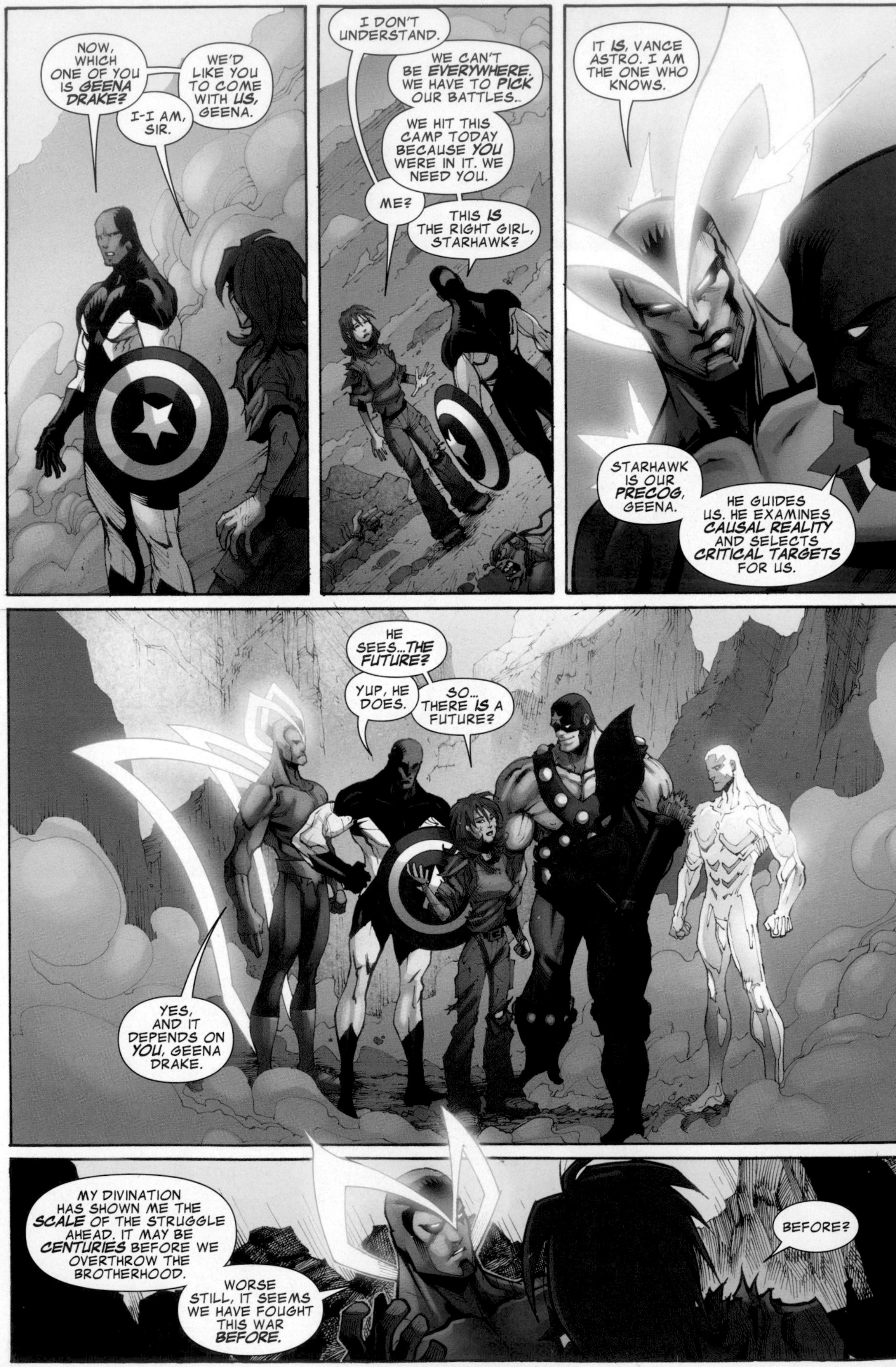
NOW, WHICH ONE OF YOU IS GEENA DRAKE?
WE'D LIKE YOU TO COME WITH US, GEENA.
I-I AM, SIR.
I DON'T UNDERSTAND.
WE CAN'T BE EVERYWHERE. WE HAVE TO PICK OUR BATTLES..
WE HIT THIS CAMP TODAY BECAUSE YOU WERE IN IT. WE NEED YOU.
ME?
THIS IS THE RIGHT GIRL, STARHAWK?
IT IS, VANCE ASTRO. I AM THE ONE WHO KNOWS.
STARHAWK IS OUR PRECOG, GEENA.
HE GUIDES US. HE EXAMINES CAUSAL REALITY AND SELECTS CRITICAL TARGETS FOR US.
HE SEES...THE FUTURE?
YUP, HE DOES.
SO... THERE IS A FUTURE?
YES, AND IT DEPENDS ON YOU, GEENA DRAKE.
MY DIVINATION HAS SHOWN ME THE SCALE OF THE STRUGGLE AHEAD. IT MAY BE CENTURIES BEFORE WE OVERTHROW THE BROTHERHOOD.
WORSE STILL, IT SEEMS WE HAVE FOUGHT THIS WAR BEFORE.
BEFORE?

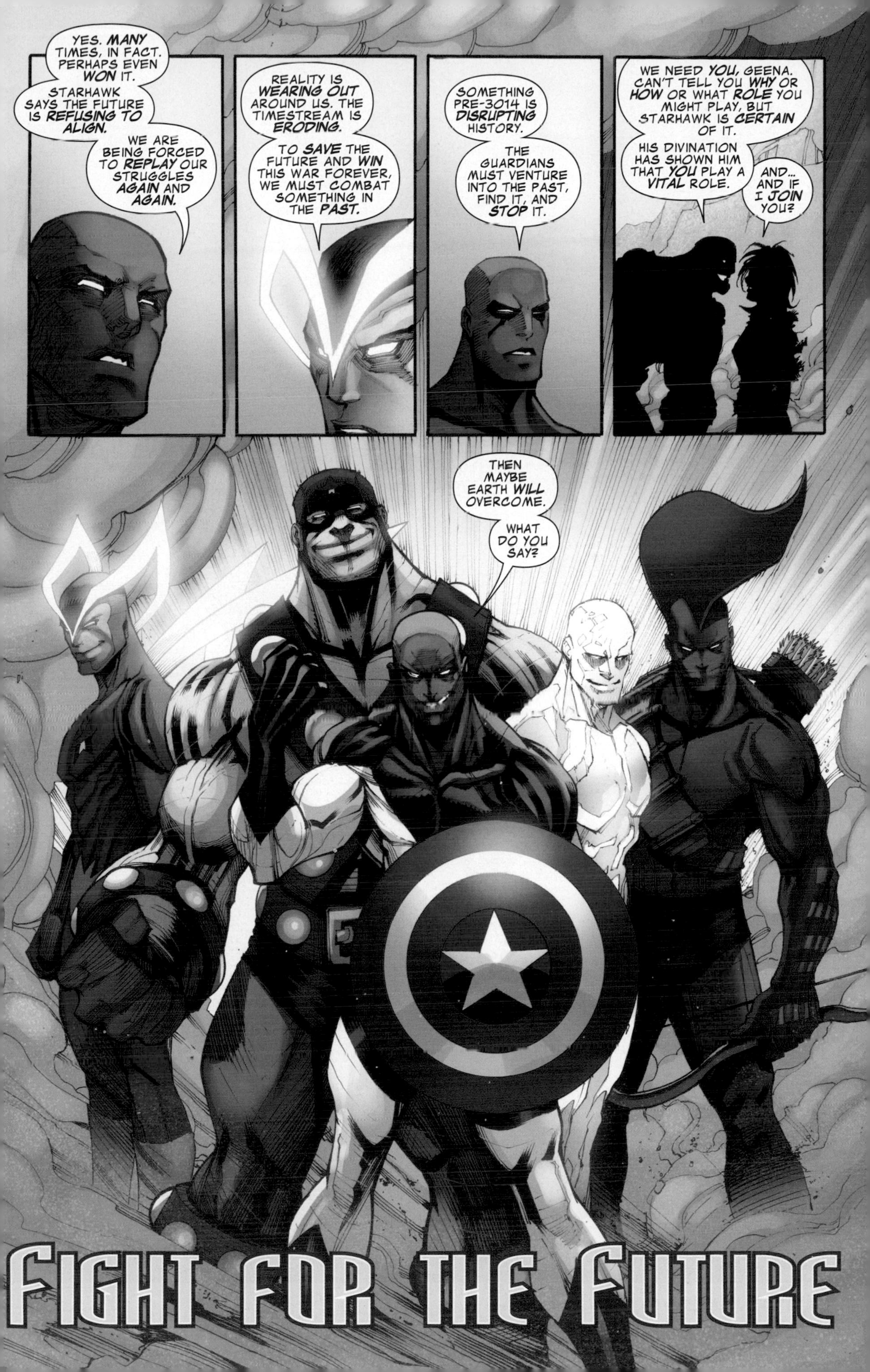
YES. MANY TIMES, IN FACT. PERHAPS EVEN WON IT.
STARHAWK SAYS THE FUTURE IS REFUSING TO ALIGN.
WE ARE BEING FORCED TO REPLAY OUR STRUGGLES AGAIN AND AGAIN.
REALITY IS WEARING OUT AROUND US. THE TIMESTREAM IS ERODING.
TO SAVE THE FUTURE AND WIN THIS WAR FOREVER, WE MUST COMBAT SOMETHING IN THE PAST.
SOMETHING PRE-3014 IS DISRUPTING HISTORY.
THE GUARDIANS MUST VENTURE INTO THE PAST, FIND IT, AND STOP IT.
WE NEED YOU, GEENA. CAN'T TELL YOU WHY OR HOW OR WHAT ROLE YOU MIGHT PLAY, BUT STARHAWK IS CERTAIN OF IT.
HIS DIVINATION HAS SHOWN HIM THAT YOU PLAY A VITAL ROLE.
AND... AND IF I JOIN YOU?
THEN MAYBE EARTH WILL OVERCOME.
WHAT DO YOU SAY?
FIGHT FOR THE FUTURE

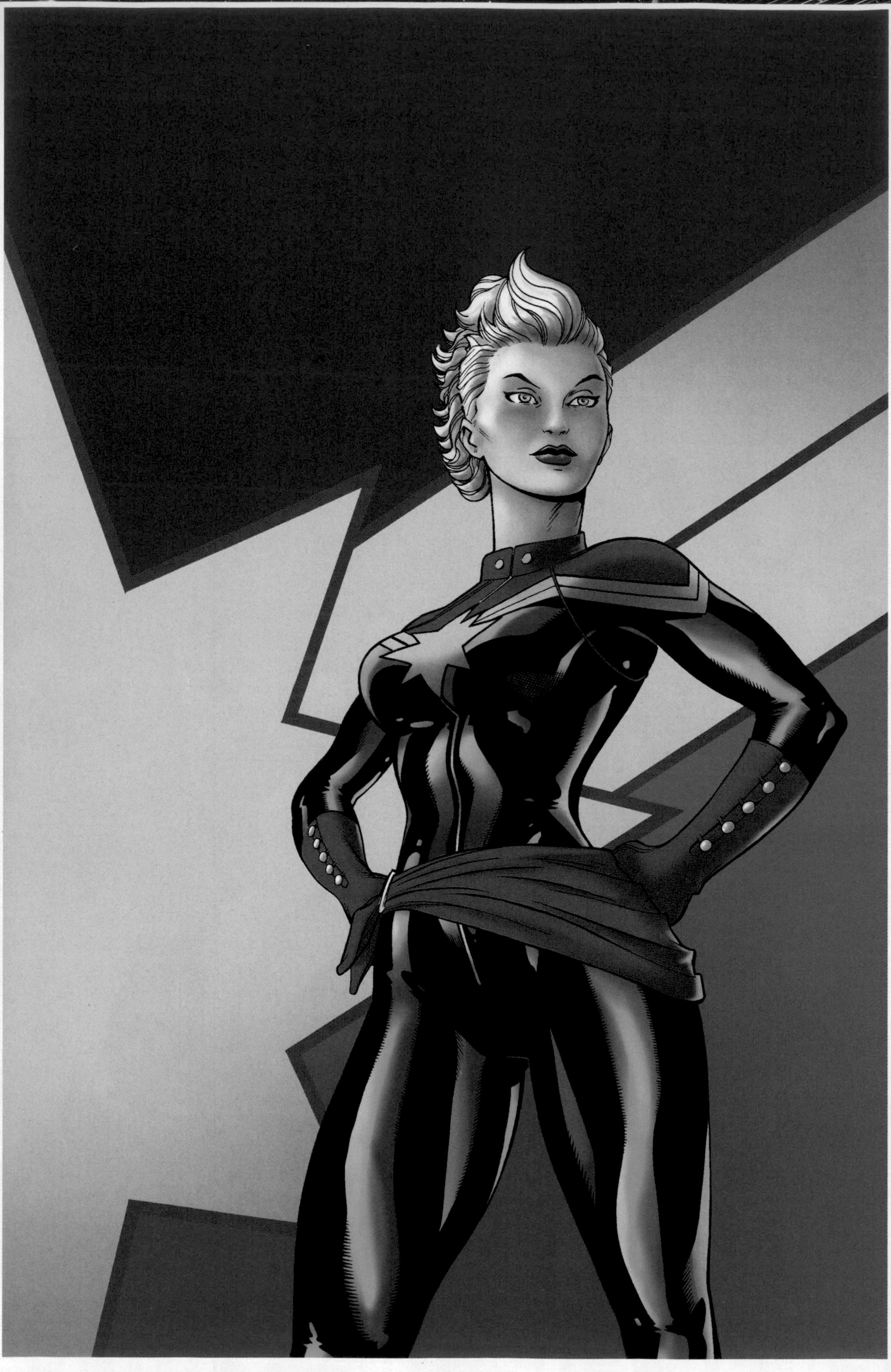

CAPTAIN MARVEL #1 (2012)
CAROL DANVERS TAKES UP THE MANTLE OF CAPTAIN MARVEL!

FINAL ☆☆☆☆

DAILY BUGLE

SINCE 1897 ☆☆☆☆
$1.00 (in NYC)
$1.50 (outside city)

SPECIAL COMMEMORATIVE ISSUE!

INSIDE: BLONDE BOMBSHELL BRAVES BOSTON! DAREDEVIL SPOTTINGS CONFIRMED IN LATVERIA! LIZARDS LOOSE IN MANHATTAN! MORE...

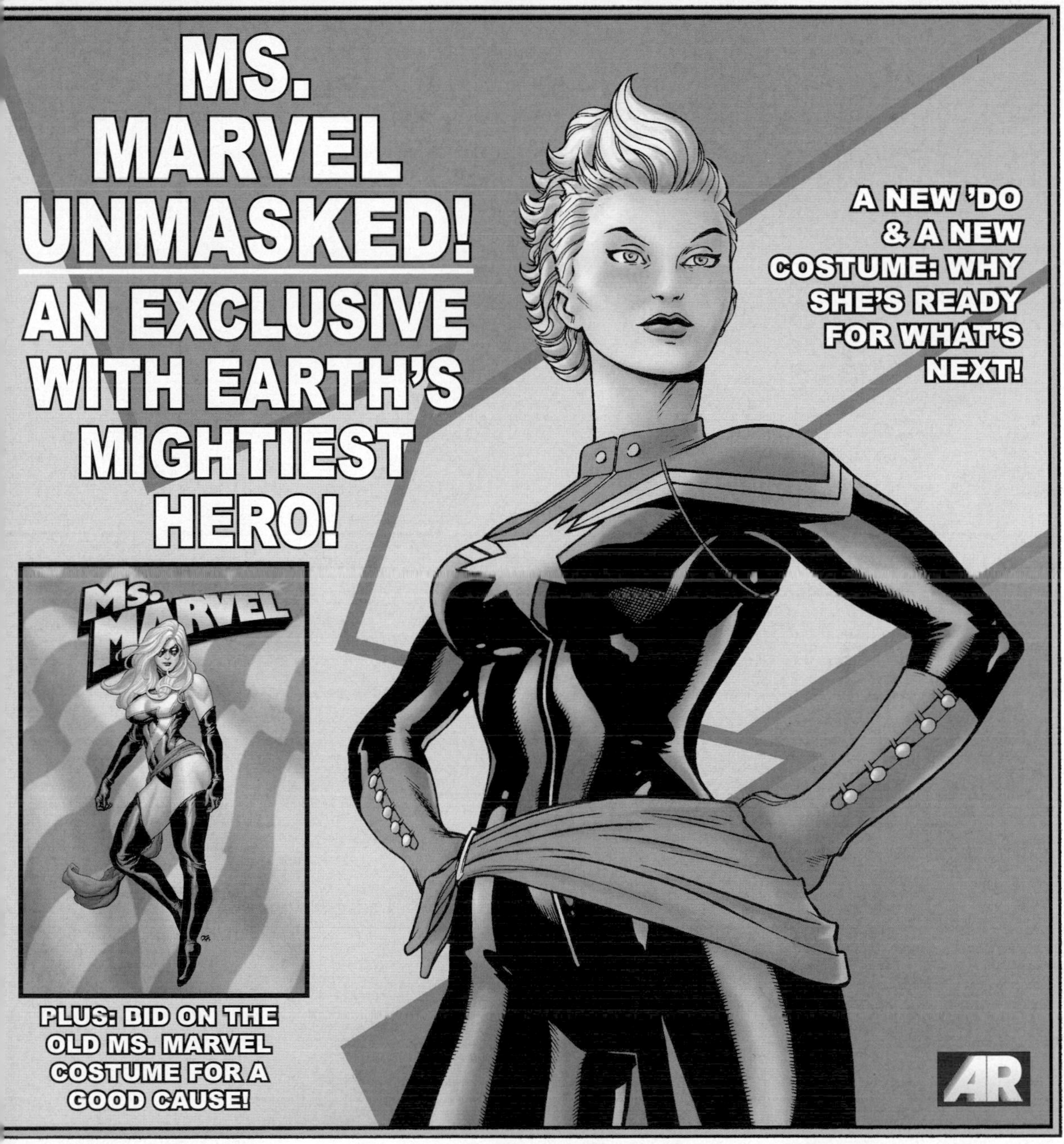

MS. MARVEL UNMASKED!
AN EXCLUSIVE WITH EARTH'S MIGHTIEST HERO!
A NEW 'DO & A NEW COSTUME: WHY SHE'S READY FOR WHAT'S NEXT!
MS. MARVEL
PLUS: BID ON THE OLD MS. MARVEL COSTUME FOR A GOOD CAUSE!
AR

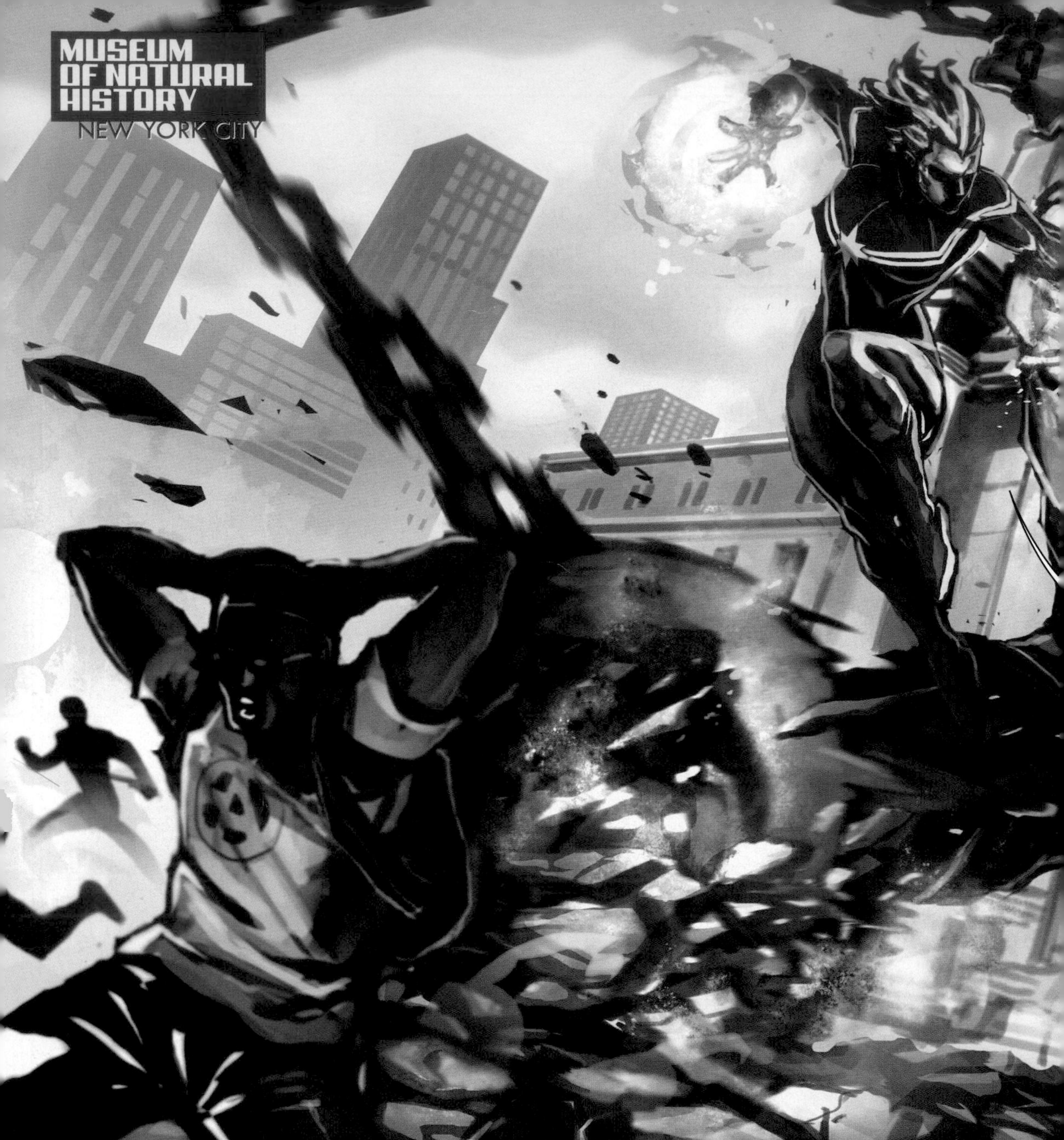
MUSEUM OF NATURAL HISTORY
NEW YORK CITY

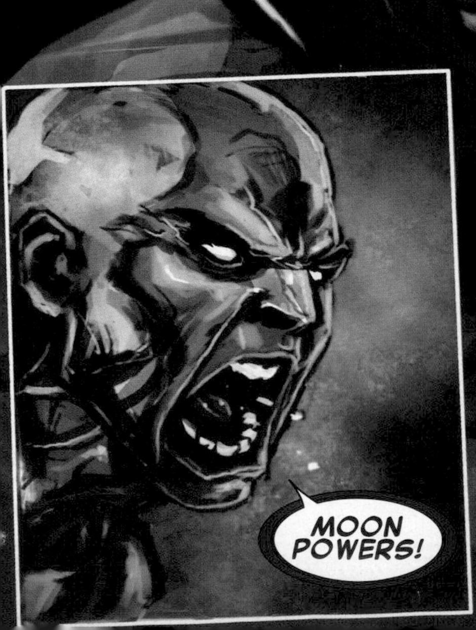
MOON POWERS!

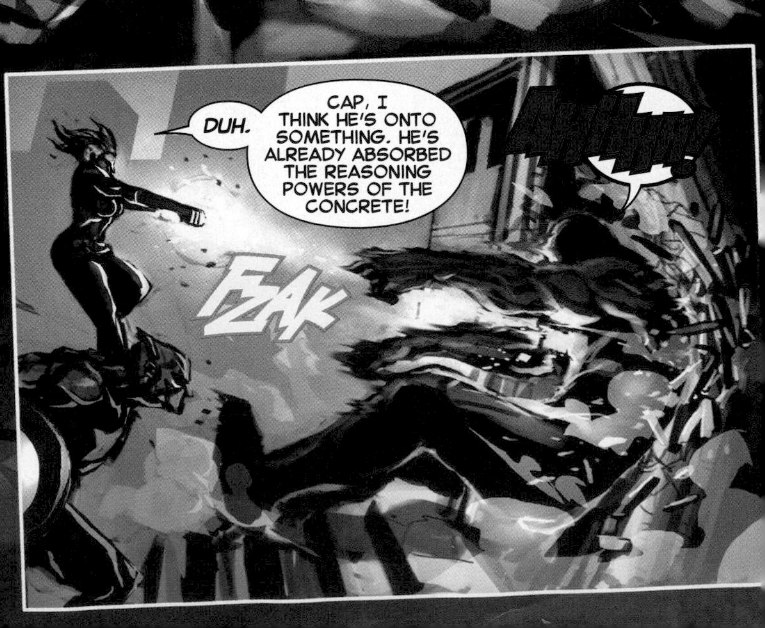
DUH.
CAP, I THINK HE'S ONTO SOMETHING. HE'S ALREADY ABSORBED THE REASONING POWERS OF THE CONCRETE!
FZAK

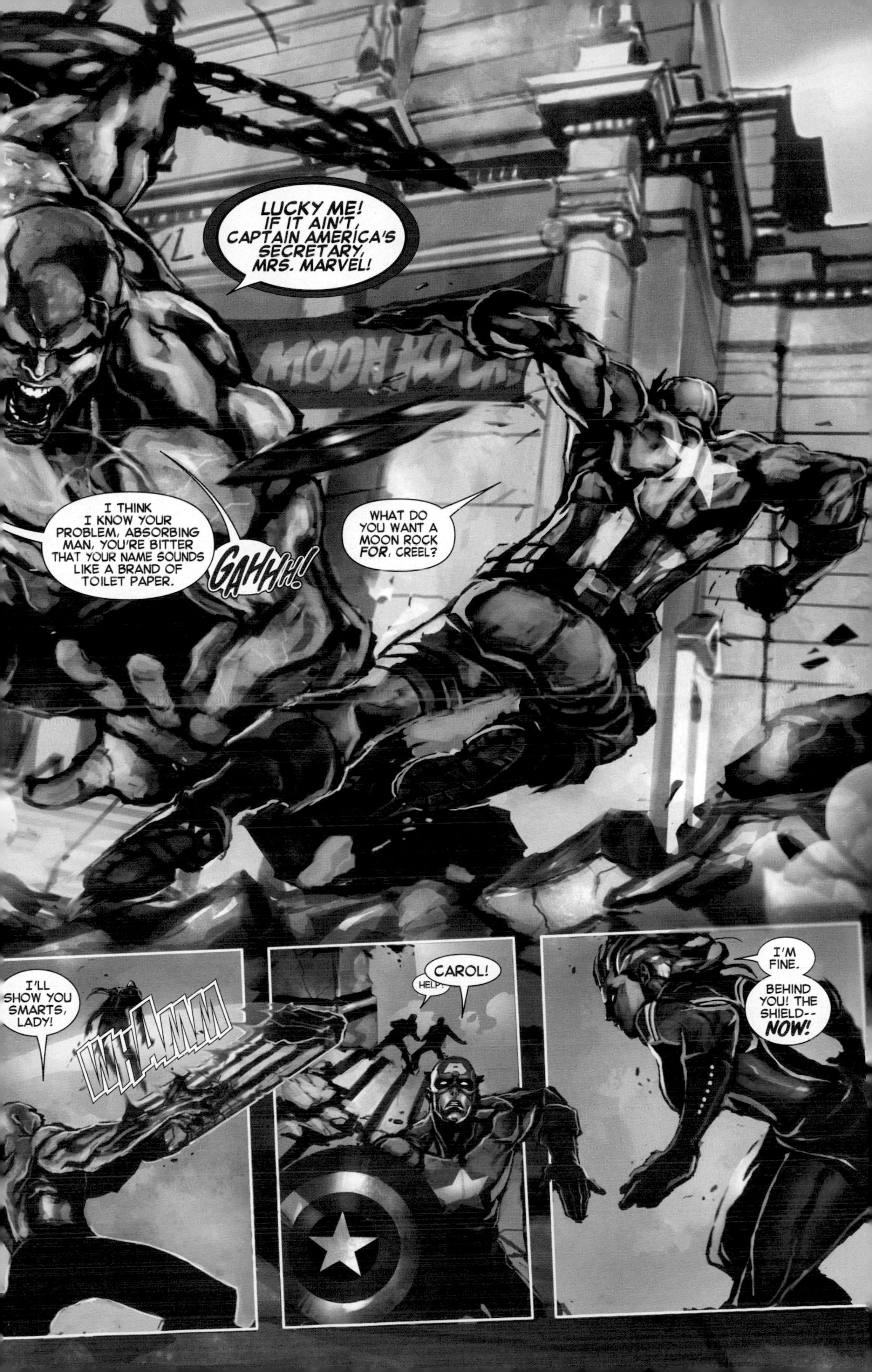
LUCKY ME! IF IT AIN'T, CAPTAIN AMERICA'S SECRETARY, MRS. MARVEL!
MOON ROCK
I THINK I KNOW YOUR PROBLEM, ABSORBING MAN. YOU'RE BITTER THAT YOUR NAME SOUNDS LIKE A BRAND OF TOILET PAPER.
GAHHH!
WHAT DO YOU WANT A MOON ROCK FOR, CREEL?
I'LL SHOW YOU SMARTS, LADY!
WHAMM
HELP!
CAROL!
I'M FINE.
BEHIND YOU! THE SHIELD-- NOW!

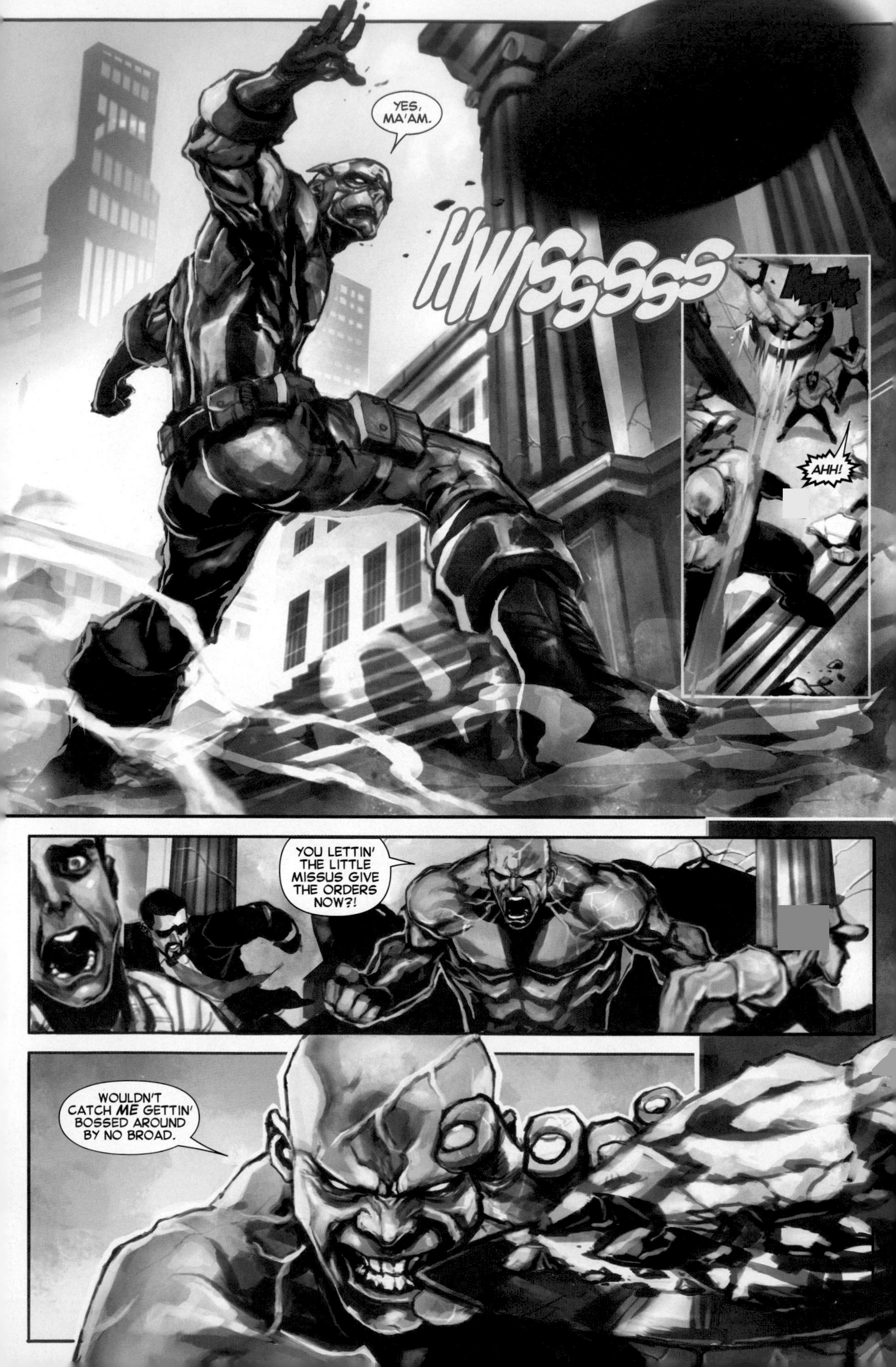
YES, MA'AM.
HWISSSSS
AHH!
YOU LETTIN' THE LITTLE MISSUS GIVE THE ORDERS NOW?!
WOULDN'T CATCH ME GETTIN' BOSSED AROUND BY NO BROAD.

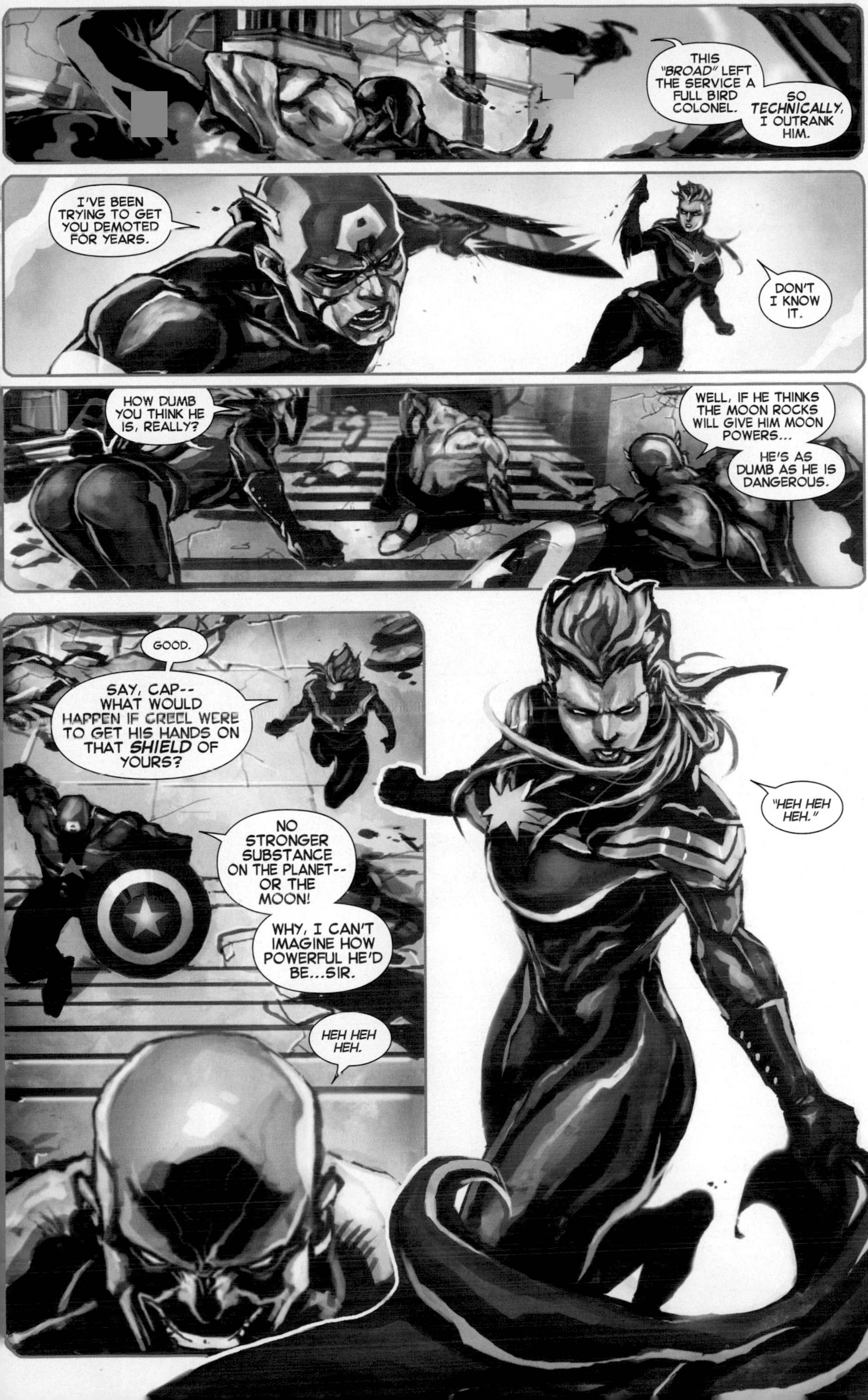
THIS "BROAD" LEFT THE SERVICE A FULL BIRD COLONEL.
SO TECHNICALLY, I OUTRANK HIM.
I'VE BEEN TRYING TO GET YOU DEMOTED FOR YEARS.
DON'T I KNOW IT.
HOW DUMB YOU THINK HE IS, REALLY?
WELL, IF HE THINKS THE MOON ROCKS WILL GIVE HIM MOON POWERS...
HE'S AS DUMB AS HE IS DANGEROUS.
GOOD.
SAY, CAP-- WHAT WOULD HAPPEN IF CREEL WERE TO GET HIS HANDS ON THAT SHIELD OF YOURS?
NO STRONGER SUBSTANCE ON THE PLANET-- OR THE MOON!
WHY, I CAN'T IMAGINE HOW POWERFUL HE'D BE...SIR.
HEH HEH HEH.
"HEH HEH HEH."

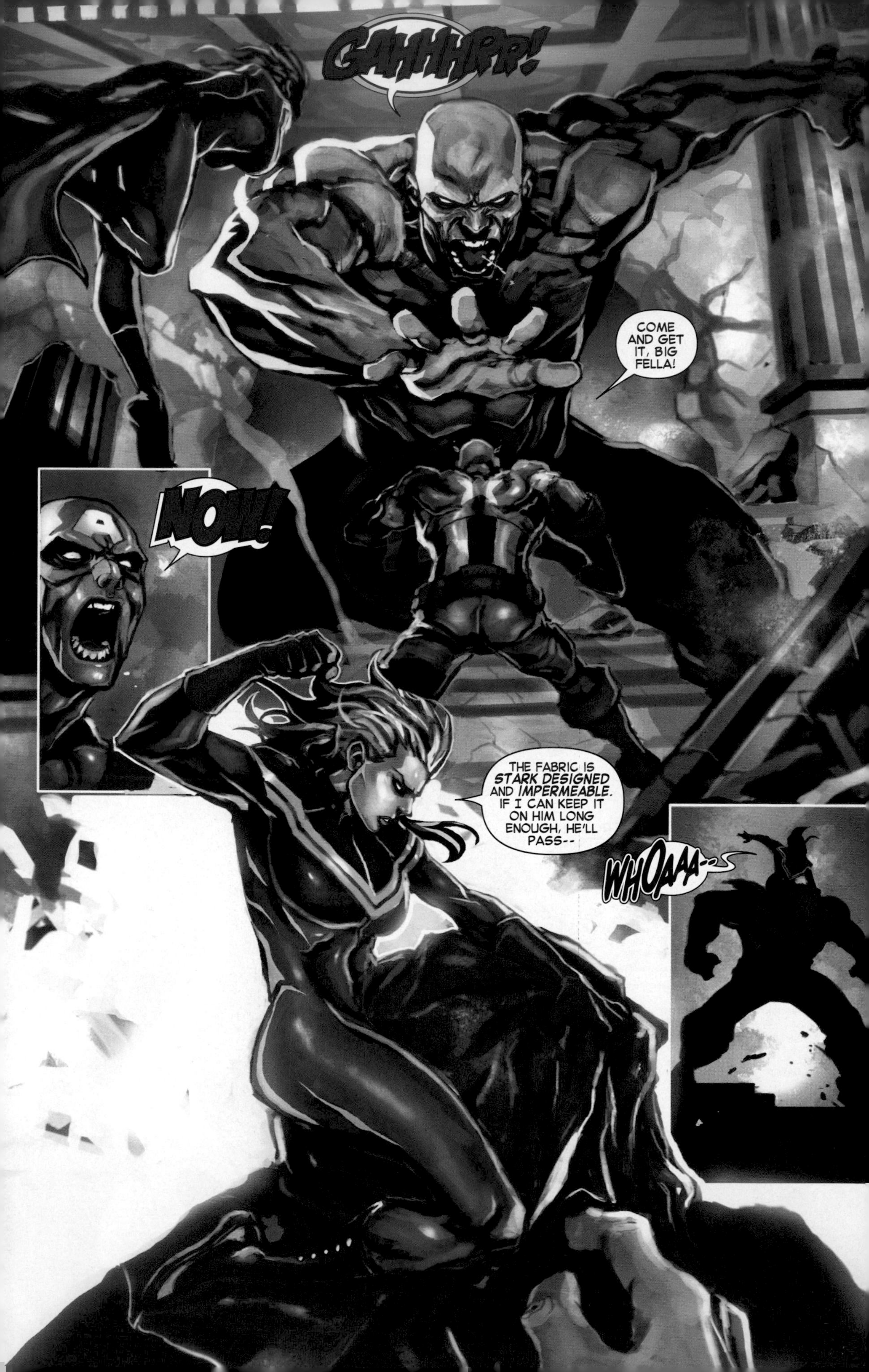

GAHHHPR!
COME AND GET IT, BIG FELLA!
NOW!
THE FABRIC IS STARK DESIGNED AND IMPERMEABLE. IF I CAN KEEP IT ON HIM LONG ENOUGH, HE'LL PASS--
WHOAAA--

JUST LIKE A WOMAN...

...SHE DON'T KNOW WHEN TO LET GO!

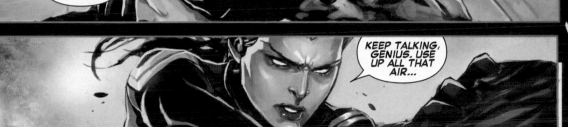

KEEP TALKING, GENIUS. USE UP ALL THAT AIR...

KRDSHHHHHH

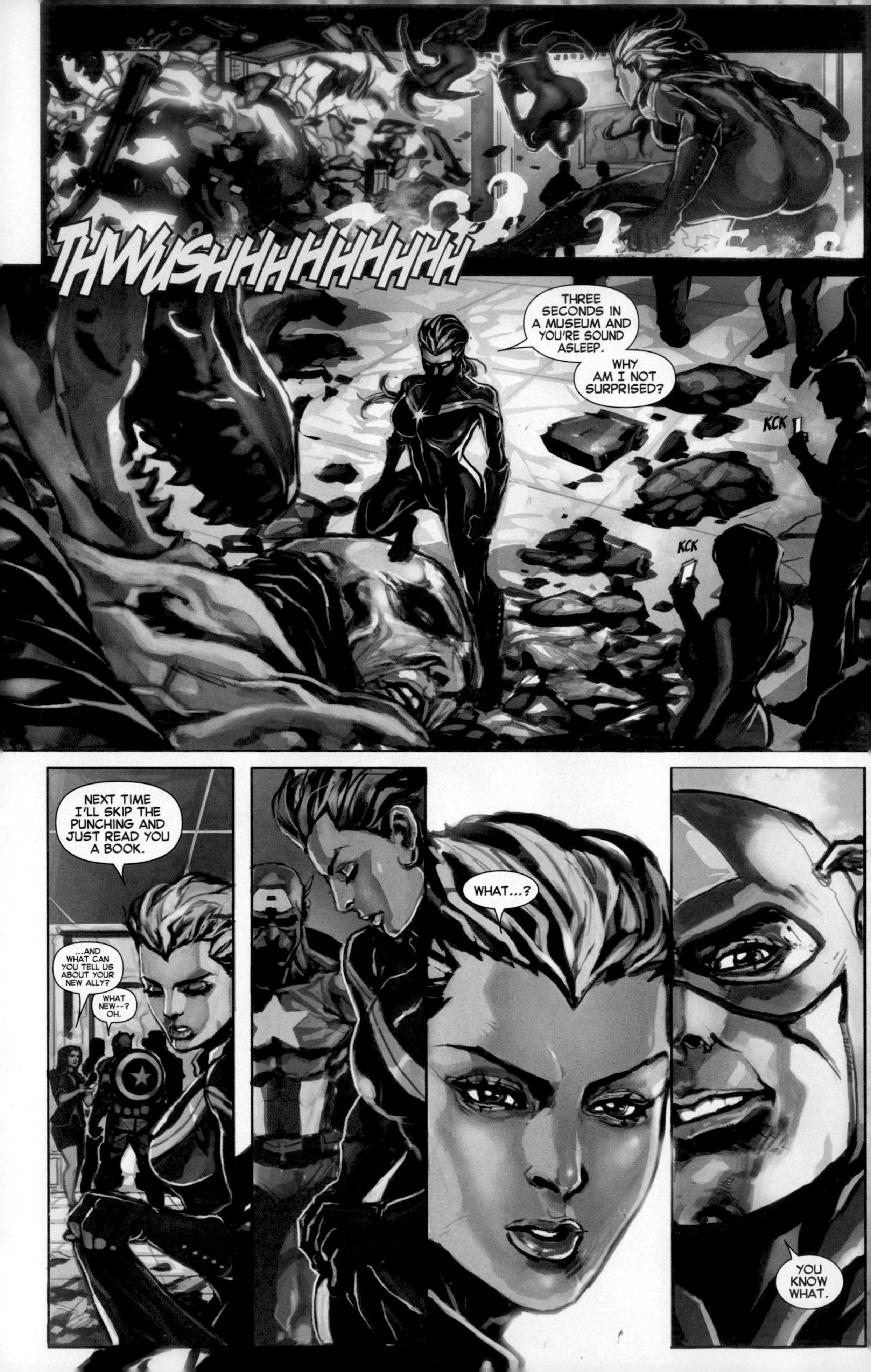
THWUSHHHHHHHHH
THREE SECONDS IN A MUSEUM AND YOU'RE SOUND ASLEEP.
WHY AM I NOT SURPRISED?
KCK
KCK
NEXT TIME I'LL SKIP THE PUNCHING AND JUST READ YOU A BOOK.
...AND WHAT CAN YOU TELL US ABOUT YOUR NEW ALLY?
WHAT NEW--? OH.
WHAT...?
YOU KNOW WHAT.

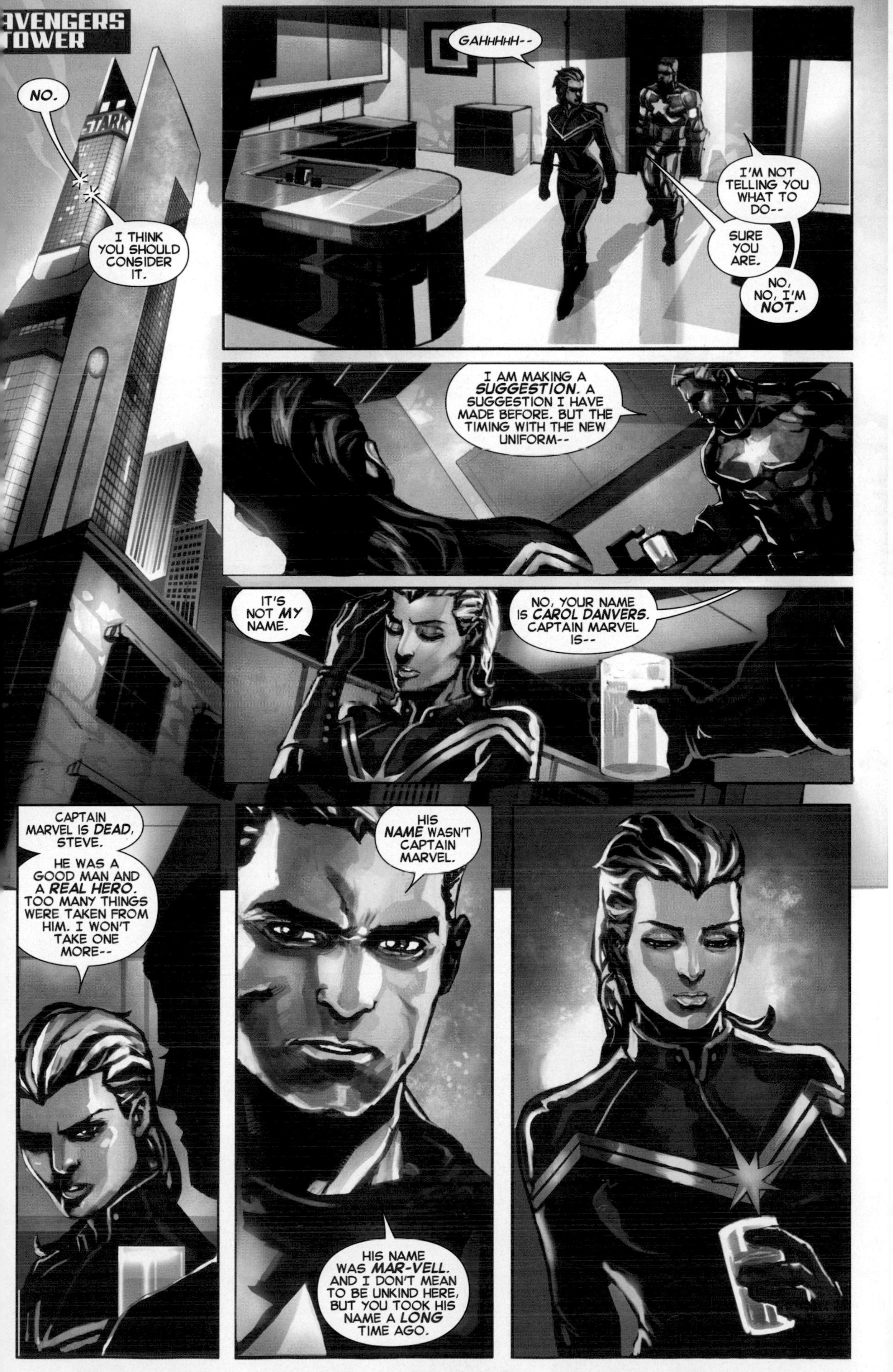
AVENGERS TOWER
STARK
NO.
I THINK YOU SHOULD CONSIDER IT.
GAHHHHH--
I'M NOT TELLING YOU WHAT TO DO--
SURE YOU ARE.
NO, NO, I'M NOT.
I AM MAKING A SUGGESTION. A SUGGESTION I HAVE MADE BEFORE. BUT THE TIMING WITH THE NEW UNIFORM--
IT'S NOT MY NAME.
NO, YOUR NAME IS CAROL DANVERS. CAPTAIN MARVEL IS--
CAPTAIN MARVEL IS DEAD, STEVE.
HE WAS A GOOD MAN AND A REAL HERO. TOO MANY THINGS WERE TAKEN FROM HIM. I WON'T TAKE ONE MORE--
HIS NAME WASN'T CAPTAIN MARVEL.
HIS NAME WAS MAR-VELL. AND I DON'T MEAN TO BE UNKIND HERE, BUT YOU TOOK HIS NAME A LONG TIME AGO.

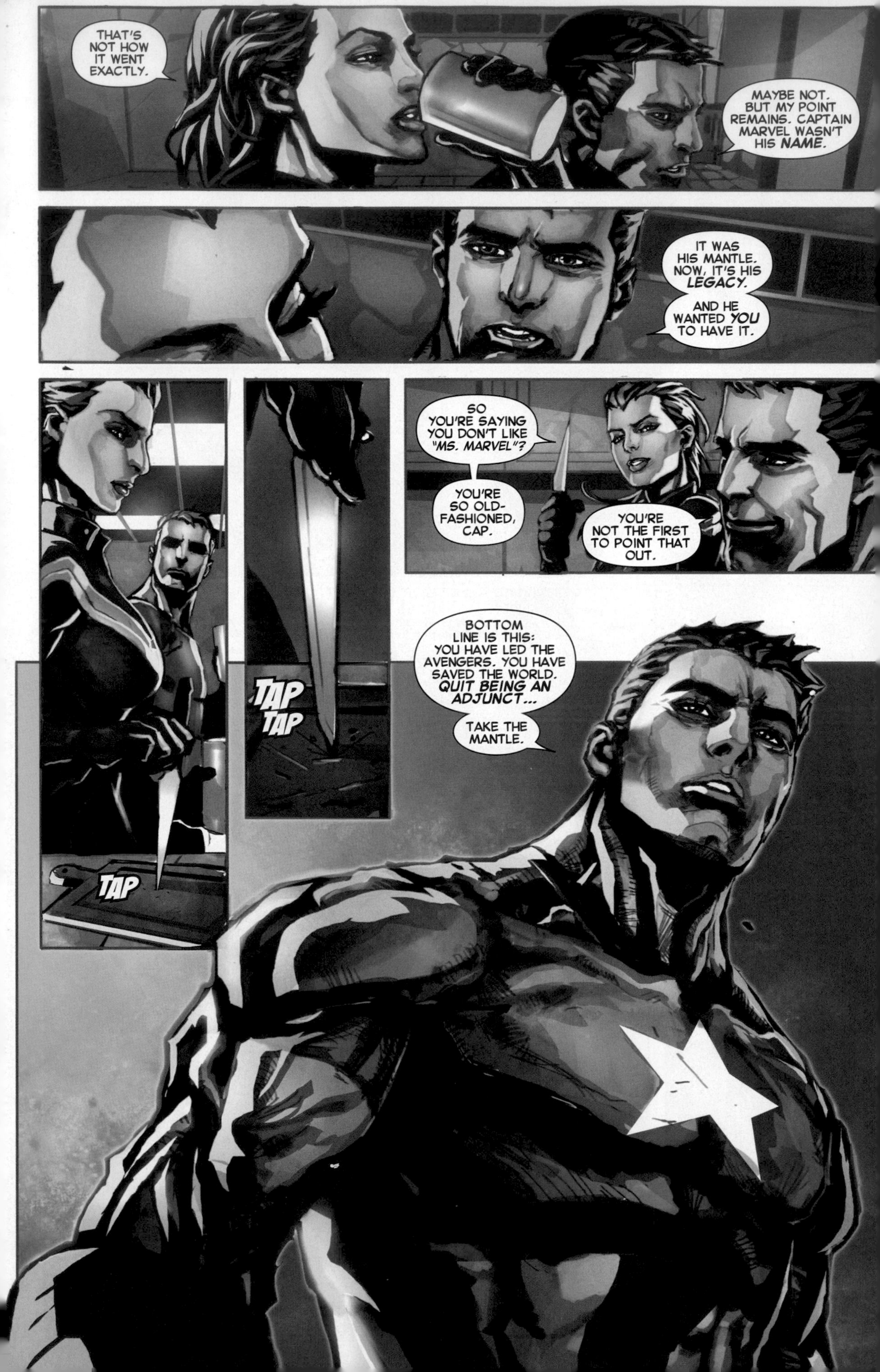
THAT'S NOT HOW IT WENT EXACTLY.
MAYBE NOT. BUT MY POINT REMAINS. CAPTAIN MARVEL WASN'T HIS *NAME.*
IT WAS HIS MANTLE. NOW, IT'S HIS *LEGACY.*
AND HE WANTED *YOU* TO HAVE IT.
TAP
TAP TAP
SO YOU'RE SAYING YOU DON'T LIKE "MS. MARVEL"?
YOU'RE SO OLD-FASHIONED, CAP.
YOU'RE NOT THE FIRST TO POINT THAT OUT.
BOTTOM LINE IS THIS: YOU HAVE LED THE AVENGERS. YOU HAVE SAVED THE WORLD. *QUIT BEING AN ADJUNCT...*
TAKE THE MANTLE.

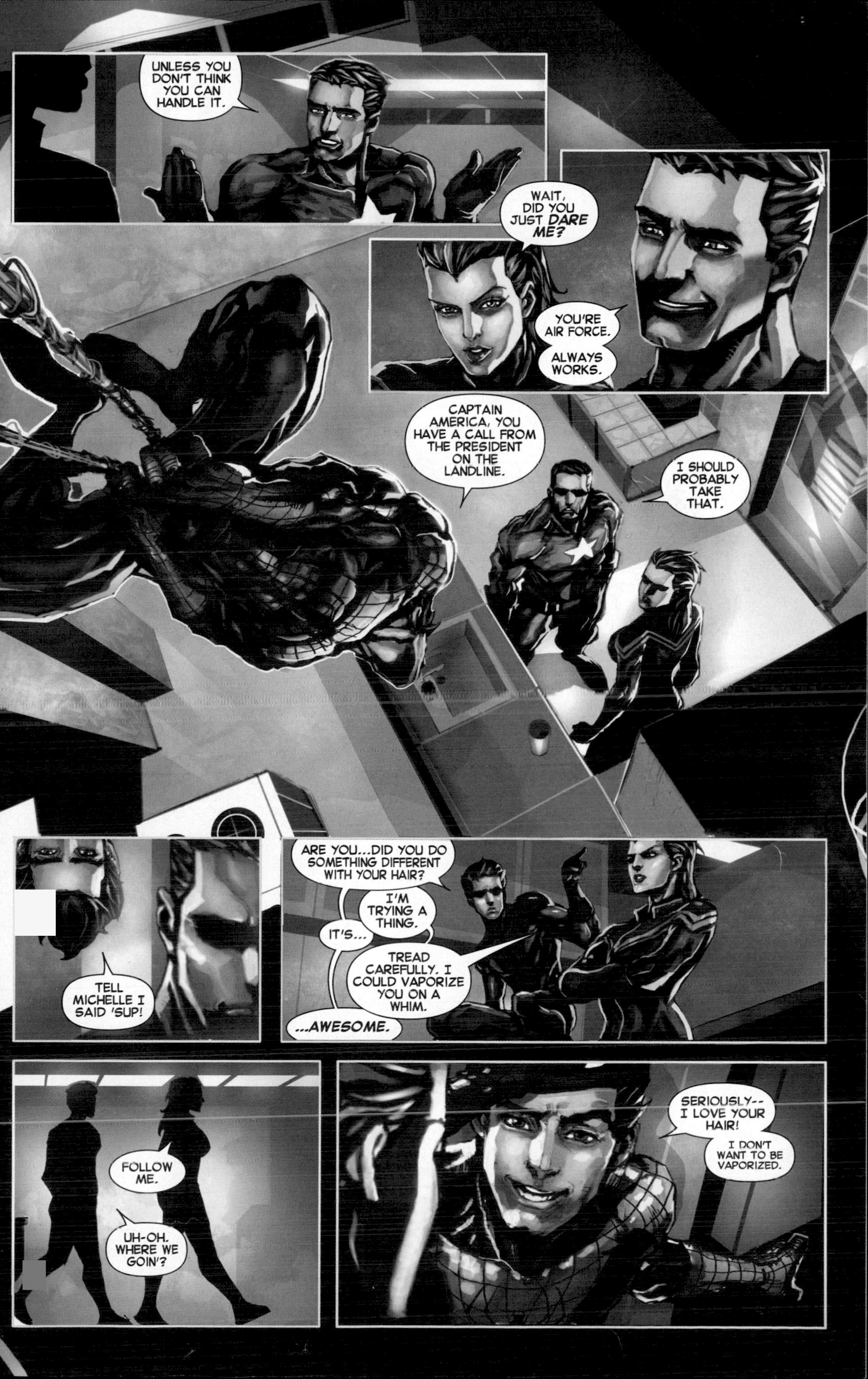

UNLESS YOU DON'T THINK YOU CAN HANDLE IT.
WAIT, DID YOU JUST DARE ME?
YOU'RE AIR FORCE.
ALWAYS WORKS.
CAPTAIN AMERICA, YOU HAVE A CALL FROM THE PRESIDENT ON THE LANDLINE.
I SHOULD PROBABLY TAKE THAT.
TELL MICHELLE I SAID 'SUP!
ARE YOU...DID YOU DO SOMETHING DIFFERENT WITH YOUR HAIR?
I'M TRYING A THING.
IT'S...
TREAD CAREFULLY. I COULD VAPORIZE YOU ON A WHIM.
...AWESOME.
FOLLOW ME.
UH-OH. WHERE WE GOIN'?
SERIOUSLY-- I LOVE YOUR HAIR!
I DON'T WANT TO BE VAPORIZED.

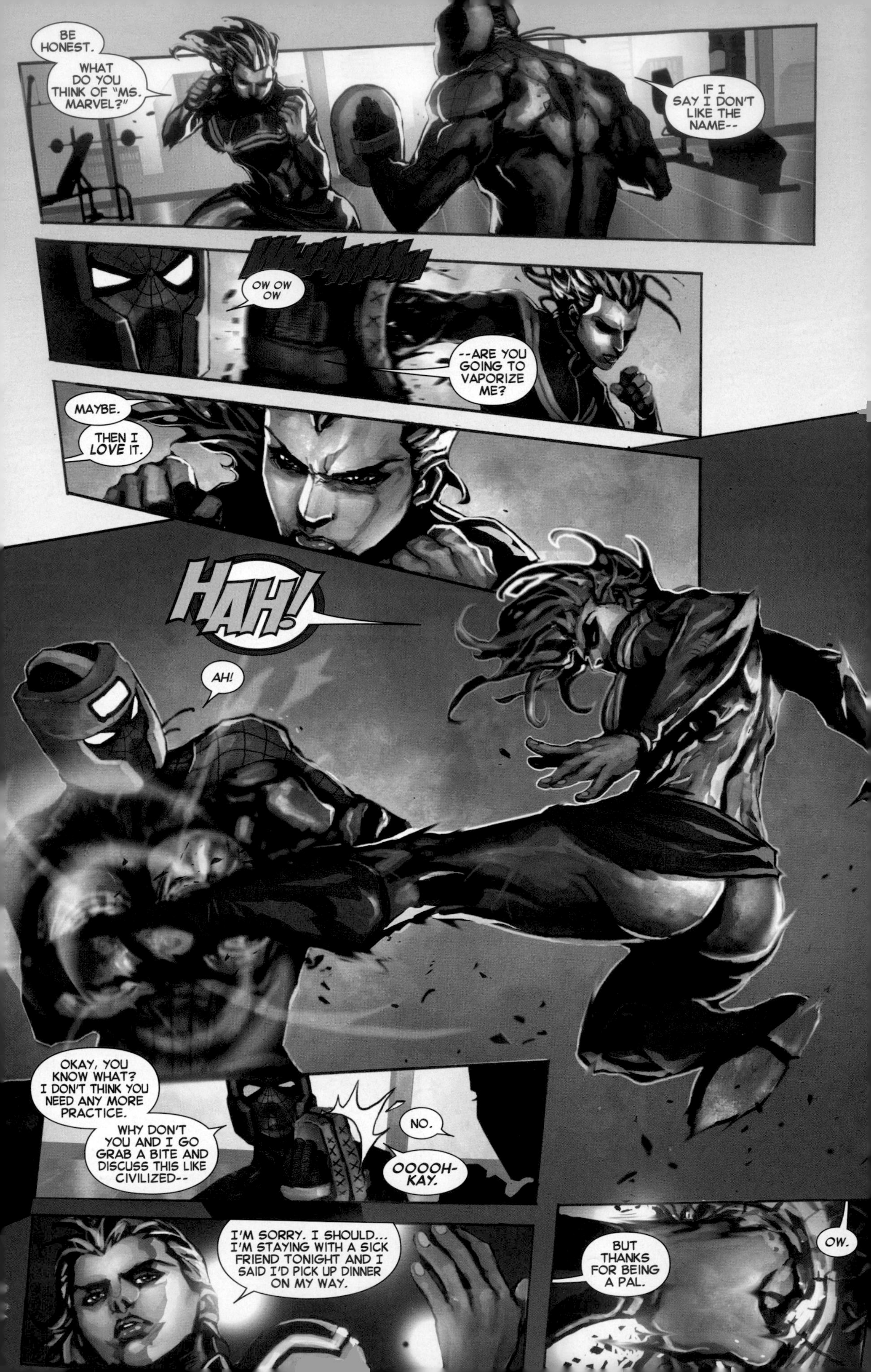
BE HONEST.
WHAT DO YOU THINK OF "MS. MARVEL?"
IF I SAY I DON'T LIKE THE NAME--
OW OW OW
--ARE YOU GOING TO VAPORIZE ME?
MAYBE.
THEN I LOVE IT.
HAH!
AH!
OKAY, YOU KNOW WHAT? I DON'T THINK YOU NEED ANY MORE PRACTICE.
WHY DON'T YOU AND I GO GRAB A BITE AND DISCUSS THIS LIKE CIVILIZED--
NO.
OOOOH-KAY.
I'M SORRY. I SHOULD... I'M STAYING WITH A SICK FRIEND TONIGHT AND I SAID I'D PICK UP DINNER ON MY WAY.
BUT THANKS FOR BEING A PAL.
OW.

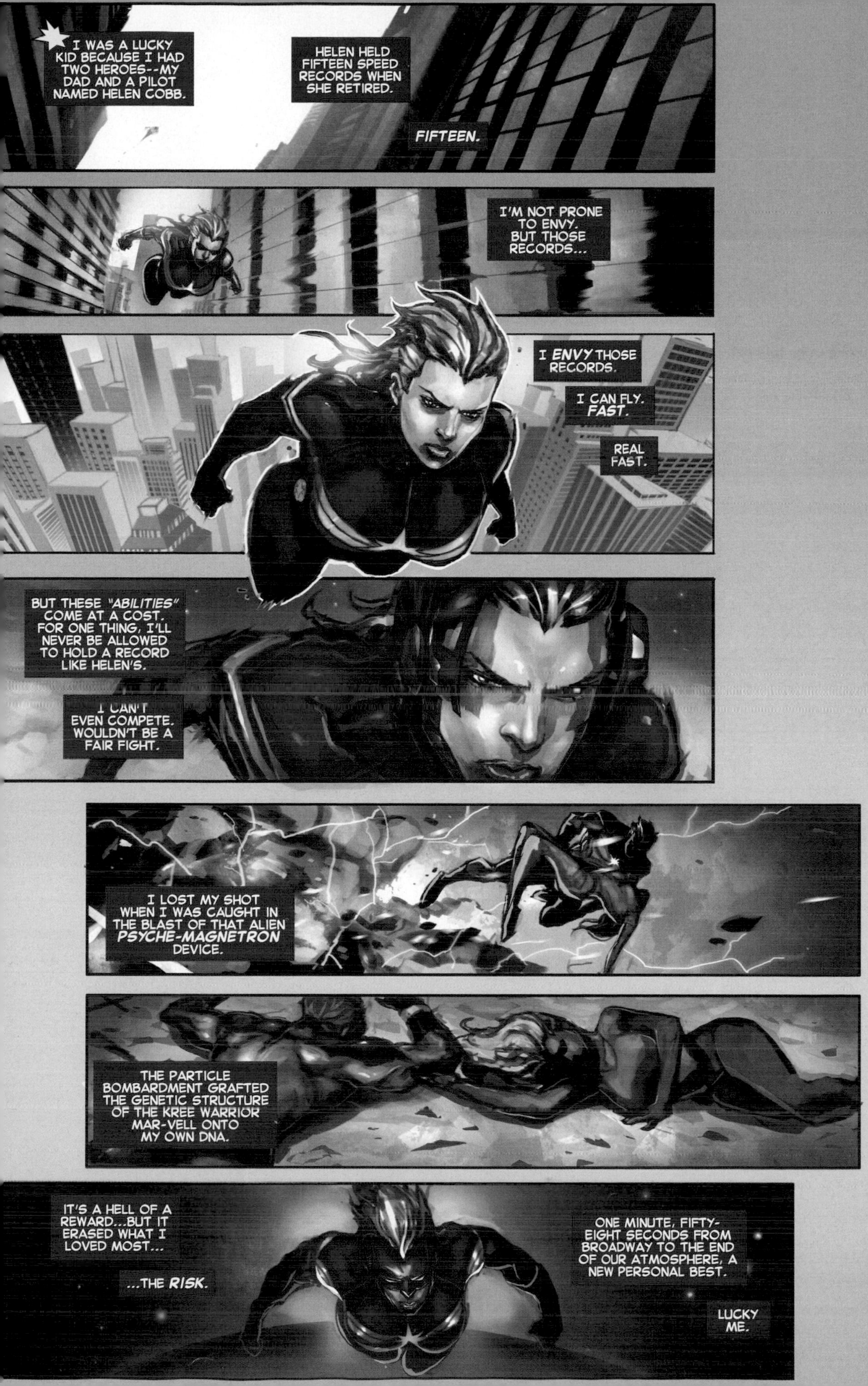
I WAS A LUCKY KID BECAUSE I HAD TWO HEROES--MY DAD AND A PILOT NAMED HELEN COBB.
HELEN HELD FIFTEEN SPEED RECORDS WHEN SHE RETIRED.
FIFTEEN.
I'M NOT PRONE TO ENVY. BUT THOSE RECORDS...
I ENVY THOSE RECORDS.
I CAN FLY. FAST.
REAL FAST.
BUT THESE "ABILITIES" COME AT A COST. FOR ONE THING, I'LL NEVER BE ALLOWED TO HOLD A RECORD LIKE HELEN'S.
I CAN'T EVEN COMPETE. WOULDN'T BE A FAIR FIGHT.
I LOST MY SHOT WHEN I WAS CAUGHT IN THE BLAST OF THAT ALIEN PSYCHE-MAGNETRON DEVICE.
THE PARTICLE BOMBARDMENT GRAFTED THE GENETIC STRUCTURE OF THE KREE WARRIOR MAR-VELL ONTO MY OWN DNA.
IT'S A HELL OF A REWARD...BUT IT ERASED WHAT I LOVED MOST...
...THE RISK.
ONE MINUTE, FIFTY-EIGHT SECONDS FROM BROADWAY TO THE END OF OUR ATMOSPHERE, A NEW PERSONAL BEST.
LUCKY ME.

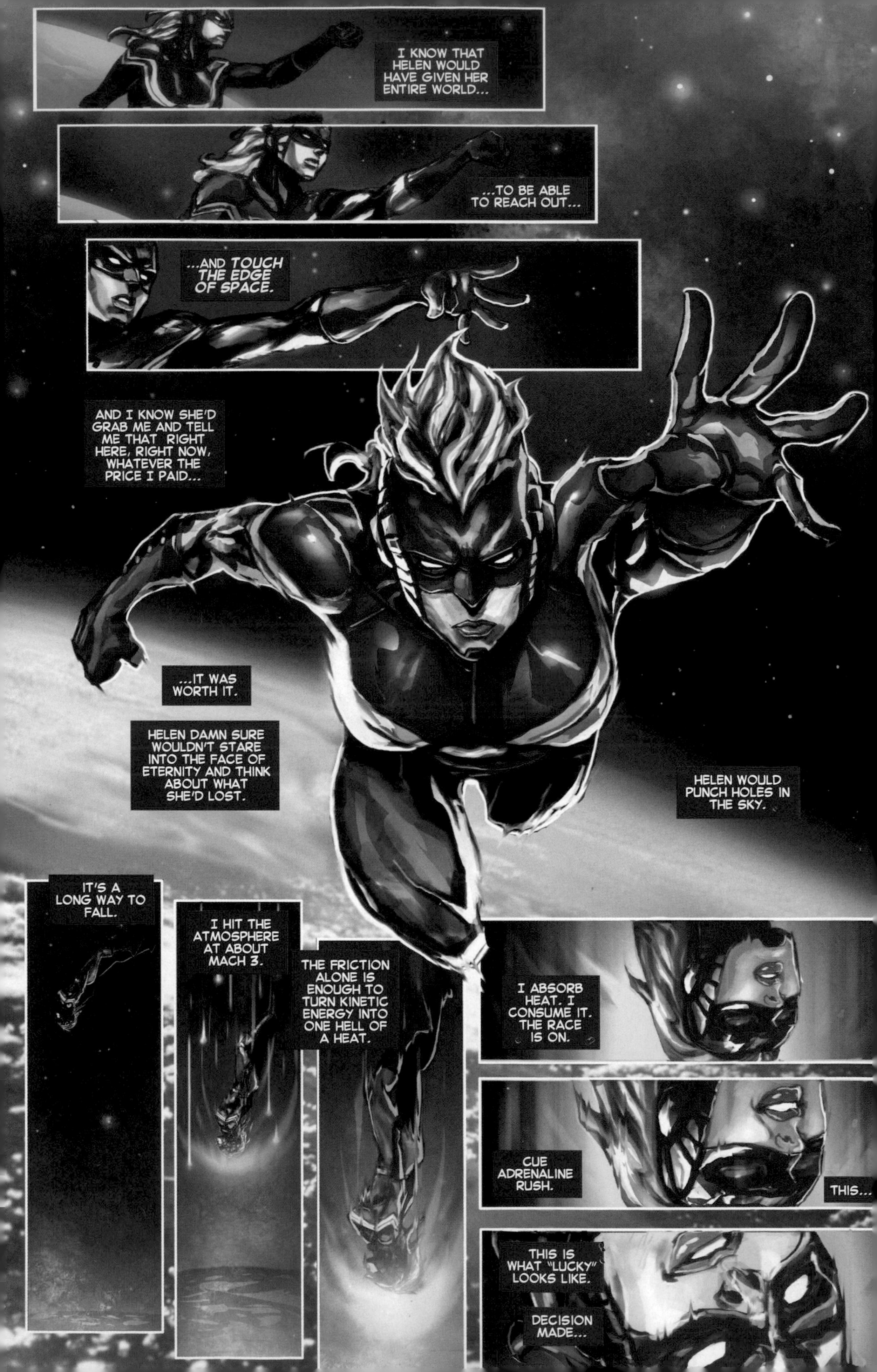
I KNOW THAT HELEN WOULD HAVE GIVEN HER ENTIRE WORLD...
...TO BE ABLE TO REACH OUT...
...AND TOUCH THE EDGE OF SPACE.
AND I KNOW SHE'D GRAB ME AND TELL ME THAT RIGHT HERE, RIGHT NOW, WHATEVER THE PRICE I PAID...
...IT WAS WORTH IT.
HELEN DAMN SURE WOULDN'T STARE INTO THE FACE OF ETERNITY AND THINK ABOUT WHAT SHE'D LOST.
HELEN WOULD PUNCH HOLES IN THE SKY.
IT'S A LONG WAY TO FALL.
I HIT THE ATMOSPHERE AT ABOUT MACH 3.
THE FRICTION ALONE IS ENOUGH TO TURN KINETIC ENERGY INTO ONE HELL OF A HEAT.
I ABSORB HEAT. I CONSUME IT. THE RACE IS ON.
CUE ADRENALINE RUSH.
THIS...
THIS IS WHAT "LUCKY" LOOKS LIKE.
DECISION MADE...

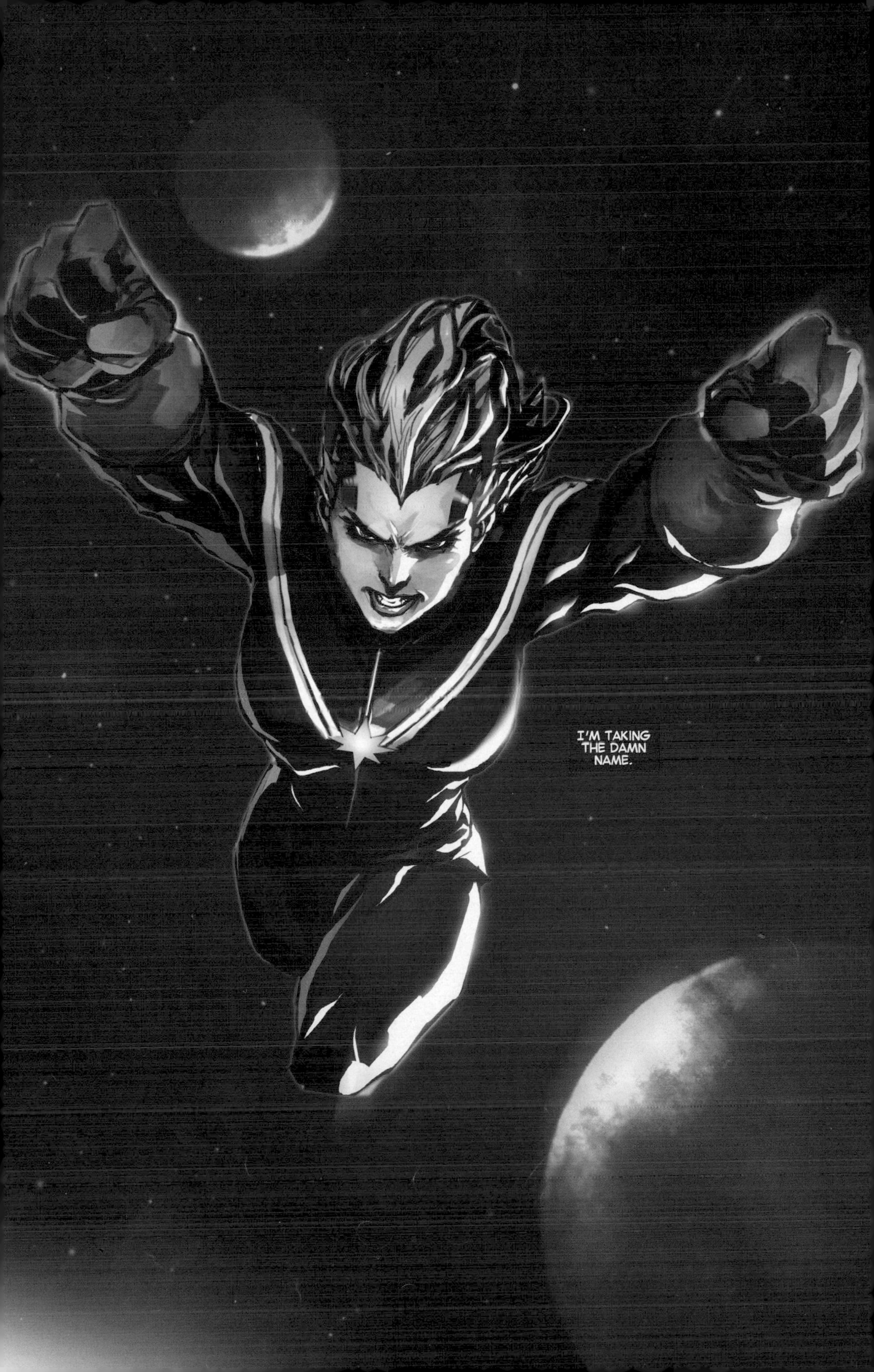
I'M TAKING THE DAMN NAME.

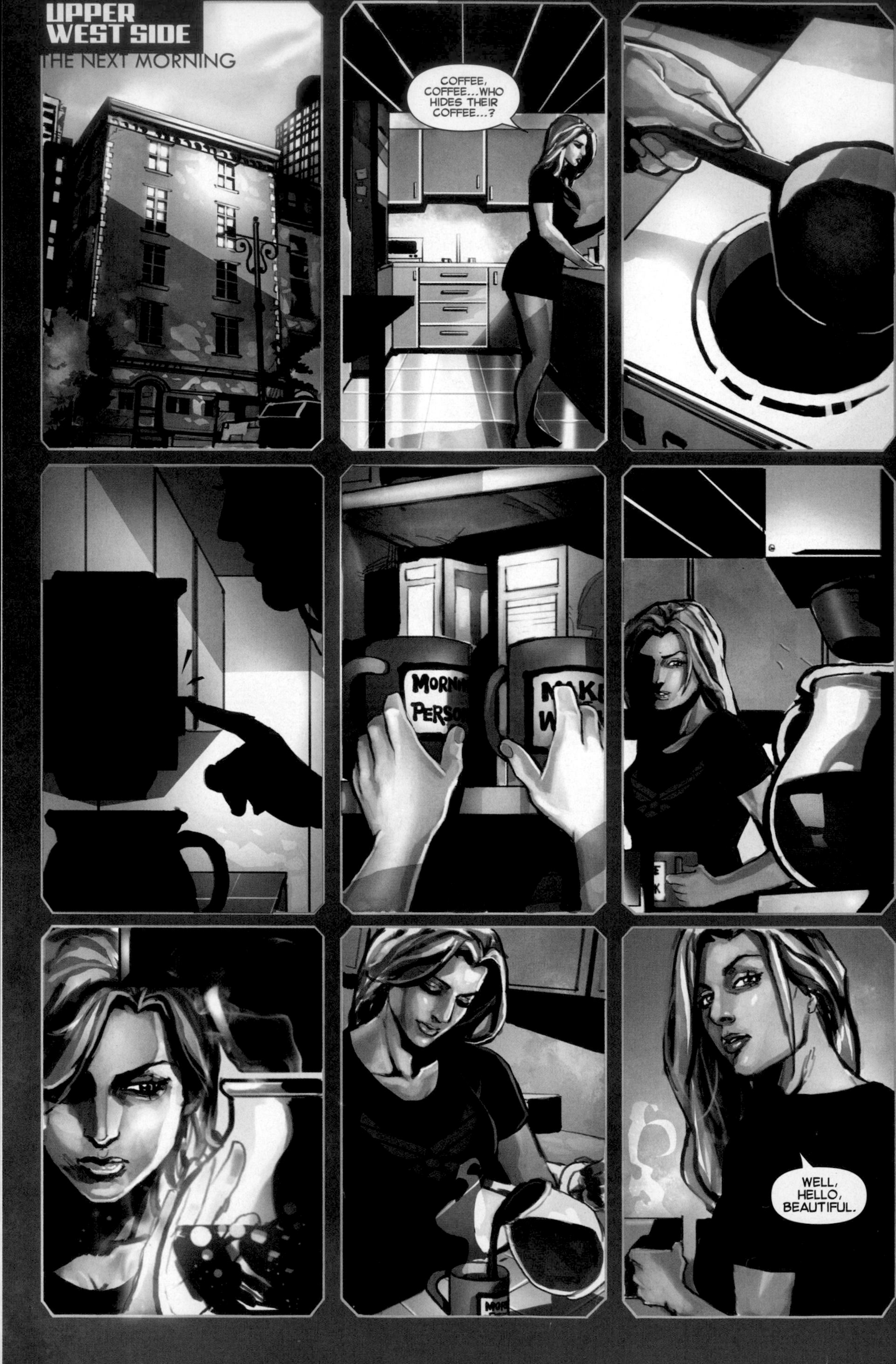
UPPER WEST SIDE
THE NEXT MORNING
COFFEE, COFFEE...WHO HIDES THEIR COFFEE...?
WELL, HELLO, BEAUTIFUL.

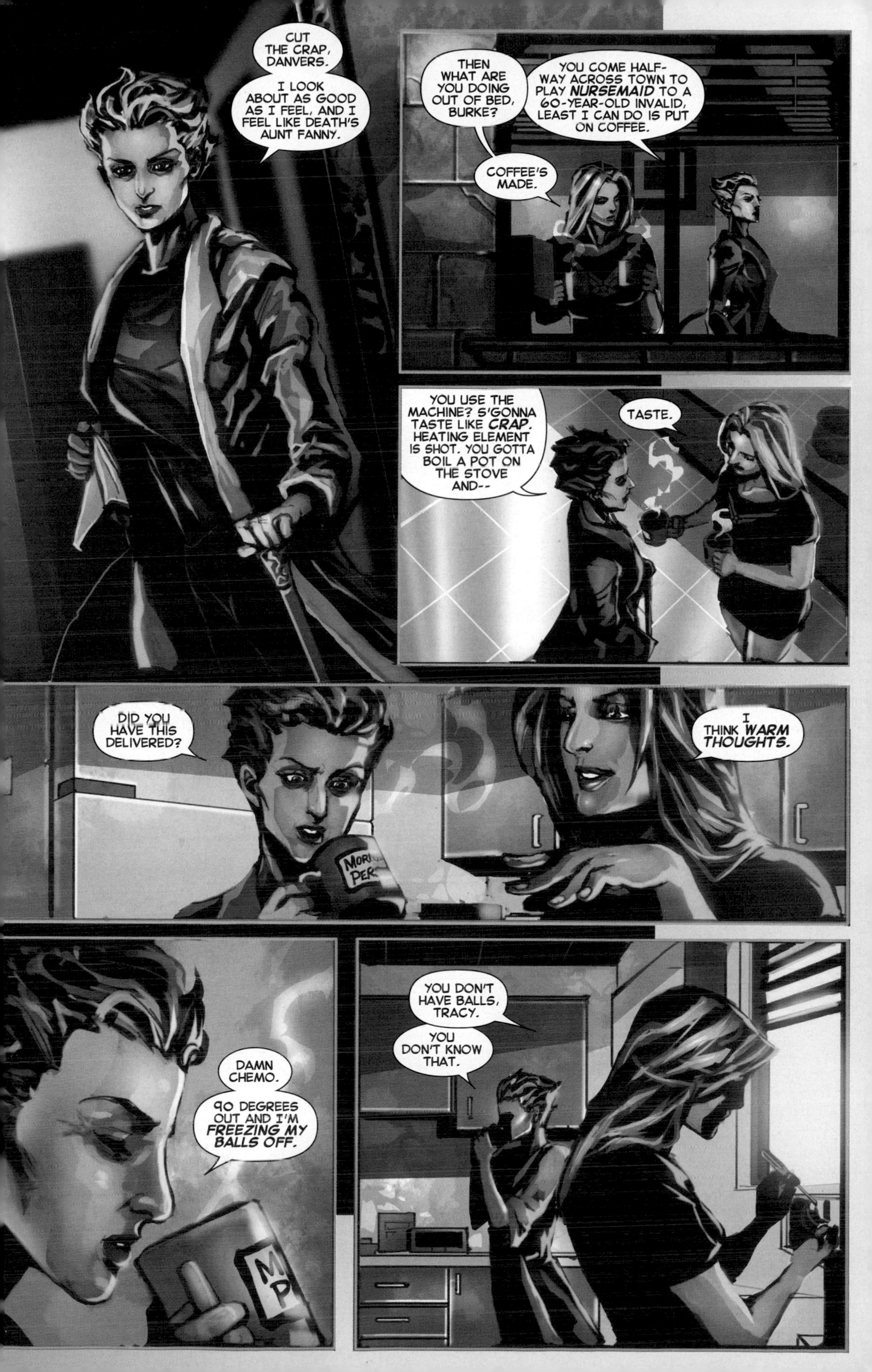

CUT THE CRAP, DANVERS.
I LOOK ABOUT AS GOOD AS I FEEL, AND I FEEL LIKE DEATH'S AUNT FANNY.
THEN WHAT ARE YOU DOING OUT OF BED, BURKE?
COFFEE'S MADE.
YOU COME HALF-WAY ACROSS TOWN TO PLAY NURSEMAID TO A 60-YEAR-OLD INVALID, LEAST I CAN DO IS PUT ON COFFEE.
YOU USE THE MACHINE? S'GONNA TASTE LIKE CRAP. HEATING ELEMENT IS SHOT. YOU GOTTA BOIL A POT ON THE STOVE AND--
TASTE.
DID YOU HAVE THIS DELIVERED?
I THINK WARM THOUGHTS.
DAMN CHEMO.
90 DEGREES OUT AND I'M FREEZING MY BALLS OFF.
YOU DON'T HAVE BALLS, TRACY.
YOU DON'T KNOW THAT.

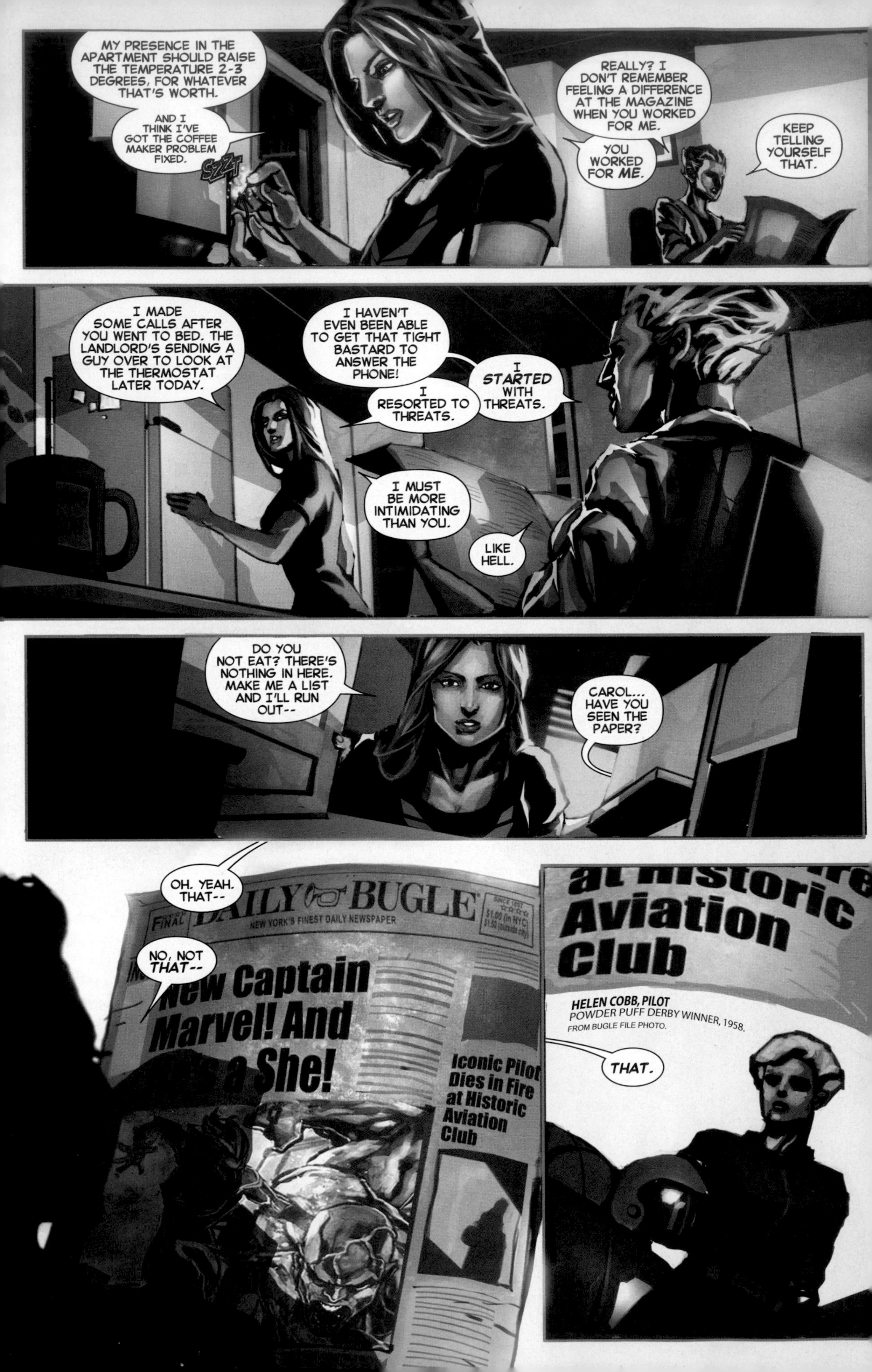
MY PRESENCE IN THE APARTMENT SHOULD RAISE THE TEMPERATURE 2-3 DEGREES, FOR WHATEVER THAT'S WORTH.
AND I THINK I'VE GOT THE COFFEE MAKER PROBLEM FIXED.
SZZT
REALLY? I DON'T REMEMBER FEELING A DIFFERENCE AT THE MAGAZINE WHEN YOU WORKED FOR ME.
YOU WORKED FOR *ME*.
KEEP TELLING YOURSELF THAT.
I MADE SOME CALLS AFTER YOU WENT TO BED. THE LANDLORD'S SENDING A GUY OVER TO LOOK AT THE THERMOSTAT LATER TODAY.
I HAVEN'T EVEN BEEN ABLE TO GET THAT TIGHT BASTARD TO ANSWER THE PHONE!
I RESORTED TO THREATS.
I *STARTED* WITH THREATS.
I MUST BE MORE INTIMIDATING THAN YOU.
LIKE HELL.
DO YOU NOT EAT? THERE'S NOTHING IN HERE. MAKE ME A LIST AND I'LL RUN OUT--
CAROL... HAVE YOU SEEN THE PAPER?
OH. YEAH. THAT--
DAILY BUGLE
NEW YORK'S FINEST DAILY NEWSPAPER
FINAL
$1.00 (in NYC) $1.50 (outside city)
NO, NOT *THAT*--
New Captain Marvel! And ... a She!
Iconic Pilot Dies in Fire at Historic Aviation Club
at Historic Aviation Club
HELEN COBB, PILOT
POWDER PUFF DERBY WINNER, 1958.
FROM BUGLE FILE PHOTO.
THAT.

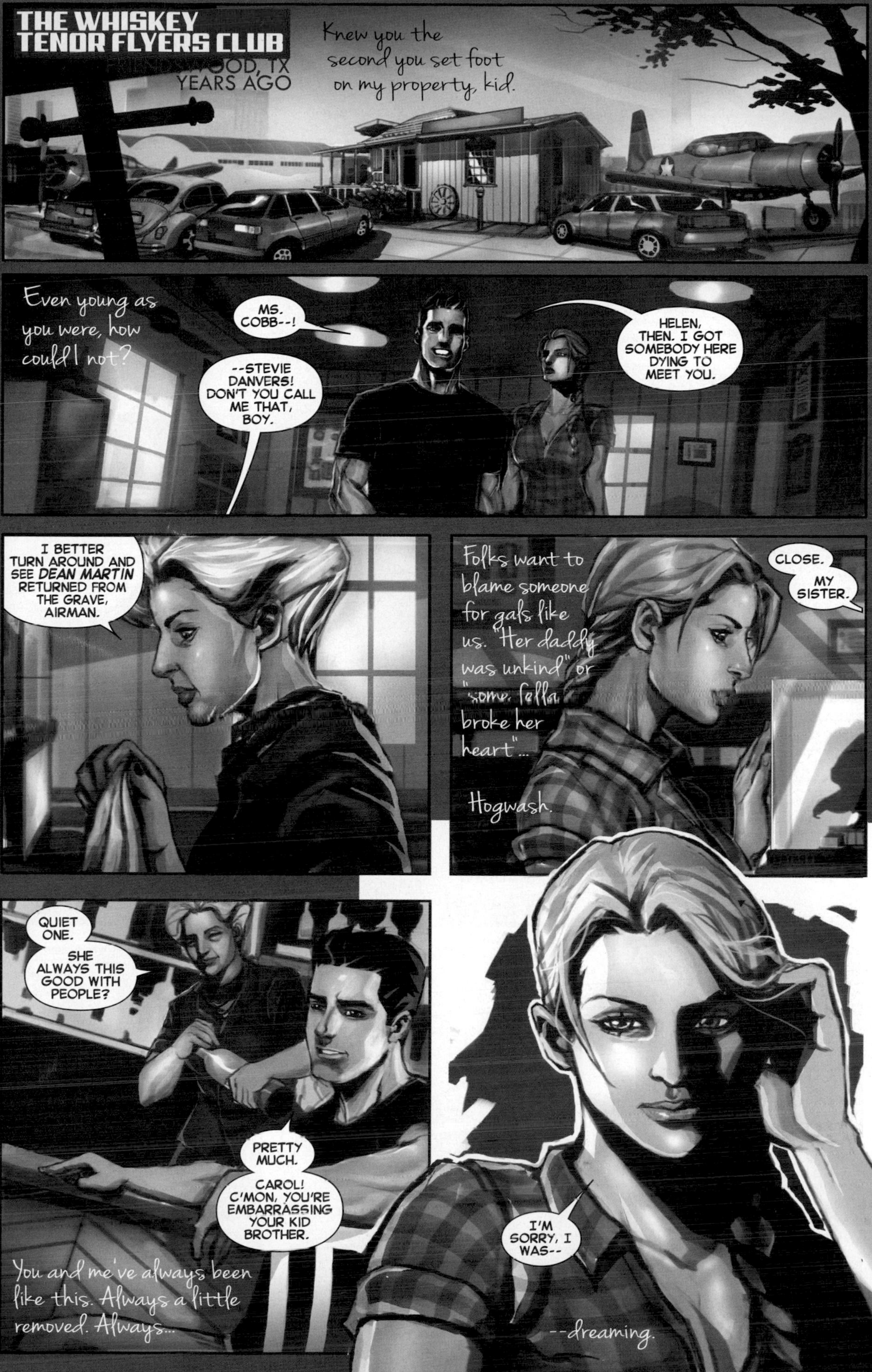

THE WHISKEY TENOR FLYERS CLUB
DSWOOD, TX
YEARS AGO
Knew you the second you set foot on my property, kid.
Even young as you were, how could I not?
MS. COBB--!
--STEVIE DANVERS! DON'T YOU CALL ME THAT, BOY.
HELEN, THEN. I GOT SOMEBODY HERE DYING TO MEET YOU.
I BETTER TURN AROUND AND SEE DEAN MARTIN RETURNED FROM THE GRAVE, AIRMAN.
Folks want to blame someone for gals like us. "Her daddy was unkind" or "some fella broke her heart"...
Hogwash.
CLOSE.
MY SISTER.
QUIET ONE.
SHE ALWAYS THIS GOOD WITH PEOPLE?
PRETTY MUCH.
CAROL! C'MON, YOU'RE EMBARRASSING YOUR KID BROTHER.
I'M SORRY, I WAS--
You and me've always been like this. Always a little removed. Always...
--dreaming.

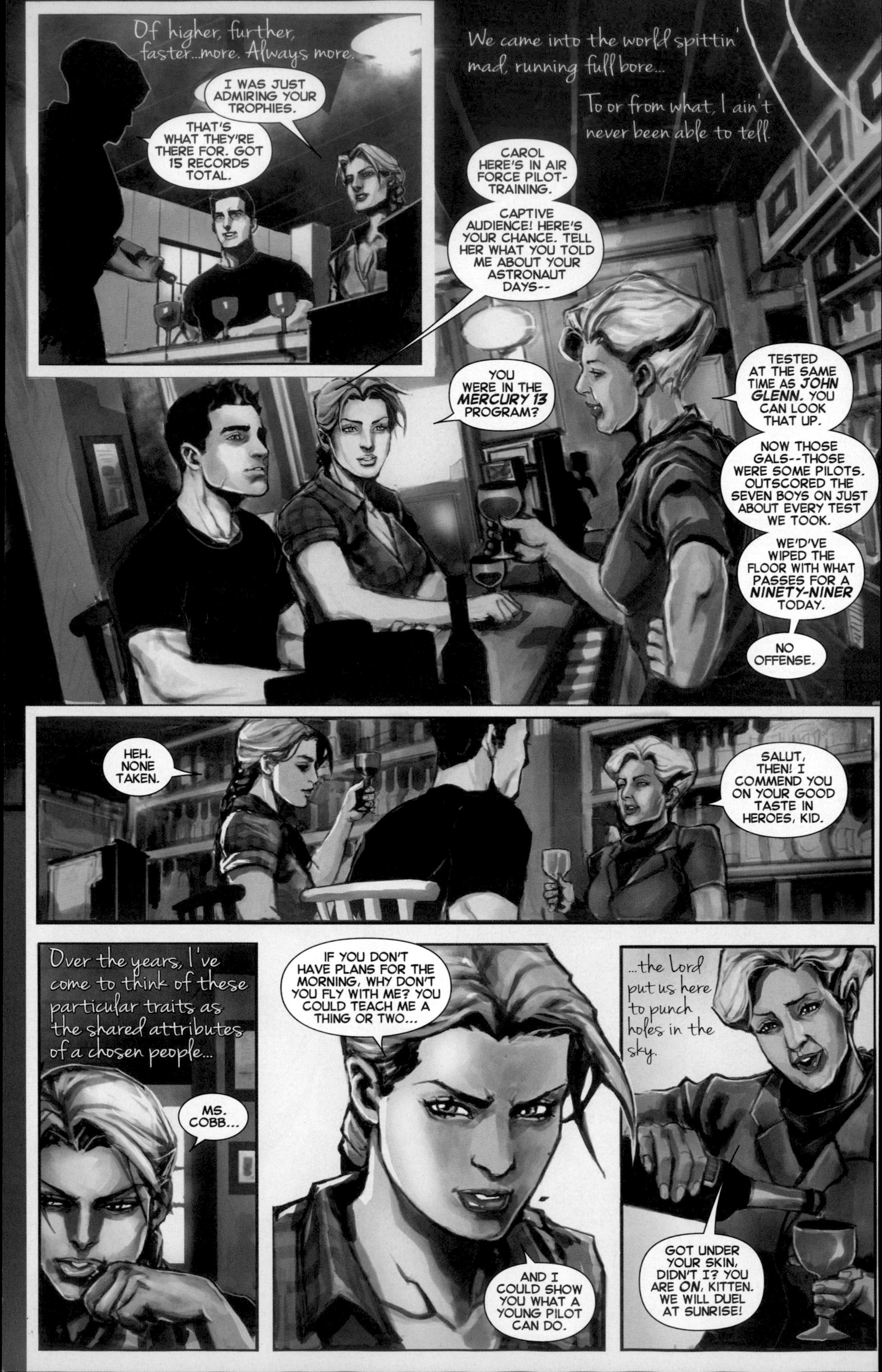

Of higher, further, faster...more. Always more.
I WAS JUST ADMIRING YOUR TROPHIES.
THAT'S WHAT THEY'RE THERE FOR. GOT 15 RECORDS TOTAL.
We came into the world spittin' mad, running full bore...
To or from what, I ain't never been able to tell.
CAROL HERE'S IN AIR FORCE PILOT-TRAINING.
CAPTIVE AUDIENCE! HERE'S YOUR CHANCE. TELL HER WHAT YOU TOLD ME ABOUT YOUR ASTRONAUT DAYS--
YOU WERE IN THE MERCURY 13 PROGRAM?
TESTED AT THE SAME TIME AS JOHN GLENN. YOU CAN LOOK THAT UP.
NOW THOSE GALS--THOSE WERE SOME PILOTS. OUTSCORED THE SEVEN BOYS ON JUST ABOUT EVERY TEST WE TOOK.
WE'D'VE WIPED THE FLOOR WITH WHAT PASSES FOR A NINETY-NINER TODAY.
NO OFFENSE.
HEH. NONE TAKEN.
SALUT, THEN! I COMMEND YOU ON YOUR GOOD TASTE IN HEROES, KID.
Over the years, I've come to think of these particular traits as the shared attributes of a chosen people...
MS. COBB...
IF YOU DON'T HAVE PLANS FOR THE MORNING, WHY DON'T YOU FLY WITH ME? YOU COULD TEACH ME A THING OR TWO...
AND I COULD SHOW YOU WHAT A YOUNG PILOT CAN DO.
...the Lord put us here to punch holes in the sky.
GOT UNDER YOUR SKIN, DIDN'T I? YOU ARE ON, KITTEN. WE WILL DUEL AT SUNRISE!

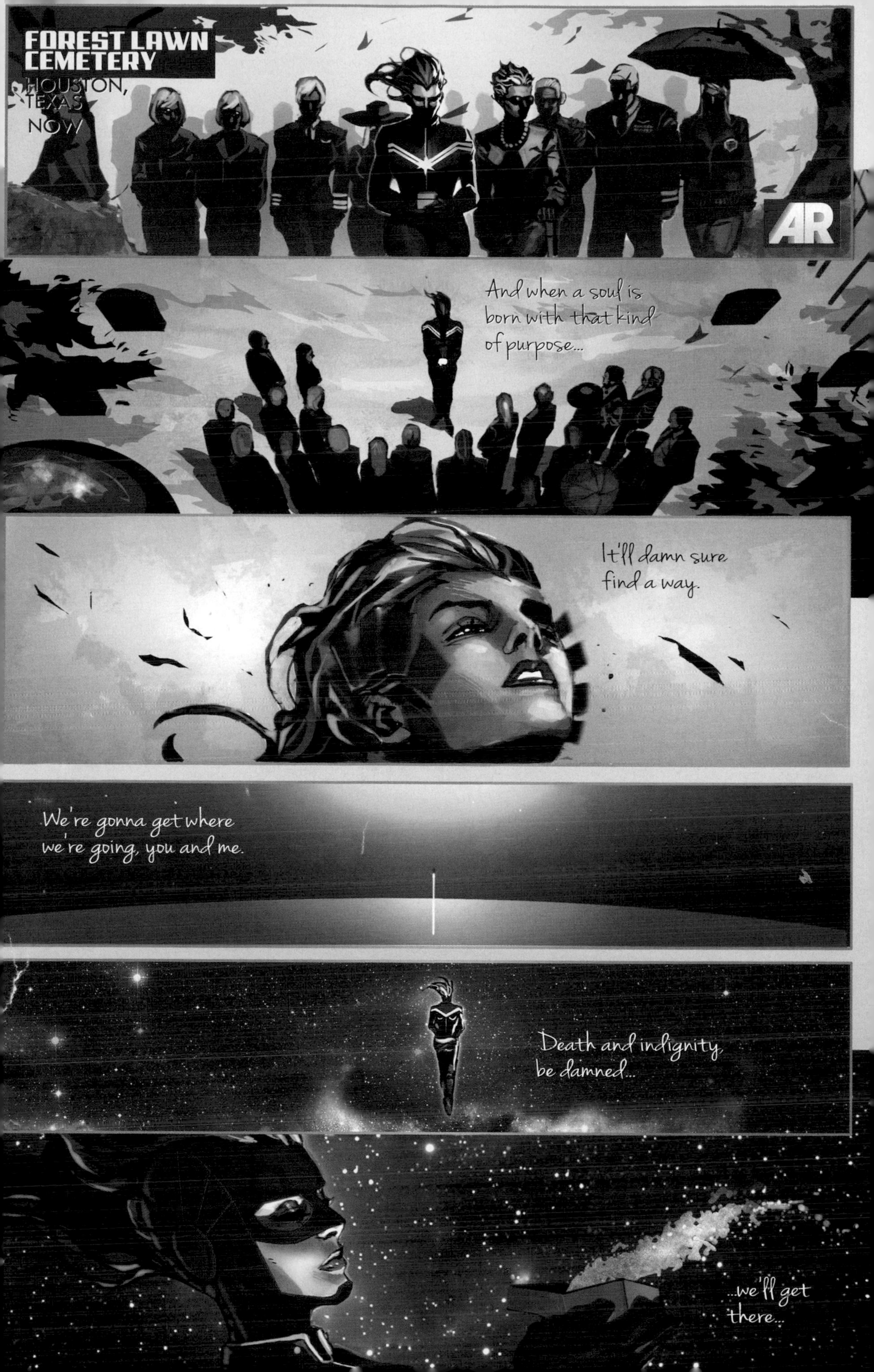

FOREST LAWN CEMETERY
HOUSTON, TEXAS NOW
AR
And when a soul is born with that kind of purpose...
It'll damn sure find a way.
We're gonna get where we're going, you and me.
Death and indignity, be damned...
...we'll get there...

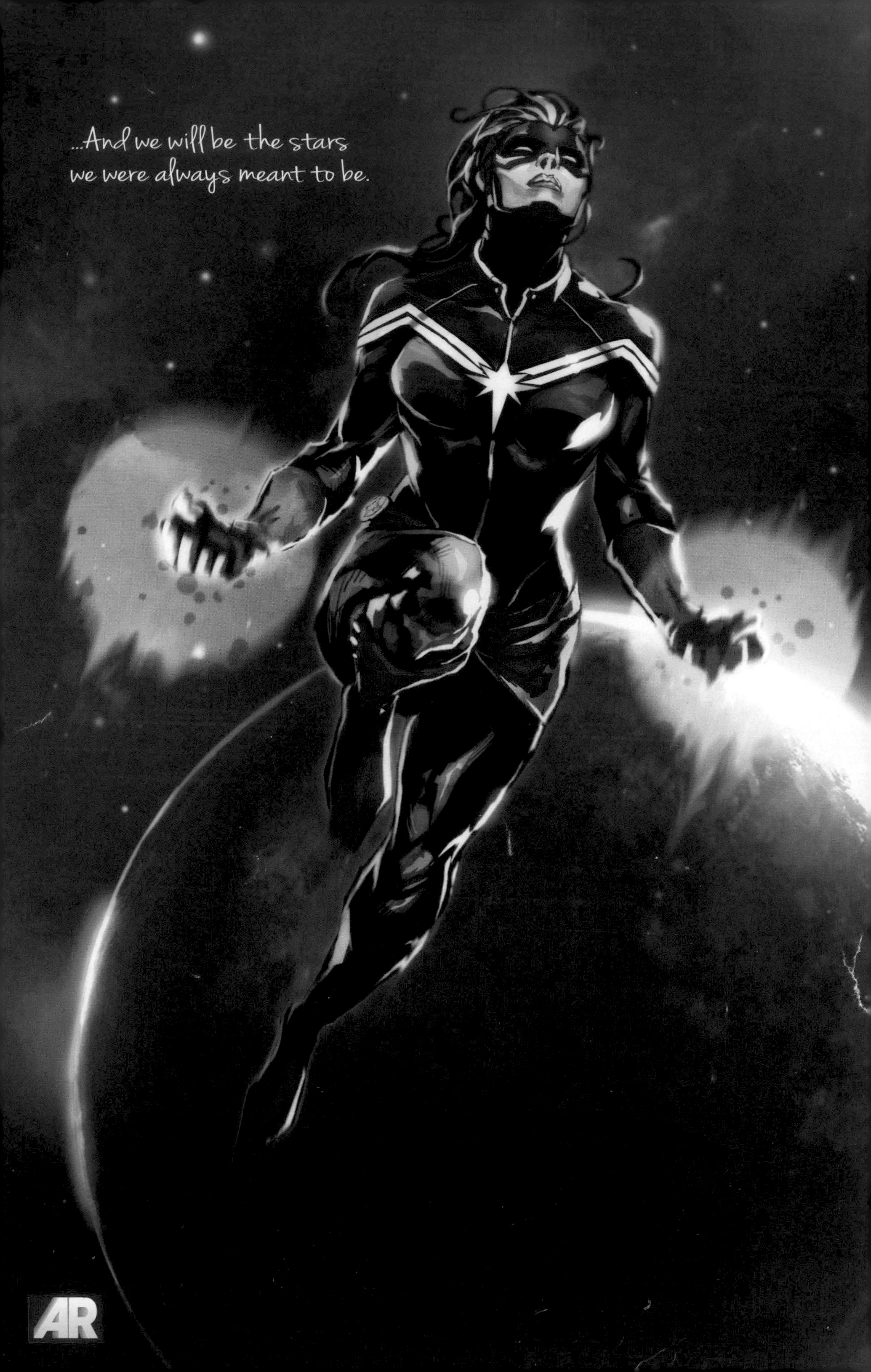
...And we will be the stars
we were always meant to be.
AR

AMAZING SPIDER-MAN #654 (2011)

FLASH THOMPSON'S FIRST APPEARANCE AS AGENT VENOM!

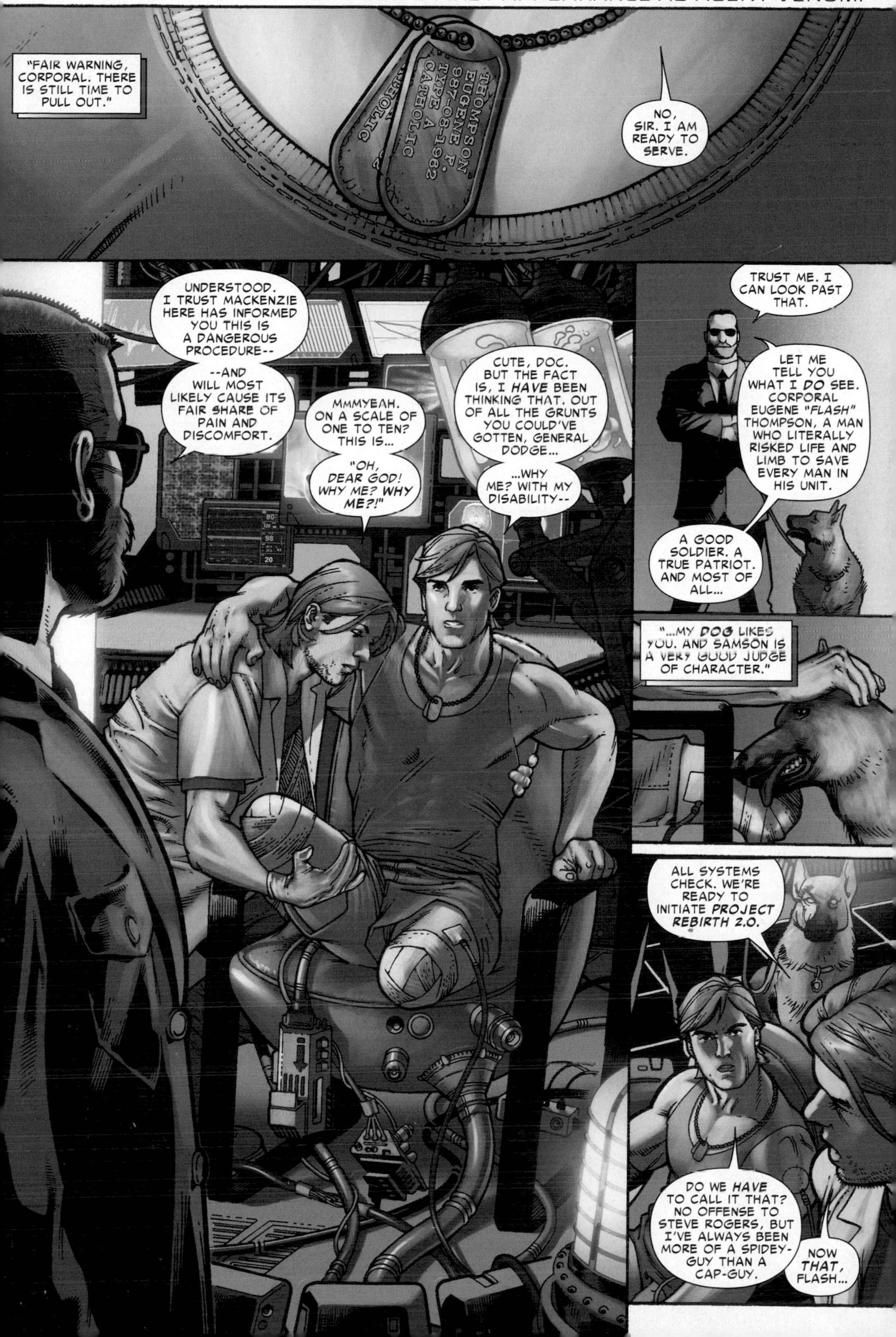
"FAIR WARNING, CORPORAL. THERE IS STILL TIME TO PULL OUT."
THOMPSON EUGENE F. 987-08-1962 TYPE A CATHOLIC
NO, SIR. I AM READY TO SERVE.
UNDERSTOOD. I TRUST MACKENZIE HERE HAS INFORMED YOU THIS IS A DANGEROUS PROCEDURE--
--AND WILL MOST LIKELY CAUSE ITS FAIR SHARE OF PAIN AND DISCOMFORT.
MMMYEAH. ON A SCALE OF ONE TO TEN? THIS IS...
"OH, DEAR GOD! WHY ME? WHY ME?!"
CUTE, DOC. BUT THE FACT IS, I HAVE BEEN THINKING THAT. OUT OF ALL THE GRUNTS YOU COULD'VE GOTTEN, GENERAL DODGE...
...WHY ME? WITH MY DISABILITY--
TRUST ME. I CAN LOOK PAST THAT.
LET ME TELL YOU WHAT I DO SEE. CORPORAL EUGENE "FLASH" THOMPSON, A MAN WHO LITERALLY RISKED LIFE AND LIMB TO SAVE EVERY MAN IN HIS UNIT.
A GOOD SOLDIER. A TRUE PATRIOT. AND MOST OF ALL...
"...MY DOG LIKES YOU. AND SAMSON IS A VERY GOOD JUDGE OF CHARACTER."
ALL SYSTEMS CHECK. WE'RE READY TO INITIATE PROJECT REBIRTH 2.0.
DO WE HAVE TO CALL IT THAT? NO OFFENSE TO STEVE ROGERS, BUT I'VE ALWAYS BEEN MORE OF A SPIDEY-GUY THAN A CAP-GUY.
NOW THAT, FLASH...

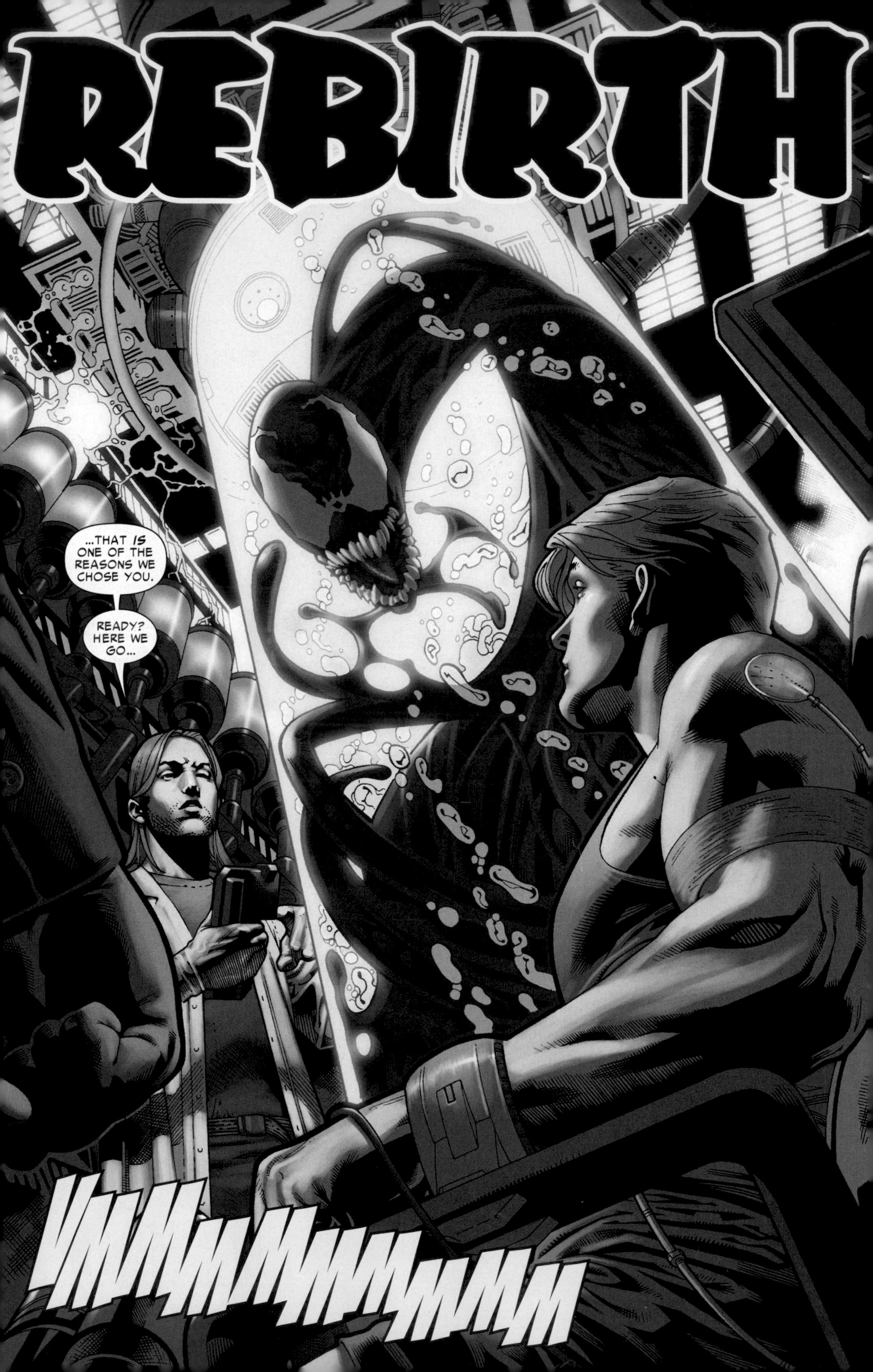
REBIRTH
...THAT IS ONE OF THE REASONS WE CHOSE YOU.
READY? HERE WE GO...
VMMMMMMMMMMMMM

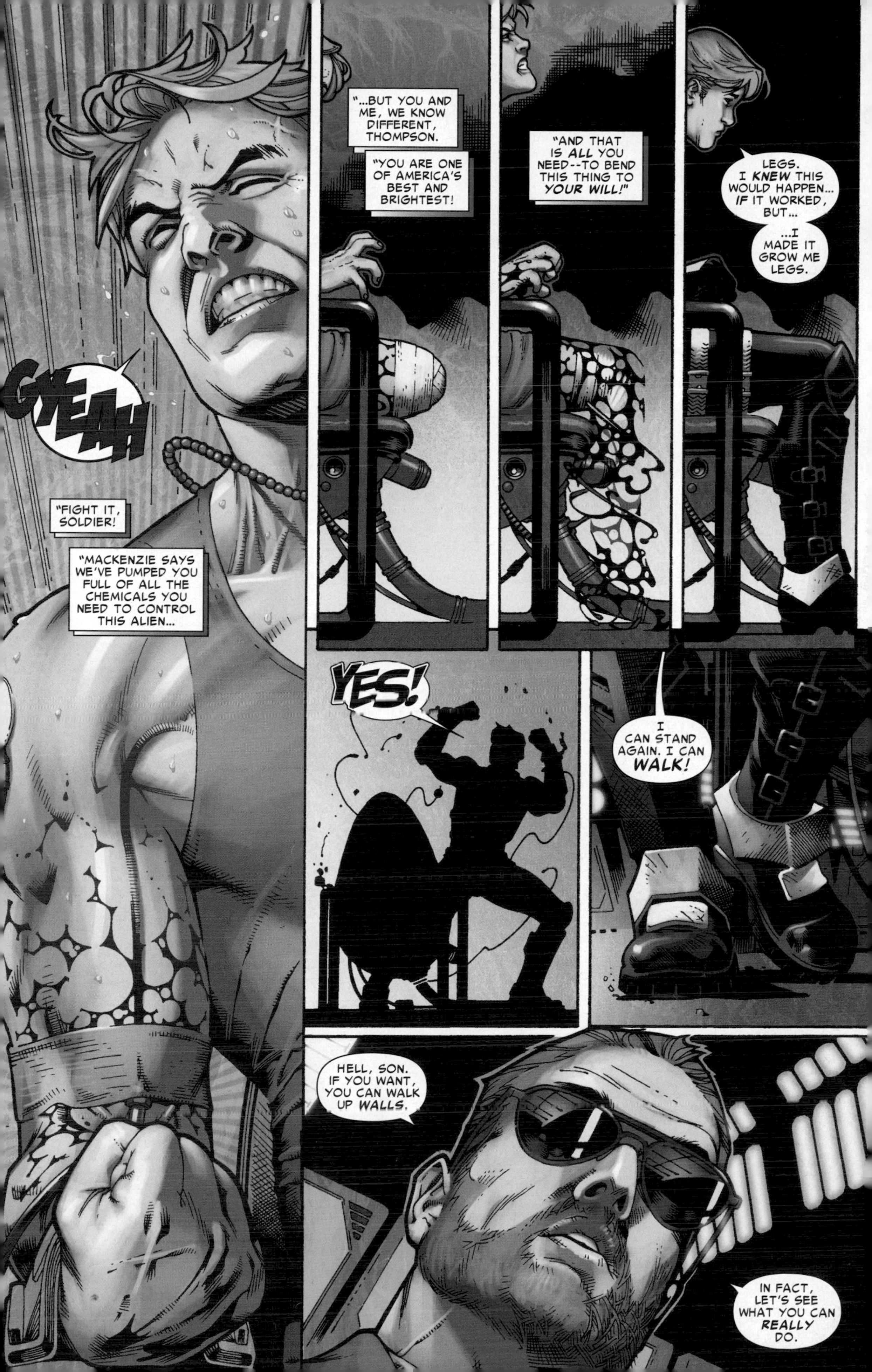
GYEAHH
"FIGHT IT, SOLDIER!
"MACKENZIE SAYS WE'VE PUMPED YOU FULL OF ALL THE CHEMICALS YOU NEED TO CONTROL THIS ALIEN...
"...BUT YOU AND ME, WE KNOW DIFFERENT, THOMPSON.
"YOU ARE ONE OF AMERICA'S BEST AND BRIGHTEST!
"AND THAT IS ALL YOU NEED--TO BEND THIS THING TO YOUR WILL!"
LEGS. I KNEW THIS WOULD HAPPEN... IF IT WORKED, BUT...
...I MADE IT GROW ME LEGS.
YES!
I CAN STAND AGAIN. I CAN WALK!
HELL, SON. IF YOU WANT, YOU CAN WALK UP WALLS.
IN FACT, LET'S SEE WHAT YOU CAN REALLY DO.

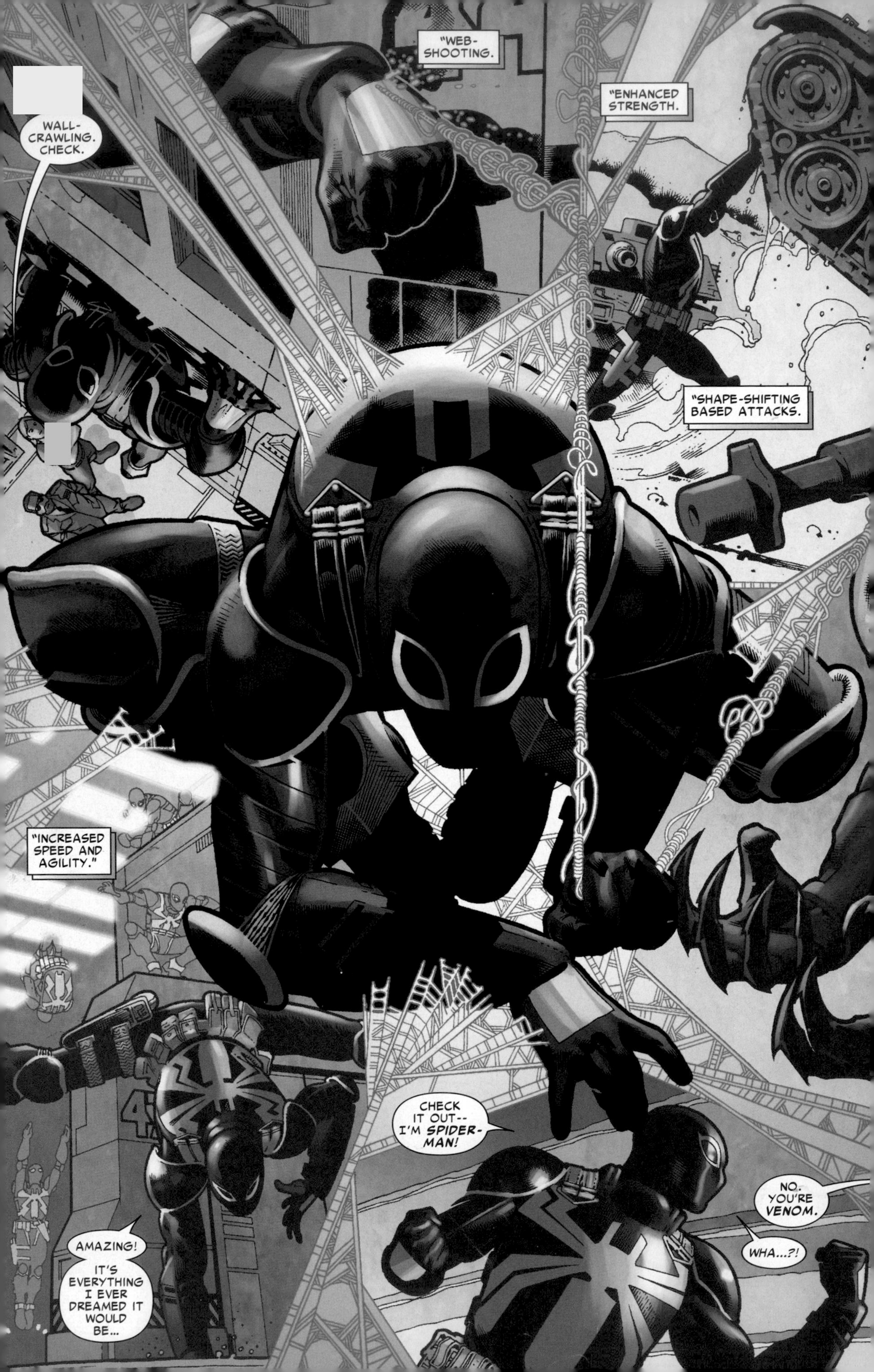
WALL-CRAWLING. CHECK.
"WEB-SHOOTING.
"ENHANCED STRENGTH.
"SHAPE-SHIFTING BASED ATTACKS.
"INCREASED SPEED AND AGILITY."
CHECK IT OUT-- I'M SPIDER-MAN!
NO. YOU'RE VENOM.
WHA...?!
AMAZING!
IT'S EVERYTHING I EVER DREAMED IT WOULD BE...

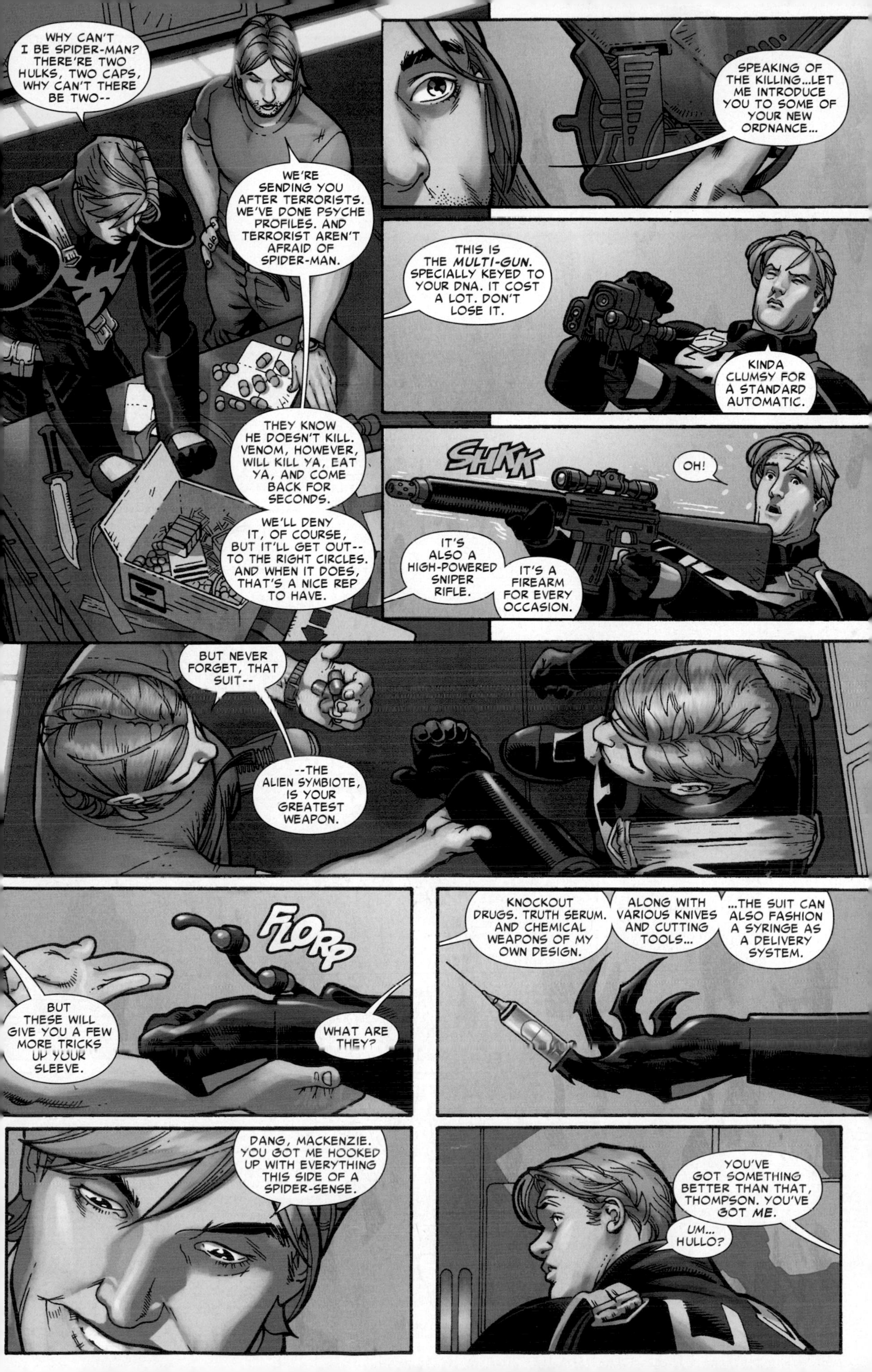

WHY CAN'T I BE SPIDER-MAN? THERE'RE TWO HULKS, TWO CAPS, WHY CAN'T THERE BE TWO--
WE'RE SENDING YOU AFTER TERRORISTS. WE'VE DONE PSYCHE PROFILES. AND TERRORIST AREN'T AFRAID OF SPIDER-MAN.
THEY KNOW HE DOESN'T KILL. VENOM, HOWEVER, WILL KILL YA, EAT YA, AND COME BACK FOR SECONDS.
WE'LL DENY IT, OF COURSE, BUT IT'LL GET OUT-- TO THE RIGHT CIRCLES. AND WHEN IT DOES, THAT'S A NICE REP TO HAVE.
SPEAKING OF THE KILLING...LET ME INTRODUCE YOU TO SOME OF YOUR NEW ORDNANCE...
THIS IS THE *MULTI-GUN.* SPECIALLY KEYED TO YOUR DNA. IT COST A LOT. DON'T LOSE IT.
KINDA CLUMSY FOR A STANDARD AUTOMATIC.
SHKK
OH!
IT'S ALSO A HIGH-POWERED SNIPER RIFLE.
IT'S A FIREARM FOR EVERY OCCASION.
BUT NEVER FORGET, THAT SUIT--
--THE ALIEN SYMBIOTE, IS YOUR GREATEST WEAPON.
FLORP
BUT THESE WILL GIVE YOU A FEW MORE TRICKS UP YOUR SLEEVE.
WHAT ARE THEY?
KNOCKOUT DRUGS. TRUTH SERUM. AND CHEMICAL WEAPONS OF MY OWN DESIGN.
ALONG WITH VARIOUS KNIVES AND CUTTING TOOLS...
...THE SUIT CAN ALSO FASHION A SYRINGE AS A DELIVERY SYSTEM.
DANG, MACKENZIE. YOU GOT ME HOOKED UP WITH EVERYTHING THIS SIDE OF A SPIDER-SENSE.
YOU'VE GOT SOMETHING BETTER THAN THAT, THOMPSON. YOU'VE GOT *ME*.
UM... HULLO?

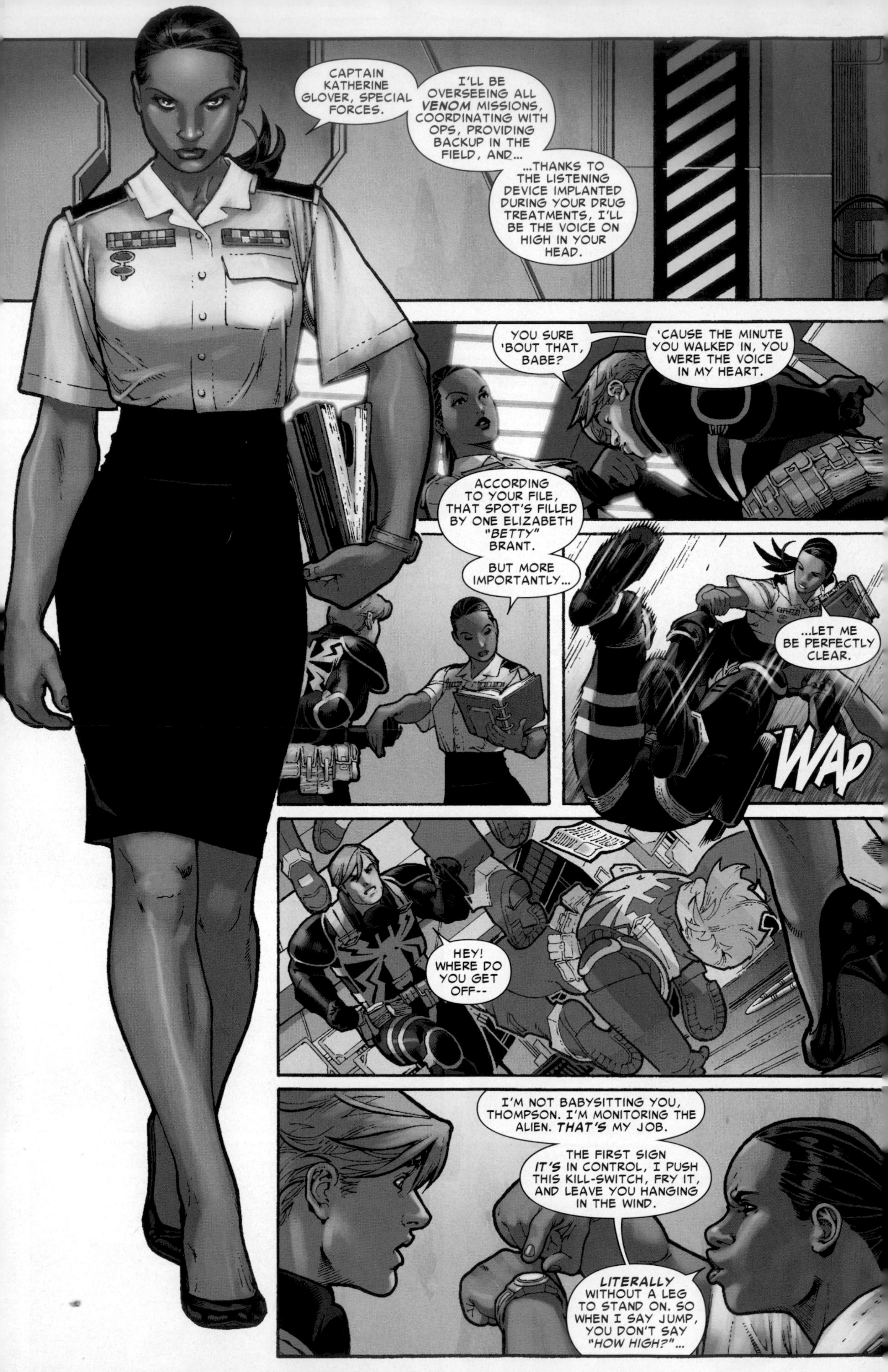
CAPTAIN KATHERINE GLOVER, SPECIAL FORCES.
I'LL BE OVERSEEING ALL VENOM MISSIONS, COORDINATING WITH OPS, PROVIDING BACKUP IN THE FIELD, AND...
...THANKS TO THE LISTENING DEVICE IMPLANTED DURING YOUR DRUG TREATMENTS, I'LL BE THE VOICE ON HIGH IN YOUR HEAD.
YOU SURE 'BOUT THAT, BABE?
'CAUSE THE MINUTE YOU WALKED IN, YOU WERE THE VOICE IN MY HEART.
ACCORDING TO YOUR FILE, THAT SPOT'S FILLED BY ONE ELIZABETH "BETTY" BRANT.
BUT MORE IMPORTANTLY...
...LET ME BE PERFECTLY CLEAR.
WAP
HEY! WHERE DO YOU GET OFF--
I'M NOT BABYSITTING YOU, THOMPSON. I'M MONITORING THE ALIEN. THAT'S MY JOB.
THE FIRST SIGN IT'S IN CONTROL, I PUSH THIS KILL-SWITCH, FRY IT, AND LEAVE YOU HANGING IN THE WIND.
LITERALLY WITHOUT A LEG TO STAND ON. SO WHEN I SAY JUMP, YOU DON'T SAY "HOW HIGH?"...

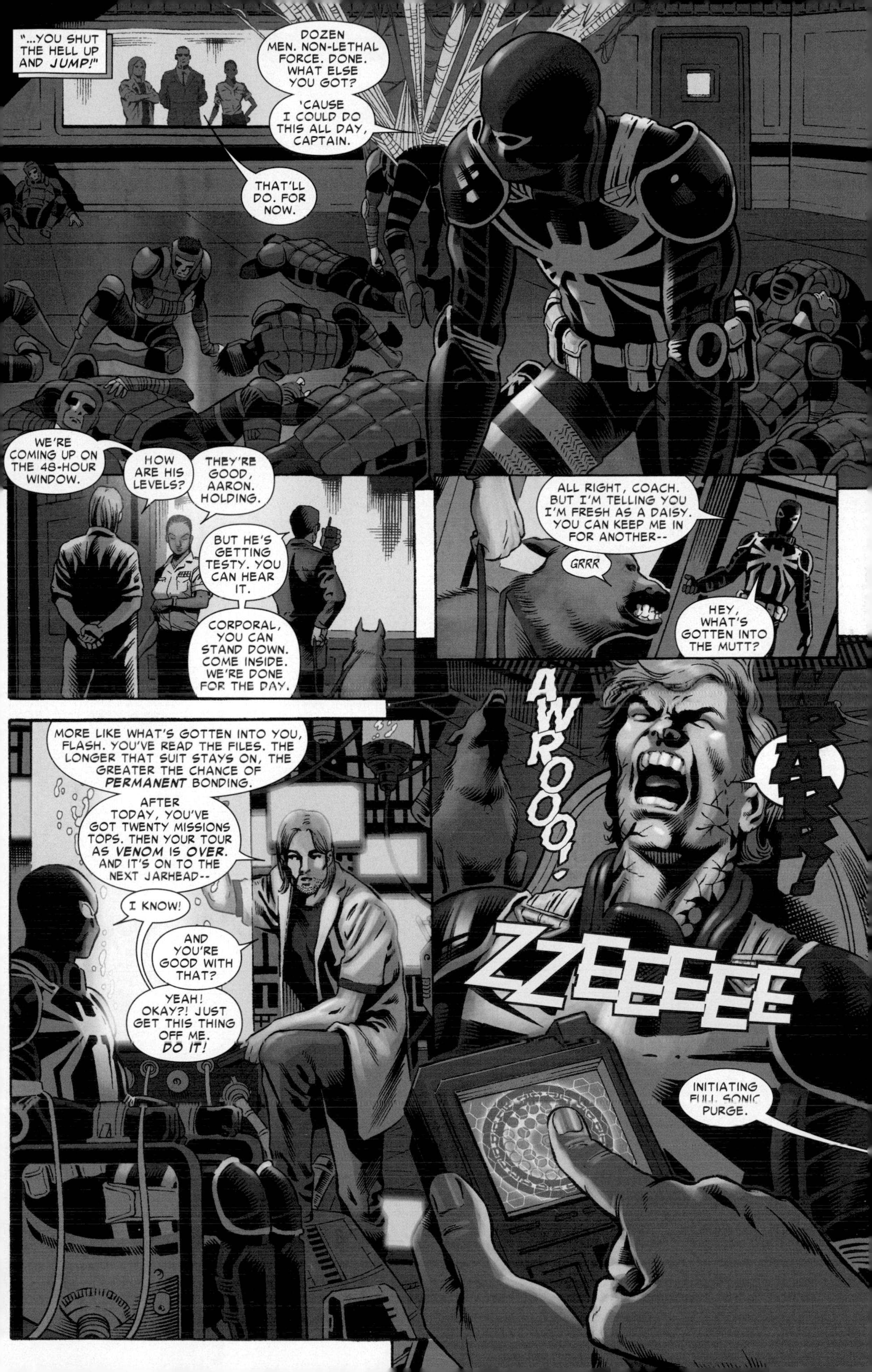
"...YOU SHUT THE HELL UP AND *JUMP!*"
DOZEN MEN. NON-LETHAL FORCE. DONE. WHAT ELSE YOU GOT?
'CAUSE I COULD DO THIS ALL DAY, CAPTAIN.
THAT'LL DO. FOR NOW.
WE'RE COMING UP ON THE 48-HOUR WINDOW.
HOW ARE HIS LEVELS?
THEY'RE GOOD, AARON. HOLDING.
BUT HE'S GETTING TESTY. YOU CAN HEAR IT.
CORPORAL, YOU CAN STAND DOWN. COME INSIDE. WE'RE DONE FOR THE DAY.
ALL RIGHT, COACH. BUT I'M TELLING YOU I'M FRESH AS A DAISY. YOU CAN KEEP ME IN FOR ANOTHER--
GRRR
HEY, WHAT'S GOTTEN INTO THE MUTT?
MORE LIKE WHAT'S GOTTEN INTO YOU, FLASH. YOU'VE READ THE FILES. THE LONGER THAT SUIT STAYS ON, THE GREATER THE CHANCE OF *PERMANENT* BONDING.
AFTER TODAY, YOU'VE GOT TWENTY MISSIONS TOPS. THEN YOUR TOUR AS *VENOM* IS *OVER*. AND IT'S ON TO THE NEXT JARHEAD--
I KNOW!
AND YOU'RE GOOD WITH THAT?
YEAH! OKAY?! JUST GET THIS THING OFF ME. *DO IT!*
AWROOO!
KRAK
ZZEEEEEE
INITIATING FULL SONIC PURGE.

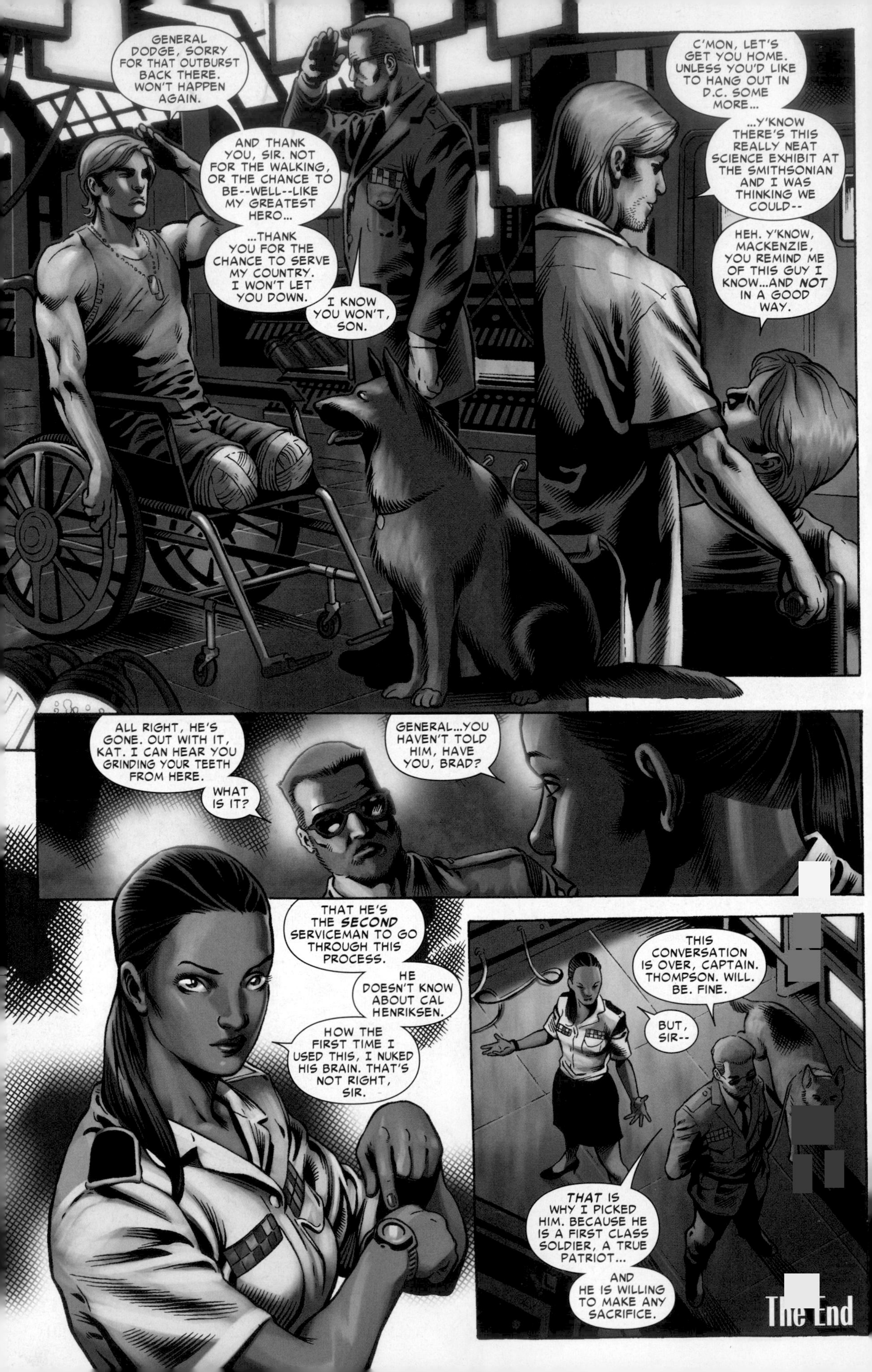
GENERAL DODGE, SORRY FOR THAT OUTBURST BACK THERE. WON'T HAPPEN AGAIN.
AND THANK YOU, SIR. NOT FOR THE WALKING, OR THE CHANCE TO BE--WELL--LIKE MY GREATEST HERO...
...THANK YOU FOR THE CHANCE TO SERVE MY COUNTRY. I WON'T LET YOU DOWN.
I KNOW YOU WON'T, SON.
C'MON, LET'S GET YOU HOME. UNLESS YOU'D LIKE TO HANG OUT IN D.C. SOME MORE...
...Y'KNOW THERE'S THIS REALLY NEAT SCIENCE EXHIBIT AT THE SMITHSONIAN AND I WAS THINKING WE COULD--
HEH. Y'KNOW, MACKENZIE, YOU REMIND ME OF THIS GUY I KNOW...AND *NOT* IN A GOOD WAY.
ALL RIGHT, HE'S GONE. OUT WITH IT, KAT. I CAN HEAR YOU GRINDING YOUR TEETH FROM HERE.
WHAT IS IT?
GENERAL...YOU HAVEN'T TOLD HIM, HAVE YOU, BRAD?
THAT HE'S THE *SECOND* SERVICEMAN TO GO THROUGH THIS PROCESS.
HE DOESN'T KNOW ABOUT CAL HENRIKSEN.
HOW THE FIRST TIME I USED THIS, I NUKED HIS BRAIN. THAT'S NOT RIGHT, SIR.
THIS CONVERSATION IS OVER, CAPTAIN. THOMPSON. WILL. BE. FINE.
BUT, SIR--
THAT IS WHY I PICKED HIM. BECAUSE HE IS A FIRST CLASS SOLDIER, A TRUE PATRIOT...
AND HE IS WILLING TO MAKE ANY SACRIFICE.
The End

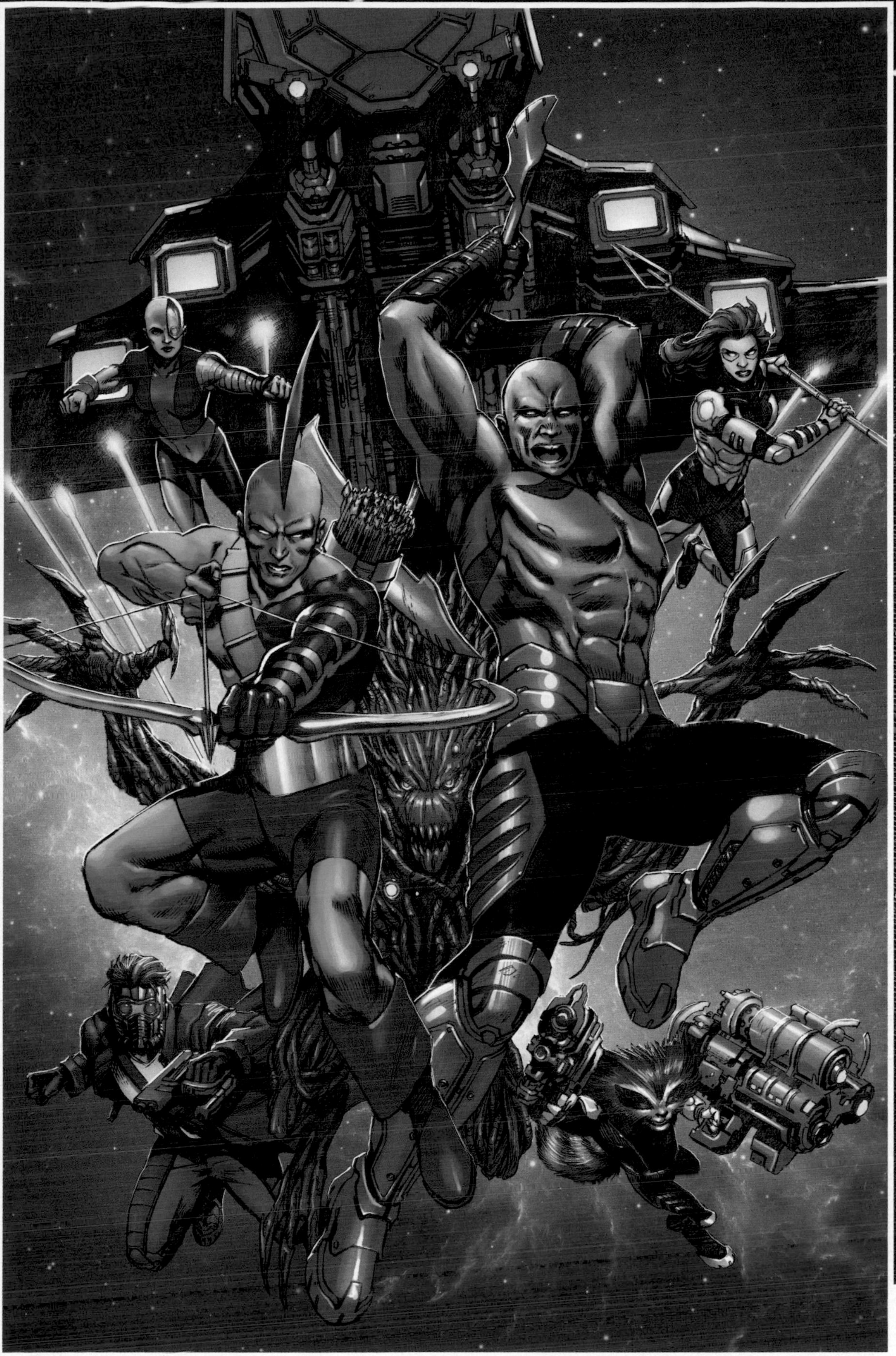

#17 WIZARD WORLD VARIANT
BY ALVARO MARTINEZ & CHRIS SOTOMAYOR

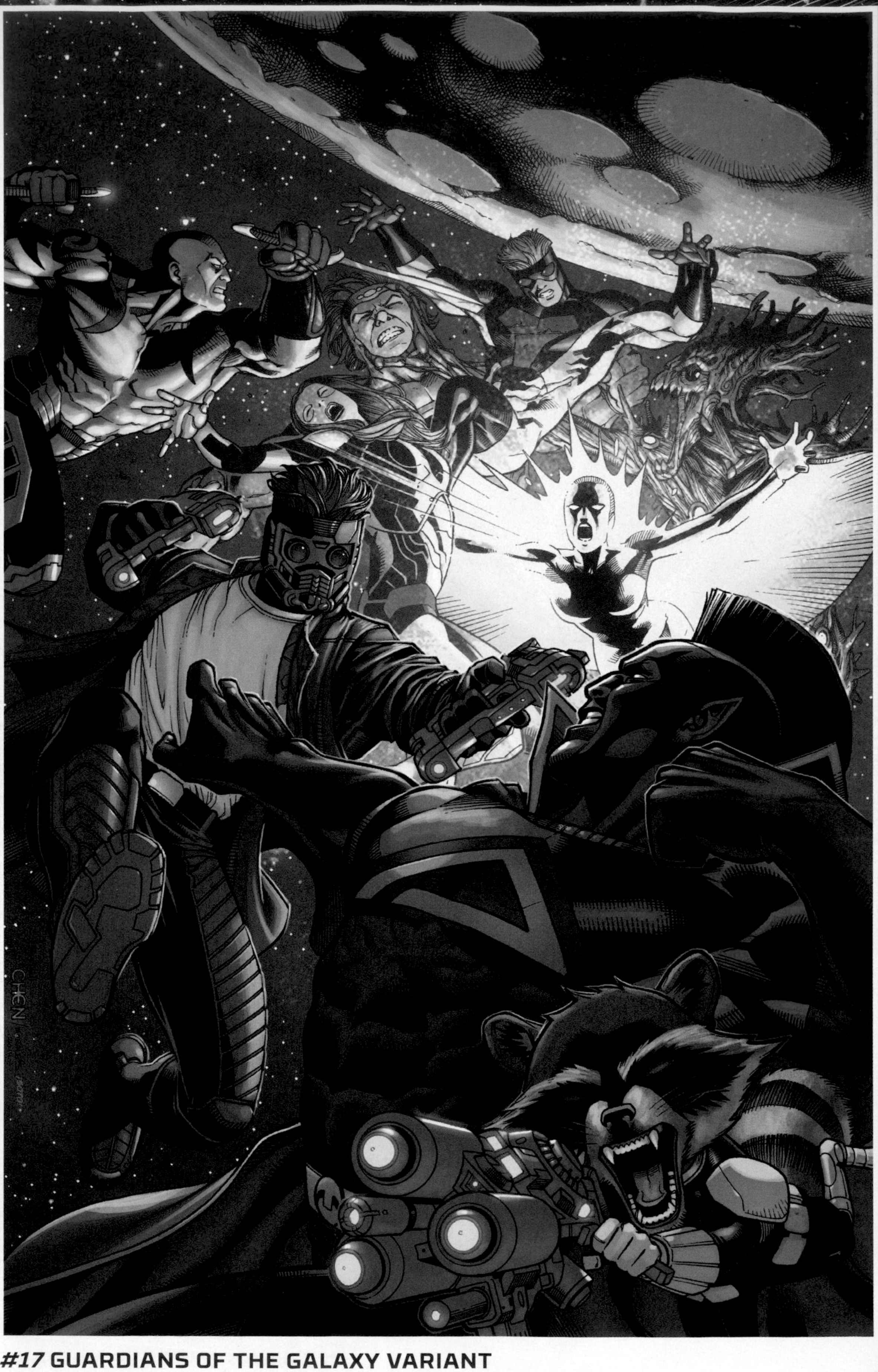
CHEN

#17 GUARDIANS OF THE GALAXY VARIANT
BY SEAN CHEN, MARK MORALES & CHRIS SOTOMAYOR

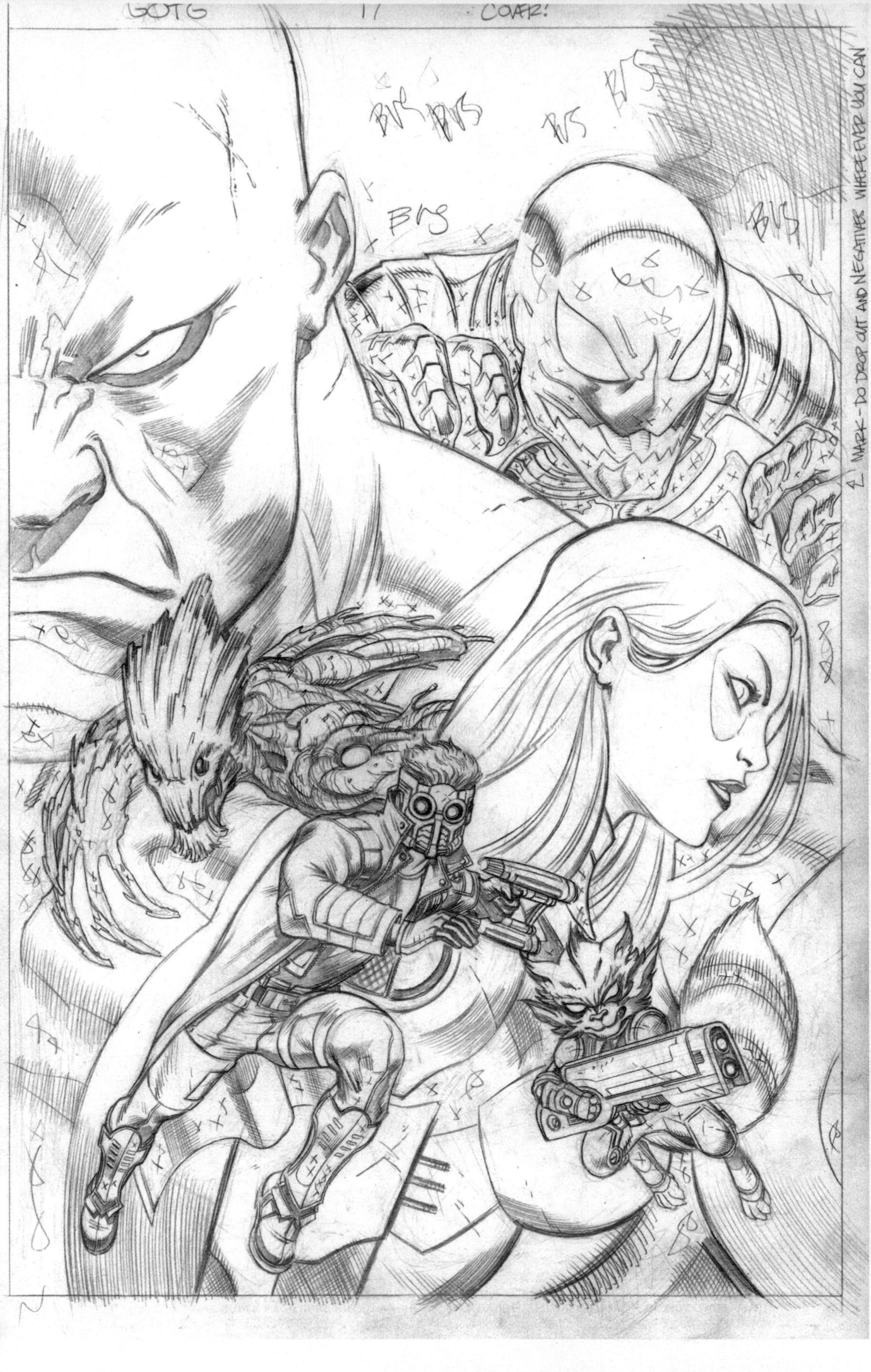
GOTG 17 COVER!
MARK - DO DROP OUT AND NEGATIVES WHERE EVER YOU CAN

#17 COVER PENCILS BY ED MCGUINNESS

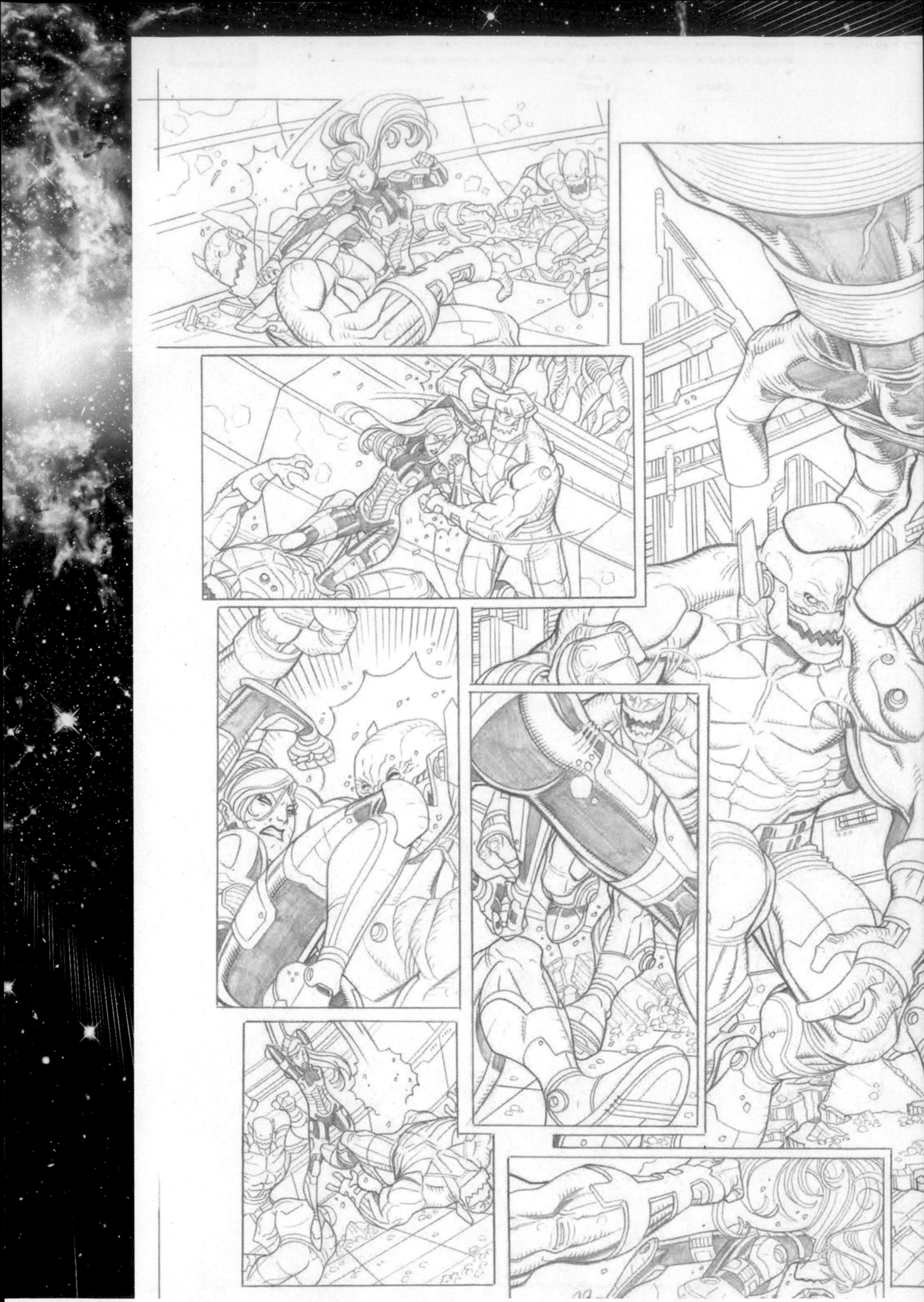

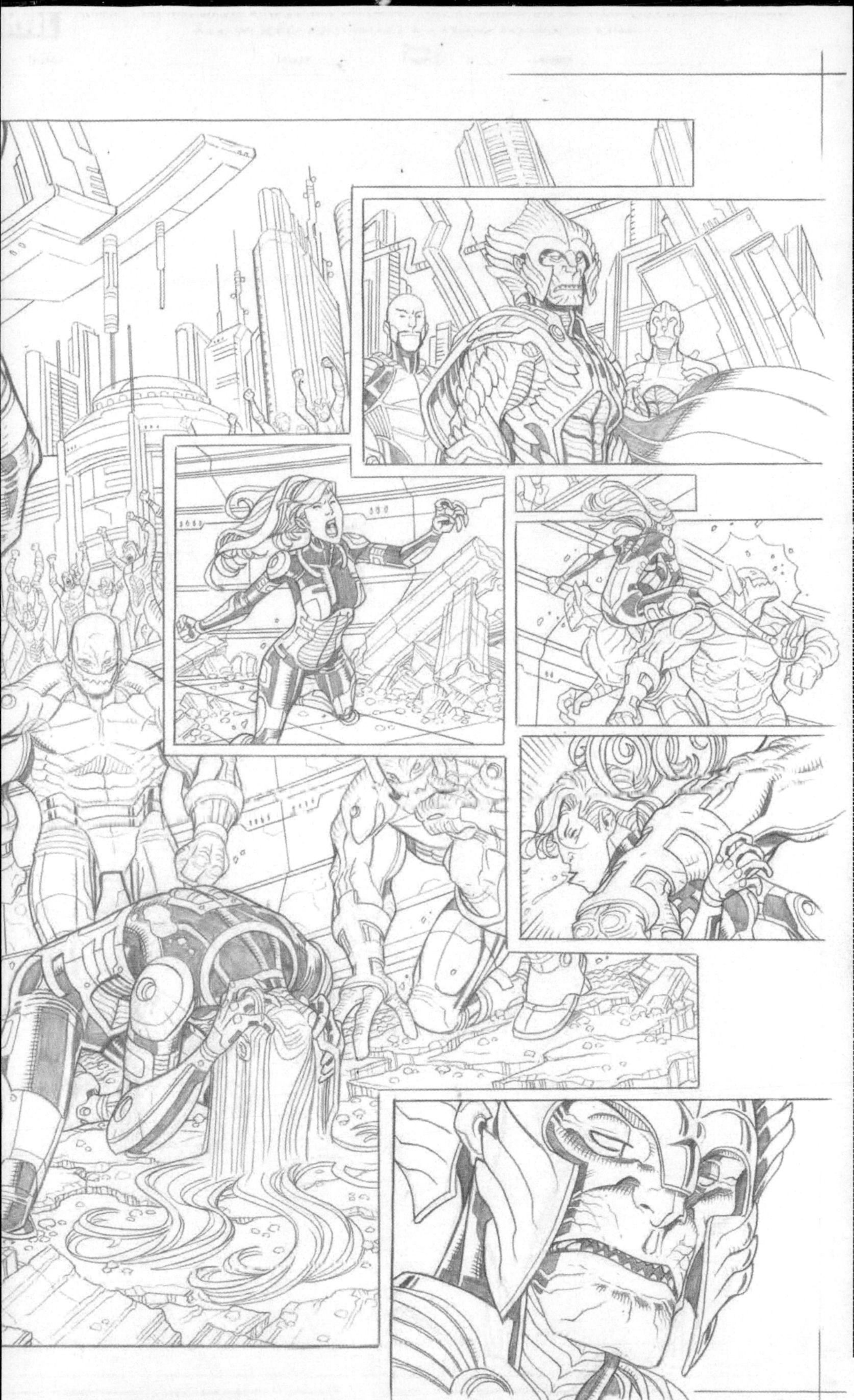

#15, PAGES 6-7 PENCILS BY NICK BRADSHAW

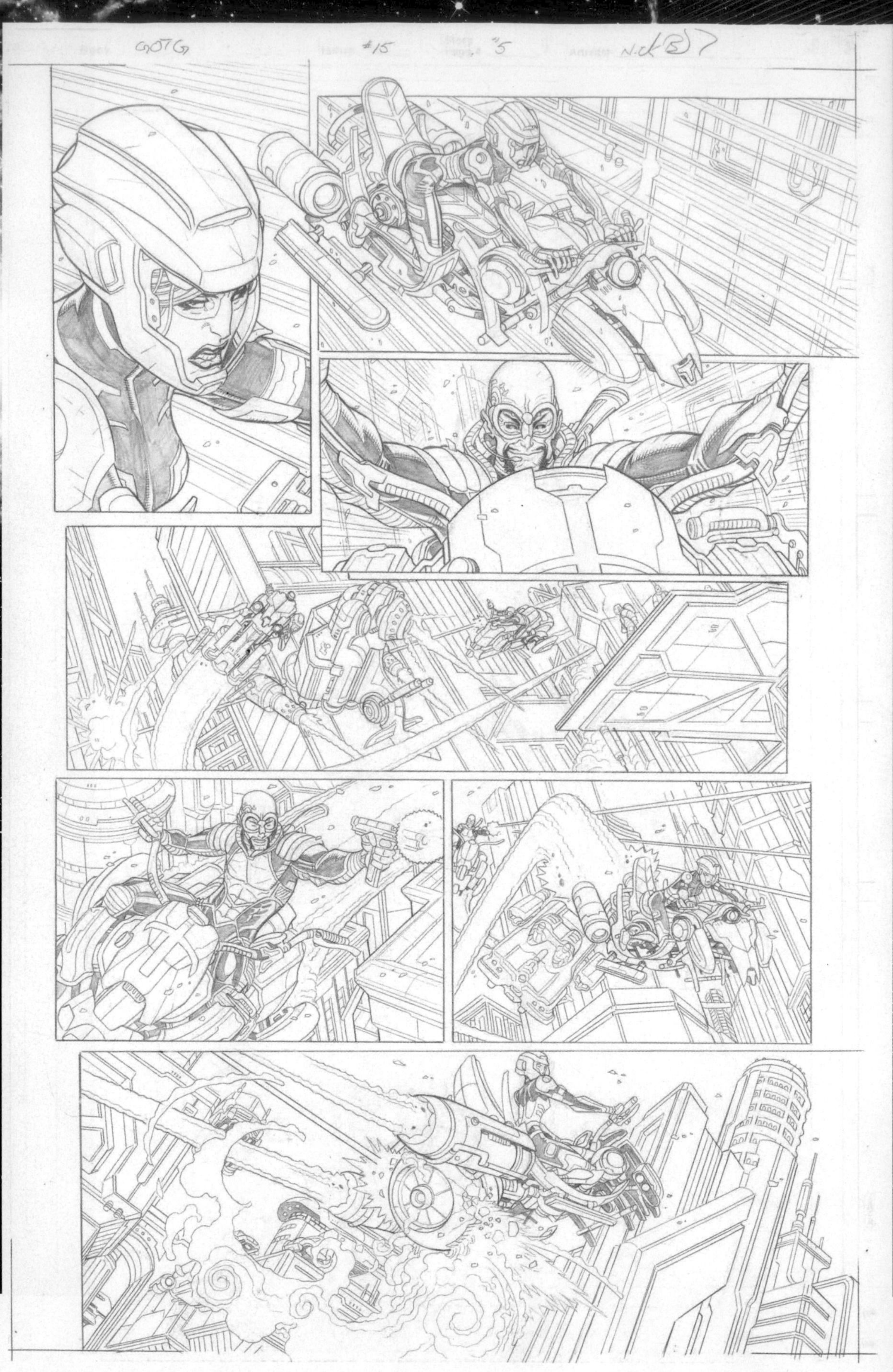
GOTG
#15

#14, PAGE 5 PENCILS BY NICK BRADSHAW

GUARDIANS OF THE GALAXY

AR INDEX